i

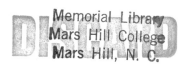

ATLAS OF RELIGIOUS CHANGE IN AMERICA, 1952-1990

by

Peter L. Halvorson and William M. Newman

ii   Atlas of Religious Change in America, 1952 - 1990

GRCA-III/P-568
May, 1994

The Glenmary Research Center was established in 1966 to help serve the research needs of the Catholic Church in rural America

ii   Atlas of Religious Change in America, 1952 - 1990

International Standard Book Number: 0-914422-23-5
Copyright © 1994 by Peter L. Halvorson and William M. Newman.
Published by the Glenmary Research Center, 750 Piedmont Ave. NE, Atlanta, GA 30308.

DEDICATION

This work is gratefully and lovingly dedicated to
Otto P. Halvorson, Adele C. Halvorson, Thomas L. Newman,
and the memory of Muriel D. Newman.

TABLE OF CONTENTS

LIST OF TABLES

ACKNOWLEDGEMENTS

This is one of a number of publications made possible by the generous support of the Lilly Endowment. We welcome this opportunity to thank the Endowment and especially Fred Hofheinz, Director of its Religion Program. We also gratefully acknowledge the superb efforts of our research assistants Danny Stewart , Tracey Smith, and Ronald Trotta. John Allen, Robert Andrle, and numerous other members of the Geography Department at the University of Connecticut have provided invaluable technical assistance and moral support. We also wish to thank Dale Jones and Richard Houseal at the Church of the Nazarene who assembled and transmitted to us over a period of many months the data for the study *Churches and Church Membership in the United States, 1990*. Of course, our work with these data would not be possible without our continuing relationship with the Church Membership Study Committee of the Association of Statisticians of American Religious Bodies (ASARB), and with our publisher, the Glenmary Research Center, its Director, Sister Mary Priniski, O.P., Ph.D., and her administrative associate, Leslie Montelongo.

INTRODUCTION

The Sociologist

I remember meeting Lauris Whitman and Glenn Trimble in the late 1960s. I visited with Lauris several times in his small office at the National Council of Churches of Christ at 475 Riverside Drive in New York City. There had not been a 1960 version of their county level census-type study *Churches and Church Membership in the United States, 1952* (Whitman and Trimble, 1956). Lauris Whitman, then near retirement, struck me as a gentle, humble, and quiet man. When I raised the subject of his study, there was a broad smile, a very definite sense of accomplishment and pride. At first, he would just smile and nod as if to say, "You understand what we did." When I departed New York City in 1969 I had no clue that Lauris' work and mine would become intertwined. I did not see him again.

In this new age of desk-top computers, laser printers, xerox, and fax machines, it is difficult to imagine the sheer logistical effort involved in administering such a study without these conveniences. Even with these conveniences Peter Halvorson and I have found that large data sets almost have a life of their own. Like dogs, cats, and little kids, these enormous collections of numbers begin to misbehave if they are out of sight for too long. It sometimes is difficult to recapture old versions of your own statistics. Peter and I have picked each other's brains trying to remember how we resolved certain problems in these data in the previous versions of this *Atlas*.

Early in the 1970s when I learned that Father Bernard Quinn, then director of the Glenmary Research Center, actually had replicated the Whitman-Trimble study, the implications seemed quite clear. Someone would have to complete the work that was begun in the early 1950s by computerizing the 1952 census-type study and merging the two data files. Today, of course, we have four studies, and as I think even the skeptics will admit, having these data mapped is revealing in ways that simply looking at the statistics is not.

This is the third and happily most elaborate version of this *Atlas*. My trip across the University of Connecticut campus in search of a geographer (I always liked maps but had never studied geography) was fortuitous. Things that in retrospect appear planned, rarely are so in fact. Initially Peter Halvorson said he had little interest in making maps of religious groups. I don't know what made me think it was worth a second trip to his office on the fourth floor of Beach Hall. He hadn't been especially giving of his time on my first visit and his disinterest in the proposed project was very clear.

This has become a close and deeply valued friendship. Together we've written a small pile of books and a big pile of occasional essays (academic journal literature). We've had lots of fun doing all this and I can only hope that readers of this *Atlas* will share in some of that fun. This edition of the *Atlas* is much like a "coffee table" book. Don't even try to read it cover to cover. Find a friend and look through some of this stuff from time to time; and have a little fun.

The Geographer

I did not immediately rise to the "bait" of helping Bill create what he described as "a few maps." I was only recently removed from graduate studies where I had focused on urban and regional development and planning. Throughout my graduate career in geography I had avoided cartography with a consistent skill. So, when Bill arrived suggesting a modest mapping project regarding a national scale cultural feature, I showed him to the door of one of my colleagues. I have since learned that Bill is remarkably skilled at dealing with rejection, a trait first made manifest to me when he reappeared in my doorway, hat still in hand. Always an easy touch for the less fortunate, but with considerably less than boundless enthusi-

asm, I signed on to help him produce his "few maps" in what I initially guessed would be a project of perhaps a few months, a momentary diversion.

What sort of credentials did I bring to that work? Well, I was familiar with the well known extended essay by geographer Wilbur Zelinsky based on the 1952 enumeration of denominational adherence, and, having served on a number of campus/student church related boards, I had dabbled in some Will Herberg as casual reading. The close work of cartographic drafting (pen and ink prevailed then) for more than an hour at a time made me queasy, irritable or both. Obviously, I was superbly qualified.

Quickly, two things became apparent. The first involved the interrelationship of some constructs from our two fields of study - most notably the interplay of sociological perspectives on assimilation and pluralism with geographic views regarding cultural regions and migration patterns in the United States. The second involved Bill's sense of the geography of the country, which conforms most closely to an old novelty map titled "A New Yorker's View of the United States," on which only Florida and Los Angeles are identified in a sea of *terra incognita*. The first of these has continued to engage my intellect, while the second has provided almost twenty years of comedic relief.

Background to the Four Studies

This *Atlas* contains maps and analysis of county level census-type data for American religious denominations for the period 1952-1990. Our primary focus is upon the data from four privately conducted census-type studies of religious adherence for the years 1952, 1971, 1980, and 1990, known as The Church Membership Studies. We begin here with the story of those studies as well as our involvement with them.

While scholars in many fields of social research long have enjoyed the luxury of government produced statistics including national census studies each decade and many Census Bureau sample studies annually, the situation regarding religious statistics has been quite different. The modern interpretation of the doctrine of church-state separation that is expressed in the Constitution of the United States has functioned to prohibit government statisticians from collecting information about the religion of Americans. There have been few deviations from this prohibition.

In the mid-19th century the federal government did begin collecting information about religion, specifically about church property. Subsequently, in the years 1890, 1906, 1916, and 1936 the Census Bureau gathered from local clergy and published comprehensive estimates of the number of churches, the seating capacity of their pews, and related data. As Finke and Stark have noted (1992:6-12), demographers appear to have ignored these data files precisely because they consist of reports by institutional leaders rather than by individual citizens. They are not census counts in the strict sense of that term (based on responses by individuals). Moreover, scholars appear to have assumed that such data, at best, are suspect.

In 1957, the Census Bureau departed from its then established practice of avoiding the topic of religion. A sample survey conducted in that year by the Bureau was published (United States Census Bureau, 1958) and quickly became the focus of an intense public debate about the Constitutional status of such a study (Petersen, 1962). While the Freedom of Information Act of 1967 (Public Act 89-489) allowed private scholars access to these materials, by then, most of the original data (based on individual responses) had been destroyed (Goldstein 1969; Mueller and Lane, 1972). More importantly, the controversy over the Bureau's 1957 sample study of religion seems to have closed the door permanently on the collection of religious statistics by the United States government. These events provide a context for understanding the significance of the four privately conducted census-type studies that are the focus of this *Atlas*.

The first of these studies, *Churches and Church Membership in the United States, 1952* (Whitman and Trimble, 1956), was collected under the auspices of the National Council of Churches of Christ (NCCC) by two staff members of the Department of Survey, Research, and Evaluation, Lauris Whitman and Glenn Trimble. While the initial focus of the study was the year 1952, the data actually contain statistics reported by denominations across the years 1952 through 1954. Data processing was done by Columbia University's Bureau of Survey and Research, and publication was in the form of a series of 80 pamphlets. The study is contained in some library collections as a single bound volume.

The 1952 study is important precisely because the United States Census Bureau has not assembled census data on religion in the contemporary period. Moreover, because a great many denominations not holding membership in the NCCC participated, the 1952 study was uniquely successful in accomplishing its goal of estimating Judaeo-Christian adherence patterns at the county level for the entire United States. The 1952 NCCC study would become the only truly comprehensive statistical portrait of religion in America at, or at least near, mid-century.

That study, as well as the three subsequent ones, report three statistics: number of full communicant, confirmed members; number of adherents; and number of churches. The adherents statistic is a more inclusive estimate of affiliation, and is the statistic we have chosen to map in this and previous versions of this *Atlas* (Halvorson and Newman, 1978, 1987). Religious communities count "adherents" by a wide range of criteria, including the practice of the single largest communion in these studies, the Catholic Church, of counting children as adherents. Clearly, using the more inclusive "adherents" rather than the "members" statistic for Protestant groups offers the best opportunity for minimizing differences in how different religious communities do their counting.

The Jewish data in the 1952 study consist of a county level allocation of the 1954 data reported in the *American Jewish Yearbook*. The original data are population estimates for communities reported by local Council of Jewish Federation agencies. Whitman and Trimble allocated these data to county units. These population estimates seem more similar to the "adherents" than the "members" data in the several Church Membership Studies. We have duplicated this procedure for each of the subsequent data points in order to provide a comparable data set for American Jews.

As was noted previously, during the 1960s there was not a replication of the 1952 study. However, in 1971, three religious agencies, the National Council of Churches of Christ, the Glenmary Research Center (a Catholic agency), and the Lutheran Church-Missouri Synod, provided funding for a new version of the study to be conducted under the direction of Father Bernard Quinn of the Glenmary Research Center. These efforts led to the second of the Church Membership Studies, and also resulted in the formation of the Church Membership Study Committee. The latter planned the administration of the 1980 version of the study, which coincided with the 1980 decennial census.

The 1980 version of the study (Quinn, *et al.*, 1984) was administered at the Glenmary Research Center, and was sponsored by the Glenmary Research Center, the Office of Research, Planning, and Evaluation of the National Council of Churches of Christ, the Department of Research and Records of the African Methodist Episcopal Zion Church, the Sunday School Board of the Southern Baptist Convention, and the Lutheran Council in the U.S.A.. Proceeds from the 1980 study established a fund for financing the 1990 study.

The 1990 Church Membership Study (Bradley *et al.*, 1992) was administered by The Church Membership Study Committee, which during the previous decade had evolved from an *ad hoc* group into a formal committee of the Association of Statisticians of American Religious Bodies (ASARB). Data processing tasks were accomplished under the direction of Dale Jones at the Church of the Nazarene. Funding was supplemented by a Lilly Endowment grant.

If an earlier generation of scholars eschewed such data (Census Bureau studies of 1890, 1906, 1916, and 1936) because they are based on the reports of clergymen, modern researchers have taken a much more realistic view. A growing body of scholars have used the 1952, 1971, and 1980 versions of the Church Membership Study (Zelinsky, 1961; Sopher, 1967; Shortridge 1976, 1977; Carroll, Johnson, and Marty, 1979; Halvorson and Newman, 1978, 1987; Newman and Halvorson, 1980). The appearance of a 1990 study does more than simply provide an "update" for the decade of the 80s. Rather, in conjunction with the earlier three studies, it creates a time-series data file that chronicles the patterns of denominational change within the nation over most of the second half of the 20th century. Accordingly, this publication has a dual focus. First, it provides an updating of the two earlier *Atlas* publications for the decade 1980-1990. More importantly, it also provides a nearly forty year view of adherents trends in the American religious population.

The Longitudinal Archive

Thus far, the four census-type studies of religious adherents have been described only in the most general terms. A closer inspection may be obtained by addressing three questions. First, how consistent is participation across the four studies? Second, exactly which denominations are available for time-series analysis in this *Atlas*? Third, what proportion of the religious or general population of the United States do these studies represent?

Participation in the four studies has varied from a high of 130 denominations in 1990 to a low of 53 denominations in 1971. The original 1952 study involved some 114 denominations, while the 1980 version included 111 denominations. Regrettably, not all of the denominations participating in these studies can be employed in a forty year analysis. As is seen in Table 1, there are two sets of denominations (labeled complete sets and partial sets) that provide time-series data for use in this *Atlas*. The complete set denominations provide data at all four time points. These 31 denominations account for over 115 million of the 137 million adherents (84%) reported in the 1990 study.

There are 26 denominations providing data only for 1980 and 1990. While the complete set denominations continue to represent primarily white religious bodies, the participation of the AME Zion Church in 1980 and 1990 and their inclusion in the partial set begins to repair this flaw. We have not included in this *Atlas* the survey type data for black Baptists that are contained in the 1990 Church Membership Study because of a desire to avoid mixing census-type and survey data. Additionally, for denominations providing data only in 1980 and 1990, we have chosen to map only those that report more than 10,000 adherents at least once during the study period.

Among the complete set denominations the more evangelical brands of Protestantism are somewhat under-represented. Although the Christian Church (Disciples of Christ) participated in all four studies, they provided "churches" but not "members" data in 1952. Similarly, a substantial change in enumeration procedures in 1971 by the Assemblies of God render their 1971 data incompatible with those for 1952, 1980, and 1990. Both are included in the partial set. Finally, Mormon data for 1952 cover only the western states, with national data appearing only in 1971 and later years. As a result, this denomination also has been included in the more limited subset.

Among a substantial number of the smaller evangelical denominations we encountered inconsistencies in counting and reporting procedures that have required their deletion from the

TABLE 1
LONGITUDINAL ARCHIVE OF AMERICAN RELIGIOUS DENOMINATIONS

Complete sets: Participation in 1952, 1971, 1980, 1990
American Baptist Churches in the U.S.A.
Baptist General Conference
Brethren in Christ Church
Catholic Church
Christian Reformed Church
Church of God (Anderson, Indiana)
Church of God (Cleveland, Tennessee)
Church of the Brethren
Church of the Nazarene
Cumberland Presbyterian Church
Episcopal Church
Evangelical Congregational Church
Evangelical Lutheran Church in America
Free Methodist Church of North America
Friends
International Church of the Foursquare Gospel
Jewish Population
Lutheran Church - Missouri Synod
Mennonite Church
Moravian Church in America, UF
North American Baptist Conference
Pentecostal Holiness Church, Inc.
Presbyterian Church (U.S.A.)
Reformed Church in America
Seventh-Day Adventists
Seventh Day Baptist General Conference
Southern Baptist Convention
Unitarian Universalist Association
United Church of Christ
United Methodist Church
Wisconsin Evangelical Lutheran Synod

Partial Sets: Participation in 1980 and 1990
Advent Christian Church
African Methodist Episcopal Zion Church
Assemblies of God
Associate Reformed Presbyterian Church (General Synod)
Baptist Missionary Association of America
Brethren Church (Ashland, Ohio)
Christian and Missionary Alliance
Christian Church (Disciples of Christ)
Christian Churches and Churches of Christ
Christian (Plymouth) Brethren
Church of God in Christ (Mennonite)
Church of Jesus Christ of Latter-Day Saints
Church of the Lutheran Brethren of America
Churches of Christ
Congregational Christian Churches, National Association of
Conservative Congregational Christian Conference
Evangelical Lutheran Synod
Evangelical Methodist Church
Free Lutheran Congregations, The Association of
General Conference of Mennonite Brethren Churches
Latvian Evangelical Lutheran Church in America
Mennonite Church, The General Conference
Missionary Church
Old Order Amish Church
Presbyterian Church in America
Salvation Army

TABLE 2
DESCRIPTIVE STATISTICS FOR THE CHURCH MEMBERSHIP ARCHIVE
1952, 1971, 1980, AND 1990

	Year 1952	1971	1980	1990
Number of Adherents (Millions)	70.4	100.0	113.3	123.1
Percent of Yearbook Membership[a]	80.9	80.1	84.1	84.7
Percent of U.S. Population[b]	47.0	49.8	50.0	49.8

[a]**Based on the following National Council of Churches of Christ Yearbook "inclusive membership" totals: In 1952, 87,027,507; In 1971, 124, 829,551; In 1980, 134,816,943; and in 1990, 145, 383, 738.**
[b]**Based on the following United States Census counts: 150,696,361 in 1952; 203,212,877 in 1971; 226,504,825 in 1980; and 249,975,000 in 1990.**

two lists of denominations shown in Table 1. A variety of data adjustment techniques have allowed us to repair others for which we encountered irregularities. Among them are the Church of God (Anderson) and the Church of the Nazarene in 1971, 1980, and 1990, the Free Methodist Church for 1980, and the Unitarian Universalist Association for 1980. A convenient remedy has been to apply the Glenmary Research Center's estimation technique to the reported members data to create longitudinally comparable adherents statistics.

Table 2 provides a comparison of the usable longitudinal data for denominations in Table 1 from the four studies with reference to the United States Census population counts, and the National Council of Churches of Christ *Yearbook of American and Canadian Churches* (Jacquet, 1990). Variations in the participating bodies between the several studies are greatly offset by the recurring participation of a large number of religious communities, and especially by most Protestant denominations numbering over a million members. As we've reported elsewhere (Newman and Halvorson, 1993) differences in the original enumerations notwithstanding, at each of the four dates, the archive contains a very substantial portion (80.1% to 84.7%) of the aggregate religious memberships reported in the corresponding editions of the *Yearbook,* with the 1990 enumeration standing as the most inclusive. These studies also represent a sizable proportion (47% to 50%) of the American population as reported by the United States Census.

Mergers, Schisms, Reunions, Divisions

Organizational mergers, schisms, reunions, and divisions are at once the delight of historians and the nemesis of demographers. In earlier versions of this *Atlas* we opted to have later versions of these organizations reflect their earlier constituencies. Thus, for example, we added the Congregational Christian Churches into the merged denomination the United Church of Christ, even though the former did not participate in the merger that created the latter. With some coaching and urging from religionists, we have thought better of that strategy, and in the present version of the *Atlas* schisms are counted as real membership losses. Two denominations included here in the partial set (Table 1), the Congregational Christian Churches and the Presbyterian Church in America, are nonmerging branches of denominations that participated in 1952, 1971, 1980, and 1990. We've treated them as independent denominations (which they are) and have not added them into the groups from which they divided or the mergers from which they abstained.

Some denominations in this version of the *Atlas* represent mergers of groups that appeared as individual organizations in

earlier versions of the *Atlas.* The Presbyterian Church (U.S.A.) is a merger of the United Presbyterian Church and the Presbyterian Church in America. The Evangelical Lutheran Church in America (ELCA) is a merger of the Lutheran Church in America (LCA) and the American Lutheran Church (ALC). A small denomination, the Association of Evangelical Lutheran Churches, that previously divided from the Lutheran Church Missouri Synod also participated in the ELCA merger.

Statistics for certain denominations that have merged since 1952 were combined in earlier data sets to provide uniform measurement from 1952 through 1990. Thus, for 1952, the Congregational Christian Churches and the Evangelical and Reformed Church are merged to become the United Church of Christ. In 1952, The Methodist Church and the Evangelical United Brethren are merged to become the United Methodist Church. In 1952, denominations that became the Lutheran Church in America and the American Lutheran Church are merged to become the Evangelical Lutheran Church in America; and in 1971 and 1980 the ALC and LCA are merged to become the ELCA. For 1952, 1971, and 1980 the Presbyterian Church in the United States and the Presbyterian Church (U.S.A.) (later called the United Presbyterian Church) are merged to become the Presbyterian Church (U.S.A.) In all cases the Moravian Church North and Moravian Church South are merged to become the Moravian Church. These and several additional instances are summarized in Table 3.

While it may be confusing to follow these changes over this period of time, the net effect of all of them may be summarized quite simply. A smaller number of denominations in 1990 represents the same constituencies that populated a larger number of denominational organizations in 1952. Once the mergers are "tracked" and the organizational units aligned, the consistency of participation from study to study becomes clear. The mergers are summarized in Table 3. Finally, as is shown in Table 4, in addition to organizational mergers, some denominations simply have changed their name over this nearly forty year period. We've adopted the present names of denominations, and for the record, the changes are given in Table 4.

An Overview of the Trends

Most students of American religious trends recognize that the "religious revival" of the 1950s had abated sometime in the 1960s. Thus, the available data for the period 1952-1971 missed the assumed peak in that trend. By 1971, annual statistics for many denominations already were headed in a downward direction, and the overall rate of growth surely had slowed. In spite of this, there is little question that it is mean-

TABLE 3
DENOMINATIONAL MERGERS, 1952-1990

United Church of Christ
    Congregational Christian Churches
    Evangelical and Reformed Church
United Methodist Church
Evangelical Church of North America
    Methodist Church
    Evangelical United Brethren
Wesleyan Church
    Wesleyan Methodist Church of America
    Pilgrim Holiness Church
Unitarian Universalist Association
    Unitarian Churches
    Universalist Association
Mennonite Church
    Mennonite Church
Conservative Mennonite Conference
Missionary Church
    Missionary Church Association
    United Missionary Church
Evangelical Lutheran Church of America
Association of Evangelical Lutheran Churches
(American Lutheran Church)
    American Lutheran Church
    Evangelical Lutheran Church
    United Evangelical Lutheran Churches
(Lutheran Church in America)
    American Evangelical Lutheran Church in America
    Augustana Evangelical Lutheran Church
    Finnish Evangelical Lutheran Church
    United Lutheran Church in America
Lutheran Church - Missouri Synod
    Lutheran Church - Missouri Synod
    Slovak Evangelical Lutheran Church
Presbyterian Church (U.S.A.)
    Presbyterian Church in the United States
(United Presbyterian Church USA)
    Presbyterian Church in the USA
    United Presbyterian Church of North America
Religious Society of Friends
    Various associations in different time periods

---

ingful to compare the data from these four studies in terms of two roughly 20 year intervals with 1971 as a midpoint. How may the performances of individual denominations be characterized in terms of these two relatively distinct periods?

Three different patterns readily are apparent. As depicted in Table 5, a first group of denominations reports 1952 to 1990 change rates that range from negative numbers (-5%) to modest increases (16.5%). For the most part, these denominations grew modestly from 1951 to 1971 and then tended to decline from 1971 to 1990. Anglo-Protestant denominations centered in the northeastern states predominate in this group. A second group of denominations record moderately strong growth rates (22.4% to 86.9%) for the entire 1952 to 1990 period. Generally, these denominations approximate the level of growth of the entire United States population (65%) during the period. These denominations appear to have participated in the growth spurt of the 1950s and 1960s, but then experienced stability or modest increase between 1971 and 1990. Continental European Protestant communities that are most prevalent in the American Midwest seem to characterize this group which also includes Catholics. Finally, a third group of denominations

report very strong change rates (115.9% to 406.8%) for the entire period. These communions experienced sustained growth rates in both the 1952-1971 and 1971-1990 periods. Native American denominations from southern and western states are most common in this group. The three distinctly different patterns of denominational change serve as a useful conceptual grid against which to read and interpret the more detailed patterns of change for individual denominations and are so employed throughout this *Atlas*.

Mapping Procedures

The longitudinal archive of religious adherence data based on the four Church Membership Studies provides more information than is readily comprehensible even in cartographic form. Obviously, the amount of data, or number of variables that may be depicted on a single map is limited. However, the important question is what are the most revealing cartographic configurations for these data?

The first map for each denomination in both the complete set and partial set displays at the county level "Total Adherents, 1990." Since this map is the point of reference for all others, it

TABLE 4
DENOMINATIONS WITH NEW NAMES, 1952-1990

American Baptist Churches in the U.S.A.
  American Baptist Convention
Episcopal Church
  Protestant Episcopal Church
Evangelical Covenant Church of America
  Evangelical Mission Covenant Church of America
Christian Churches (Disciples of Christ)
  Disciples of Christ
Christian Reformed Church
  Christian Reformed Church of North America
Moravian Church North and South
  Moravian Church in America, UF
Wisconsin Evangelical Lutheran Synod
  Evangelical Lutheran Joint Synod of Wisconsin & Other States

---

has been portrayed in a full page size. It repeats a format used in earlier versions of the *Atlas* with the distribution of adherents at the county level divided into thirds. For each denomination the color scheme shows the most populous third of counties in the darkest shade, orange, and the remaining thirds in gold and yellow respectively. Counties in which no adherents are reported for a denomination are left unshaded. The key for each map of Total Adherents 1990 contains the range of adherents at the county level represented by each third of counties. These statistics, of course, differ from denomination to denomination, and also allow a rough estimate of the median size of congregations in that denomination (the middle of the middle range). A comparative listing of the upper limits of the categories on all Total Adherents, 1990 maps is provided in tabular form (Table 7A&B) in the Appendix of this volume.

The second map for each denomination portrays "Percent Change in Adherents, 1980-1990." Again, the same shading scheme has been used, with the highest positive rates of change being depicted in orange. The value ranges of the percentages mapped are provided in the key. These value ranges provide a useful clue to whether adherence gains or losses are characteristic for a given denomination for the decade. For instance, denominations for which slight percentage increase statistics provide the upper limit of the middle category are communions that lost, rather than gained adherents in most counties. The third map depicts the denomination's "Percent Share of Population, 1990" at the county level as reported by the United States Census. The mapping scheme is identical to that of the first two maps. The second and third maps in each denominational set are produced in half page format and along with the 1990 distribution map form a series of three maps that is provided for all 57 denominations in this *Atlas*.

For those denominations included in the complete set two additional maps are provided. These maps utilize a different format than the others. The first of these depicts "Percent Change in Adherents, 1952-1971 and 1971-1990." Treating 1971 as a midpoint in these data, for each denomination four occurrences are mapped. They are counties in which denominations report:

A. Below median level change for 1952-1971 and 1971-1990. These counties are colored yellow.

B. Above median level change for 1952-1971 and below for 1971-1990. These counties are colored gold.

C. Below median level change for 1952-1971, and above

for 1971-1990. These counties are colored orange.

D. Above median level change for both 1952-1971 and 1971-1990. These counties are colored red.

The fifth and final map in each series of maps focuses upon how denominational shares of county populations have changed over the entire 1952-1990 period. The median rates of change for each denomination's share of county population for the time periods 1952-1971 and 1971-1990 have been calculated. For this measure, a value of 1.00 indicates a constant share of county population over time. Scores below 1.00 reflect declining shares of county population, while those above 1.00 register increasing shares. As with the map for Percent Change in Adherents, 1952-1971 and 1971-1990, the map for Shift in Share of Population, 1952-1971 and 1971-1990 differentiates counties in each time period in which a denomination either fell above or below the median statistic, in this case median change in the denomination's share of county level population. Both maps four and five employ the same four color shading scheme, with yellow indicating counties in which a denomination experienced relative weak performance throughout the entire 40 year period, and with red designating those counties in which a denomination experienced strong relative performances throughout the nearly 40 year period. Both appear in half page format.

Tables 5 and 6 on the following pages contain the adherents and county statistics for all the denominations in both sets (1952-1990 and 1980-1990) for which maps are provided in this *Atlas*. Additionally, several tables in the Appendix to this volume contain the value ranges and median rates from the keys on the various maps (Tables 7 through 10). These tables allow comparative examination of denominational trends in a tabular format .

Obviously, the accompanying text for the maps in this *Atlas* focuses upon the description of basic denominational patterns and changes in them, as well as the nature of denominational trends when viewed in the context of general population trends. There remains much to be gleaned from more detailed examinations and comparisons of the maps and the keys for the maps both within and between denominational map sets. To some extent, ours is an "outsiders" attempt to discern the general shapes and patterns in these data. There is little question that those with an "insiders" perspective will approach these data with an eye for the richness of detail they supply.

REFERENCES

American Jewish Committee
1990 *American Jewish Yearbook.* New York, American Jewish Committee.

Bradley, Martin *et al.*
1992 *Churches and Church Membership in the United States, 1990.* Atlanta, Georgia, Glenmary Research Center.

Carroll, Jackson W., Douglas W. Johnson and Martin Marty
1979 *Religion in America: 1950 to the Present.* San Francisco, Harper & Row Publishers.

Finke, Roger and Rodney Stark
1992 *The Churching of America, 1776-1990: Winners and and Losers in Our Religious Economy.* New Brunswick, New Jersey, Rutgers University Press.

Goldstein, Sidney
1969 "Socioeconomic differentials among religious groups in the United States," *American Journal of Sociology*, Volume 74, 612-631.

Halvorson, Peter L. and William M. Newman
1978 *Atlas of Religious Change in America, 1952-1971.*Washington, D. C., Glenmary Research Center.
1987 *Atlas of Religious Change in America, 1971-1980.*Atlanta, Georgia, Glenmary Research Center.

Irwin, Leonard G.
1976 *Churches and Church Membership in the United States, Supplementary Data, 1971.* Atlanta, Georgia, Southern Baptist Convention.

Jacquet, Constant (Ed.)
1990 *Yearbook of American & Canadian Churches.* Nashville, Tennessee, Abingdon Press.

Johnson, Douglas, Paul Picard, and Bernard Quinn
1974 *Churches and Church Membership in the United States, 1971.* Washington, D. C., Glenmary Research Center.

Mueller, Samuel, and Angela Lane
1972 "Tabulations from the 1957 'Current Population Survey on Religion,'" *Journal for the Scientific Study of Religion*, Volume 11, 76-98.

Newman, William M. and Peter L. Halvorson
1982 "Updating an archive: 'Churches and Church Membership in the United States,' 1952-1980", *Review of Religious Research*, Volume 24, Number 1, 54-58.

Newman, William M. and Peter L. Halvorson
1993 "The Church Membership Studies: Four decades of institutional research," *Review of Religious Research*, Volume 35, Number 1, 74-80.

Newman, William M., Peter L. Halvorson, and Jennifer Brown
1977 "Problems and potential uses of the 1952 and 1971 National Council of Churches' 'Churches and Church Membership in the United States' studies'," *Review of Religious Research*, Volume 18, Number 2, 167-173.

Petersen, William
1962 "Religious statistics in the United States", *Journal for the Scientific Study of Religion*, Volume 2, 165-178.

Quinn, Bernard, *et al.*
1982 *Churches and Church Membership in the United States, 1980.* Atlanta, Georgia, Glenmary Research Center.

Shortridge, James
1976 "Patterns of religion in the United States", *Geographical Review.* Volume 66, Number 4, 420-434.
1977 "A new regionalization of American religion", *Journal for the Scientific Study of Religion*, Volume 16, Number 2, 143-154.

Sopher, David
1967 *Geography of Religions.* Englewood Cliffs, New Jersey, Prentice-Hall Inc.

United States Census Bureau
1958 *Religion Reported by the Civilian Population of the United States, March 1957*, Series P-20, Number 79, Washington D.C., United States Department of Commerce.

Whitman, Lauris, and Glen Trimble
1956 *Churches and Church Membership in the United States, 1952.* New York, National Council of Churches of Christ.

Zelinsky, Wilbur
1961 "An approach to the religious geography of the United States: Patterns of church membership in 1952", *Annals of the Association of American Geographers*, Volume 51, Number 2, 139-193.

TABLE 5

NUMBER OF ADHERENTS AND PERCENT CHANGE FOR DENOMINATIONS PROVIDING COUNTY LEVEL DATA *
IN 1952, 1971, 1980, AND 1990

DENOMINATION	ADHERENTS				PERCENT CHANGE			
	1952	1971	1980	1990	1952-71	1971-80	1980-90	1952-90
American Baptist Churches in the U.S.A.	1,528,850	1,692,284	1,920,955	1,870,923	10.7	13.5	-2.6	22.4
Baptist General Conference	49,127	125,678	150,509	167,300	155.8	19.8	11.2	240.5
Brethren in Christ Church	6,007	11,458	18,443	19,769	90.7	61.0	7.2	229.1
Catholic Church	29,689,148	44,619,259	47,252,474	53,108,015	50.3	5.9	12.4	78.9
Christian Reformed Church	155,355	208,689	211,633	225,852	34.3	1.4	6.7	45.4
Church of God (Anderson, Indiana)	105,564	186,509	217,831	227,887	76.7	16.8	4.6	115.9
Church of God (Cleveland, Tennessee)	136,461	368,009	472,383	691,563	169.7	28.4	46.4	406.8
Church of the Brethren	189,277	220,813	207,980	186,588	16.7	-5.8	-10.3	-1.4
Church of the Nazarene	249,033	486,431	577,805	683,245	95.3	18.8	18.2	174.4
Cumberland Presbyterian Church	92,656	104,006	90,691	91,040	12.2	-12.8	0.4	-1.7
Episcopal Church	2,554,976	3,007,483	2,808,144	2,427,350	17.7	-6.6	-13.6	-5.0
Evangelical Congregational Church	28,596	35,742	34,085	33,166	25.0	-4.6	-2.7	16.0
Evangelical Lutheran Church in America	4,225,210	5,492,588	5,265,178	5,213,164	30.0	-4.1	-1.0	23.4
Free Methodist Church of North America	49,052	63,487	62,159	70,296	29.4	-2.1	13.1	43.3
Friends	95,029	128,161	133,405	127,533	34.9	4.1	-4.4	34.2
International Church of the Foursquare Gospel	66,181	101,522	160,074	250,250	53.4	57.7	56.3	278.1
Jewish Population	5,146,634	5,641,589	5,005,957	5,982,529	9.6	6.5	-0.4	16.2
Lutheran Church - Missouri Synod	1,856,638	2,768,539	2,617,936	2,598,469	49.1	-5.4	-0.7	40.0
Mennonite Church	66,652	108,048	118,239	154,257	62.1	9.4	30.5	131.4
Moravian Church in America, UF	48,618	57,121	53,647	52,519	17.5	-6.1	-2.0	8.0
North American Baptist Conference	35,431	50,555	51,726	54,010	42.7	2.3	4.4	52.4
Pentecostal Holiness Church, Inc.	41,541	87,789	121,879	156,431	111.3	38.8	28.3	276.6
Presbyterian Church (U.S.A.)	3,415,837	4,687,228	4,005,950	3,545,264	37.2	-14.5	-11.5	3.8
Reformed Church in America	194,157	370,508	371,048	362,932	90.8	0.1	-2.2	86.9
Seventh-Day Adventists	252,917	531,191	662,261	894,170	110.0	24.7	35.0	253.5
Seventh Day Baptist General Conference	6,425	6,178	6,145	6,439	-3.8	-0.5	4.8	0.2
Southern Baptist Convention	8,121,045	14,460,873	15,251,268	18,891,633	78.1	12.4	16.2	132.6
Unitarian Universalist Association	160,336	193,997	159,336	174,004	21.0	-17.9	9.2	8.5
United Church of Christ	2,009,642	2,296,566	2,075,227	1,970,607	14.3	-9.6	-5.0	-1.9
United Methodist Church	9,509,244	11,542,198	11,540,616	11,077,728	21.4	0.0	-4.0	16.5
Wisconsin Evangelical Lutheran Synod	316,692	381,735	403,854	418,820	20.5	5.8	3.7	32.2
Totals Table 5:	70,403,031	100,036,237	104,028,818	111,876,272	42.1	4.0	7.5	58.9
Total U.S. Population:	149,770,238	201,007,084	226,471,172	247,051,601	34.2	12.7	9.1	65.0
Percentage U.S. Population:	47.0	49.8	46.0	45.3	2.8	-3.8	-0.7	-1.4

* Does not include Alaska and Hawaii

9

TABLE 5A

NUMBER OF ADHERENTS AND PERCENT CHANGE FOR DENOMINATIONS PROVIDING COUNTY LEVEL DATA *
IN 1980 AND 1990

| DENOMINATION | ADHERENTS | | PERCENT CHANGE |
	1980	1990	1980-90
Advent Christian Church	35,448	23,794	-32.9
African Methodist Episcopal Zion Church	1,092,389	1,141,650	4.5
Assemblies of God	1,598,963	2,139,826	33.8
Associate Reformed Presbyterian Church (General Synod)	31,984	37,988	18.8
Baptist Missionary Association of America	274,515	289,919	5.6
Brethren Church (Ashland, Ohio)	18,372	16,331	-11.1
Christian and Missionary Alliance	169,459	269,284	58.9
Christian Church (Disciples of Christ)	1,211,889	1,037,205	-14.4
Christian Churches and Churches of Christ	1,126,500	1,210,319	7.4
Christian (Plymouth) Brethren	65,490	84,966	29.7
Church of God in Christ (Mennonite)	7,454	12,535	68.2
Church of Jesus Christ of Latter-Day Saints	2,647,940	3,486,766	31.7
Church of the Lutheran Brethren of America	10,935	17,793	62.7
Churches of Christ	1,597,189	1,677,711	5.0
Congregational Christian Churches, National Association of	119,002	98,457	-17.3
Conservative Congregational Christian Conference	27,781	35,574	28.1
Evangelical Lutheran Synod	20,044	21,523	7.4
Evangelical Methodist Church	11,788	11,105	-5.8
Free Lutheran Congregations, The Association of	14,462	27,316	88.9
General Conference of Mennonite Brethren Churches	19,268	22,097	14.7
Latvian Evangelical Lutheran Church in America	13,617	14,299	5.0
Mennonite Church, The General Conference	46,891	40,951	-12.7
Missionary Church	30,697	38,580	25.7
Old Order Amish Church	85,676	121,750	42.1
Presbyterian Church in America	86,631	221,295	155.4
Salvation Army	144,032	136,752	-5.1
Totals Table 5A:	10,511,425	12,235,786	16.4
Totals Tables 5 and 5A:	114,540,243	124,112,058	8.4
Total U.S. Population:	226,471,172	247,051,601	9.1
Percentage U.S Population (Table 5A):	4.6	5.0	0.4
Percentage U.S. Population (Tables 5 and 5A):	50.6	50.2	-0.4

* Does not include Alaska and Hawaii

TABLE 6

COUNTY STATISTICS FOR DENOMINATIONS *
1952, 1971, 1980, AND 1990

DENOMINATION	1952	1971	1980	1990	PERCENT CHANGE			
					1952-71	1971-80	1980-90	1952-90
American Baptist Churches in the U.S.A.	1,067	1,058	1,100	1,094	-0.8	4.0	-0.5	2.5
Baptist General Conference	181	277	324	348	53.0	17.0	0.7	79.0
Brethren in Christ Church	57	73	83	90	28.1	13.7	8.4	57.9
Catholic Church	2,563	2,816	2,837	2,937	9.9	0.7	3.5	14.6
Christian Reformed Church	121	181	221	235	49.6	22.1	6.3	94.0
Church of God (Anderson, Indiana)	990	993	1,016	1,020	0.3	2.3	0.4	3.0
Church of God (Cleveland, Tennessee)	1,073	1,416	1,510	1,497	32.0	6.6	-0.9	39.5
Church of the Brethren	460	427	417	420	-7.2	-2.3	0.7	-8.7
Church of the Nazarene	1,680	1,733	1,781	1,852	3.2	2.8	4.0	10.2
Cumberland Presbyterian Church	307	288	292	275	-6.2	1.4	-5.8	-10.4
Episcopal Church	1,945	2,032	1,989	2,069	4.5	-2.1	4.0	6.4
Evangelical Congregational Church	34	30	34	36	-11.8	13.3	5.9	5.9
Evangelical Lutheran Church in America	1,420	1,577	1,620	1,693	11.1	2.7	4.5	19.2
Free Methodist Church of North America	577	549	535	514	-4.9	-2.6	-3.9	-10.9
Friends	260	460	497	657	76.9	8.0	32.2	152.7
International Church of the Foursquare Gospel	290	350	399	537	20.7	14.0	34.6	85.2
Jewish Population	481	503	770	748	4.6	53.1	-2.9	55.5
Lutheran Church - Missouri Synod	1,423	1,649	1,679	1,769	15.9	1.8	5.4	24.3
Mennonite Church	230	358	376	444	55.7	5.0	18.1	93.0
Moravian Church in America, UF	50	53	56	64	6.0	5.7	14.3	28.0
North American Baptist Conference	146	152	159	163	4.1	4.6	2.5	11.6
Pentecostal Holiness Church, Inc.	371	489	459	509	31.8	-6.1	10.9	37.2
Presbyterian Church (U.S.A.)	2,434	2,428	2,381	2,366	-0.2	-1.9	-0.6	-2.8
Reformed Church in America	150	203	208	232	35.3	2.5	11.5	54.7
Seventh-Day Adventists	1,466	1,624	1,734	1,781	10.8	6.8	2.7	21.5
Seventh Day Baptist General Conference	46	45	49	69	-2.2	8.9	40.8	50.0
Southern Baptist Convention	1,788	2,212	2,365	2,495	23.7	6.9	5.5	39.5
Unitarian Universalist Association	365	520	511	541	42.5	-1.7	5.9	48.2
United Church of Christ	1,401	1,272	1,266	1,265	-9.2	-0.5	-0.1	-9.7
United Methodist Church	2,889	2,950	2,957	2,952	2.1	0.2	-0.2	2.2
Wisconsin Evangelical Lutheran Synod	248	352	444	503	41.9	26.1	13.3	102.8

* Does not include Alaska and Hawaii

TABLE 6A

COUNTY STATISTICS FOR DENOMINATIONS *
1980 AND 1990

DENOMINATION	1980	1990	PERCENT CHANGE 1980-90
Advent Christian Church	192	185	-3.6
African Methodist Episcopal Zion Church	404	445	10.1
Assemblies of God	2,424	2,546	5.0
Associate Reformed Presbyterian Church (General Synod)	68	86	26.5
Baptist Missionary Association of America	374	351	-6.1
Brethren Church (Ashland, Ohio)	71	73	2.8
Christian and Missionary Alliance	601	722	20.1
Christian Church (Disciples of Christ)	1,422	1,377	-3.2
Christian Churches and Churches of Christ	1,584	1,524	-3.8
Christian (Plymouth) Brethren	417	420	0.7
Church of God in Christ (Mennonite)	51	61	19.6
Church of Jesus Christ of Latter-Day Saints	1,502	1,646	9.6
Church of the Lutheran Brethren of America	82	87	6.1
Churches of Christ	2,345	2,397	2.2
Congregational Christian Churches, National Association of	215	217	0.9
Conservative Congregational Christian Conference	92	127	38.0
Evangelical Lutheran Synod	73	92	26.0
Evangelical Methodist Church	100	104	4.0
Free Lutheran Congregations, The Association of	75	118	57.3
General Conference of Mennonite Brethren Churches	79	78	-1.3
Latvian Evangelical Lutheran Church in America	50	49	-2.0
Mennonite Church, The General Conference	113	134	18.6
Missionary Church	128	123	-3.9
Old Order Amish Church	107	166	55.1
Presbyterian Church of America	252	530	110.3
Salvation Army	730	761	4.2

* Does not include Alaska and Hawaii

DENOMINATIONAL MAPS: 1952 - 1990

AMERICAN BAPTIST CHURCHES IN THE U.S.A.

Independent Baptist churches formed associations in the colonies of Virginia, Rhode Island, New Jersey, and Pennsylvania well before the American Revolution. By the early 19th century, a number of sizable Baptist missionary societies had emerged. Subsequently, during the Great Awakenings, Baptist fellowships spread throughout the nation. This group and its counterpart, the Southern Baptist Convention, split on a regional basis just prior to the Civil War (1845). Initially known as the Northern Baptist Convention (1907), and subsequently as the American Baptist Convention (1950), this denomination adopted its present name in 1972. Theological and especially social issues continue to separate the two major Baptist bodies, with the American Baptist Churches in the U.S.A. being the more socially liberal denomination.

	1952	1971	1980	1990
Adherents:	1,528,850	1,692,284	1,920,955	1,870,923
Counties:	1,067	1,058	1,100	1,094

For the entire 1952-1990 period the American Baptist Churches record a modest growth rate (22.4%) which lagged well behind the national population growth trend (64.9%). In the decade of the 1980s, the American Baptists experienced a small decline in adherents of less than 3%. These trends also are reflected in the number of counties occupied, which peaked at 1,100 in 1980, and grew by only 27 over the entire 1952-1990 period. Similarly, the American Baptists' number of churches was 5,871 in 1952, peaked at 5,933 in 1971, and was 5,801 in 1990. The American Baptist Churches fall within that set of denominations exhibiting modest growth throughout the nearly 40 years encompassed by these data.

The map of Total Adherents, 1990 reveals a denomination that occupies bands of contiguous counties throughout the northern portion of the nation. The distribution pattern begins in the Northeast (New England, New York, and Pennsylvania), stretches across the Midwest (Ohio, Indiana, Michigan, and Illinois) and does not begin to thin until it reaches the Great Plains. The pattern returns in strength on the West Coast, where it extends from California to Washington. While the American Baptists are present in very few counties in the home turf of their sister denomination the Southern Baptist Convention, the American Baptists nonetheless are a national denomination. They can be found from coast to coast in more than a thousand counties.

The map for Percent Change in Adherents, 1980-1990, shows that counties in all categories are scattered throughout the nation, with no particular regional component evident. While the aggregate pattern is best understood as a stable one (2.6% decline in adherents nationally) it is clear that during the decade of the 1980s, more than half of all counties for this denomination lost adherents (the middle category ranges from -18.99% loss to a modest 2.83% gain).

Some additional clues to the pattern are provided by the map for Share of Population, 1990. The category values indicate that the American Baptists represent less than 3% of the population in two-thirds of the counties where they are present. The significance of the top third of counties must be interpreted with care, as the values in this category range from as little as 2% to as much as 50% of county populations. However, many of these high share counties are decidedly non-urban, including locations in Maine, New Hampshire, Vermont, upstate New York, West Virginia, southern Indiana, and Kansas.

The map for Percent Change in Adherents, 1952-1971 and 1971-1990 indicates a modest but positive median county change value for the earlier period (+ 14.36%) and a negative value (-11.0%) for the more recent period. Thus, many counties that bettered the denomination's median performance for both periods may have registered virtually no overall gain. Such counties are widely distributed throughout the nation, with perhaps some predominance shown in areas of high population share, such as New Hampshire, Vermont, West Virginia, and southern Indiana.

The map for Shift in Share of Population also highlights some of the very same general areas, and follows the same sequence over time. While the median county change in share rate indicates modest growth in the 1952-1971 period (1.01), declining shares (.80) are indicated in the more recent period. Thus, even where the American Baptists have done best, they may be declining in their share of total county populations.

In summary, the American Baptist Churches in the U.S.A. are a major Anglo-Protestant community that settled here during the colonial period and has become widely dispersed into a national distribution. Only the mid-19th century division between Northern and Southern Baptists has changed this pattern. For the period 1952-1990 the American Baptist Churches in the U.S.A. recorded a modest numerical growth rate in the context of very little spatial expansion. In the decade of the 1980s some modest declines occurred. Even in places of relative numeric strength, the American Baptists have had difficulty retaining population share.

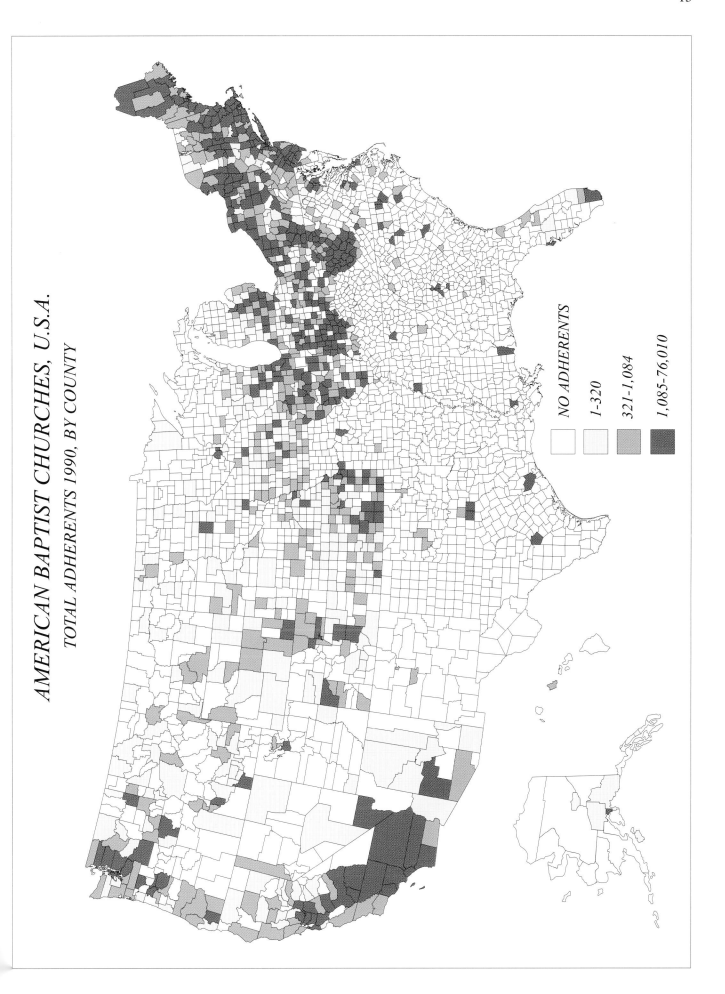

AMERICAN BAPTIST CHURCHES, U.S.A.
TOTAL ADHERENTS 1990, BY COUNTY

NO ADHERENTS

1-320

321-1,084

1,085-76,010

15

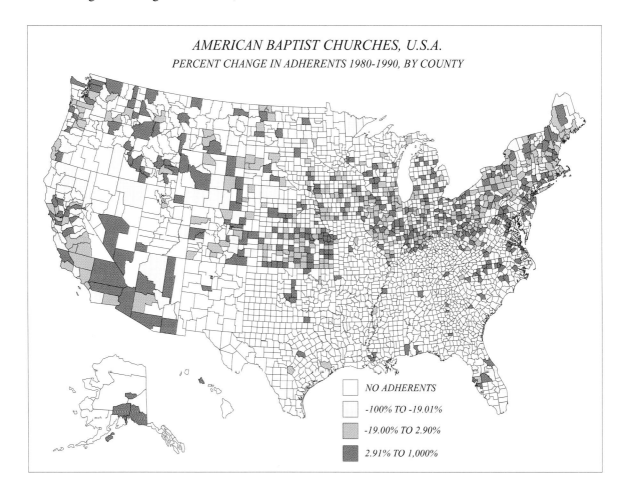

AMERICAN BAPTIST CHURCHES, U.S.A.
PERCENT CHANGE IN ADHERENTS 1980-1990, BY COUNTY

NO ADHERENTS
-100% TO -19.01%
-19.00% TO 2.90%
2.91% TO 1,000%

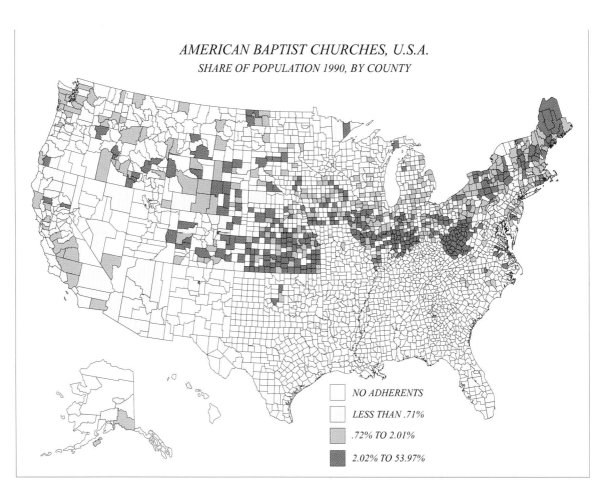

AMERICAN BAPTIST CHURCHES, U.S.A.
SHARE OF POPULATION 1990, BY COUNTY

NO ADHERENTS
LESS THAN .71%
.72% TO 2.01%
2.02% TO 53.97%

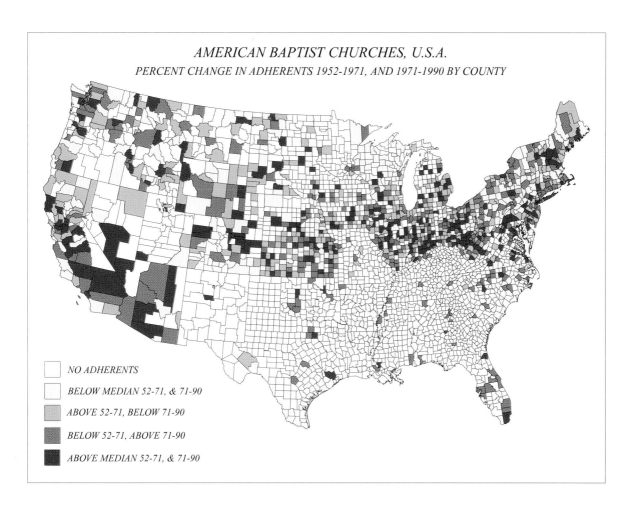

AMERICAN BAPTIST CHURCHES, U.S.A.

PERCENT CHANGE IN ADHERENTS 1952-1971, AND 1971-1990 BY COUNTY

NO ADHERENTS

BELOW MEDIAN 52-71, & 71-90

ABOVE 52-71, BELOW 71-90

BELOW 52-71, ABOVE 71-90

ABOVE MEDIAN 52-71, & 71-90

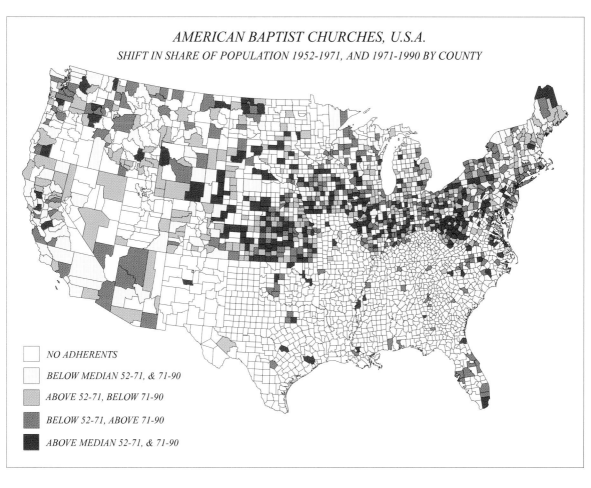

AMERICAN BAPTIST CHURCHES, U.S.A.

SHIFT IN SHARE OF POPULATION 1952-1971, AND 1971-1990 BY COUNTY

NO ADHERENTS

BELOW MEDIAN 52-71, & 71-90

ABOVE 52-71, BELOW 71-90

BELOW 52-71, ABOVE 71-90

ABOVE MEDIAN 52-71, & 71-90

BAPTIST GENERAL CONFERENCE

The Baptist General Conference is a relatively small, once highly ethnic, denomination. This group was founded in 1852 by an immigrant Swedish school teacher named Gustaf Palmquist, and in 1879 the name Swedish Baptist General Conference of America was adopted. Between 1888 and 1944, this denomination was affiliated with the Northern Baptists (now American Baptist Churches in the U.S.A.). In 1945 the word "Swedish" was dropped from its name. Maintenance of a fairly conservative brand of Baptist doctrines has reinforced its independent denominational status.

	1952	1971	1980	1990
Adherents:	49,127	125,678	150,509	167,300
Counties:	181	277	324	348

Although the Baptist General Conference remains a relatively small church, its growth has been quite impressive. Between 1952 and 1990, its number of adherents more than tripled (from 49,127 to 167,300) and the number of counties it occupies nearly doubled (from 181 to 348). Similarly, between 1952 and 1990, the number of congregations more than doubled (from 343 to 786). These rates of expansion place the Baptist General Conference among that group of denominations that grew most rapidly during the 1951-1990 period.

The map of Total Adherents, 1990 continues to reflect the historic settlement patterns of this group's Swedish and German immigrant founders, with a distribution centered in the upper Midwest, especially in Wisconsin and Minnesota. Smaller isolated clusters of contiguous counties are found in Colorado, Oregon, California, and the Boston metropolitan area. A comparison of the numeric category limits on the map of Total Adherents, 1990 and its 1952 counterpart suggests that growth has been evenly distributed throughout the denomination's county locations. For example, in 1952, the middle third of counties for this denomination ranged from

89 to 210 adherents per county. In 1990, the middle third of counties report adherents levels between 114 and 307.

The map for Percent Change in Adherents, 1980-1990 indicates a process of redistribution of adherents within the several core areas. High growth counties (the upper third of counties) representing increases in excess of 42% typically are located adjacent to those counties registering the highest levels of incidence on the map of Total Adherents, 1990. It is difficult to escape the impression that the Baptist General Conference is shifting in a suburban direction.

However, as indicated on the map for Share of Population, 1990, even in its strongest share counties, this denomination never reaches as much as 10% of a county's total population. Given that this core area is so strongly dominated by Lutheran churches, this Baptist denomination most likely represents only a secondary cultural force, even though its adherents share a common ethnic heritage with many of their neighbors.

The remaining two maps provide longer term views of these same patterns. The map for Percent Change in Adherents, 1952-1971 and 1971-1990 quite clearly indicates a filling-in pattern, in which counties that consistently performed above the denomination's median county rate of growth (218.96% for 1952-1971 and 43.45% for 1971-1990) are located adjacent to previously occupied counties in the several historic core areas. Similarly, the map for Shift in Share of Population, 1952-1971 and 1971-1990 indicates consistently growing denominational populations in counties of "new" entry since 1952, especially along the front range of the Rockies, in Arizona, and in California.

In summary, the Baptist General Conference provides a classic pattern of contagion diffusion, in which growth occurs in locations adjoining previously established centers. This is a communion for which numeric and spatial growth have occurred in tandem. Yet, impressive growth rates have not changed the general impression that this is a single region church. Moreover, in 1990, the denomination does not yet claim a substantial share of the total population even in its places of highest incidence.

BAPTIST GENERAL CONFERENCE
TOTAL ADHERENTS 1990, BY COUNTY

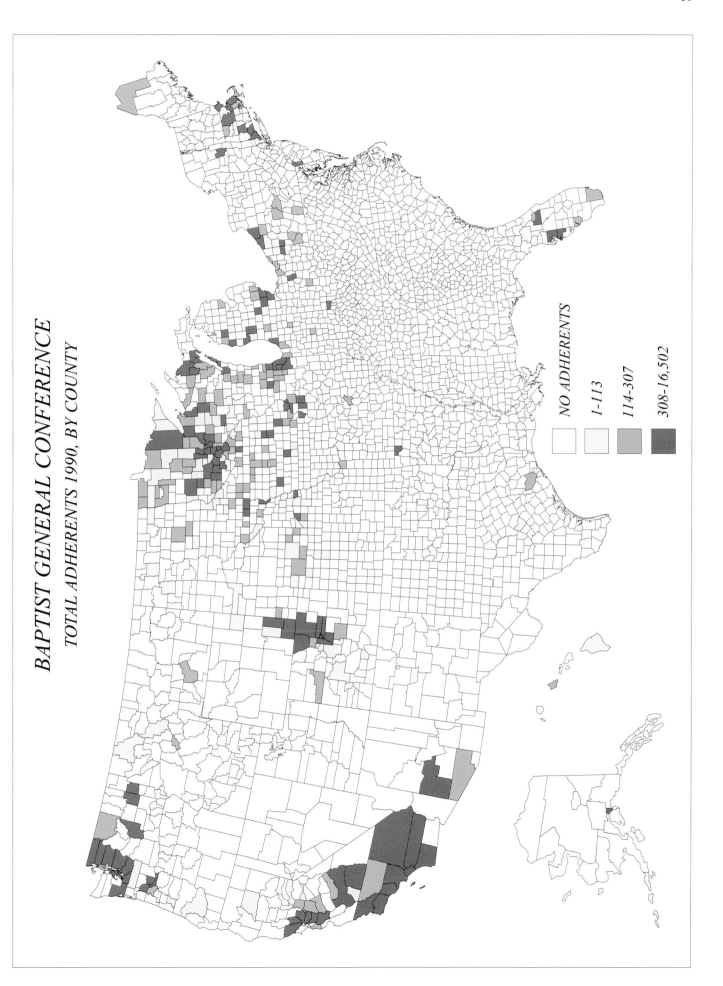

NO ADHERENTS

1-113

114-307

308-16,502

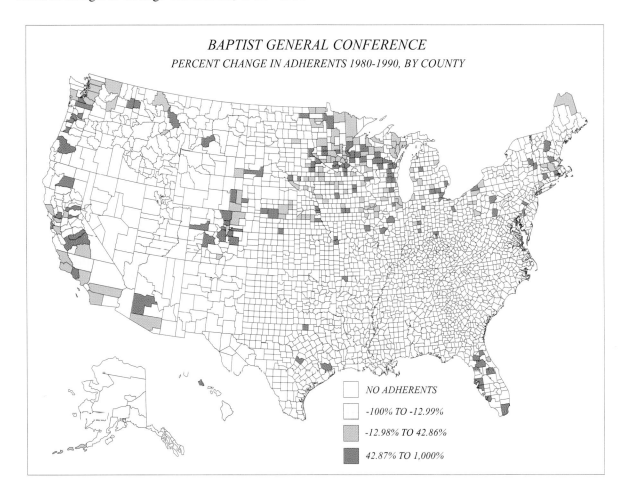

BAPTIST GENERAL CONFERENCE
PERCENT CHANGE IN ADHERENTS 1980-1990, BY COUNTY

NO ADHERENTS
-100% TO -12.99%
-12.98% TO 42.86%
42.87% TO 1,000%

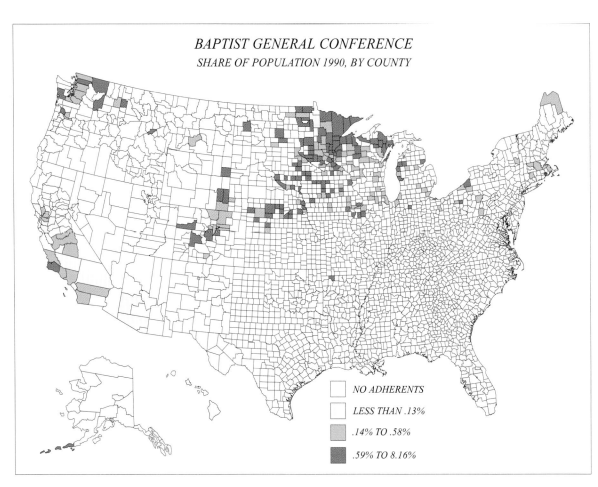

BAPTIST GENERAL CONFERENCE
SHARE OF POPULATION 1990, BY COUNTY

NO ADHERENTS
LESS THAN .13%
.14% TO .58%
.59% TO 8.16%

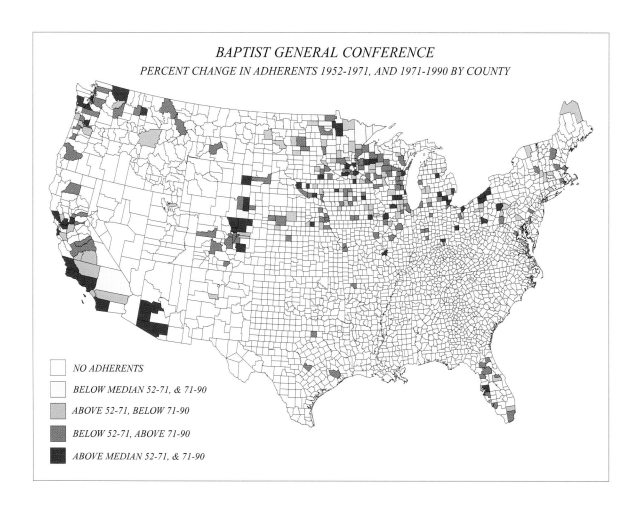

BAPTIST GENERAL CONFERENCE

PERCENT CHANGE IN ADHERENTS 1952-1971, AND 1971-1990 BY COUNTY

NO ADHERENTS
BELOW MEDIAN 52-71, & 71-90
ABOVE 52-71, BELOW 71-90
BELOW 52-71, ABOVE 71-90
ABOVE MEDIAN 52-71, & 71-90

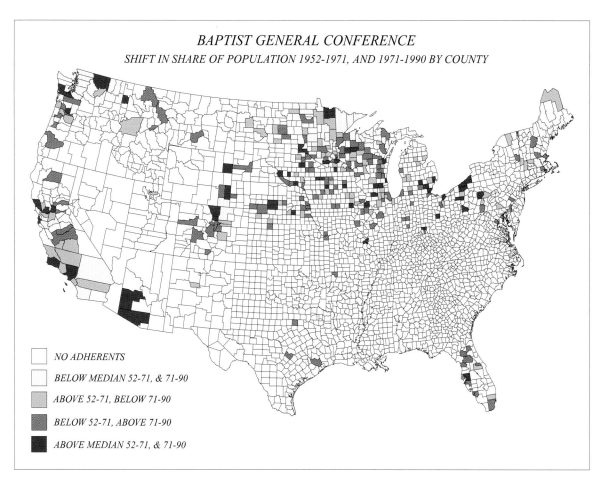

BAPTIST GENERAL CONFERENCE

SHIFT IN SHARE OF POPULATION 1952-1971, AND 1971-1990 BY COUNTY

NO ADHERENTS
BELOW MEDIAN 52-71, & 71-90
ABOVE 52-71, BELOW 71-90
BELOW 52-71, ABOVE 71-90
ABOVE MEDIAN 52-71, & 71-90

BRETHREN IN CHRIST CHURCH

Religious persecution in Europe during the 1700s caused many small religious sects to flee to the colonies. Numerous German Pietist groups chose to settle in the most tolerant of the colonies, Pennsylvania. During the late 1700s, one small community, later to be known as the "River Brethren," dissented on certain theological matters and separated themselves from other Brethren groups. In 1863, the descendants of the River Brethren renamed themselves the Brethren in Christ. Members of this small religious body practice conscientious objection. They are one of a number of closely related religious groups characterized in the public mind by the most distinctive of them, the Amish.

	1952	1971	1980	1990
Adherents:	6,007	11,458	18,443	19,769
Counties:	57	73	83	90

This is a highly localized religious sect. In 1952, 67% of its 6,000 adherents were situated in the State of Pennsylvania. In 1990, 66% of its 19,800 adherents were still in Pennsylvania, with 17.3% found in Lancaster County. The impressive growth rate of 229% increase between 1952 and 1990 must be viewed in the context of the small size of the communion at the beginning of this period. Although in 1990 this group remains quite small both in adherents and geographic extent, nonetheless, it is accurate to characterize these Brethren as a high growth rate community for the entire 1952-1990 period.

The map of Total Adherents, 1990 clearly delineates the group's traditional core area, as well as a scattering of small clusters of counties and even isolated counties elsewhere in the nation. Even the largest third of counties for this denomination may represent communities of less than 150 (141 to 3,412) adherents.

The map for Percent Change in Adherents, 1980-1990 must be viewed in terms of the modest overall increase for these Brethren during the decade (8%). The category values for this map indicate that over half of all counties declined in adherents, with a median county rate of - 19.23%. The upper third of counties begins at just under an 11% rate of increase. Counties in this upper third are located across the geographic distribution, both within the historic core and

elsewhere.

As might be expected, the map for Share of Population, 1990 indicates that this small sect nowhere accounts for as much as 2% of county populations. Nonetheless, the preponderance of the historic core area in Pennsylvania still is defined sharply on this map.

The map for Percent Change in Adherents, 1952-1971 and 1971-1990 is based on median county change rates of 97.67% and 132.43%. This set of values represents a counter trend, as most denominations in this *Atlas* grew more aggressively between 1952 and 1971. The median county change rates for this community reflect the fact that its most substantial growth occurred between 1971 and 1980. Counties that performed consistently at or above the median rate for this later period appear to represent isolated situations, perhaps representing individual congregations both within and outside the traditional eastern Pennsylvania core area.

The map portraying Shift in Share of Population 1952-1971 and 1971-1990 is nearly identical to that for Percent Change in Adherents. The median county change rates of 1.62 and 1.71 indicate that growth in adherents has translated into stronger shares of population at the county level, more so in the later 1971-1990 period. However, it must be remembered that between 1971 and 1990 this small sect added 17 new counties, and that those 17 counties represent 18% of all counties in 1990. Moreover, in their places of greatest relative strength, the Brethren in Christ represent only 2% of total county populations. Thus, while it is not surprising that the median share rate increase is high, it also is somewhat misleading because of the small absolute numbers involved.

In summary, the Brethren in Christ Church is substantially more dispersed (58% more counties) in 1990 than it was in 1952. Yet, the proportion of its adherents located both in Lancaster County and in the state of Pennsylvania is virtually unchanged. This remains a highly localized (eastern Pennsylvania) religious sect with a distinctive theology and social ethic. Its aggressive growth pattern of the 1970s was not sustained in the 1980s. Alone, it represents minuscule population shares. However, in combination with other related groups such as the Mennonite Church, the Church of the Brethren, the Evangelical Congregational Church, and the various Amish communities, it surely has a cultural significance in eastern Pennsylvania's "Dutch country."

BRETHREN IN CHRIST CHURCH
TOTAL ADHERENTS 1990, BY COUNTY

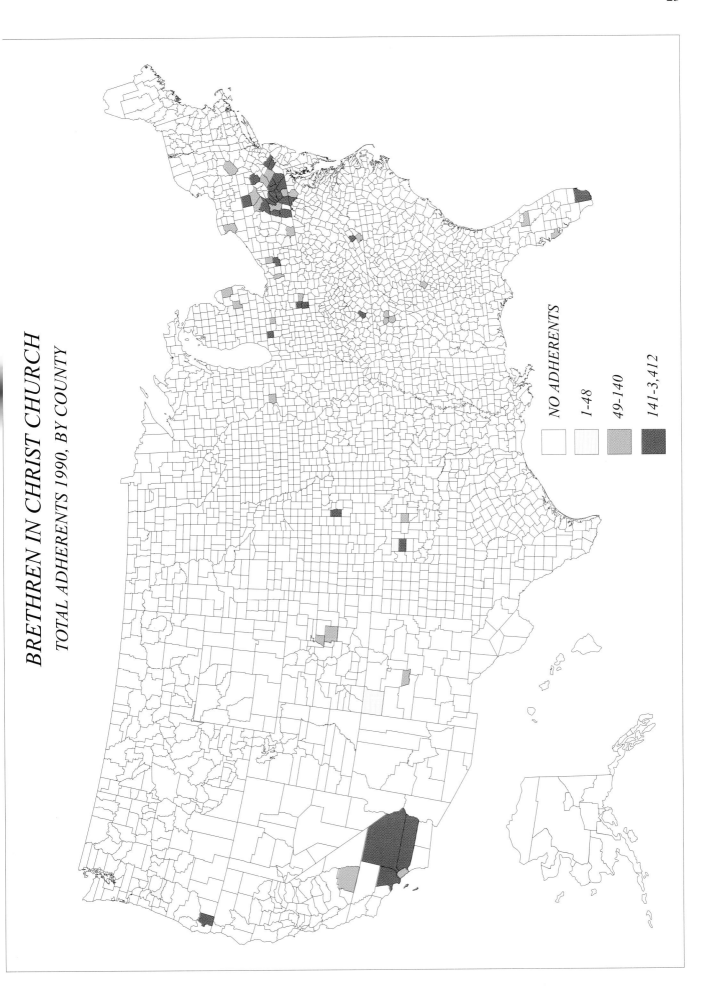

NO ADHERENTS

1-48

49-140

141-3,412

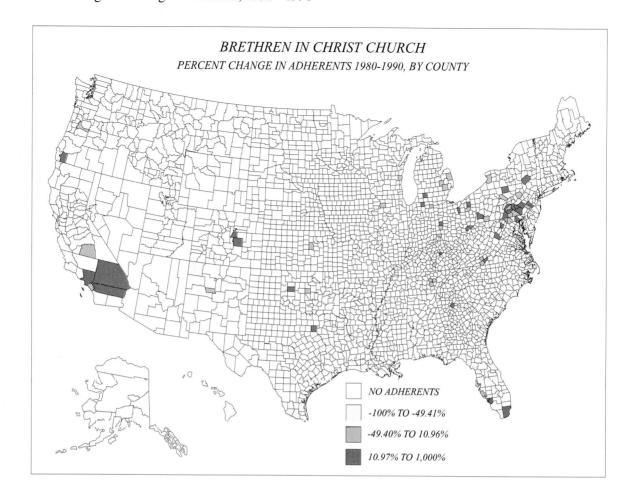

BRETHREN IN CHRIST CHURCH
PERCENT CHANGE IN ADHERENTS 1980-1990, BY COUNTY

NO ADHERENTS
-100% TO -49.41%
-49.40% TO 10.96%
10.97% TO 1,000%

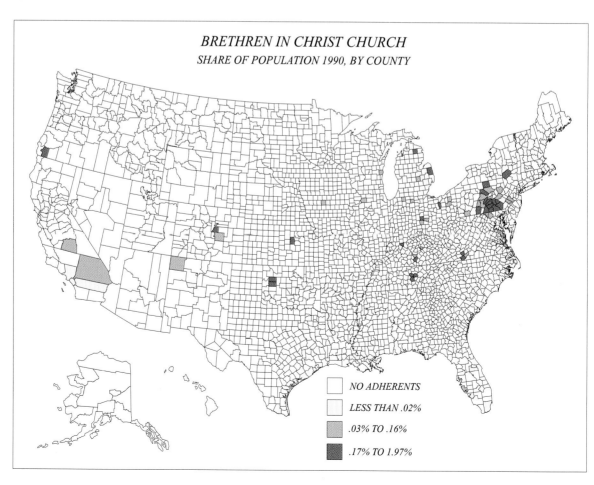

BRETHREN IN CHRIST CHURCH
SHARE OF POPULATION 1990, BY COUNTY

NO ADHERENTS
LESS THAN .02%
.03% TO .16%
.17% TO 1.97%

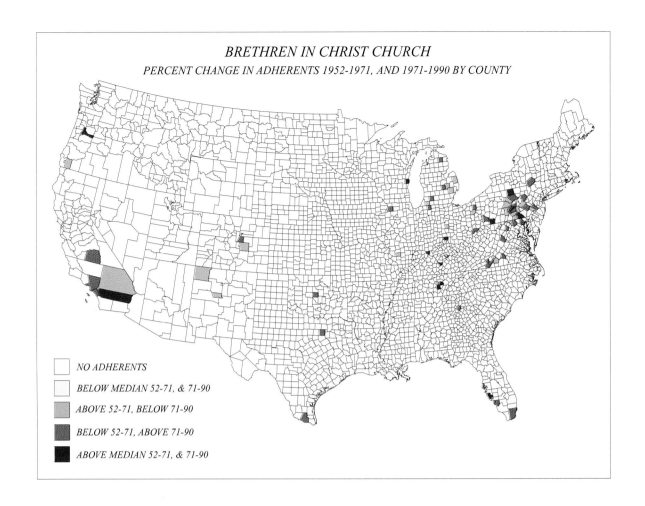

BRETHREN IN CHRIST CHURCH

PERCENT CHANGE IN ADHERENTS 1952-1971, AND 1971-1990 BY COUNTY

NO ADHERENTS

BELOW MEDIAN 52-71, & 71-90

ABOVE 52-71, BELOW 71-90

BELOW 52-71, ABOVE 71-90

ABOVE MEDIAN 52-71, & 71-90

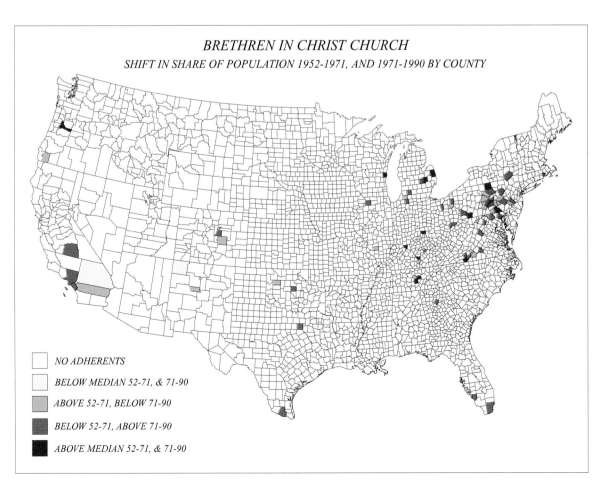

BRETHREN IN CHRIST CHURCH

SHIFT IN SHARE OF POPULATION 1952-1971, AND 1971-1990 BY COUNTY

NO ADHERENTS

BELOW MEDIAN 52-71, & 71-90

ABOVE 52-71, BELOW 71-90

BELOW 52-71, ABOVE 71-90

ABOVE MEDIAN 52-71, & 71-90

CATHOLIC CHURCH

Worldwide, there are over 20 different forms of Catholicism, with the so-called Eastern Rite groups accounting for nearly one million adherents in the United States. In the United States, these other branches of Catholicism together are dwarfed by the Roman Catholic Church, which by 1990, had over 53 million adherents. Between 1952 and 1990, the number of adherents in the Catholic Church increased 78.9%, a rate somewhat greater than that for the total United States population (65%). Between 1971 and 1990, the Catholic growth rate of 19% was slightly below the national population growth rate of 22.9%. By 1990, Catholics were situated in 96 percent of all counties. This is America's largest Christian denomination. It accounts for almost 40% of all religious adherents in the study *Churches and Church Membership in the United States, 1990*, and approximately 20% of the total national population. Given the very large numbers involved, it is not surprising that the patterns of change for this denomination mirror those of the general population, nor that the Catholic Church occupies a position close to the median statistics of many of the denominations portrayed in this *Atlas*.

	1952	1971	1980	1990
Adherents:	29,689,148	44,619,259	47,252,474	53,108,015
Counties:	2,563	2,816	2,837	2,937

The map for Total Adherents, 1990 reveals that very few counties lack Catholic adherents. However, counties in the upper third (from 3,991 to 3,077,114 adherents per county) distinguish the core of Euro-Catholicism in the Northeast and upper Midwest, from that of Latino-Catholicism in the Southwest and West. Between 1980 and 1990, Los Angeles County, California replaced Cook County (Chicago), Illinois as Catholicism's most populous county. This clearly reflects current immigration trends from Latin America. Despite this impressive national pattern, in 1990, 9 states contained 57.9% of all Roman Catholics. The Catholic distribution thins most perceptibly in the Mormon-dominated interior West and in the traditional Anglo-Protestant interior South. Almost 22 million Catholics can be found in a six state corridor stretching from Massachusetts, through New York and into Illinois (New York-7.3 million, Pennsylvania-3.7, Illinois-3.7, Massachusetts-3.6, Michigan-3.0, and Ohio-2.2). Another 12 million Catholics are situated in a less continuous band of counties across the southern tier of states (California-7.1 million, Texas-3.6, and Florida-1.6).

The map for Percent Change in Adherents, 1980-1990 suggests that Catholic population increases and decreases both had distinct regional features. Counties that lost Catholic adherents (-100% to -5.51%) during the 1980s are most strongly clustered in the northeastern manufacturing belt from New England through the Ohio Valley. In contrast, counties with the strongest growth rates are clustered in both the interior South and in the West. These two regions represent rather different phenomenon. In the West, growth largely results from Latin American immigration. Alternatively, in the interior South, growth most likely stems from internal migration form the northeastern and the north central states. Moreover, such counties registered growth rates that minimally were three times as great as that for the United States general population (over 25% as compared to 8%). Counties in the middle third with a median change rate of nearly 10% increase (-5.5% to +25.44%) are widely distributed.

The map for Share of Population, 1990 is very similar to the map of Total Adherents, 1990, and might even be viewed as a "clarified" version of it. Catholics still are a small population element (less than 4%) in the interior South and in much of Mormonism's mountain states turf. European Catholics account for strong shares in both the Northeast and upper Midwest. Traditional Hispanic Catholic communities are major population components (15% and higher) from Texas to California across the Southwest, as are Creole Catholics in Louisiana, and Cuban Catholics in lower Florida. Interestingly, because people may commute from home to church across county lines, the upper limit on this map is greater than 100% of county population.

The map for Percent Change in Adherents 1952-1971 and 1971-1990 is based on median county change values of 52.63% and 21.80% respectively. These rates indicate that even counties that did not perform at or above the median county rate for both periods could have increased substantially in Catholic population. However, those counties at or above these median an county change rates are most evident in the South. A comparison of this map with the 1980-1990 map confirms the impression that Catholic gains in the South are strongest in the more recent period. For the entire 1952-1990 period it is clear that rural counties in the central Plains and upper Midwest, as well as those in the urban Northeast and in New England, report the weakest relative performances.

The map for Shift in Share of Population, 1952-1971 and 1971-1990 is based on median county change rates of 1.37 and 1.07. These rates in part reflect the fact that in absolute numbers Catholics grew more between 1952 and 1971 (15 million adherents) than in the years 1971 through 1990 (9 million adherents). The continued upward trend for the Catholic share of population is quite impressive, and underscores the growing cultural significance of Catholic communities in many areas of the nation. Clearly, counties performing at or above these median county change in share rates in both periods are disproportionately southern. A second cluster of counties can be found in the central Plains where population generally has been thinning. Two regions seem to lag in Catholic share change performance: New England and the Northeast, where the Catholic share declines; and in the fast-growing states of the South and West, where Catholic populations apparently have increased, but not as fast as the general population.

In summary, by 1990 the Roman Catholic Church was situated in all but a few counties in the United States, and had increased in adherents by a factor of nearly 80% since 1952. While Catholic incursions into "new" regions, most notably the South, are quite dramatic, in 1990, a disproportionate share of the Catholic population still is concentrated in two distinct clusters of states. Thus, while Catholicism has become virtually ubiquitous, it is most prominent culturally in a series of more defined pockets. These diverse pockets continue to reflect, at least in part, the ethnic and cultural pluralism of the Catholic Church and its distinctive representations in America.

27

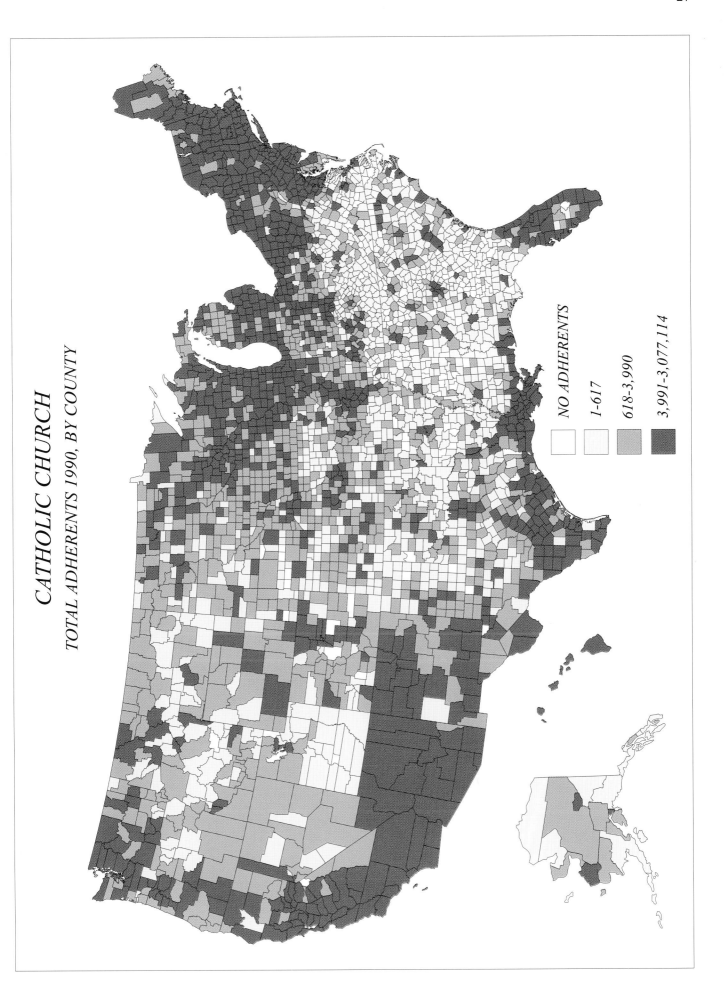

CATHOLIC CHURCH
TOTAL ADHERENTS 1990, BY COUNTY

NO ADHERENTS

1-617

618-3,990

3,991-3,077,114

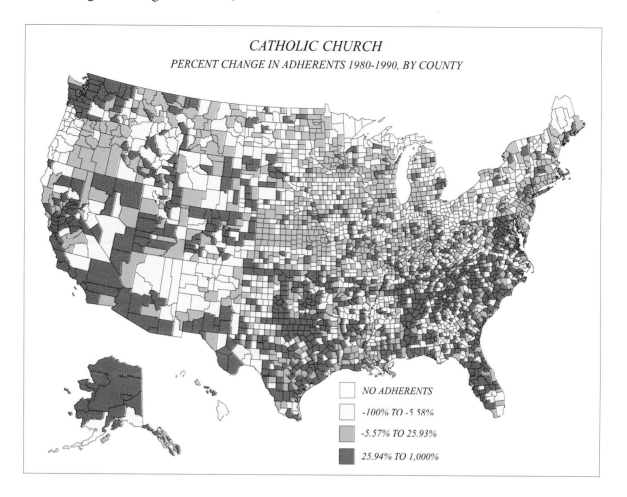

CATHOLIC CHURCH

PERCENT CHANGE IN ADHERENTS 1980-1990, BY COUNTY

NO ADHERENTS

-100% TO -5.58%

-5.57% TO 25.93%

25.94% TO 1,000%

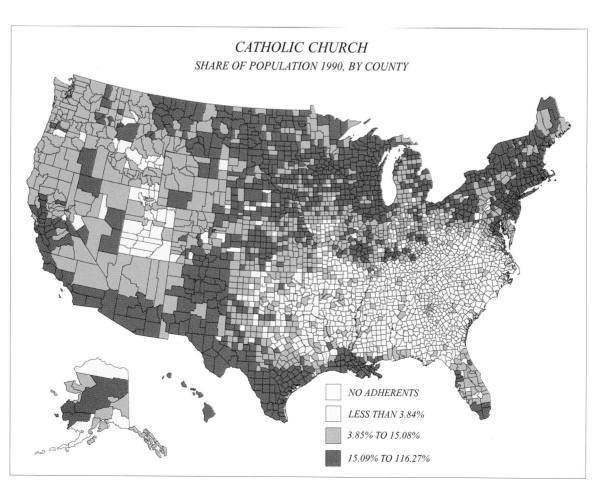

CATHOLIC CHURCH

SHARE OF POPULATION 1990, BY COUNTY

NO ADHERENTS

LESS THAN 3.84%

3.85% TO 15.08%

15.09% TO 116.27%

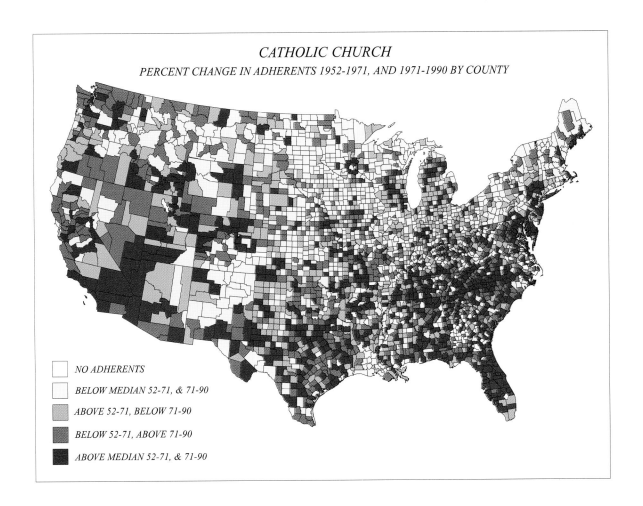

CATHOLIC CHURCH
PERCENT CHANGE IN ADHERENTS 1952-1971, AND 1971-1990 BY COUNTY

- NO ADHERENTS
- BELOW MEDIAN 52-71, & 71-90
- ABOVE 52-71, BELOW 71-90
- BELOW 52-71, ABOVE 71-90
- ABOVE MEDIAN 52-71, & 71-90

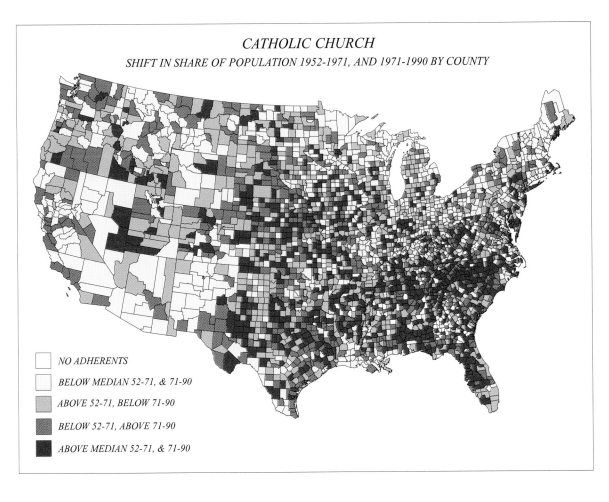

CATHOLIC CHURCH
SHIFT IN SHARE OF POPULATION 1952-1971, AND 1971-1990 BY COUNTY

- NO ADHERENTS
- BELOW MEDIAN 52-71, & 71-90
- ABOVE 52-71, BELOW 71-90
- BELOW 52-71, ABOVE 71-90
- ABOVE MEDIAN 52-71, & 71-90

CHRISTIAN REFORMED CHURCH

When the Reformation theologies spread into the European countries of Switzerland, Germany, and Holland, those groups following the teachings of John Calvin took the name "Reformed." Their counterparts in the British Isles became known as "Presbyterian." The group which today is called the Christian Reformed Church began in Michigan in the late 1840s. After a brief affiliation between 1850 and 1857 with the Reformed Church in America, it severed ties with that denomination, taking the name True Holland Reformed Church. Today, largely as a result of its home missionary activities, its churches reflect a diversity of ethnic traditions including various native American and Asian American cultures.

	1952	1971	1980	1990
Adherents:	155,355	208,689	211,633	225,852
Counties:	121	181	221	235

This branch of the Reformed tradition grew by 45.4% between 1952 and 1990, and also increased its county coverage by an impressive 94%. This small denomination reflects the general religious growth trend, in that its rapid growth in the earlier 1952-1971 period (34%) was followed by modest growth (6.2%) in the 1971-1990 period. In this regard, the Christian Reformed Church exhibits a general pattern shared by many of the Continental European Protestant groups in this *Atlas*.

The map for Total Adherents, 1990 must be read in the context of the fact that one county in Michigan (Kent) contains nearly 20% of the denomination's adherents, and 45% of adherents were reported in one state (Michigan). Outside this highly concentrated midwestern core, there are smaller clusters of counties in the West (California, New Mexico, and Arizona), the Northwest (Washington, and Idaho), elsewhere in the upper Midwest (Wisconsin, Minnesota, and Iowa), in New England, New York-New Jersey, Virginia, and Florida.

The map for Percent Change in Adherents, 1980-1990 is centered on a median county change rate of approximately 14% growth. The upper third of counties with growth rates beginning at over 32% are scattered both within the historic Michigan core area and in all other regions. Counties that decreased in adherents in the decade of the 1980s are predominantly in

the central Plains, Michigan, and in the Southwest. Because both growth and loss patterns are so widely dispersed, it is likely that in most locales, county trends reflect the experiences of individual churches.

The map for Share of Population, 1990 must be interpreted in terms of the wide range of values in the upper third of counties. While the Christian Reformed Church represents over 26% of the population in one county (Kent, Michigan), in over two-thirds of all counties where it is present it accounts for less than half of one percent (.05) of population! Thus, while this church generally is a very small component in county populations, in a small number of cases it is a genuine force in defining the local culture.

The map for Percent Change in Adherents, 1952-1971 and 1971-1990 is based on median county percent change rates (68.08% and 25.30%) that reflect more impressive growth in the earlier than the later period. For this denomination, many counties that performed below the median change rates in either or both periods actually may have gained adherents. Generally, the consistent percentage leaders for the Christian Reformed Church are outside the historic core area, most clearly in the Southwest, in California, and in Florida.

A very similar pattern is revealed by the map for Shift in Share of Population, 1952-1971 and 1971-1990. The median county change rates of 1.34 and 1.07 reflect a denomination that more than held its share of county populations in at least half of its locations. In general, this denomination seems to have done best in rural counties, a feature that reflects both its historical settlement patterns in America, as well as its recent missionary work among Native American communities.

In summary, it is difficult to contend that the distribution pattern for the Christian Reformed Church has changed much over the nearly forty year period between 1952 and 1990. A disproportionate number of adherents remain concentrated in one geographic pocket in Michigan. Outside that pocket this small religious community is but a trace population element in counties where it is found. However, unlike it's sister communion, the Reformed Church in America, the Christian Reformed Church has continued to grow both in adherents and county coverage as a result of aggressive home missions work. Accordingly, this once Dutch church has become both more geographically dispersed and more ethnically diverse.

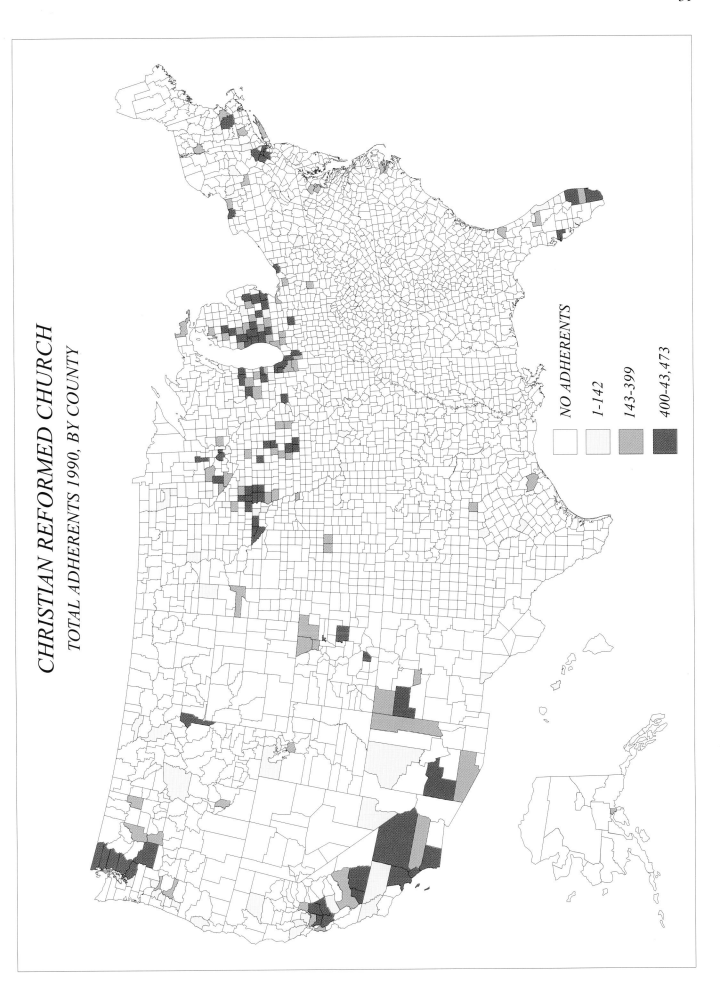

CHRISTIAN REFORMED CHURCH
TOTAL ADHERENTS 1990, BY COUNTY

NO ADHERENTS

1-142

143-399

400-43,473

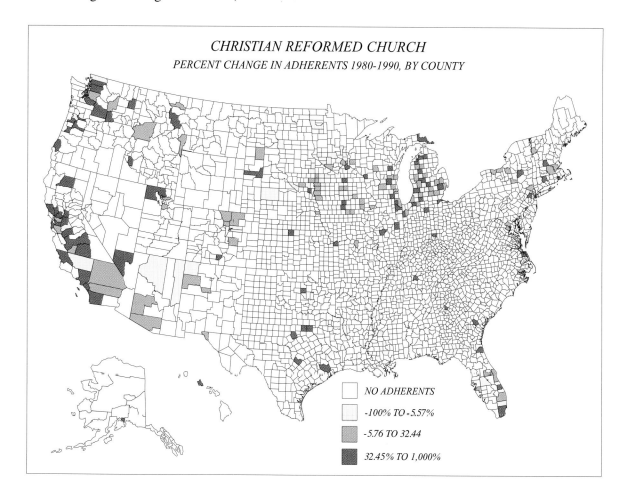

CHRISTIAN REFORMED CHURCH

PERCENT CHANGE IN ADHERENTS 1980-1990, BY COUNTY

NO ADHERENTS

-100% TO -5.57%

-5.76 TO 32.44

32.45% TO 1,000%

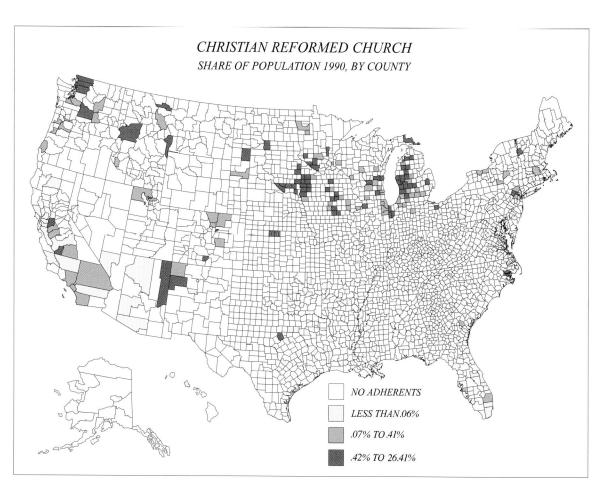

CHRISTIAN REFORMED CHURCH

SHARE OF POPULATION 1990, BY COUNTY

NO ADHERENTS

LESS THAN .06%

.07% TO .41%

.42% TO 26.41%

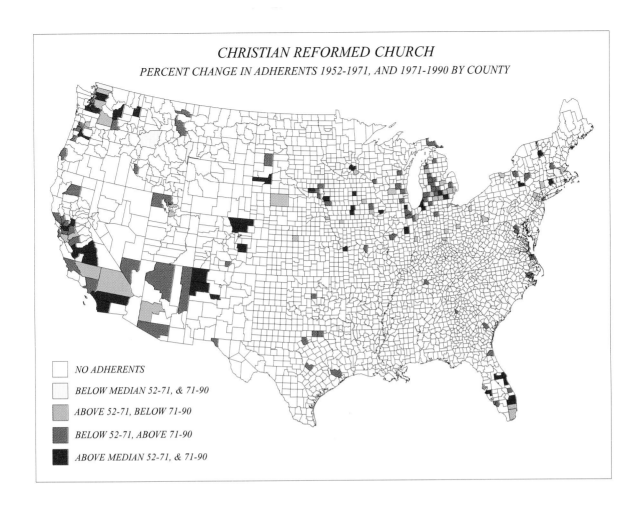

CHRISTIAN REFORMED CHURCH
PERCENT CHANGE IN ADHERENTS 1952-1971, AND 1971-1990 BY COUNTY

NO ADHERENTS

BELOW MEDIAN 52-71, & 71-90

ABOVE 52-71, BELOW 71-90

BELOW 52-71, ABOVE 71-90

ABOVE MEDIAN 52-71, & 71-90

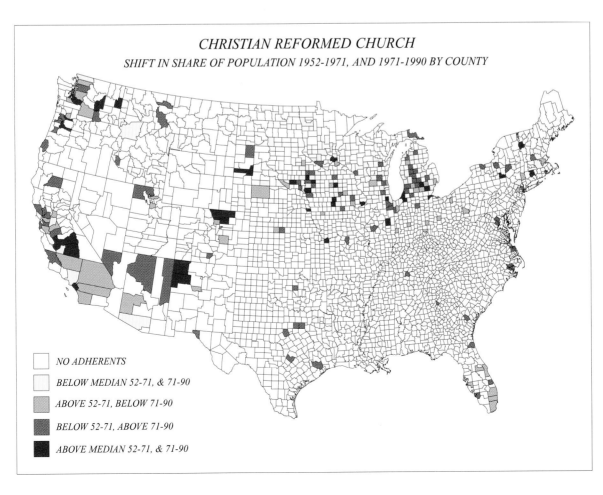

CHRISTIAN REFORMED CHURCH
SHIFT IN SHARE OF POPULATION 1952-1971, AND 1971-1990 BY COUNTY

NO ADHERENTS

BELOW MEDIAN 52-71, & 71-90

ABOVE 52-71, BELOW 71-90

BELOW 52-71, ABOVE 71-90

ABOVE MEDIAN 52-71, & 71-90

CHURCH OF GOD (ANDERSON, INDIANA)

There are over 200 independent religious groups in the United States that use the name "Church of God" in some form. Most of these churches trace their origins to the 19th century. These variously named Spiritualist, Holiness, Adventist, and Pentecostal bodies tend to be either Baptist or Methodist in their theological character, and generally practice foot washing, immersion, and in some cases, speaking in tongues. The Church of God (Anderson, Indiana) is not related historically to the Holiness Movement and it strongly opposes such practices that are common among Pentecostal churches such as speaking in tongues. The Church of God (Anderson, Indiana) began as a secession from the General Eldership of the Church of God in 1880. Following the teachings of its founder Daniel Warner, the Church of God, (Anderson, Indiana) views itself as a movement or association, not a denomination. Local congregations are autonomous, and persons are admitted into local associations by their experience of salvation, not through formal membership procedures. The polity is congregational, and the emergence of state level offices among these associations is only a recent development.

	1952	1971	1980	1990
Adherents:	105,564	186,509	217,831	227,887
Counties:	990	993	1,016	1,020

Because of a change in the estimation procedure used within this association, its 1990 adherents data are not consistent with those reported by it in earlier versions of the study *Churches and Church Membership in the United States*. We have employed the standard estimation technique described in that study to estimate adherents from the reported "members" data. Thus, the adherents data used here differ from the published source but are entirely consistent with adherents data in earlier versions of that study. Even though this estimation is more conservative than that in the published source, its still shows the Church of God (Anderson, Indiana) registering very substantial growth over the nearly forty year period between 1952 and 1990.

The Church of God, (Anderson, Indiana) has increased at a rate of growth well above that of the general population and actually more than doubles its numbers in adherents between 1952 and 1990. Like many of the denominations in this *Atlas*, this association's growth between 1971 and 1990 has been much more modest than it was during the period of the so-called religious revival (1952 to 1971).

The map of Total Adherents, 1990 reveals the traditional regional core of this association, which is centered in Indiana, Ohio, and Michigan, and stretches into western Pennsylvania and Kentucky. Outside of that region, the distribution thins until reaching migratory destinations that have been important for midwesterners, specifically Florida and the West Coast. Throughout its distribution, the map of Total Adherents, 1990 seems to indicate rather small county level adherents numbers for this branch of the Church of God. Where they are present, two-thirds of counties contain fewer than 171 adherents.

Between 1980 and 1990, the Church of God (Anderson, Indiana) increased in adherents at the modest rate of 4.6%, and expanded spatially by entering only four new counties. However, the map for Percent Change in Adherents, 1980-1990 suggests that this aggregate pattern of relative stability masks the diversity of contrasting experiences for different congregations. Between 1980 and 1990, fully one-third of all county locations declined by 30% or more, while in another third of counties associations grew by at least 20%. Moreover, counties

both declining and gaining in adherents are widely scattered within and outside the traditional midwestern core region.

The map portraying Share of Population, 1980-1990 reveals that these Churches of God rarely account for a major share of county populations, never more than 7%. High share counties are most readily apparent in the traditional midwestern core area. However, a comparison of this map and the map of Total Adherents, 1990 also is revealing. On the West Coast, many counties that register high levels of adherents also register low population shares. This suggests that the Church of God (Anderson, Indiana) is highly metropolitan in character in those settings. Second, in the Great Plains, the Church of God (Anderson, Indiana) tends to register high relative shares, but low absolute numbers of adherents. This suggests that these congregations are in rural locations. Numerous other smaller denominations in this *Atlas*, exhibit this same pattern, including several of the Brethren communities.

The map for Percent Change in Adherents, 1952-1971 and 1971-1990 clearly shows that these two time periods produced very different trends for the Church of God (Anderson, Indiana). Between 1952 and 1971, an impressive median county change rate of 72.1% was accompanied by an increase of only three counties. This pattern reflects a religious group that grew within its established congregations or communities, not through migration or missionary outreach. In the more recent period, 1971-1990, the median county growth rate dropped to only 3.2%. Perhaps the most revealing feature of the map for Percent Change in Adherents, 1952-1971 and 1971-1990 is the wide geographic dispersion of counties in all four categories of performance. Both within the traditional core areas in Indiana, Ohio, and Michigan, as well as outside that core, counties that perform at or above the median rates in both time periods are along side those that consistently perform below the median change rates.

Finally, the map for Shift in Share of Population, 1952-1971 and 1971-1990 also contains patterns that defy simple regional characterization. Additionally, the median county change in share rates for the two time periods are quite different. While the median county share rate of 1.44 in the early period signals a community that was increasing its shares of county population, the rate in the 1971-1990 period of .86 indicates declining population shares. While the South and West report strong performances on the Percent Change in Adherents maps, these regions do not register such strong increases on the Shift in Share of Population map. Obviously, in these regions, growth in adherents has not kept pace with the growth of the general population. Conversely, in both the Midwest and on the central Great Plains, where the general population is declining, the Church of God (Anderson, Indiana) has been increasing its population shares.

In summary, the Church of God (Anderson, Indiana) has more than doubled its numbers of adherents between 1952 and 1990. In this regard, its trend resembles that of many of the Anglo-Protestant groups in this *Atlas* that are of American origins. However, like most groups that are centered spatially in the America Midwest, the Church of God (Anderson, Indiana) saw its more impressive growth in the earlier period, followed by very modest growth in the second period. They have not even kept pace with the growth of the general population between 1971 and 1990. This contrasts sharply with the continued growth of the Church of God (Cleveland, Tennessee), which is much more southern in its spatial orientation, and which also maintains a more traditional form of denominational organization. When comparing these two groups, it is difficult to escape the impression that in a time of more moderate religious change trends, both the regional setting and the style of organization have more favored some forms of Protestantism than others growing out of the 19th century.

CHURCH OF GOD (ANDERSON, INDIANA)

TOTAL ADHERENTS 1990, BY COUNTY

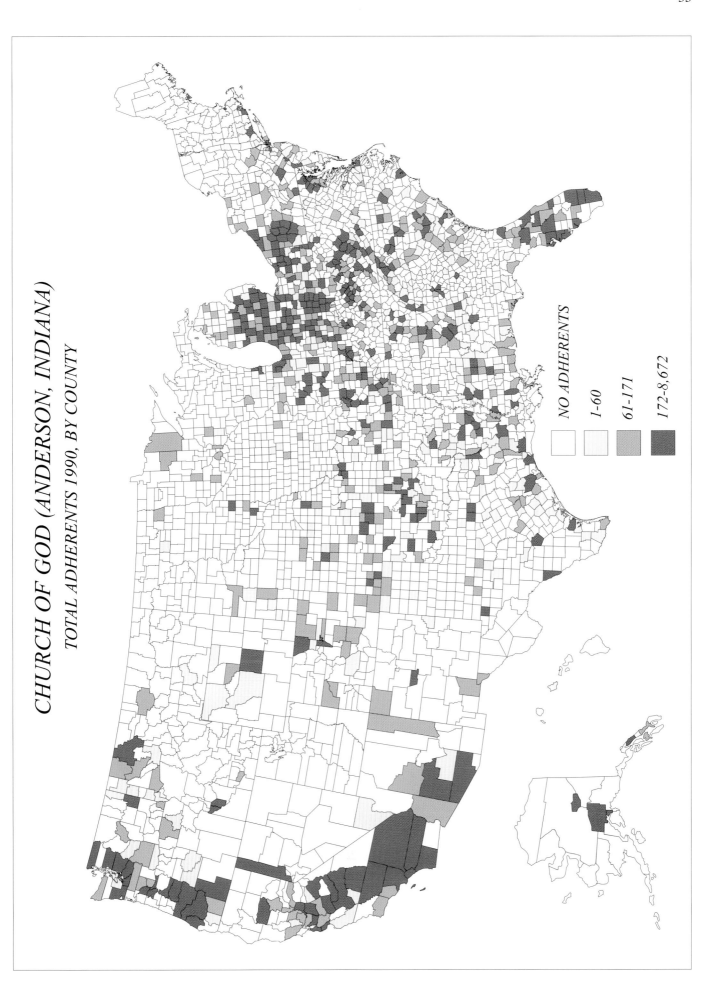

NO ADHERENTS

1-60

61-171

172-8,672

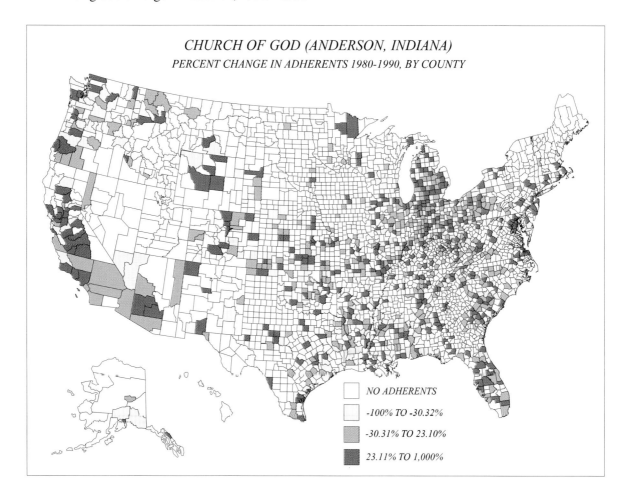

CHURCH OF GOD (ANDERSON, INDIANA)
PERCENT CHANGE IN ADHERENTS 1980-1990, BY COUNTY

NO ADHERENTS
-100% TO -30.32%
-30.31% TO 23.10%
23.11% TO 1,000%

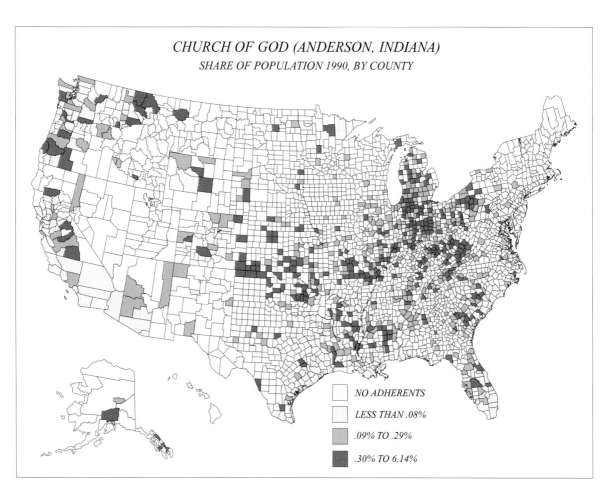

CHURCH OF GOD (ANDERSON, INDIANA)
SHARE OF POPULATION 1990, BY COUNTY

NO ADHERENTS
LESS THAN .08%
.09% TO .29%
.30% TO 6.14%

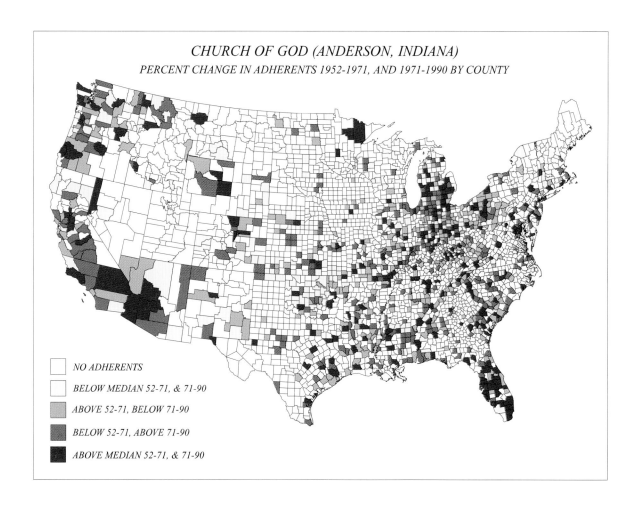

CHURCH OF GOD (ANDERSON, INDIANA)

PERCENT CHANGE IN ADHERENTS 1952-1971, AND 1971-1990 BY COUNTY

NO ADHERENTS
BELOW MEDIAN 52-71, & 71-90
ABOVE 52-71, BELOW 71-90
BELOW 52-71, ABOVE 71-90
ABOVE MEDIAN 52-71, & 71-90

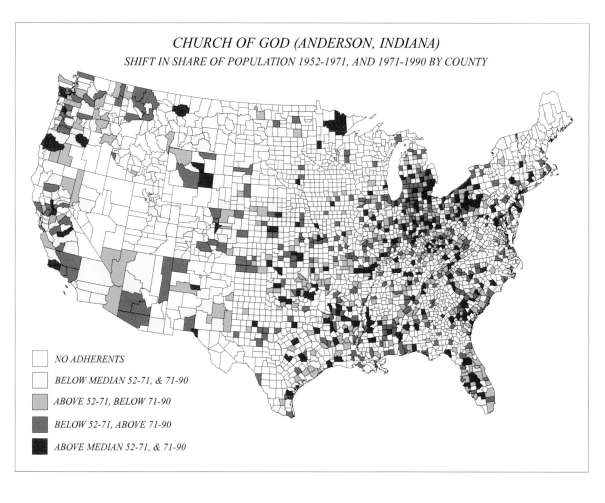

CHURCH OF GOD (ANDERSON, INDIANA)

SHIFT IN SHARE OF POPULATION 1952-1971, AND 1971-1990 BY COUNTY

NO ADHERENTS
BELOW MEDIAN 52-71, & 71-90
ABOVE 52-71, BELOW 71-90
BELOW 52-71, ABOVE 71-90
ABOVE MEDIAN 52-71, & 71-90

CHURCH OF GOD (CLEVELAND, TENNESSEE)

This is one of several hundred groups bearing the name "Church of God," all of which were created during the Second Great Awakening. The Church of God (Cleveland, Tennessee) is the major present-day descendent of Richard Spurling's "Christian Union" of the 1880s and of A.J. Thomlinson's "The Holiness Church" of the early 1900s. When the latter experienced a series of schisms in the 1920s the Church of God (Cleveland, Tennessee) emerged as the largest surviving body. This is "born again" Christianity complete with divine healing and speaking in tongues.

	1952	1971	1980	1990
Adherents:	136,461	368,009	472,383	691,563
Counties:	1,073	1,416	1,510	1,497

The statistics for adherents and counties indicate that the numerical and geographic expansion of the Church of God (Cleveland, Tennessee) have followed different patterns. The number of counties occupied reached a plateau by the end of the decade of the 1970s. However, even as this denomination's geographic coverage stabilized, it continued to grow in adherents impressively during the decade of the 1980s. For the entire 1952-1990 period the Church of God (Cleveland, Tennessee) had a 406% rate of increase, the highest such rate reported among the denominations portrayed in this *Atlas*.

The map for Total Adherents, 1990 reveals a denomination that has broad geographic coverage throughout the eastern third of the nation, excepting in the New England states and the most northern reaches of the Midwest. This may be viewed as a previously Southern-based denomination that has extended significantly its geographical range, especially into eastern urban-industrial areas during the years encompassed by these data. It should be noted that this is a thinly-spread denomination, as illustrated by the value limits of the middle category of the map of Total Adherents, 1990. The latter range from 102 to 341 adherents per county. This also suggests that the denomination is characterized by smaller, not larger, local churches.

The map showing Percent Change in Adherents, 1980-1990 has two predominant features. First, this denomination's sustained growth is reflected in the fact that the lowest percent change category has an upper limit of nearly 10% increase. Clearly, strong growth has characterized the denomination. Second, strong growth has characterized the denomination's traditional core locations, including southern Florida, metropolitan Atlanta, Mobile, Alabama, Texas, and Louisiana; while also occurring in more dispersed areas,

including those in northern Kentucky and southern Ohio, the Chicago metropolitan area, and even in Tucson, Arizona. Thus, there has been substantial growth through evangelism both on "home turf," as well as in new territory.

The map for Share of Population, 1990 indicates that the denomination's strongest population shares are in its traditional southeastern core regions. However, with some of these high share counties representing less than 1% of population, and never representing as much as 10% of the county population, it cannot be argued that this denomination is culturally dominant even in its core areas. Secondarily, there is a wide scatter of isolated counties in this highest category in all other regions where the denomination has churches.

The median county change rate for the Church of God (Cleveland, Tennessee) was an increase of 221.21% between 1952 and 1971, and 78.99% between 1971 and 1990. Counties performing above these median rates in both periods are especially evident in the industrial Midwest, and in the urban corridor from Washington D.C. to Boston. Moderate to weak county performance in relation to these impressive median change statistics characterize the denomination's older core area. However, these core areas may have experienced considerable growth in adherents even though they do not consistently register high in relative terms. The map portraying Percent Change in Adherents, 1952-1971 and 1971-1990 gives the distinct impression that the Church of God (Cleveland, Tennessee) followed the general population movement during the immediate Post-War years into the industrial areas of the Northeast and Midwest, while continuing to grow in its original core region as well. Throughout the entire period, this Church of God has grown much more rapidly than the general population.

The map showing Shift in Share of Population, 1952-1971 and 1971-1990, much like that for Percent Change in Adherents, 1952-1971 and 1971-1990, contains many high performance counties throughout the eastern third of the United States, as well as some on the West Coast. The Church of God (Cleveland, Tennessee) registered the second highest shift in share median change rate (2.7%) of all denominations for the 1952-1971 period, and the fifth highest such rate (1.43%) during the 1971-1990 period.

In summary, throughout the 1952-1990 period, the Church of God (Cleveland, Tennessee) reported an impressive sustained rate of growth in adherents. On the other hand, the rate of geographic expansion achieved in the 1952-1971 period appears to have slowed during the 1970s and 1980s. This denomination's geographic and numeric growth patterns seem to reflect general population migration trends, although the rates of increase reported for this Church of God far surpass those of the general population.

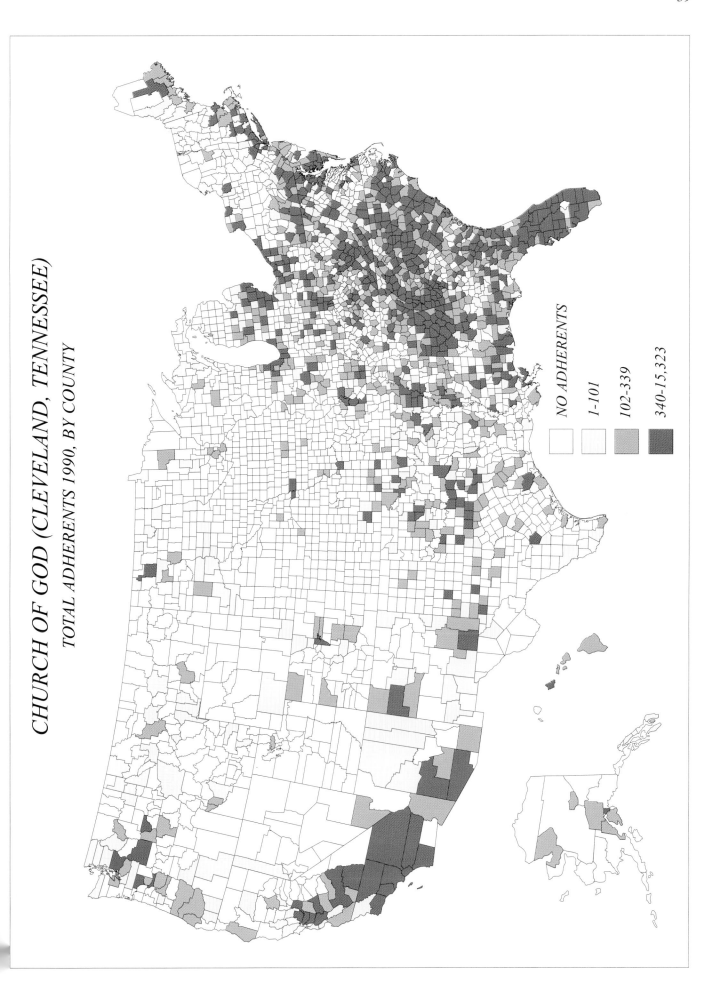

CHURCH OF GOD (CLEVELAND, TENNESSEE)
TOTAL ADHERENTS 1990, BY COUNTY

NO ADHERENTS

1-101

102-339

340-15,323

39

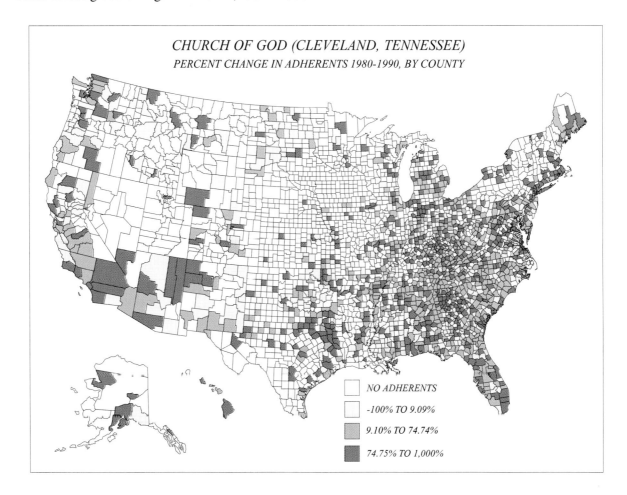

CHURCH OF GOD (CLEVELAND, TENNESSEE)
PERCENT CHANGE IN ADHERENTS 1980-1990, BY COUNTY

NO ADHERENTS
-100% TO 9.09%
9.10% TO 74.74%
74.75% TO 1,000%

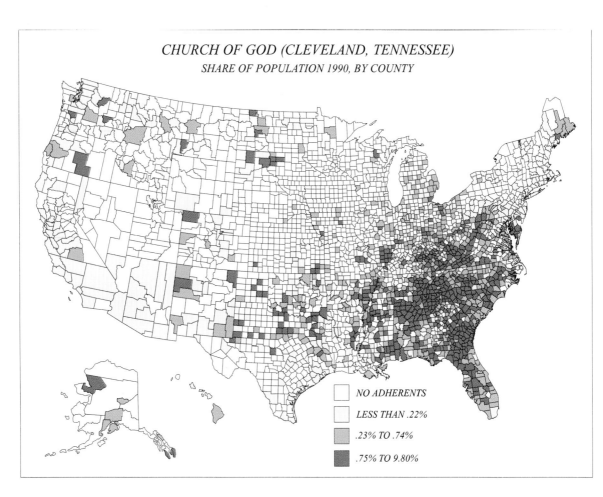

CHURCH OF GOD (CLEVELAND, TENNESSEE)
SHARE OF POPULATION 1990, BY COUNTY

NO ADHERENTS
LESS THAN .22%
.23% TO .74%
.75% TO 9.80%

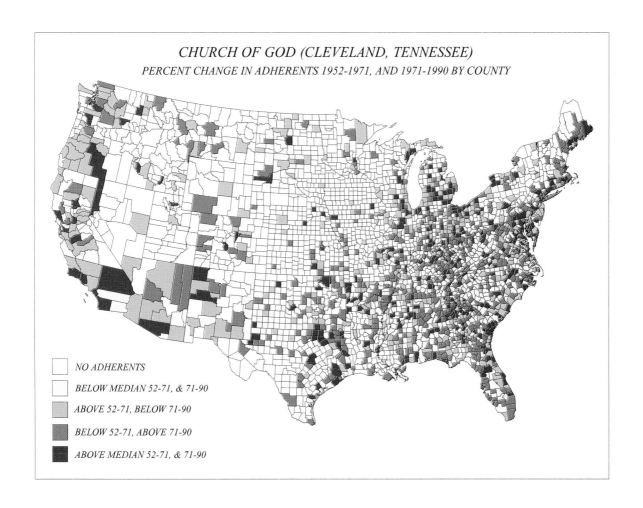

CHURCH OF GOD (CLEVELAND, TENNESSEE)

PERCENT CHANGE IN ADHERENTS 1952-1971, AND 1971-1990 BY COUNTY

NO ADHERENTS

BELOW MEDIAN 52-71, & 71-90

ABOVE 52-71, BELOW 71-90

BELOW 52-71, ABOVE 71-90

ABOVE MEDIAN 52-71, & 71-90

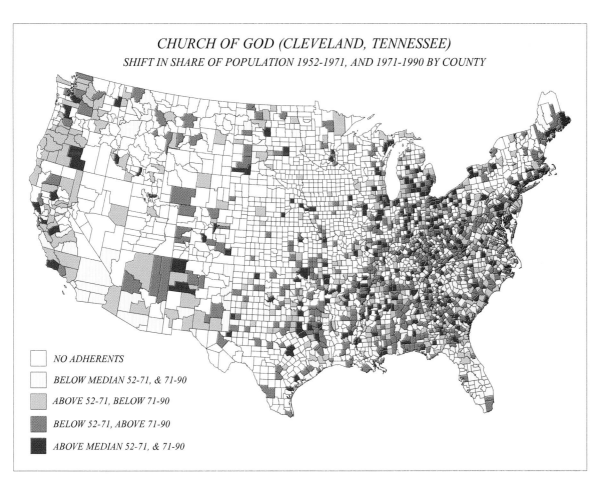

CHURCH OF GOD (CLEVELAND, TENNESSEE)

SHIFT IN SHARE OF POPULATION 1952-1971, AND 1971-1990 BY COUNTY

NO ADHERENTS

BELOW MEDIAN 52-71, & 71-90

ABOVE 52-71, BELOW 71-90

BELOW 52-71, ABOVE 71-90

ABOVE MEDIAN 52-71, & 71-90

CHURCH OF THE BRETHREN

Brethren (i.e. German Pietist) groups were the object of severe religious persecution in Europe during the early 1700s. Many of these groups fled to the colonies, especially to Pennsylvania. The Church of the Brethren is the parent group from which a large number of native American sects were created through schisms. Among these are the Seventh Day Baptists, the Church of God (New Dunkers), the Progressive Brethren, the Old Order Dunkers, the River Brethren (now called Brethren in Christ), and others. In spite of their theological differences, most of these groups share an emphasis on the "simple life" and a belief in pacifism.

	1952	1971	1980	1990
Adherents:	189,277	220,813	207,980	186,588
Counties:	460	427	417	420

From 1952 to 1971, the Church of the Brethren grew at only half the growth rate for the general population. In the 1971-1990 period, they decreased at a substantial rate (-16.7%). During the entire 1952-1990 period, they declined slightly in adherents (-1.4%) and also diminished in their geographic coverage, appearing in fifty-four fewer counties, a decline of nearly 10%. The denomination fits the general pattern characteristic of many groups centered in the northeastern United States, with modest growth (1952-1971) followed by decline (1971-1990).

The map for Total Adherents, 1990 clearly emphasizes the Church of the Brethren's historic core area reaching from Pennsylvania into the Shenandoah Valley. It is noteworthy that over the years covered by these data, the three state area of Pennsylvania, Maryland, and Virginia accounts for increasing shares of the Brethren's national adherents (48% in 1952, 52% in 1971, and 54% in 1990). The map of Total Adherents, 1990 also identifies two secondary core areas that developed as a result of the 19th century westward migration in the Midwest and Northwest. It is clear from the modest values of the lower category ranges on the map of Total Adherents, 1990 (1 to 81, and 82 to 242) that this group is characterized by small sized communities.

The map for Percent Change in Adherents, 1980-1990 reflects a general pattern of decline. The middle third of counties (-29.19% to 2.21%) indicates a negative median county change rate of approximately -15%, and also indicates that counties declining in adherents are scattered throughout the areas occupied by the group, most especially across the historic prima-

ry core area.

The map for Share of Population, 1990 very much resembles the map of Total Adherents, 1990 in its emphasis of the primary and two secondary historic core areas. The highest third of share counties represent a wide range of values, from below 1% to almost 20% of county populations. This suggests or the one hand, that many of the isolated high share counties outside the historic core areas are in fact, rural, lightly populated counties. It also suggests that this community, by itself, occasionally is a culturally significant factor at the county level. Moreover, in combination with other ethnically and theologically similar groups (for example, see The Mennonite Church) the Church of the Brethren surely imparts a significant cultural imprint on the life of the "Pennsylvania Dutch" country.

The map for Percent Change in Adherents, 1952-1971 and 1971-1990 reflects median county percent change values of 5.36% and -22.72% in the two time periods. Thus, even the relatively small number of counties that performed above the median county level for both periods (shown in red) may have lost adherents over the entire period, and probably did so in the more recent period. Given the nature of these trends, and the apparent extent of declining counties in the traditional core areas, it seems likely that out-migration, mortality, and perhaps even denominational switching all are affecting a distinctive religious community that simply is not replacing its diminishing numbers of adherents.

The map for Shift in Share of Population, 1952-1971 and 1971-1990 depicts virtually the same relative spatial patterns as the Percent Change in Adherents map. However, because the Shift in Share of Population map is based on median county change rates of .87 for 1952-1971 and .68 for 1971-1990, the picture it paints is even more negative than the Percent Change in Adherents map. The share map shows that even counties that performed above the median county rate of share change in both time periods could have lost as much as 40% of population share between 1952 and 1990.

In summary, the Church of the Brethren is a culturally distinctive denomination that has declined both in adherents and in geographic extent between 1952 and 1990. Additionally, its original geographic core area represents a greater share of the group's national adherents in 1990 (54%) than it did in 1952 (48%). Together, these facts portray a religious community that is contracting numerically and geographically into a weakened core area. In the context of even gradual national population growth rates, the trends here suggest that this religious community and the cultural nitch of which it is a part is in decline.

43

CHURCH OF THE BRETHREN
TOTAL ADHERENTS 1990, BY COUNTY

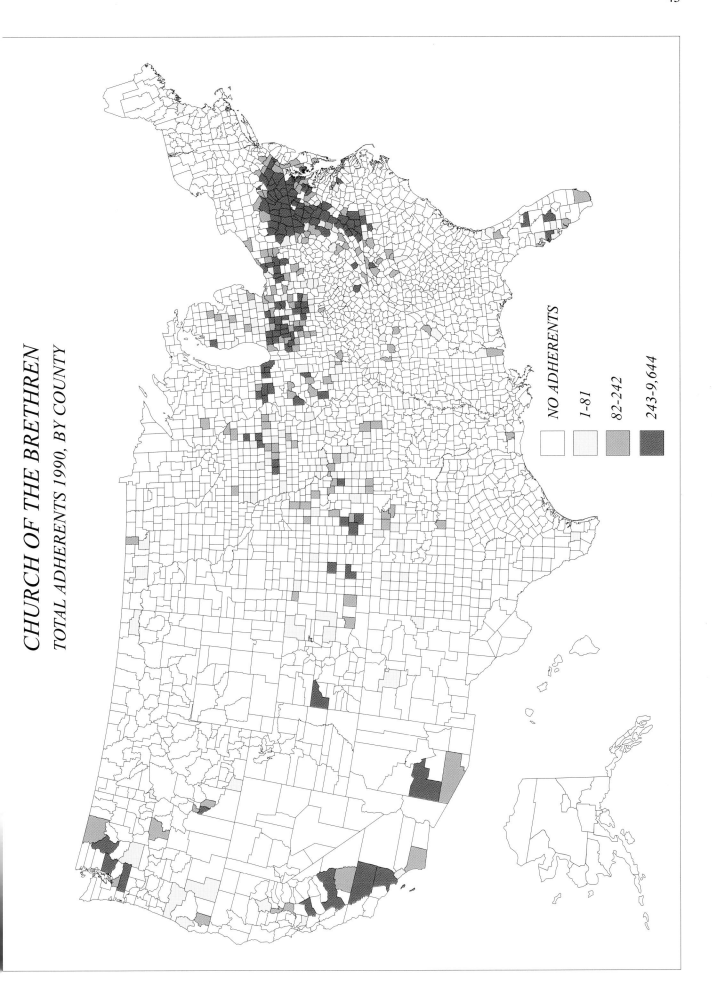

NO ADHERENTS

1-81

82-242

243-9,644

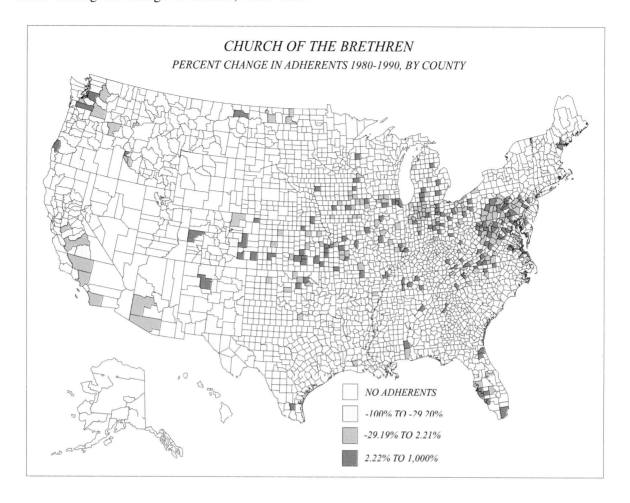

CHURCH OF THE BRETHREN

PERCENT CHANGE IN ADHERENTS 1980-1990, BY COUNTY

NO ADHERENTS

-100% TO -29.20%

-29.19% TO 2.21%

2.22% TO 1,000%

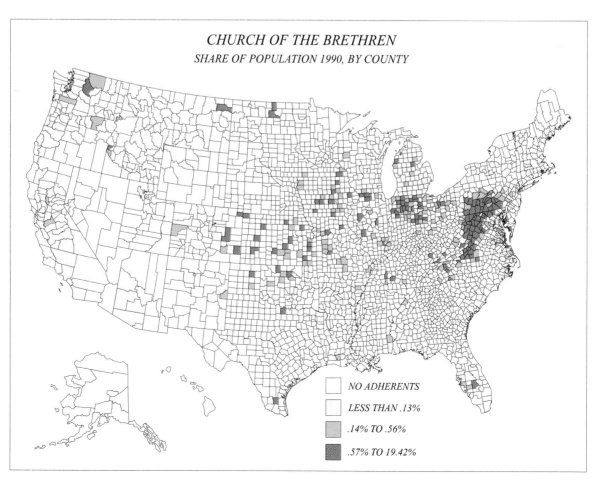

CHURCH OF THE BRETHREN

SHARE OF POPULATION 1990, BY COUNTY

NO ADHERENTS

LESS THAN .13%

.14% TO .56%

.57% TO 19.42%

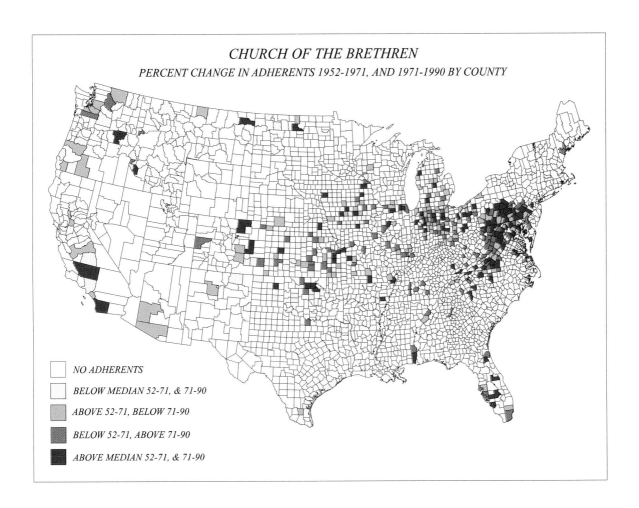

CHURCH OF THE BRETHREN
PERCENT CHANGE IN ADHERENTS 1952-1971, AND 1971-1990 BY COUNTY

NO ADHERENTS

BELOW MEDIAN 52-71, & 71-90

ABOVE 52-71, BELOW 71-90

BELOW 52-71, ABOVE 71-90

ABOVE MEDIAN 52-71, & 71-90

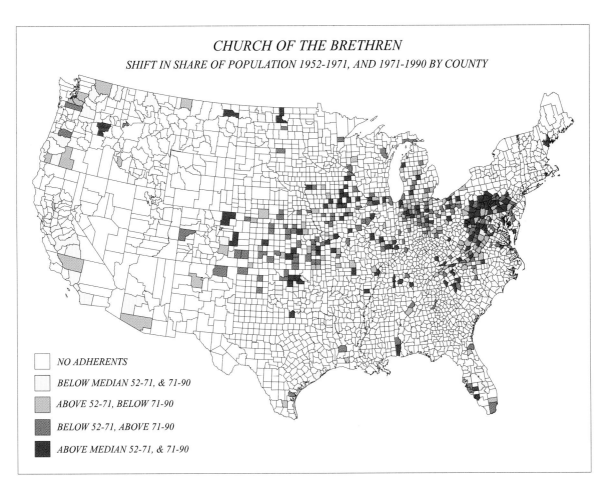

CHURCH OF THE BRETHREN
SHIFT IN SHARE OF POPULATION 1952-1971, AND 1971-1990 BY COUNTY

NO ADHERENTS

BELOW MEDIAN 52-71, & 71-90

ABOVE 52-71, BELOW 71-90

BELOW 52-71, ABOVE 71-90

ABOVE MEDIAN 52-71, & 71-90

CHURCH OF THE NAZARENE

The Church of the Nazarene resulted from a series of mergers between native American holiness-type denominations. The National Holiness Movement spawned many such groups in the middle of the 19th century. In 1907, the Association of Pentecostal Churches in America, with churches primarily in New England and New York, merged with a California-based group, the Church of the Nazarene. A new name, Pentecostal Church of the Nazarene, was adopted at that time. In the following year, a southern group, the Holiness Church of Christ, merged with this body. In 1919 the term "Pentecostal" was deleted from their name. These diverse regional origins may be viewed either as having set the pattern for an association of small regional sects, or as having planted the seeds for a multiregional denomination. The Church of the Nazarene follows Methodist-type theology and polity.

	1952	1971	1980	1990
Adherents:	249,033	486,431	577,805	683,245
Counties:	1,680	1,733	1,781	1,852

Throughout the years from 1952 to 1990, the Church of the Nazarene grew in its number of adherents by an impressive 175%, doubling its adherents between 1952 and 1971 and nearly doing so again between 1971 and 1990. Additionally, it expanded its geographical reach by an additional 100 counties over the years encompassed by these data. The Nazarenes typify the pattern of sustained growth characteristic of many of the native Protestant groups included in this *Atlas*.

The map of Total Adherents, 1990 reveals a widely-dispersed denomination with adherents in well over half of the nation's counties. Two-thirds of these counties report fewer than 400 adherents, and it seems likely that in this instance counties are surrogates for individual congregations. High category counties are prevalent in the Midwest reaching from western Pennsylvania into Illinois. A second band of counties forms a ring in the western states which stretches from Arizona along the West Coast to Canada surrounding the Mormon stronghold. Additionally, clusters of high category counties appear in the southern Plains and in Florida. Counties reporting Nazarene adherents are located in every region of the nation.

The map for Percent Change in Adherents, 1980-1990 clearly depicts the continued growth of the Church of the Nazarene. The upper third of counties grew in adherents by rates in excess of 35%, and are readily apparent in both the Sunbelt and the northwestern states, in the denomination's traditional midwestern core, and even in the Great Plains states. The medi-

an county percent change rate of 20% indicates that growth was a county level norm for this denomination. Yet, counties that increased in adherents as well as those that declined appear adjacent to one another in all regions. This pattern suggests that the success of evangelism efforts varies by congregation, not by region.

The map for Share of Population, 1990 indicates that the Church of the Nazarene rarely constitutes a prominent element in county populations. The upper third of counties may represent less than 1% of county population and never reaches as much as 7%. These "high" share counties seem to be located disproportionately in small town and rural environments, a feature that is consistent with the denomination's historical development. Such counties appear in the Midwest from West Virginia to Indiana, in the southern Plains of Oklahoma and Kansas, and in the mountain interior of the Northwest in Idaho, Washington, Oregon, and California.

The map for Percent Change in Adherents, 1952-1971 and 1971-1990 is based on median county percent change rates of 96% for the earlier period and 34% for the later period. These impressive rates place this denomination in the top third of denominations in this *Atlas* for this measure. Counties that performed at or above these median county rates in both time periods are widely distributed, although they are perhaps more apparent in areas of general population increase, such as in Florida and in the Southwest, and less so in the Midwest.

The map for Shift in Share of Population, 1952-1971 and 1971-1990 portrays a bit more complex set of patterns. Again, the median county change rates are impressively high, in this case 1.63 for the period 1952-1971 and 1.12 for the years 1971-1990. However, there are distinct regional variations. In the Southwest and in Florida, where general population increase has been substantial, it is clear that in spite of their absolute growth, the Nazarenes have not greatly expanded their share of total population. However, they are more than holding their relative position in these areas. Conversely, in areas of declining population, such as in West Virginia and in southern Missouri, the Nazarenes consistently perform at rates above the median county share increase rates. The maps in this series demonstrate the extent to which absolute growth and population share growth can be disassociated.

In summary, in terms of both growth in adherents and growth in county coverage, the Church of the Nazarene represents one of the more impressive success stories in this *Atlas*. It seems reasonable to conclude that between 1952 and 1990, the Church of the Nazarene established itself as a national religious body, though one of relatively small size. Given its traditional strength in small towns and rural settings, it remains to be seen if in future decades it will become more of a presence in growing metropolitan areas.

CHURCH OF THE NAZARENE
TOTAL ADHERENTS 1990, BY COUNTY

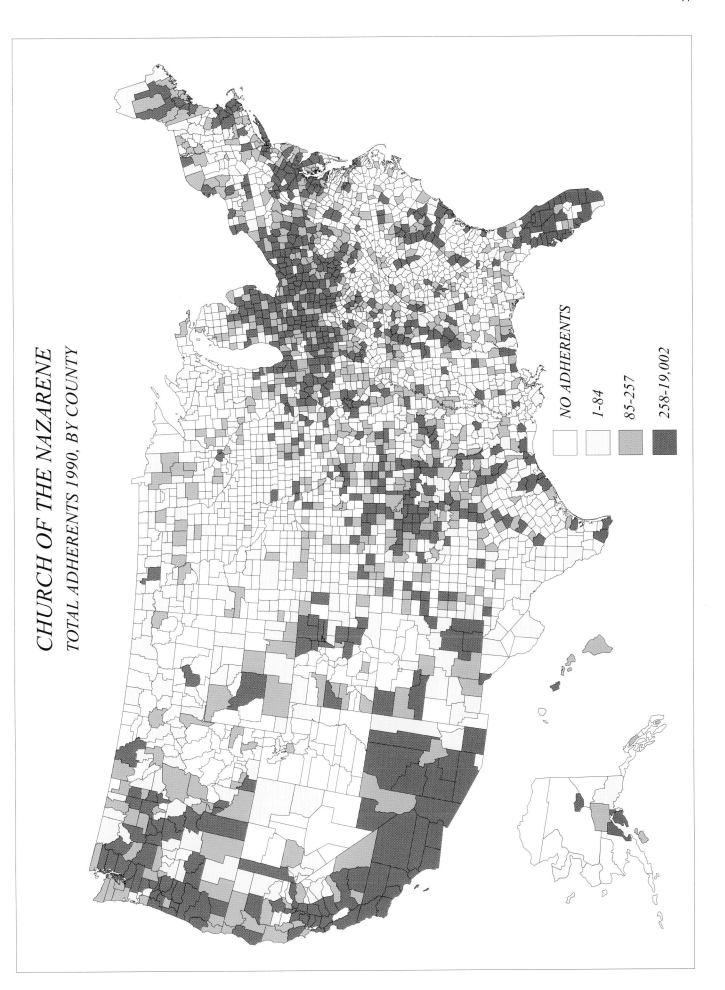

NO ADHERENTS

1-84

85-257

258-19,002

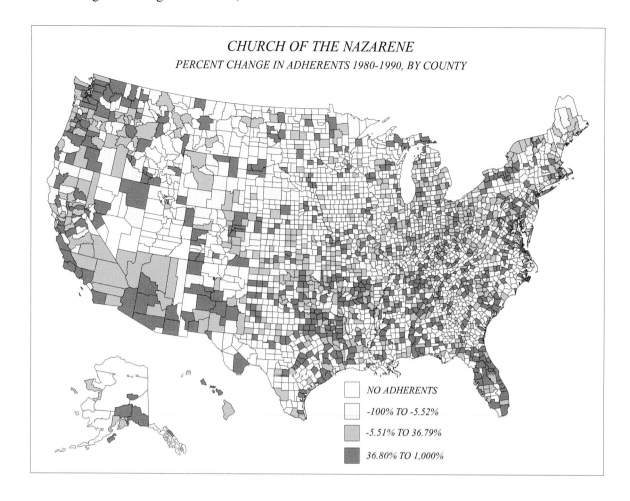

CHURCH OF THE NAZARENE

PERCENT CHANGE IN ADHERENTS 1980-1990, BY COUNTY

NO ADHERENTS

-100% TO -5.52%

-5.51% TO 36.79%

36.80% TO 1,000%

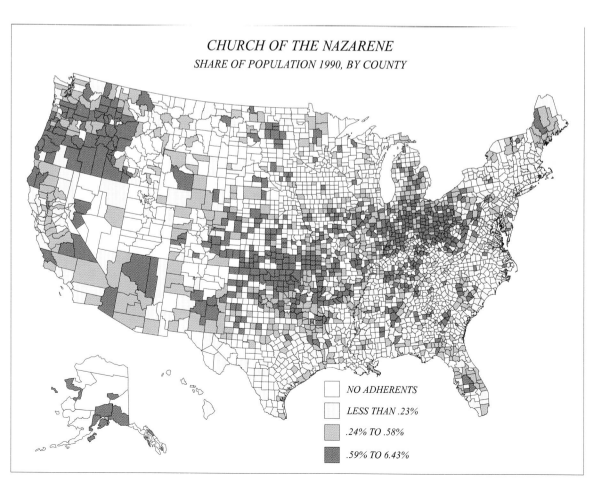

CHURCH OF THE NAZARENE

SHARE OF POPULATION 1990, BY COUNTY

NO ADHERENTS

LESS THAN .23%

.24% TO .58%

.59% TO 6.43%

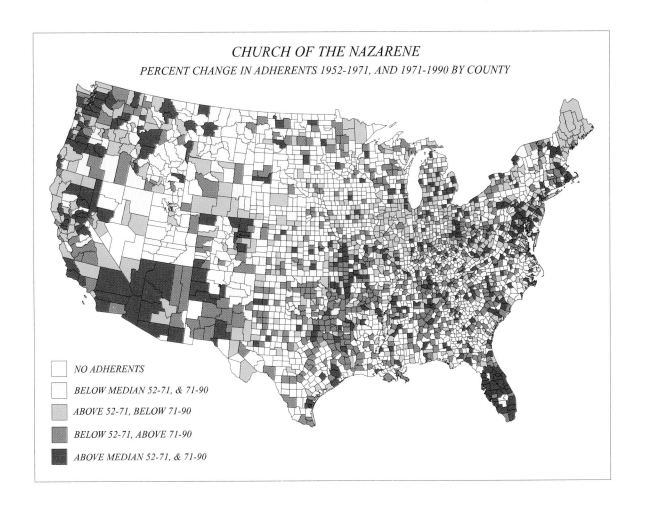

CHURCH OF THE NAZARENE

PERCENT CHANGE IN ADHERENTS 1952-1971, AND 1971-1990 BY COUNTY

NO ADHERENTS

BELOW MEDIAN 52-71, & 71-90

ABOVE 52-71, BELOW 71-90

BELOW 52-71, ABOVE 71-90

ABOVE MEDIAN 52-71, & 71-90

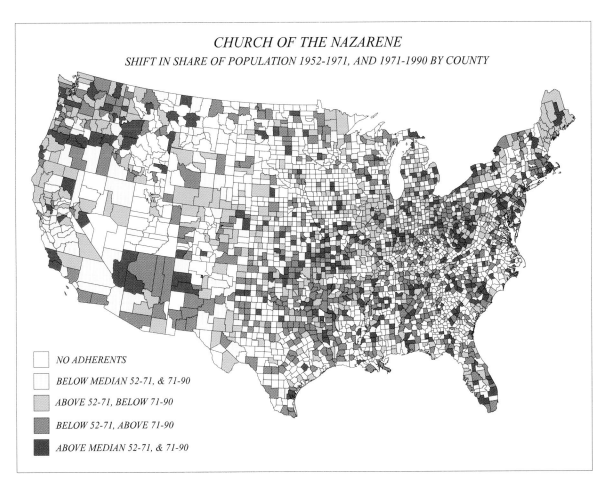

CHURCH OF THE NAZARENE

SHIFT IN SHARE OF POPULATION 1952-1971, AND 1971-1990 BY COUNTY

NO ADHERENTS

BELOW MEDIAN 52-71, & 71-90

ABOVE 52-71, BELOW 71-90

BELOW 52-71, ABOVE 71-90

ABOVE MEDIAN 52-71, & 71-90

CUMBERLAND PRESBYTERIAN CHURCH

The Cumberland Presbytery was organized in 1810 in Tennessee by ministers who felt that the churches of the frontier needed greater freedom to adapt to their unique circumstances. The doctrine of double predestination and the unwillingness of the parent body to relax certain educational requirements for clergy were key to these disagreements. A General Assembly was formed for the Cumberland branch of Presbyterianism by 1829. When the Cumberland Presbyterian Church and the Presbyterian Church U.S.A. merged in 1906, a dissenting group of churches withdrew from that merger and perpetuated a then greatly reduced Cumberland Presbyterian Church as a separate denomination.

	1952	1971	1980	1990
Adherents:	92,656	104,006	90,691	91,040
Counties:	307	288	292	275

The long term trend for the Cumberland Presbyterian Church has been relative stability (a modest decline of 1.4% in adherents between 1952 and 1990) in the context of shrinking geographical coverage, as indicated by a10.4% decline in counties from 1952 to 1990. Even at the beginning of the era (1952) this small denomination was present in barely 10% of all counties.

The map for Total Adherents, 1990 reveals the primary core area for this group in the Cumberland Plateau of western Kentucky and Tennessee. Secondary pockets of counties appear in Alabama and Mississippi, and in Oklahoma and Texas. Isolated counties, most likely representing single congregations, are located in Florida, California, and Arizona, as well as in Detroit and Chicago. A third of all counties reporting for this denomination contain fewer than 100 adherents.

Turning to the map for Percent Change in Adherents, 1980-1990, the middle third of counties represents change rates from just under 27% losses to just above 10% gains in adherents. These values reflect a denomination that is barely retaining a stable size. Many of the counties with declining adherents during the 1980s are located in the historic core area. However, the high growth rate counties (which at the lower threshold represent as small an increase as 10%) are apparent throughout the geographic distribution.

The map for Share of Population, 1990 has a top category range of less than 1% to just over 5% of county populations. This suggests that even where it is numerically strongest, the Cumberland Presbyterian Church is not a dominant cultural force. As would be expected, those areas with the strongest shares of population are in the denomination's historic core area in Tennessee and Kentucky.

The map for Percent Change in Adherents, 1952-1971 and 1971-1990 again emphasizes counties within and along the geographic fringes of the historic core area. Here, the median county rates of change were 5.53% between 1952 and 1971, and -21.28% from 1971 to 1990. Thus, some of those counties colored red on this map, indicating performance above the median change rate for both periods, actually lost adherents between 1952 and 1990.

Similarly, the map for Shift in Share of Population, 1952-1971 and 1971-1990 conveys a very similar picture. The respective median county change rates of 1.05 for 1952-1971 and .64 for 1971-1990 mean that some counties performing above the median rates for both periods either lost population or were, at best, stable. These frequently are the very same counties described in similar terms in relation to the map for Percent Change in Adherents for the same nearly forty year period.

In summary, by virtue of having remained outside the 1906 Presbyterian merger, the Cumberland Presbyterian Church became a highly regionalized small denomination. Nearly a half century later (1952), that pattern had not changed. Between 1952 and 1990, the Cumberland Presbyterians remained essentially stable in numerical terms, but had begun contracting spatially. During the decade of the 1980s, the Cumberland Presbyterians once again remained outside of a merger of larger Presbyterian denominations. Given that the home turf of this small denomination is not characterized by population growth, it is reasonable to expect that maintaining stability of adherents into the 21st century will be a challenge for the Cumberland Presbyterian Church.

51

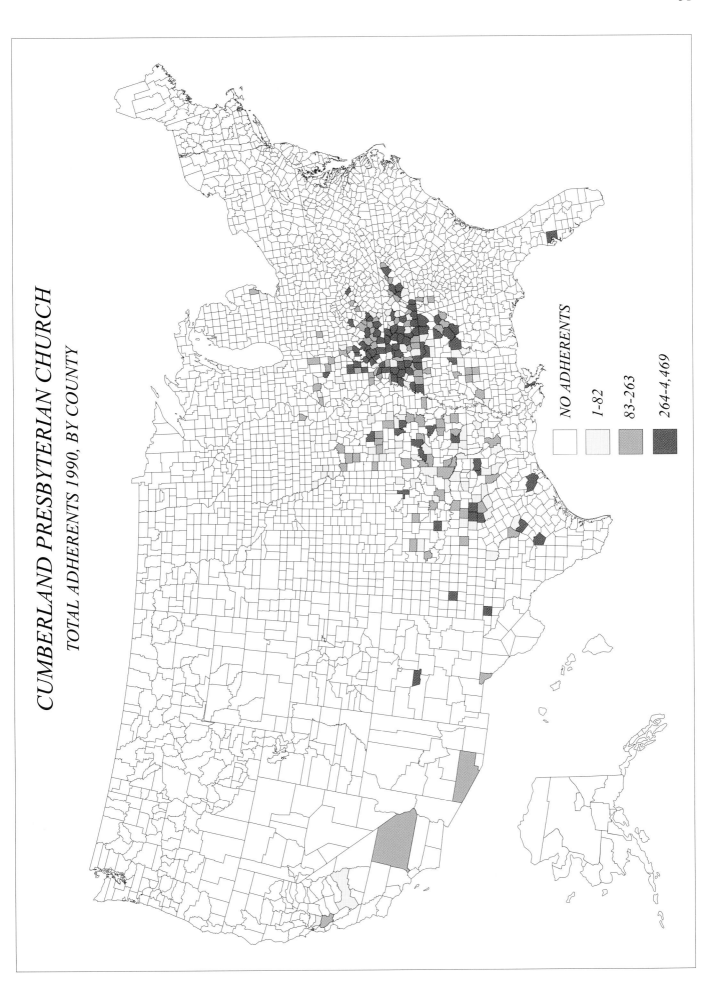

CUMBERLAND PRESBYTERIAN CHURCH
TOTAL ADHERENTS 1990, BY COUNTY

NO ADHERENTS

1-82

83-263

264-4,469

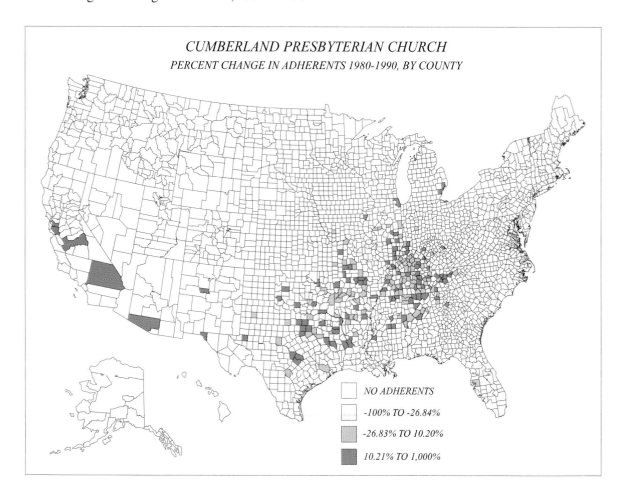

CUMBERLAND PRESBYTERIAN CHURCH
PERCENT CHANGE IN ADHERENTS 1980-1990, BY COUNTY

NO ADHERENTS

-100% TO -26.84%

-26.83% TO 10.20%

10.21% TO 1,000%

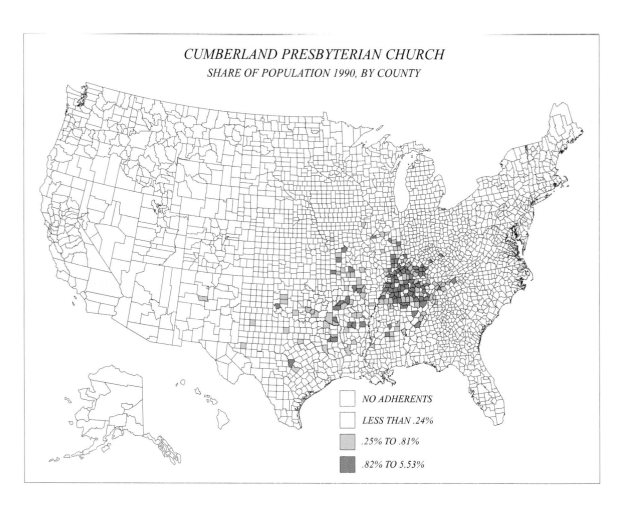

CUMBERLAND PRESBYTERIAN CHURCH
SHARE OF POPULATION 1990, BY COUNTY

NO ADHERENTS

LESS THAN .24%

.25% TO .81%

.82% TO 5.53%

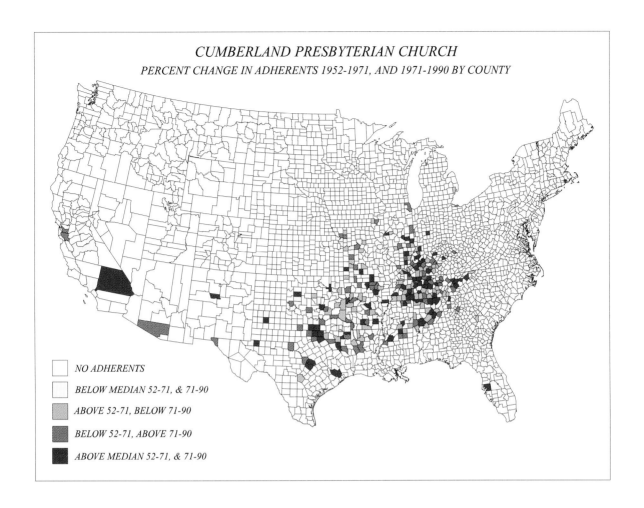

CUMBERLAND PRESBYTERIAN CHURCH

PERCENT CHANGE IN ADHERENTS 1952-1971, AND 1971-1990 BY COUNTY

NO ADHERENTS

BELOW MEDIAN 52-71, & 71-90

ABOVE 52-71, BELOW 71-90

BELOW 52-71, ABOVE 71-90

ABOVE MEDIAN 52-71, & 71-90

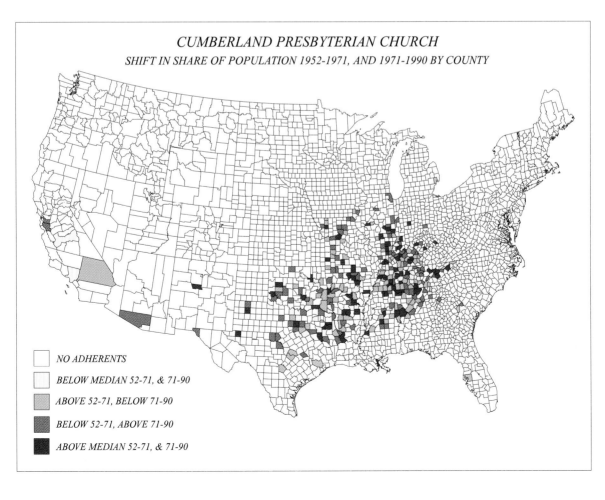

CUMBERLAND PRESBYTERIAN CHURCH

SHIFT IN SHARE OF POPULATION 1952-1971, AND 1971-1990 BY COUNTY

NO ADHERENTS

BELOW MEDIAN 52-71, & 71-90

ABOVE 52-71, BELOW 71-90

BELOW 52-71, ABOVE 71-90

ABOVE MEDIAN 52-71, & 71-90

EPISCOPAL CHURCH

The Protestant Episcopal Church is, of course, the Anglican Church or Church of England transplanted to the colonies. In terms of both its longevity on these shores and the social standing of its membership, it became the most "elite" of all Anglo-Protestant churches in America. The Episcopal Church is a truly national denomination, with churches in virtually every state. Yet, historically, its strongest concentrations have been throughout the northeastern region.

	1952	1971	1980	1990
Adherents:	2,554,976	3,007,483	2,808,144	2,427,350
Counties:	1,945	2,032	1,989	2,069

Over the nearly forty year period encompassed by these data, the Episcopal Church exhibits a pattern shared by other Anglo-Protestant groups historically centered in the northeastern states. When American denominations grew aggressively (42.1% between 1952 and 1971), the Episcopal Church grew modestly (17.7%). When the religious growth trend moderated (12% increase between 1971 and 1990), the Episcopal Church experienced significant decline (-19.3%), losing more than half a million adherents. In 1990, the Episcopal Church was slightly smaller than it was in 1952, but was situated in a slightly larger number of counties.

The map of Total Adherents, 1990 reveals a nationally dispersed denomination with its traditional core areas (those in orange) in New England, the mid-Atlantic states, and urbanized portions of the Midwest. Secondary pockets of strength are discernible in Florida, on the West Coast (California to Washington), and in the Rocky Mountain states (Colorado and Wyoming). This denomination is least in evidence in the rural counties of the central and eastern Great Plains. In 1990, fully two-thirds of all this denomination's counties contain populations of less than 500 adherents, while one-third of all counties contain fewer than 125 Episcopalians. Small numbers are a norm for the Episcopal Church in most localities.

The map for Percent Change in Adherents, 1980-1990 shows that growth counties are located predominantly in the Sunbelt tier of southern and western states, especially in Florida,

Texas, California, and the interior South. Moreover, nearly two-thirds of counties (the top third begins at only a 4.63% gain) register decline between 1980 and 1990. The denomination's traditional home turf is declining in adherents. The map for Share of Population, 1990 demonstrates that while the Episcopal Church is national in its distribution, it represents a very minor share of population in most places.

The map for Percent Change in Adherents, 1952-1971 and 1971-1990 shows that counties performing above the median for both periods were disproportionately outside the historic core areas. Counties with red coloring are located in the Sunbelt, in north central California, and in Florida. Moreover, while the median county change rate for the Episcopal Church was a 29.01% increase between 1952 and 1971, it was -17.35% between 1971 and 1990. Thus, many of the counties shaded red on this map represent either stability or slight increases for the entire period.

This impression is reinforced by the map for Shift in Share of Population, 1952-1971 and 1971-1990. The mean change in share rate between 1952 and 1971 was only 1.08, nearly stable, while the rate for 1970-1990 is .67, indicating that the median performance was a substantial decline in population share. For the more recent period, the Episcopal Church has reported the second weakest performance in terms of this measure for all groups contained in this *Atlas*. Only the Presbyterian Church (U.S.A.) had a lower share change rate between 1971 and 1990 (.64).

In summary, while the Episcopal Church continues to be a nationally dispersed large communion, it also represents an exceedingly small population component in most communities where it is found. While there has been some shift of adherents away from the old northeastern and mid-Atlantic core areas into the Sunbelt, this denomination is not keeping pace with population growth. During a nearly 40 year period when the United States population grew by almost 40%, the Episcopal Church declined by 5%. If it is correct to suspect that such factors as an aging adherents base, small family size, and an inability to retain offspring within the denomination all are contributing elements, then it is probable that the weak performance of the Episcopal Church in the 1980s (-13.6% decline) will continue and perhaps even be accelerated in the 1990s.

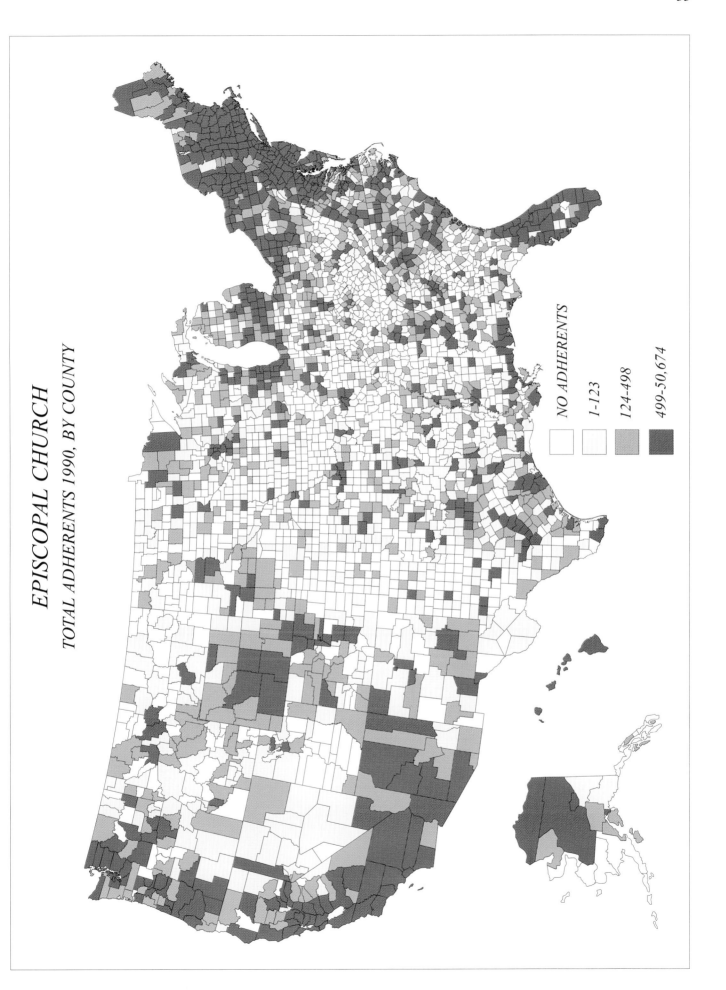

EPISCOPAL CHURCH
TOTAL ADHERENTS 1990, BY COUNTY

NO ADHERENTS
1-123
124-498
499-50,674

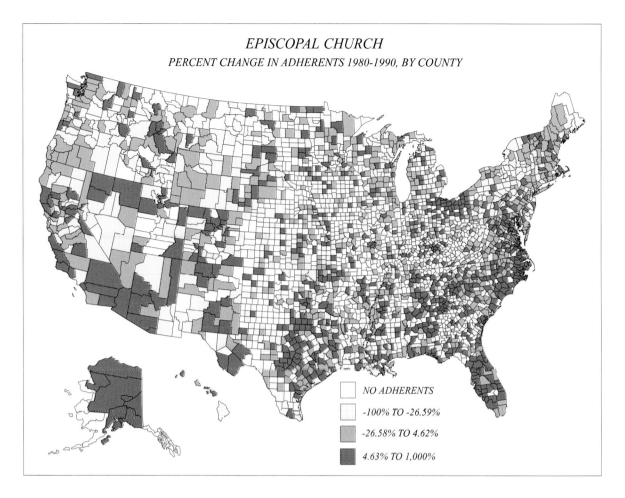

EPISCOPAL CHURCH

PERCENT CHANGE IN ADHERENTS 1980-1990, BY COUNTY

NO ADHERENTS
-100% TO -26.59%
-26.58% TO 4.62%
4.63% TO 1,000%

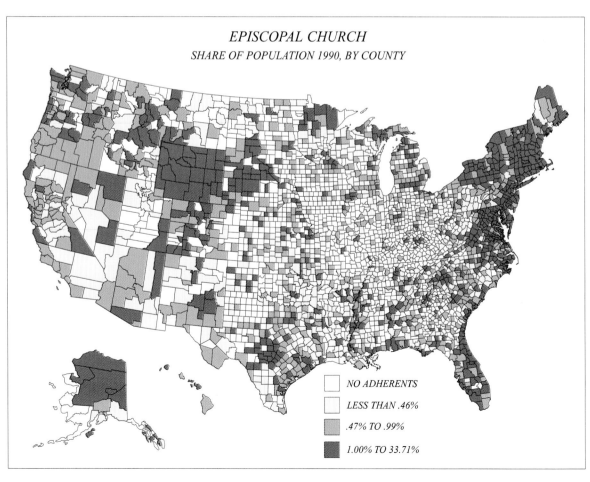

EPISCOPAL CHURCH

SHARE OF POPULATION 1990, BY COUNTY

NO ADHERENTS
LESS THAN .46%
.47% TO .99%
1.00% TO 33.71%

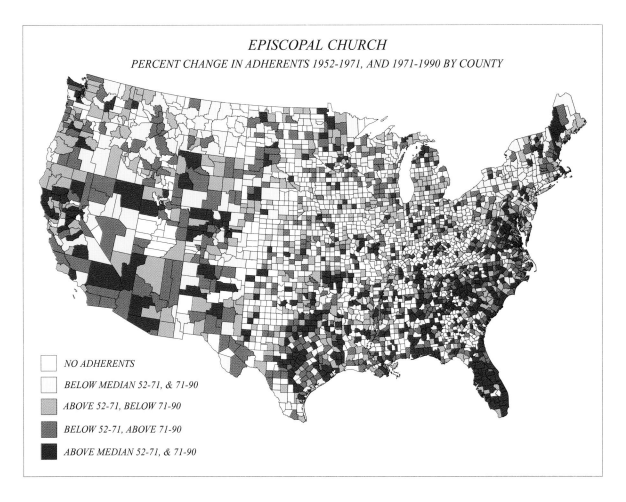

EPISCOPAL CHURCH

PERCENT CHANGE IN ADHERENTS 1952-1971, AND 1971-1990 BY COUNTY

NO ADHERENTS

BELOW MEDIAN 52-71, & 71-90

ABOVE 52-71, BELOW 71-90

BELOW 52-71, ABOVE 71-90

ABOVE MEDIAN 52-71, & 71-90

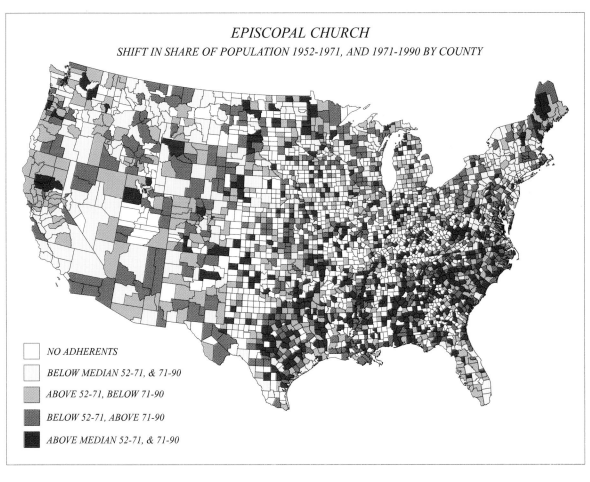

EPISCOPAL CHURCH

SHIFT IN SHARE OF POPULATION 1952-1971, AND 1971-1990 BY COUNTY

NO ADHERENTS

BELOW MEDIAN 52-71, & 71-90

ABOVE 52-71, BELOW 71-90

BELOW 52-71, ABOVE 71-90

ABOVE MEDIAN 52-71, & 71-90

EVANGELICAL CONGREGATIONAL CHURCH

In 1894, a dispute over polity issues developed within the Evangelical Association (later known as the Evangelical Church), resulting in the formation of a splinter group called the United Evangelical Church. When, in 1922, it seemed that these differences were resolved and the two denominations were reuniting, a minority of congregations in the United Evangelical Church dissented, refusing to participate in the reunion. These churches, primarily located in eastern Pennsylvania and the Pittsburgh area, became the Evangelical Congregational Church. Theologically this group falls within the Methodist tradition. This church maintains a program of summer camp meetings, and is active in foreign missions.

	1952	1971	1980	1990
Adherents:	28,596	35,742	34,085	33,166
Counties:	34	30	34	36

The map of Total Adherents, 1990 clearly identifies this as a small sub-regional denomination with a single major cluster of counties in eastern Pennsylvania, and only two secondary clusters in Illinois and Ohio. There are isolated counties in both Virginia and New Jersey. The map of Total Adherents, 1990 must be read in light of two facts. Eighty percent of adherents reside in the State of Pennsylvania and over 20% of adherents are reported in Lancaster County. For the entire nearly 40 year period between 1952 and 1990, the total adherents in this small splinter group increased by less than 5,000 adherents, with all of the increase occurring in the earlier 1952 to 1971 period.

The map for Percent Change in Adherents, 1980-1990 is centered on a median county change rate of 0%, reflecting the relative stability of this small communion. The weakest performing counties are in the Pennsylvania core area. Indeed, between 1980 and 1990, Lancaster County's share of the denomination decreased from 25% to 20%.

The map for Share of Population, 1990 again highlights the eastern Pennsylvania core. However, even here the denomination never accounts for as much as 2.5% of the population of any county. In fact, in a third of its locations this communion represents less than one tenth of one percent (actually .09%).

The map for Percent Change in Adherents, 1952-1971 and 1980-1990 greatly resembles that for 1980-1990 with the weaker performing counties strongly in evidence in the eastern Pennsylvania core. Median county percent change rates of 19% and 1.92% reflect the familiar pattern of modest growth in the earlier period followed by relative stability. The map for Shift in Share of Population, 1952-1971 and 1971-1990 reveals virtually the same pattern, except that its median county values are 1.07 and 1.01, indicating that even where it experienced modest growth, this group barely held its share of county populations.

In summary, to the extent that this small denomination grew in adherents during the years 1952-1971 (23%), and remained nearly stable in the years 1971-1990 (-3%), it reflects the first of the three general patterns for denominations discussed in the introduction to this *Atlas*. However, it does not mirror the growth trend of other Pietist or theologically conservative denominations with which it shares both theological tradition and territory. For example, between 1952 and 1990, the Mennonite Church grew an impressive 134%, and the Brethren in Christ increased by 229%. Both of these "Pennsylvania Dutch" communions grew in the 1971-1990 period as well. The Evangelical Congregational Church exhibits a change pattern more typical of the Anglo-Protestant groups that predominate in the northeastern states. The Evangelical Congregational Church may be characterized as a sect-like religious community that in 1990 was slightly larger and barely more geographically dispersed than it was in 1952. Moreover, in the context of declining adherents since 1971, the historic core of Lancaster County accounted for a smaller proportion of the denomination in 1990 than it did in 1980. One is led to speculate that this is an aging population that is neither reproducing itself, nor, despite it name, growing though evangelism.

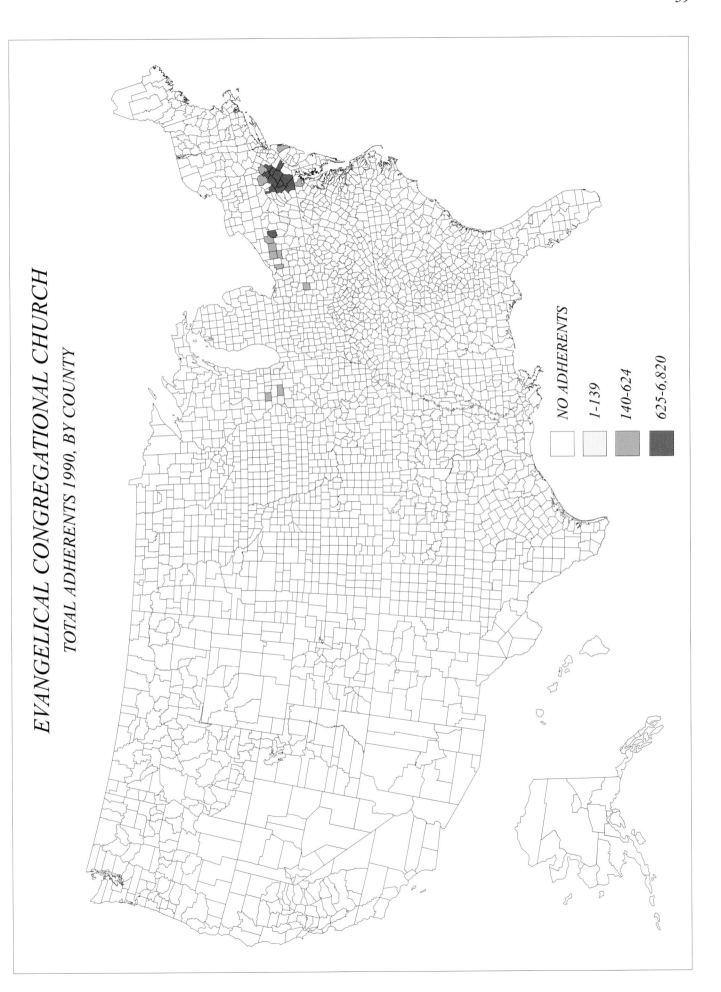

EVANGELICAL CONGREGATIONAL CHURCH
TOTAL ADHERENTS 1990, BY COUNTY

NO ADHERENTS

1-139

140-624

625-6,820

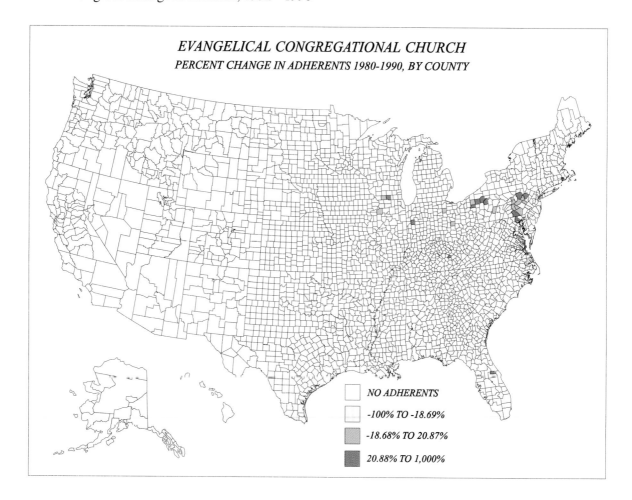

EVANGELICAL CONGREGATIONAL CHURCH
PERCENT CHANGE IN ADHERENTS 1980-1990, BY COUNTY

NO ADHERENTS

-100% TO -18.69%

-18.68% TO 20.87%

20.88% TO 1,000%

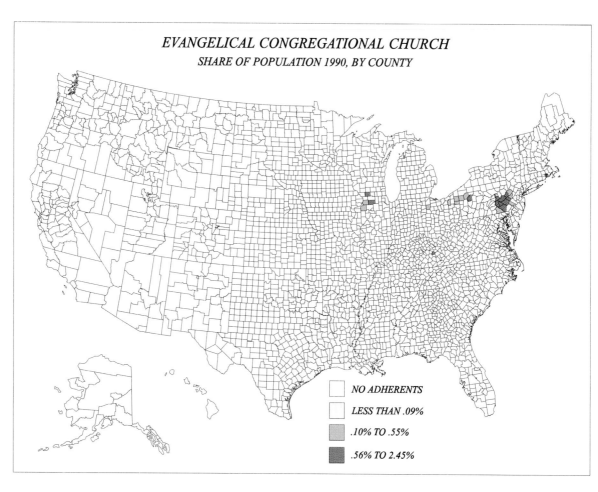

EVANGELICAL CONGREGATIONAL CHURCH
SHARE OF POPULATION 1990, BY COUNTY

NO ADHERENTS

LESS THAN .09%

.10% TO .55%

.56% TO 2.45%

61

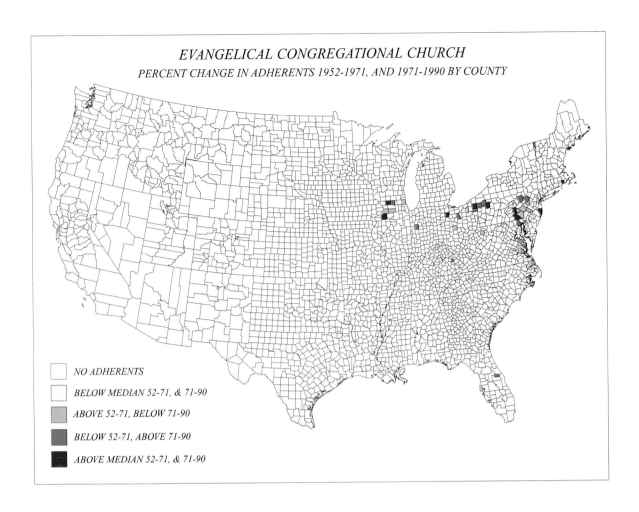

EVANGELICAL CONGREGATIONAL CHURCH
PERCENT CHANGE IN ADHERENTS 1952-1971, AND 1971-1990 BY COUNTY

NO ADHERENTS

BELOW MEDIAN 52-71, & 71-90

ABOVE 52-71, BELOW 71-90

BELOW 52-71, ABOVE 71-90

ABOVE MEDIAN 52-71, & 71-90

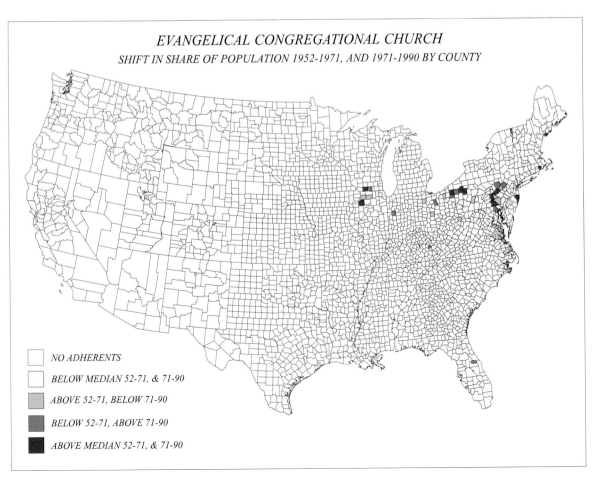

EVANGELICAL CONGREGATIONAL CHURCH
SHIFT IN SHARE OF POPULATION 1952-1971, AND 1971-1990 BY COUNTY

NO ADHERENTS

BELOW MEDIAN 52-71, & 71-90

ABOVE 52-71, BELOW 71-90

BELOW 52-71, ABOVE 71-90

ABOVE MEDIAN 52-71, & 71-90

EVANGELICAL LUTHERAN CHURCH IN AMERICA

The form of Protestantism that took Martin Luther's name would become a predominant religious force in Germany and throughout Scandinavia. Many of these national Lutheran churches were transplanted to the United States. The formation in 1988 of the Evangelical Lutheran Church in America (ELCA) marked the culmination of long series of mergers and unions among diverse ethnic immigrant Lutheran religious bodies. The ELCA was created from three denominations: the Lutheran Church in America (LCA), American Lutheran Church (ALC), and the Association of Evangelical Lutheran Churches.

Prior to the ELCA merger, the Lutheran Church in America (LCA) had been the largest branch of American Lutheranism. This denomination, which was located primarily across the northeastern quadrant of the county was created in 1962 through a union of four denominations: the Augustana Evangelical Lutheran Church (Swedish), the American Evangelical Lutheran Church (Danish), the Finnish Evangelical Church (Suomi Synod), and the United Lutheran Church. The United Lutheran Church was formed in 1918 through a merger of some 45 different synods, including a predominantly southern branch of American Lutheranism. At the time of the 1988 ELCA union, the LCA consisted of over 3 million adherents and nearly 5,000 congregations.

The American Lutheran Church (ALC) began in the early 1800s as the Ohio Synod, primarily a German group. A 1960 merger united the American Lutheran Church (German), the Evangelical Lutheran Church (Norwegian), and the United Evangelical Lutheran Church (Danish). In 1963, the Lutheran Free Church (also Norwegian) was absorbed into the American Lutheran Church. By the time of the ELCA merger, the ALC had seen its traditional core area in the upper Midwest and northern Plains states of Illinois, Wisconsin, Iowa, Minnesota, and the Dakotas expanded into Colorado, Montana, and states along the Pacific Coast. The ALC brought over 2 million adherents and 4,958 congregations into the ELCA merger.

Of the three communions uniting in 1988, the smallest was the Association of Evangelical Lutheran Churches, which numbered just over 100,000 members in 250 congregations. It was formed in 1976 through a separation from the Lutheran Church-Missouri Synod. ELCA statistics for the years prior to 1990 are statistical mergers of data for the various constituent bodies.

	1952	1971	1980	1990
Adherents:	4,225,210	5,492,588	5,265,178	5,213,164
Counties:	1,420	1,577	1,620	1,693

In 1990, the ELCA was the third largest American Protestant denomination (next to the Southern Baptist Convention and the United Methodist Church). Like its sister communion the Lutheran Church-Missouri Synod, between 1952 and 1990, the ELCA registered a modest increase in adherents (23.4%) accompanied by a gradual spatial expansion (19.2% new counties). Moreover, spatial expansion continued even as the number of adherents contracted during the period from 1971 to 1990. This pattern of expansion followed by relative stability is characteristic of many of the Continental European Protestant groups that immigrated to the United States in the 19th century and subsequently predominated in the American Midwest.

The map of Total Adherents, 1990 clearly reveals the two previous core areas of the old LCA in the eastern states of New York, New Jersey, Pennsylvania, and Ohio, and the old Scandinavian-dominated ALC throughout the upper Midwest. The ELCA also has substantial strength in clusters of counties along the West Coast, in Florida, and in Texas, and clearly is a multiregional denomination. Additionally, in the counties of highest incidence, much higher levels of adherents (2,324 to 160,979 persons) are reported than is so for most Anglo-Calvinist denominations such as the Episcopal Church, the Presbyterian Church (U.S.A.), the American Baptist Churches, and the United Church of Christ.

The map for Percent Change in Adherents, 1980-1990 reveals a highly diffuse pattern of high change rate counties. However, retirement areas in Florida, California, and Arizona unquestionably are among the places of highest growth during the 1980s. For the ELCA, the upper third of counties has a lower limit of 12.49% growth in adherents as compared to a growth rate of 9.2% between 1980 and 1990 for the United States population. Thus, in its strongest third of counties, the ELCA is growing at a somewhat faster rate than the general population.

The map for Share of Population, 1990 is one of the most striking in this *Atlas*. Images of Garrison Keillor's "Prairie Home Companion" are brought to mind. No other American Protestant community, except perhaps the Southern Baptist Convention in the Old South, can claim such a large and highly regionalized band of contiguous high percentage share counties as does the ELCA in the upper Midwest. The counties colored orange on this map represent from nearly 5% to over 77% of county populations. This level of population share and thus, cultural influence is a rare occurrence.

The ELCA's continued expansion into locales outside its historic core areas is highlighted by the map for Percent Change in Adherents, 1952-1971 and 1971-1990. Counties that performed above the median change rates for the denomination in both periods are conspicuously outside the historic core areas. They are in New England, Florida, and California, and are scattered throughout the southern tier of states. The former core of the LCA in the middle Atlantic states had its stronger performance in the more recent 1971-1990 period, while the old ALC midwestern core region performed more strongly in the 1952-1971 period. The latter seems, in part, to reflect the shifting of population out of the nation's Rustbelt.

The map for Shift in Share of Population, 1952-1971 and 1971-1990 again emphasizes this denomination's unique position in the northern Plains states. Similar to the pattern for the United Methodist Church, the Evangelical Lutheran Church in America appears to gain share because it represents a persistently stable element in nonmetropolitan counties that are decreasing in population. However, this map also provides clear identification of counties of new entry in the states of Florida, New Mexico, Arizona, and elsewhere. When this denomination's median county change in population share rates for 1952-1990 are converted to a rate for the entire period (1952-1990) the result is quite near stability (1.07). In other words, in 1990, the ELCA's share of population across most of its counties remains virtually what it was for the total of its constituent denominations nearly forty years earlier.

In summary, the Evangelical Lutheran Church in America is a major Protestant communion (third largest) that has experienced modest increase in adherents and continuous spatial growth over the period 1952-1990. It claims a share of county populations throughout the American Midwest that is unique in its strength and breath. This clearly is a cultural residue of the enormous late 19th century migration to the United States of German and Scandinavian populations. However, because this denomination predominates in a region of stable or declining rural population, its growth potential for the coming decades may be limited.

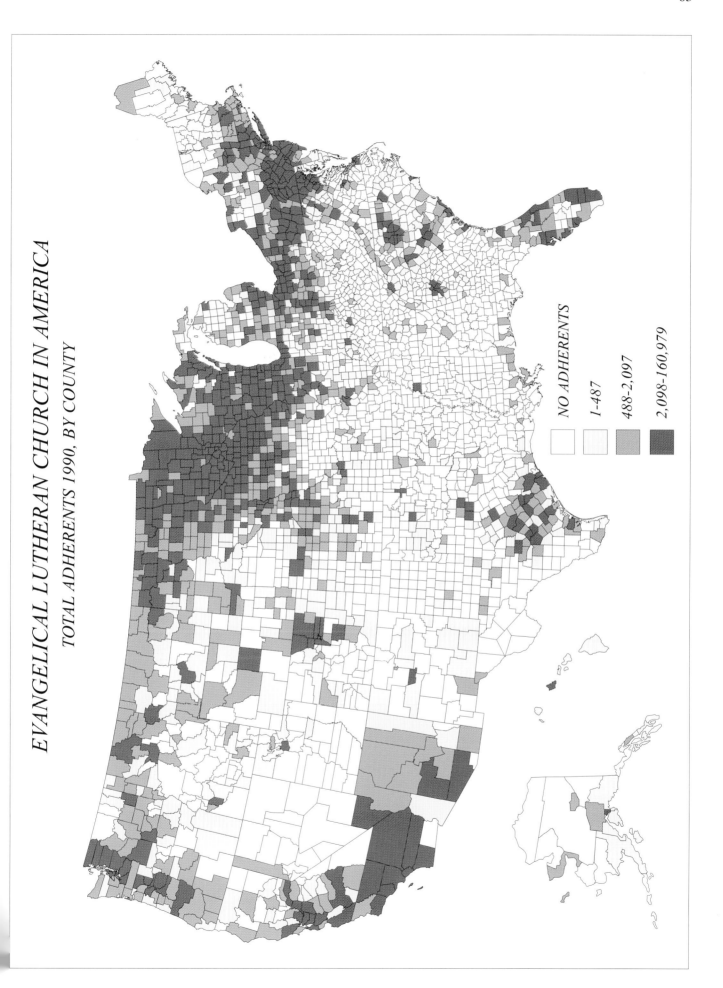

EVANGELICAL LUTHERAN CHURCH IN AMERICA

TOTAL ADHERENTS 1990, BY COUNTY

NO ADHERENTS

1-487

488-2,097

2,098-160,979

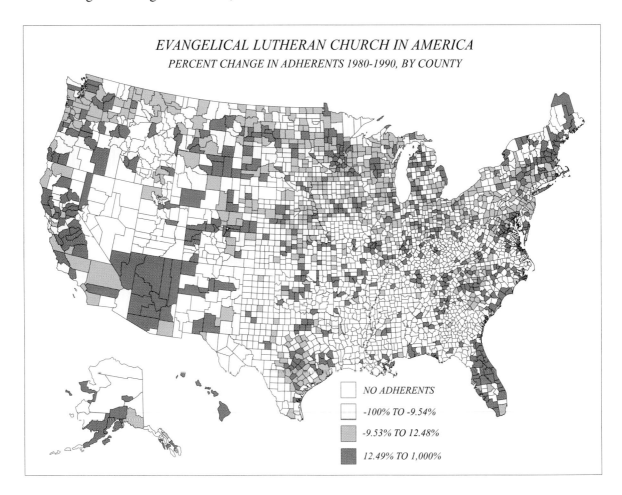

EVANGELICAL LUTHERAN CHURCH IN AMERICA
PERCENT CHANGE IN ADHERENTS 1980-1990, BY COUNTY

NO ADHERENTS
-100% TO -9.54%
-9.53% TO 12.48%
12.49% TO 1,000%

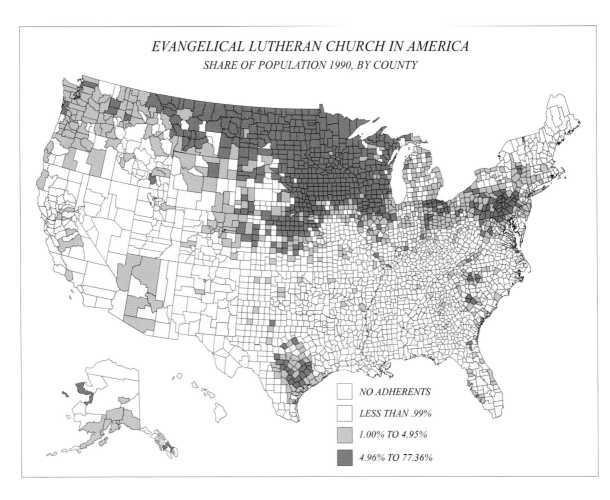

EVANGELICAL LUTHERAN CHURCH IN AMERICA
SHARE OF POPULATION 1990, BY COUNTY

NO ADHERENTS
LESS THAN .99%
1.00% TO 4.95%
4.96% TO 77.36%

65

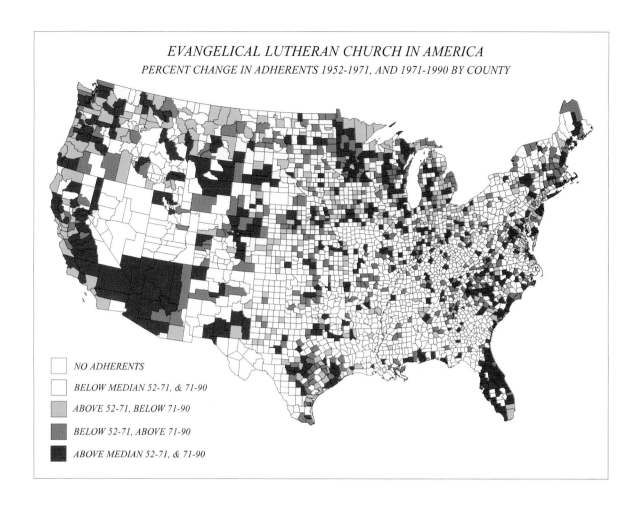

EVANGELICAL LUTHERAN CHURCH IN AMERICA
PERCENT CHANGE IN ADHERENTS 1952-1971, AND 1971-1990 BY COUNTY

- NO ADHERENTS
- BELOW MEDIAN 52-71, & 71-90
- ABOVE 52-71, BELOW 71-90
- BELOW 52-71, ABOVE 71-90
- ABOVE MEDIAN 52-71, & 71-90

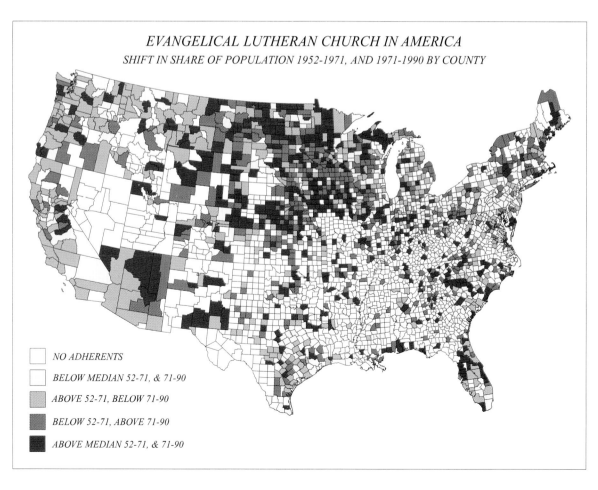

EVANGELICAL LUTHERAN CHURCH IN AMERICA
SHIFT IN SHARE OF POPULATION 1952-1971, AND 1971-1990 BY COUNTY

- NO ADHERENTS
- BELOW MEDIAN 52-71, & 71-90
- ABOVE 52-71, BELOW 71-90
- BELOW 52-71, ABOVE 71-90
- ABOVE MEDIAN 52-71, & 71-90

FREE METHODIST CHURCH OF NORTH AMERICA

The Free Methodist Church of North America was founded by B. T. Roberts in 1860 in western New York. It represented both a conservative reaction to the "new school" religious ideas and practices of the Second Great Awakening, and well as an expression of anti-slavery sentiment among northern Methodists. It remains one of the larger Methodist groups not joining in the several mergers that produced the United Methodist Church. The study *Churches and Church Membership in the United States, 1990* notes that this denomination which counted "households" in the 1980 study, now has adopted a more conventional method of counting "members" and estimating "adherents." Thus, its 1980 statistics are not entirely compatible with those for the other three time points. The 1980 numbers most likely entail an under-counting.

	1952	1971	1980	1990
Adherents:	49,052	63,487	62,139	70,296
Counties:	577	549	535	514

The Free Methodist Church of North America recorded an impressive 43.3% increase in adherents over the entire 1952-1990 period. However, within this overall trend are several different change patterns. Like most Protestant denominations, the period 1952-1971 evidenced the strongest growth rate (29.4%), while the next two decades recorded a more modest increase, in this instance composed of a slight decline (-2.1%) followed by modest growth (13.1%). For reasons we've already noted, the 1971-1980 rate is subject to question and most likely distorts the trend in a negative direction. Clearly, this denomination's growth rates fall near the middle for those groups that grew rapidly between 1952 and 1971, but only moderately between 1971 and 1990. Interestingly, the county change statistics reveal a modest but continuous pattern of spatial consolidation. This denomination experienced spatial consolidation throughout the entire period.

The map of Total Adherents, 1990 reveals that this is a denomination of rather small local churches, with a median size of 79 persons per county. The origins of this group still are evident in their contemporary patterns. Contiguous blocks of counties stretch from upstate New York, westward into Pennsylvania, Michigan, Ohio, Indiana, and Illinois. Michigan is the Free Methodists' most populous state (14,465) and in combination with New York (7,132), Pennsylvania (6,397), and Ohio (3,931) accounts for 45% of all adherents. California (7,976) represents another 11%. While local congregations are small in size, they are scattered across nearly all geographic regions, though least so in the interior South and the interior West. Outside the traditional core areas, there are groups of contiguous counties in Florida, California, Arizona, Colorado, Washington, and Oregon.

The map for Percent Change in Adherents, 1980-1990 confirms the impression of only modest increase. The median county change rate is centered on 7.7% increase, which closely approximates the national population growth rate for the decade. Moreover, small absolute numbers for this denomination have been translated into rather high percent change rates in the upper third of counties, which minimally represent growth in excess of over a third of adherents during this decade. While all three categories of event are widely distributed, counties experiencing the most severe declines are in evidence in the original New York and Pennsylvania core area. Although the center of gravity appears to be shifting westward, it must be remembered that the counting techniques were different in 1980 and 1990, and that as a consequence, analysis of the short term trend is precarious. Nonetheless, comparable statistics would not likely alter the wide geographic dispersal of counties in all three categories.

The map for Share of Population, 1990 contains some fairly predictable patterns. Because the absolute number of adherents in most counties is quite small, the county population shares are minuscule. In two-thirds of counties where they are present, the Free Methodists represent less than a fifth of one percent of population. The strongest shares predominate in its traditional core area of New York, Pennsylvania, Michigan, and Ohio. There also are isolated strong share counties in the small town and rural setting of the central Great Plains. Elsewhere, high category adherents counties register as weak share counties in such growing states as Florida and California.

Because of the change in counting procedures for 1980, the map for Percent Change in Adherents, 1952-1971, and 1971-1990 is based on a more stable set of indices than was the 1980-1990 change map. The median county change rates are 8% for 1952-1971 and -3.42% for 1971-1990. It is evident that counties performing below the median in both periods, as well as those performing above the median in the early period but below it in the later period are greatly in evidence in the traditional core states. Conversely, developing retirement areas in Florida, California, Arizona, Colorado, and the Pacific Northwest exhibit above median performances either in both time periods or in the 1971-1990 period. While it probably is accurate to attribute some of this growth to the migration of retirement-aged adherents, the continued national growth of the denomination indicates the influx of "new" adherents.

Finally, the map for Shift in Share of Population must be read against the fact that the median statistics again are very low, .87 for 1952-1971 and .83 for 1971-1990. While the patterns are widely dispersed, weak relative share performances clearly are prevalent throughout most of the western states. Elsewhere the patterns are mixed.

In summary, the anomalous character of the 1980 data for the Free Methodist Church of North America results in a less complete picture of events than has been possible for other denominations. Overall, this distinctive branch of American Methodism appears to have been shifting its population center in a westward direction. In 1990, the older core states of New York, Pennsylvania, Michigan, and Ohio account for less than half of all adherents. Precisely because this is a denomination of rather small communities of adherents, its shift to locations in the West and South do not register substantial population shares. Obviously, the Free Methodists have a limited cultural impact except as an added element in places populated by other Methodists, especially the United Methodist Church. Finally, unlike some smaller denominations that began experiencing decline once the "religious revival" of the 1950s ended, The Free Methodist Church of North America seems to have experienced relative stability in the 1970s and 1980s.

FREE METHODIST CHURCH OF NORTH AMERICA

TOTAL ADHERENTS 1990, BY COUNTY

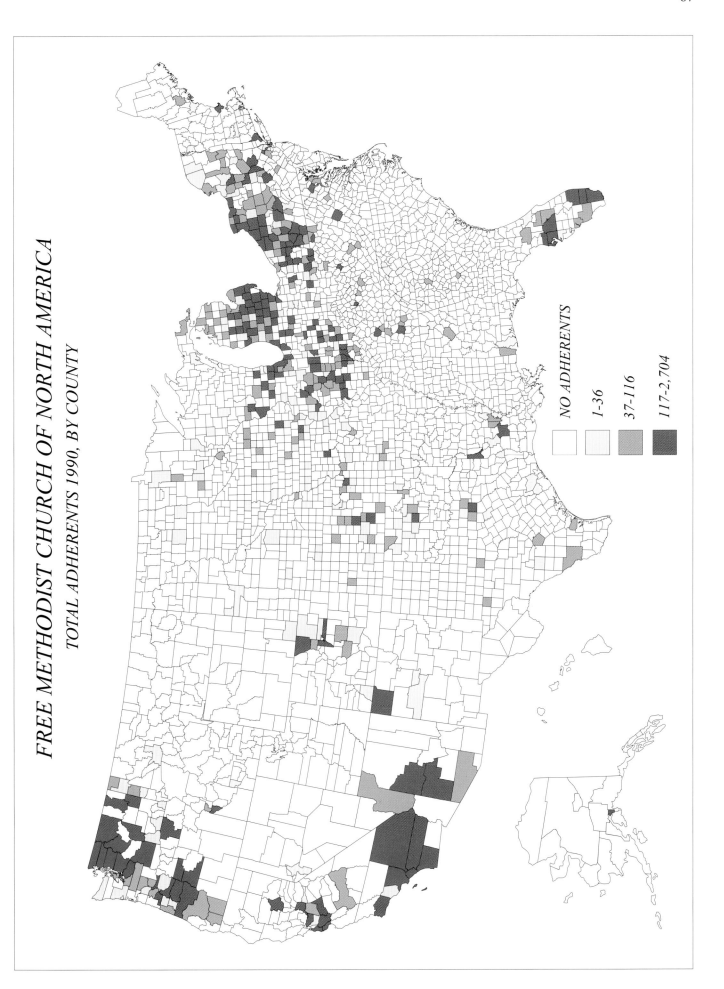

NO ADHERENTS

1-36

37-116

117-2,704

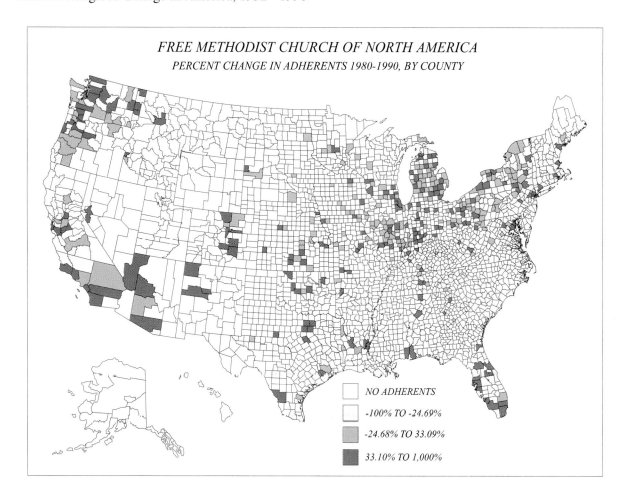

FREE METHODIST CHURCH OF NORTH AMERICA
PERCENT CHANGE IN ADHERENTS 1980-1990, BY COUNTY

NO ADHERENTS
-100% TO -24.69%
-24.68% TO 33.09%
33.10% TO 1,000%

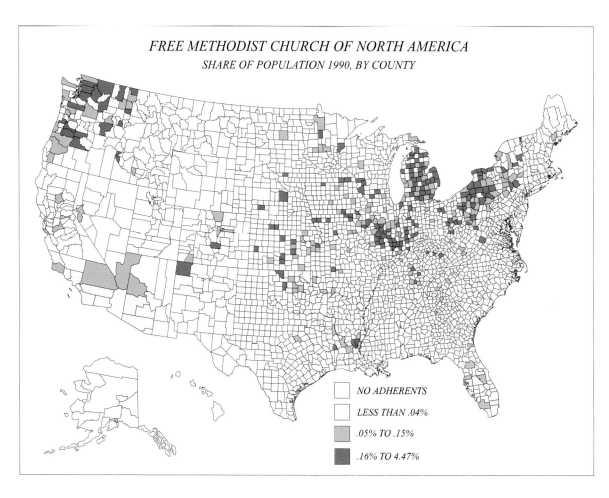

FREE METHODIST CHURCH OF NORTH AMERICA
SHARE OF POPULATION 1990, BY COUNTY

NO ADHERENTS
LESS THAN .04%
.05% TO .15%
.16% TO 4.47%

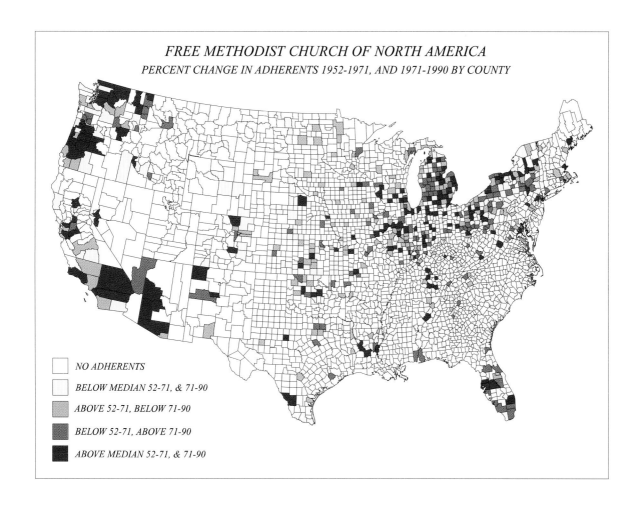

FREE METHODIST CHURCH OF NORTH AMERICA
PERCENT CHANGE IN ADHERENTS 1952-1971, AND 1971-1990 BY COUNTY

NO ADHERENTS
BELOW MEDIAN 52-71, & 71-90
ABOVE 52-71, BELOW 71-90
BELOW 52-71, ABOVE 71-90
ABOVE MEDIAN 52-71, & 71-90

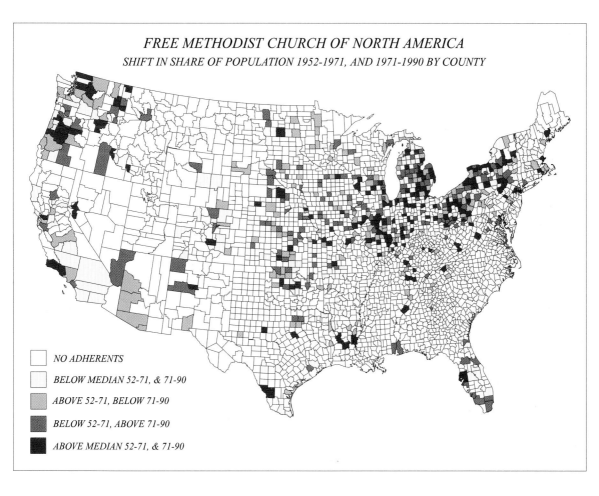

FREE METHODIST CHURCH OF NORTH AMERICA
SHIFT IN SHARE OF POPULATION 1952-1971, AND 1971-1990 BY COUNTY

NO ADHERENTS
BELOW MEDIAN 52-71, & 71-90
ABOVE 52-71, BELOW 71-90
BELOW 52-71, ABOVE 71-90
ABOVE MEDIAN 52-71, & 71-90

FRIENDS

The Friends, or Quakers, were founded in England during the 1650s by George Fox. Fleeing persecution by the Anglican Church, these "seekers of the True Light" found refuge in William Penn's Pennsylvania experiment in toleration. Some of the divisions and schisms that occurred among the Friends early in the 19th century have been repaired through 20th century reunions (in the years 1902, 1955, 1968, and 1972). Today, the Friends are widely recognized for their relief activities and their efforts on behalf of world peace through the American Friends Service Committee and the World Friends Committee.

Unfortunately, there continue to be unspecified variations in the constituencies reporting under "Friends" in the several Church Membership Studies. The major communities reporting in the several studies appear to be these: Religious Society of Friends, Conservative; Religious Society of Friends, General Conference; The Five Year Meeting; and Religious Society of Friends, Philadelphia (the latter two groups are both included in Friends United Meeting in the 1980 data.). However, there also are inconsistencies between the four studies for which no detailed comparison is provided. Since the Friends stress the autonomy of local units, some of what normally would be viewed as growth for this community also must be attributed to reporting anomalies. Given these uncertainties, we are reluctant to over-interpret the longitudinal data for this group, even though the general pattern they exhibit (growth between 1952 and 1971, followed by relative stability from 1971 to 1990), is common to a number of other denominations.

	1952	1971	1980	1990
Adherents:	95,029	128,161	133,405	127,533
Counties:	260	460	497	657

The map for Total Adherents, 1990 clearly reflects the historic migration of Quakerism across the American continent. Clusters of counties are located in southeastern Pennsylvania, in Ohio, Indiana, and the Carolinas, as well as in Iowa and on the West Coast. Florida and California would appear to represent the most recent areas of entry. Fully two-thirds of this community's locations report less than 132 adherents in 1990.

The map for Percent Change in Adherents, 1980-1990, is very much a mirror image of the map of Total Adherents, 1990. Two events seem to predominate on this map. First, many counties of high incidence on the map of Total Adherents, 1990 are reporting adherents loss on the map of Percent Change in Adherents, 1980-1990 (the entire lower third of counties). Second, 160 of the 220 counties in the highest third of counties are registering new entry dur-

ing this decade. This "explosion" of new locations is quite uncommon, especially for so small a community, and reinforces a concern for possible reporting inconsistencies between the various studies.

Predictably, the map for Share of Population, 1990 greatly resembles the 1990 incidence patterns for the Friends It should be noted that the upper third of share counties begins at less than 1% of county population. Traditional core areas in Pennsylvania, Ohio, and Indiana, the Carolinas, and in the Northwest show the strongest shares. Understandably, where high population counties are involved, as in California, high Friends incidence does not register as high shares of county population.

The next two maps must be read in the context of the inconsistent reporting procedures mentioned previously. The latter result in clearly exaggerated median change rates, especially for the change in share of county population measure. In the 1952-1971 period the Friends' median county change rate was 305.26%, and for the period 1971-1990 was 41.73%. The great number of new counties in the 1980-1990 period (160 out of 200) surely affect the median county change rate for the 1971-1990 period. Of course, none of the "new" 1980-1990 counties are reporting an above median change rate for the earlier period (they were not in the distribution then). The result then, is a widely dispersed pattern of high performance counties that defy description relative to the other maps in this series.

The median county change in population share rate between 1952 and 1971 was 3.49, while between 1971 and 1990 the median county change in population share rate was 1.19. Obviously, the small size of local "meetings" combined with the large number of counties reported here as "new entry" are reflected in this impressive statistic. Spatially, counties consistently performing above the median rate for both periods are located outside the traditional core areas. Conversely, with counties in those core areas reporting below the median performance rate for both periods, there is the distinct impression that the Friends are experiencing at least some "thinning" of their older communities.

In summary, if one can overlook the irregularities in enumeration procedures for this group, it seems that this is a relatively small religious community, which over the nearly forty years encompassed by these studies appears to have expanded spatially. In 1990, they have some representation in each region of the nation, but typically only in isolated clusters of counties or even single counties within a region or subregion. As stated previously, Friends' communities tend to be small, with two-thirds in 1990 numbering fewer than 132 persons. Their influence and recognition in the larger community is all the more impressive given the denomination's small size and diffuse distribution.

FRIENDS

TOTAL ADHERENTS 1990, BY COUNTY

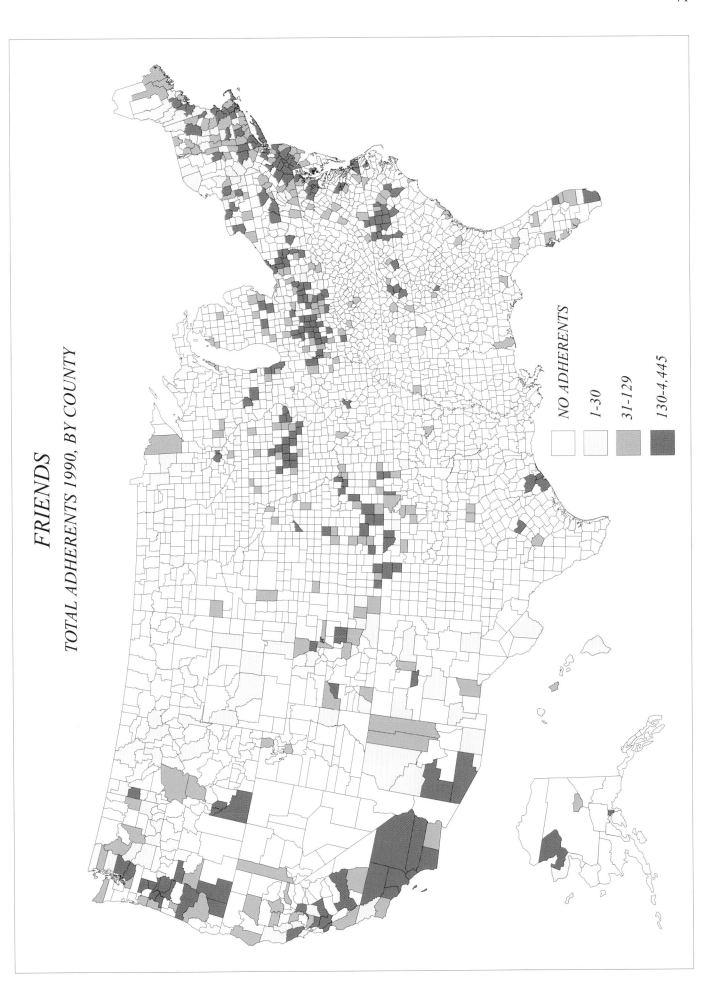

NO ADHERENTS

1-30

31-129

130-4,445

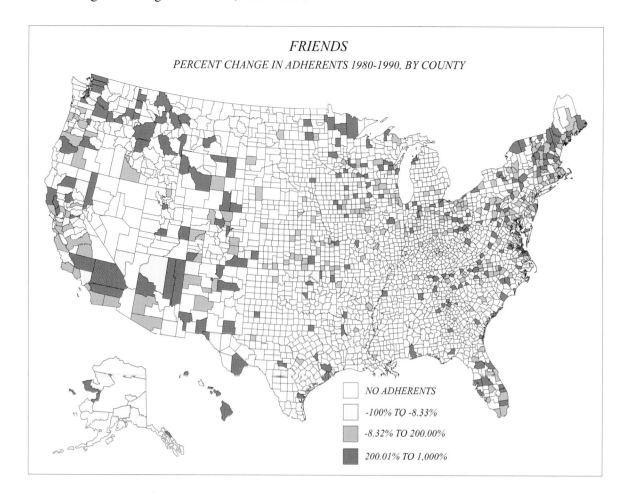

FRIENDS

PERCENT CHANGE IN ADHERENTS 1980-1990, BY COUNTY

NO ADHERENTS

-100% TO -8.33%

-8.32% TO 200.00%

200.01% TO 1,000%

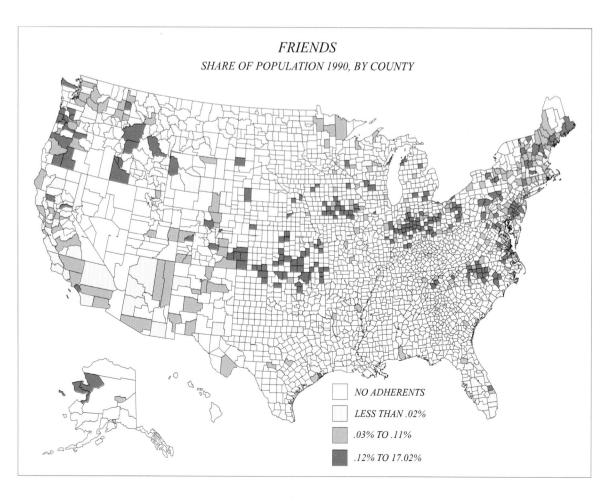

FRIENDS

SHARE OF POPULATION 1990, BY COUNTY

NO ADHERENTS

LESS THAN .02%

.03% TO .11%

.12% TO 17.02%

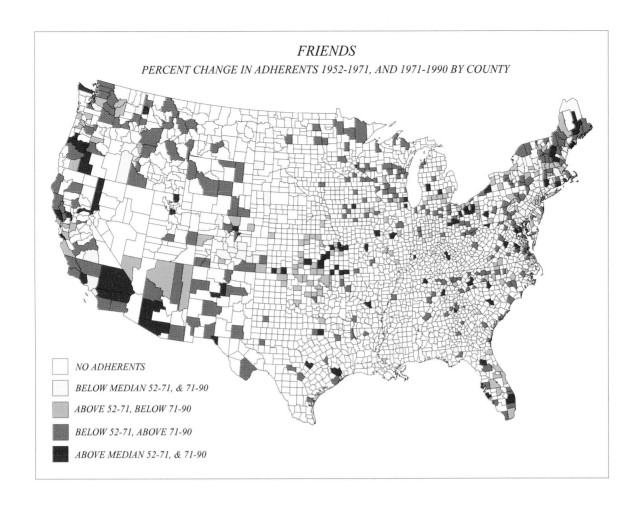

FRIENDS

PERCENT CHANGE IN ADHERENTS 1952-1971, AND 1971-1990 BY COUNTY

NO ADHERENTS

BELOW MEDIAN 52-71, & 71-90

ABOVE 52-71, BELOW 71-90

BELOW 52-71, ABOVE 71-90

ABOVE MEDIAN 52-71, & 71-90

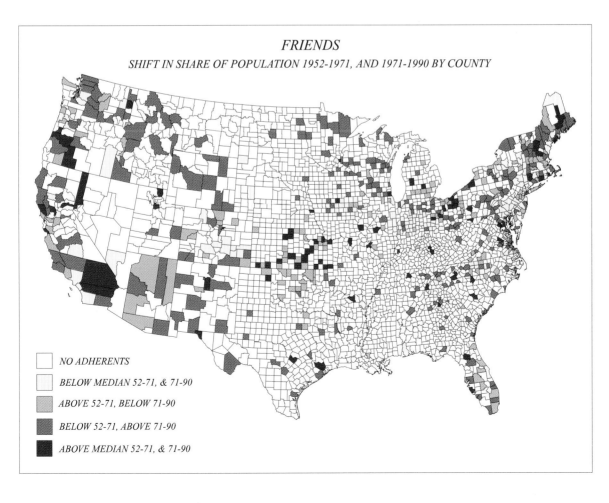

FRIENDS

SHIFT IN SHARE OF POPULATION 1952-1971, AND 1971-1990 BY COUNTY

NO ADHERENTS

BELOW MEDIAN 52-71, & 71-90

ABOVE 52-71, BELOW 71-90

BELOW 52-71, ABOVE 71-90

ABOVE MEDIAN 52-71, & 71-90

INTERNATIONAL CHURCH OF THE FOURSQUARE GOSPEL

This charismatic and evangelical native American denomination was founded in 1921 as the Echo Park Evangelistic Association, in Los Angeles, California, by Sister Aimee Semple McPherson. The International Church of the Foursquare Gospel maintains a strong evangelical orientation, and practices both faith healing and speaking in tongues. Its missionary activities have transformed it from a small American Protestant sect into a world-wide religious movement with a broad base of support here in the United States.

	1952	1971	1980	1990
Adherents:	66,181	101,522	160,074	250,250
Counties:	290	350	399	537

Over the 1952-1990 period, the International Church of the Foursquare Gospel increased in adherents by 279% and grew in its county coverage by 85%. This is the only denomination among those numbering over 100,000 adherents that reports more rapid growth between 1971 and 1990 than between 1952 and 1971 (145% as compared to 55%). Clearly, this church claims one of the most dynamic sustained growth patterns among those contained in this *Atlas*. Throughout this period, the two states of California and Arizona have anchored a disproportionate share of the denomination's national adherents (51% by 1990). Yet, the map of Total Adherents, 1990 also indicates that this group has expanded beyond its original southwestern core. In 1990, it can be found throughout the West Coast, as well as into the Chicago metropolitan area, northern Illinois, northern Ohio, the Carolinas, and in the Pennsylvania-Maryland corridor. Interestingly, with the exception of the Chicago area, this denomination's distribution outside the western states in distinctively nonmetropolitan. Nonetheless, if the International Church of the Foursquare Gospel is said to have a "home" region, it is the West, with a continuous band of counties from the Mexican border to the Canadian border.

The map for Percent Change in Adherents, 1980-1990 displays clusters of high growth counties across the West, which in this case include those from both the middle and upper thirds of counties. In other regions, apparent "plantings" of new churches appear in isolated counties across the nation. These first two maps, when viewed together, provide important additional information. On the map of Total Adherents, 1990 the lower threshold of the top third of counties represents only 205 adherents per county. Thus, it appears that many of the high growth rate counties on the map for Percent Change in Adherents, 1980-1990 actually are counties containing very small numbers of adherents in 1990.

The map for Share of Population, 1990 confirms the impression that this still is very much a West Coast-oriented denomination. The upper third of counties has an upper limit of just over 11.5% of county populations. Such counties predominate throughout the American West, excepting in the Mormon core region. These levels of population share indicate a group this is most often a secondary element in the religious culture of this region.

The International Church of the Foursquare Gospel reported a median county change rate of 122.76% for 1952-1971 and 409.45% for 1971-1990. Together these rates reflect a pace of growth that is unique among the denominations in this *Atlas*. This is a rapidly expanding denomination. Counties that bettered the denomination's median performance consistently in both time periods are scattered throughout the nation. Many of these counties likely were newly entered during the years 1952-1971 and continued to grow between 1971 and 1990. However, there are also are many counties in the western states falling below the median rates of change, but which, because of the very elevated median growth rates, could be counties that grew substantially.

Finally, the map for Shift in Share of Population, 1952-1971 and 1971-1990 is based on median change rates of 1.71 and 3.78. These medians reveal that strong relative gains in the earlier period and even stronger ones in the more recent period. A comparison of this map with that of Total Adherents, 1990 indicates that many counties of high incidence in 1990 are counties of modest populat on share increase over the entire period covered by these four studies. This seems to reflect some tendency of this denomination to be found in large and growing metropolitan areas.

In summary, this denomination has experienced impressive spatial and numerical growth between 1952 and 1990. Moreover, it is the only sizable group in this *Atlas* that grew in adherents more rapidly in the later 1971-1990 period than in the earlier 1952-1971 period. While the International Church of the Foursquare Gospel surely has expanded beyond its initial western states core area, it still is most strongly centered in that region. It might reasonably be argued that the International Church of the Foursquare Gospel already was positioned at mid-century to benefit from the in-migration of population into the western states, and that it has translated that position into impressive gains in adherents over nearly four decades.

75

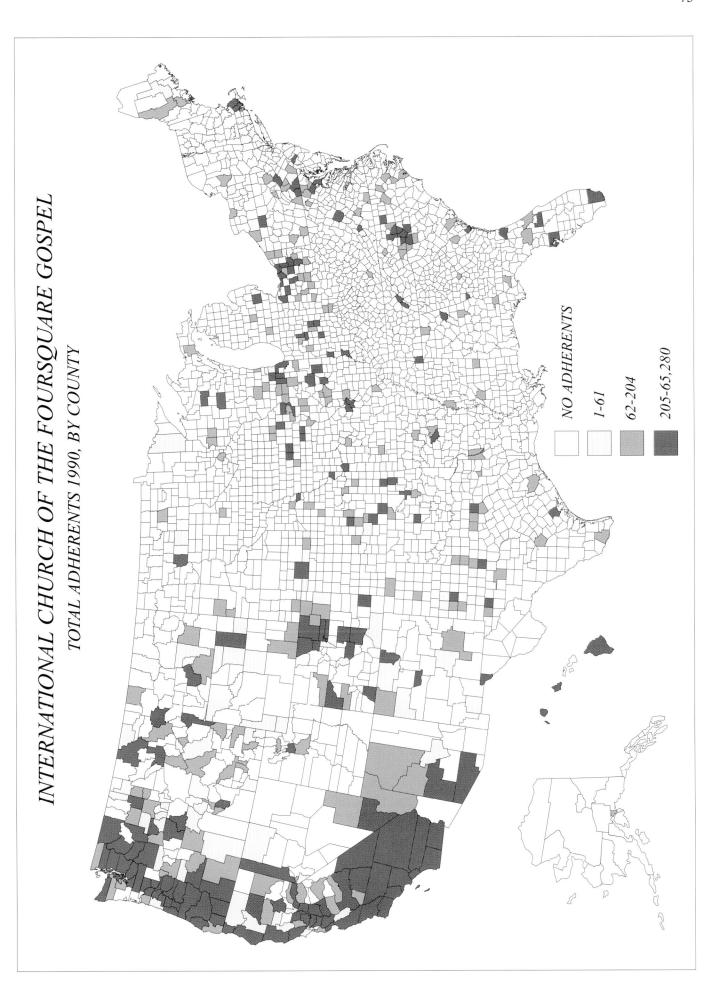

INTERNATIONAL CHURCH OF THE FOURSQUARE GOSPEL
TOTAL ADHERENTS 1990, BY COUNTY

NO ADHERENTS

1-61

62-204

205-65,280

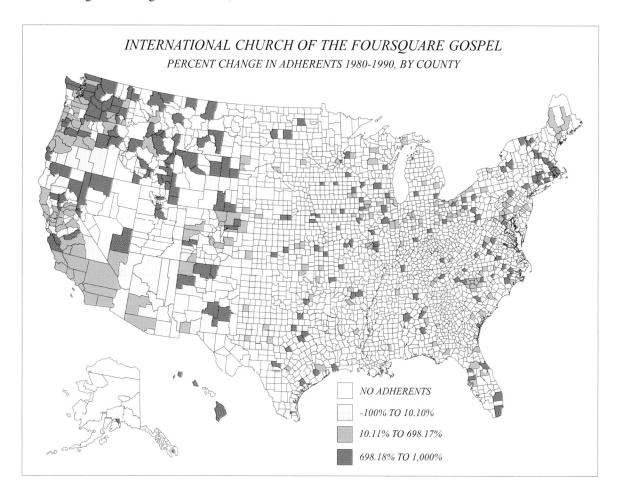

INTERNATIONAL CHURCH OF THE FOURSQUARE GOSPEL
PERCENT CHANGE IN ADHERENTS 1980-1990, BY COUNTY

NO ADHERENTS
-100% TO 10.10%
10.11% TO 698.17%
698.18% TO 1,000%

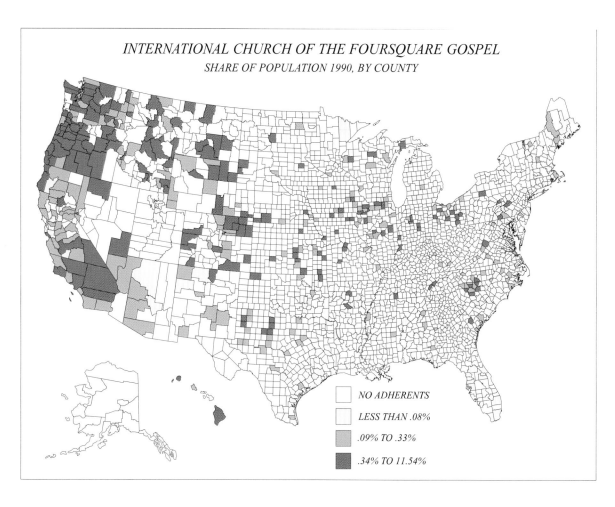

INTERNATIONAL CHURCH OF THE FOURSQUARE GOSPEL
SHARE OF POPULATION 1990, BY COUNTY

NO ADHERENTS
LESS THAN .08%
.09% TO .33%
.34% TO 11.54%

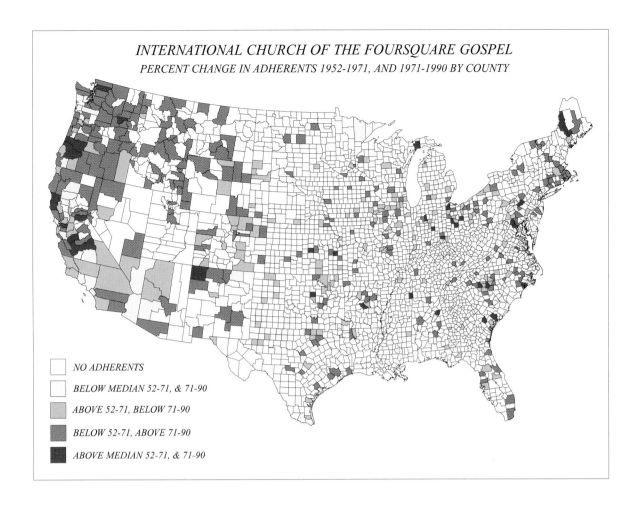

INTERNATIONAL CHURCH OF THE FOURSQUARE GOSPEL
PERCENT CHANGE IN ADHERENTS 1952-1971, AND 1971-1990 BY COUNTY

NO ADHERENTS

BELOW MEDIAN 52-71, & 71-90

ABOVE 52-71, BELOW 71-90

BELOW 52-71, ABOVE 71-90

ABOVE MEDIAN 52-71, & 71-90

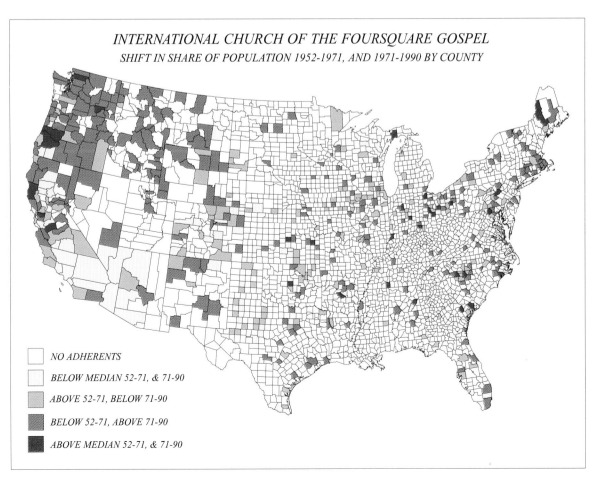

INTERNATIONAL CHURCH OF THE FOURSQUARE GOSPEL
SHIFT IN SHARE OF POPULATION 1952-1971, AND 1971-1990 BY COUNTY

NO ADHERENTS

BELOW MEDIAN 52-71, & 71-90

ABOVE 52-71, BELOW 71-90

BELOW 52-71, ABOVE 71-90

ABOVE MEDIAN 52-71, & 71-90

JEWISH POPULATION

Since their first North American settlements in the 1600s in Newport, Rhode Island and New Amsterdam (New York), Jewish Americans have become the nation's largest non-Christian religious community. In 1990 they report population in virtually every state. Over the years 1952 to 1990, this once highly immigrant population has become over 90% American born. While the northeastern states contained 67% of the Jewish population in 1952, by 1990 this region accounted for only 51%. Few religious communities exhibit this extent of spatial shift.

The data presented here consist of population estimates that are provided by a nation-wide network of some two hundred American Jewish Federation community service agencies and that are published in the *American Jewish Year Book*. The *Year Book* estimates for communities of 100 or more Jewish residents have been converted into county level data for use here and for inclusion in the study *Churches and Church Membership in the United States, 1990*. The process of allocation to counties results in some counties reporting less than 100 Jewish residents. Generally, these data may be characterized as providing a "culture count" for American Jews. Consequently, these statistics are deemed comparable to the adherents measures for Christian denominations mapped in this *Atlas*.

	1952	1971	1980	1990
Population:	5,146,634	5,641,589	6,005,957	5,982,529
Counties:	481	503	770	748

The Jewish population appears to have reached a peak size of just over six million persons in 1980, and for the entire 1952-1990, period has increased at a modest 16% rate. Clearly, this is barely one quarter the rate of increase for the general population, which was 65%. Over the most recent decade, 1980-1990 the American Jewish population remained essentially stable (-.03%). However, simultaneously the number of counties reporting Jewish population increased by 56% between 1952 and 1990, although here too ,the decade of the 1980s exhibits a modest decline (- 3%).

The map for Jewish Population in 1990 has a number of distinctive features. First, it is significant that the upper third of counties, representing communities in excess of 1,300 Jewish residents, are located throughout the nation. There is a clear implication that the geographic redistribution of American Jewry that has been on-going for several decades has created by 1990 a more even national distribution. Second, as further illustration of this regional redistribution, large bands of contiguous counties in 1990 are found in three places; throughout the northeastern Washington to Boston corridor, and also both in Florida and the West Coast corridor from Washington to Arizona. Third, elsewhere, Jewish population tends to be clustered in metropolitan areas. Nationally, this still is a predominantly metropolitan population.

The map for Percent Change in Adherents, 1980-1990 reveals a number of important features. First, the Jewish population, like many Anglo-Protestant denominations traditionally centered in the northeastern states, experienced moderate declines during the 1980s. Over a third of counties on this map report losses. Second, those counties that grew in Jewish population are of several different types. Retirement areas in Florida, Arizona, and elsewhere in the Southwest, report strong increases and surely reflect the aging of the American Jewish population, in all regions, where grow-

ing counties appear ad acent to declining counties in patterns that seem to reflect movement from cities to suburbs. Such regionally diverse metropolitan areas as New York, Nashville, Denver, and Los Angeles are included. Finally, counties declining in Jewish population between 1980 and 1990 are particularly apparent in the Rustbelt. Overall, the aggregate statistics for change between 1980 and 1990 mask a great deal of internal diversity in the movement of the American Jewish population.

The map for Share of Population, 1990 very much resembles a map of metropolitan areas. Clearly delineated are not only the major northeastern cities, but also such metropolitan centers as Atlanta, Houston, Denver, Phoenix, Miami and Seattle. While the Jewish population in 1990 in some instances represents nearly 25% of county population, in fully two-thirds of cases it barely exceeds 1% of county population. This is not surprising given the metropolitan character of the 1990 distribution pattern. All three maps portraying features of the Jewish population distribution in 1990 serve to highlight the small number of counties occupied. In this regard, the Jewish population pattern, much like that for the AME Zion Church, seems to reflect the unique historic role of segregation for this community.

The map for Percent Change in Jewish Population, 1952-1971 and 1971-1990 requires careful inspection because of the very different median county percent change rates on which it is based. The rate of 9.09% for the period 1952-1971 surely reflects the modest growth of the American Jewish population during those years. However, the addition of some 250 newly entered counties between 1971 and 1990 creates an artificially high median county change rate of 130.77% for the later period. For this reason, only a small number of counties containing Jewish population in the earlier period can attain the median rate in the later period. Conversely, counties of new entry in the later period were "empty" of Jewish population in the early period and thus are assigned to the third performance category (orange) on this map. It is precisely these counties that form suburban rings around central city counties in metropolitan areas such as Indianapolis, Minneapolis, St. Paul, Kansas City, Dallas-Fort Worth, and Nashville. They also appear in retirement communities across the southern tier of states. The few counties that report increases at or above the median county percentage change rate in both time periods are found in both some of the older northeastern suburbs and in the retirement communities of the South and Southwest.

The map for Shift in Share of Population, 1952-1971 and 1971-1990 also reflects the impact of these newly entered counties, with the median county change rates for the two time periods being .81 and 1.60 respectively. The category on this map indicating performance at or above the median county change in share rate in both time periods (red) is quite small. Included are such places as San Diego, Phoenix, the Bay area, and Palm Beach, as well as a scatter of counties in the Northeast. The third category on this map (orange) indicates counties performing at or above the median county change in share rate only in the more recent period, and therefore highlights counties of new entry since 1971. Such counties are numerous, and are present in the suburban rings of many established metropolitan areas as well as throughout the sunbelt.

In summary, since mid-century, the American Jewish population has undergone two fairly dramatic changes. While over the entire period the American Jewish population has grown slowly, there has been a significant redistribution of Jewish population away from the historic northeastern core area, and away from urban counties into suburban ones. These trends are clearly portrayed on this series of maps.

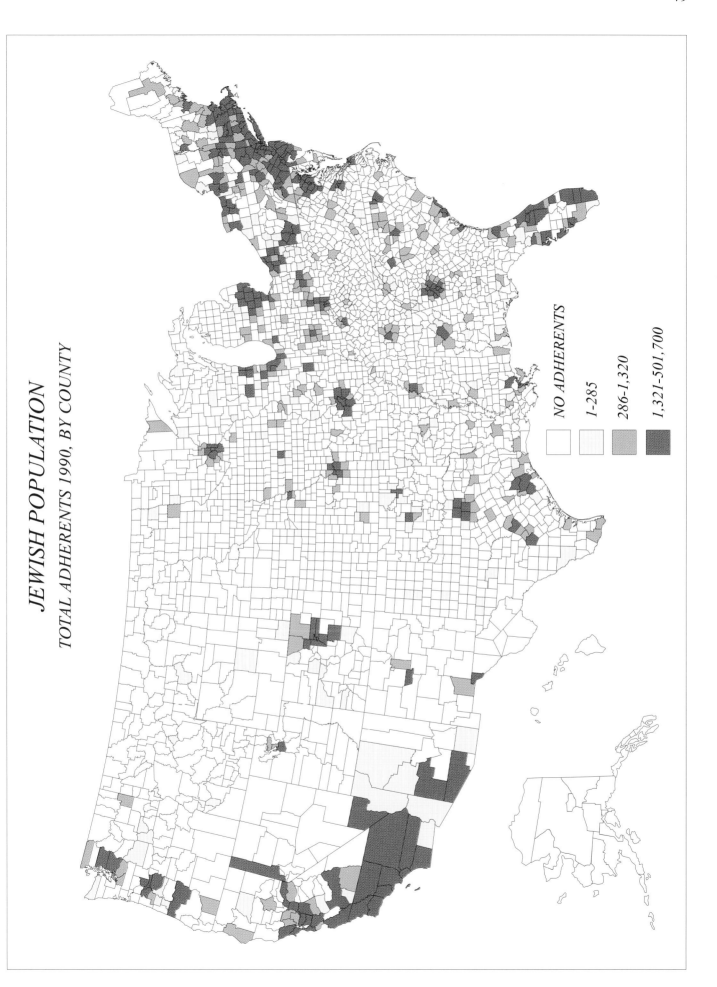

JEWISH POPULATION
TOTAL ADHERENTS 1990, BY COUNTY

NO ADHERENTS

1-285

286-1,320

1,321-501,700

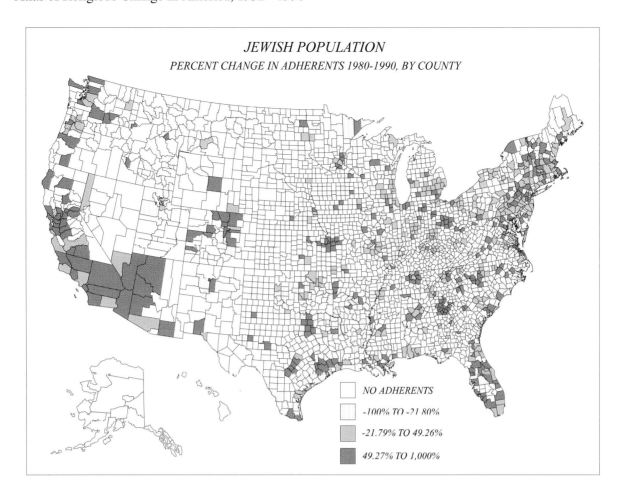

JEWISH POPULATION

PERCENT CHANGE IN ADHERENTS 1980-1990, BY COUNTY

NO ADHERENTS

-100% TO -21.80%

-21.79% TO 49.26%

49.27% TO 1,000%

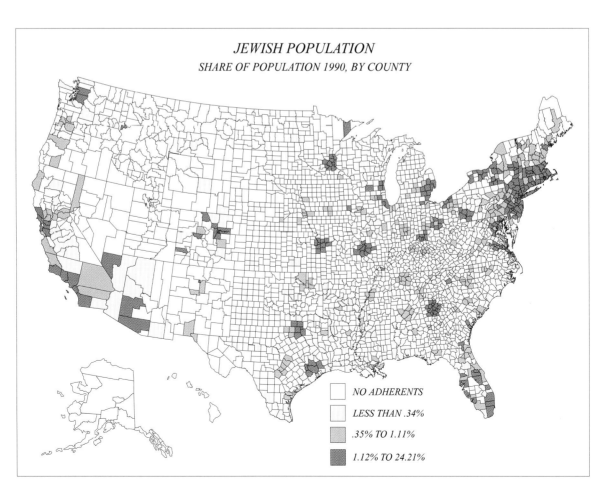

JEWISH POPULATION

SHARE OF POPULATION 1990, BY COUNTY

NO ADHERENTS

LESS THAN .34%

.35% TO 1.11%

1.12% TO 24.21%

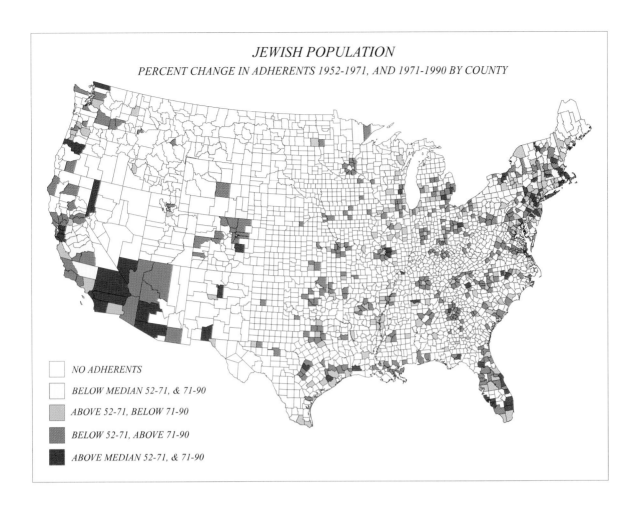

JEWISH POPULATION
PERCENT CHANGE IN ADHERENTS 1952-1971, AND 1971-1990 BY COUNTY

NO ADHERENTS

BELOW MEDIAN 52-71, & 71-90

ABOVE 52-71, BELOW 71-90

BELOW 52-71, ABOVE 71-90

ABOVE MEDIAN 52-71, & 71-90

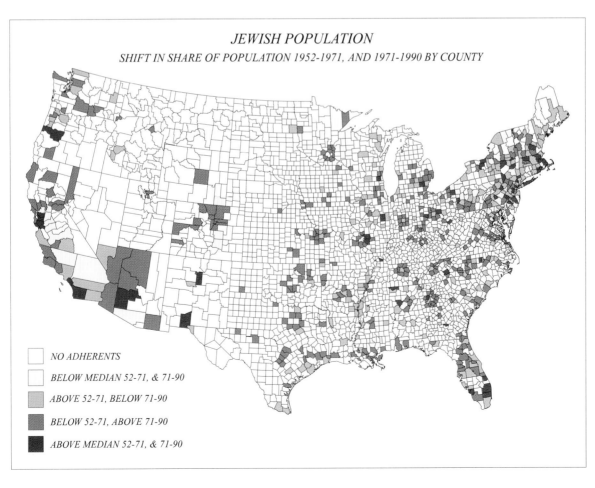

JEWISH POPULATION
SHIFT IN SHARE OF POPULATION 1952-1971, AND 1971-1990 BY COUNTY

NO ADHERENTS

BELOW MEDIAN 52-71, & 71-90

ABOVE 52-71, BELOW 71-90

BELOW 52-71, ABOVE 71-90

ABOVE MEDIAN 52-71, & 71-90

LUTHERAN CHURCH-MISSOURI SYNOD

The Lutheran Church-Missouri Synod was founded in 1847 as the German Evangelical Lutheran Synod of Wisconsin. It is more theologically conservative than any of the constituent groups that formed the Evangelical Lutheran Church in America (ELCA) in 1988, and it is about half the size of that group. During the 1970s a schism within the Missouri Lutherans resulted in the formation of a small splinter group, the Association of Evangelical Lutheran Churches. That communion later participated in the ELCA merger.

	1952	1971	1980	1990
Adherents:	1,856,638	2,768,539	2,617,936	2,598,469
Counties:	1,423	1,649	1,679	1,769

The impressive growth in adherents between 1952 and 1971 (49%) for the Lutheran Church-Missouri Synod was not sustained in the years 1971-1990, when the denomination contracted by some 200,000 adherents. Approximately half of this decline reflects the 1976 schism mentioned earlier. While the Missouri Synod did experience some declines in adherents during the 1980s, it did so in the context of continuing spatial expansion. For the entire 1952-1990 period the Lutheran Church-Missouri Synod registers a rate of growth that occupies a middle position when compared to other Lutheran communities.

In 1952, the Missouri Lutherans were a multiregional denomination. While the primary area of concentration was located in the upper Midwest and northern Plains, secondary clusters of counties were located in California and the Pacific Northwest, Colorado and in the northeastern metropolitan corridor. As seen on the map of Total Adherents, 1990, some 300 counties of new entry have created a pattern of in-filling. Contiguous bands of counties have emerged in some previously unoccupied areas including the Utah-Arizona-Nevada basin, clear across the nation's southern rim from California to Texas to Florida, as well as around Atlanta and other metropolitan areas of the "new South."

The map for Percent Change in Adherents, 1980-1990 reveals two contrasting patterns of events for this denomination in the most recent decade. Growing counties, which include slightly more than half of all cases (the middle category ranges from -6.37% to 14.43%), are prevalent in the areas of "more recent entry." The southern rim of states from Florida, to Texas, to Arizona, to California, are the "winners." In contrast, counties that have been declining in number are located predominantly in the traditional core areas, most especially in the northern Plains and the upper Midwest.

The map for Share of Population, 1990 tells a different story. In this instance, the emphasis is on the northern Plains and upper midwestern "home turf" of the Missouri Synod. Yet, the lower limit for the top third of counties (2.45%) suggests that where its greatest share of population occurs, the Missouri Synod is sharing "turf" with other denominations, most likely other Lutherans (see the population share maps for the ELCA and the Wisconsin Evangelical Lutheran Church). Alternatively, counties representing the lowest third of population shares, are disproportionately located across the South and West in areas of new entry. Here, the Lutheran Church-Missouri Synod generally accounts for slightly more than one half of one percent of county populations.

Because the rates of change in adherents for this denomination were so different in the 1952-1971 and 1971-1990 periods (medians of 60.92% and 5.37%), the map for Percent Change in Adherents, 1952-1971 and 1971-1990 must be interpreted with some care. Counties performing below the median in both periods could have grown substantially in the early period, but were likely declining in the later period. However, it is clear that between 1971 and 1990, the denomination's traditional core areas contain its weakest performers.

Similarly, the median rates for the Shift in Share of Population map indicate two very different trends for the Missouri Lutherans. In the period 1952-1971 a median county change in share rate of 1.40 reflects the denomination's strong absolute growth in adherents and geographic expansion. In the 1971-1990 period, a median county change in share of population rate of less than 1.00 (actually .95) reflects the predominance of declining share counties. The last map in this series indicates that counties performing above these median rates in both periods are predominantly in rural locations. Even in traditional core regions, "winners" are not in urbanized counties in California, in midwestern metropolitan and urban counties, or even in the most urbanized or fastest growing counties in Florida. Rather, even in areas into which its adherents have migrated, the Lutheran Church-Missouri Synod has not been keeping pace with population change.

In summary, over the years 1952-1990 this multiregional denomination expanded its geographical coverage, especially outside its historic core areas. While the Missouri Lutheran Church's growth in adherents out-paced general population growth for the early period, the years 1971-1990 have been characterized by numeric retrenchment, some of which resulted from a schism. This numeric decline, in combination with continued spatial expansion is resulting in a thinning of the denomination at the county level. Thus, while the Lutheran Church-Missouri Synod is spatially more national in character than ever before, this dispersion also may represent a potential decline in its cultural significance.

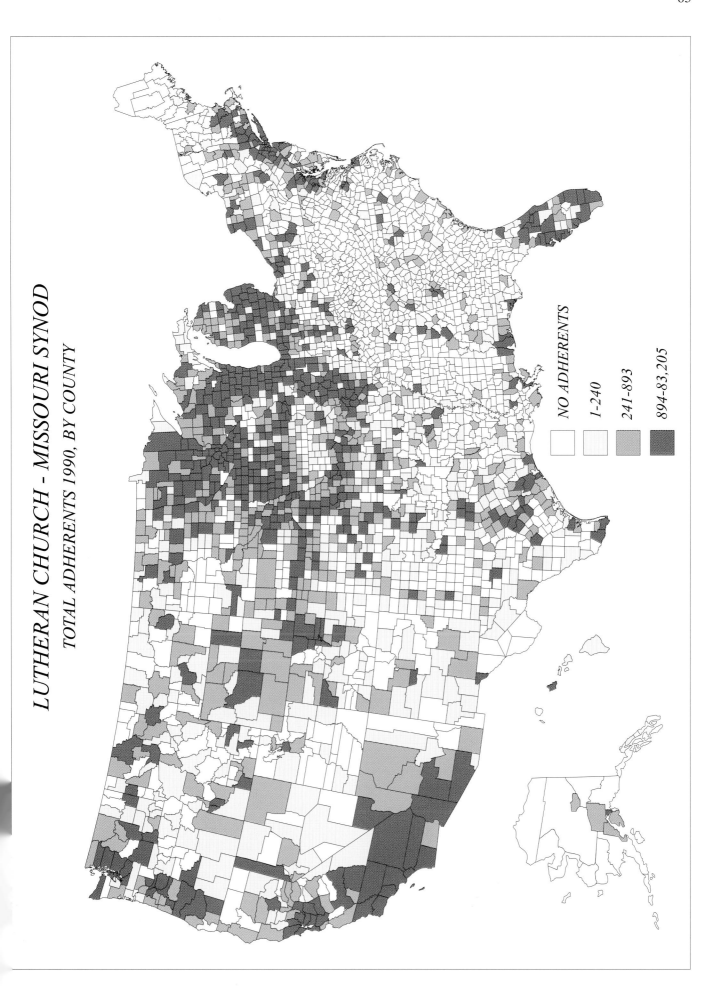

LUTHERAN CHURCH - MISSOURI SYNOD
TOTAL ADHERENTS 1990, BY COUNTY

NO ADHERENTS

1-240

241-893

894-83,205

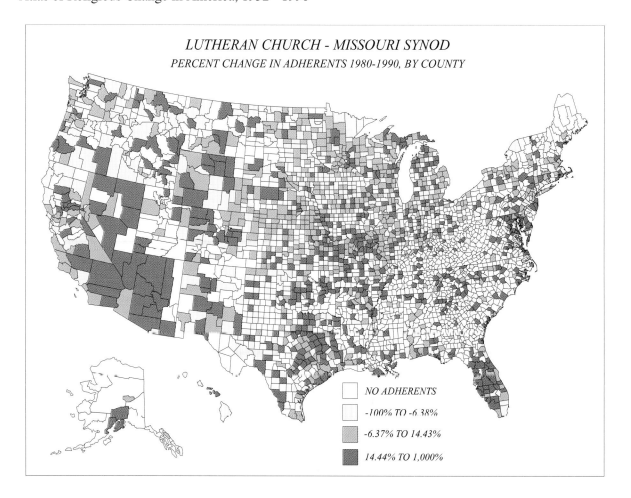

LUTHERAN CHURCH - MISSOURI SYNOD
PERCENT CHANGE IN ADHERENTS 1980-1990, BY COUNTY

NO ADHERENTS
-100% TO -6 38%
-6.37% TO 14.43%
14.44% TO 1,000%

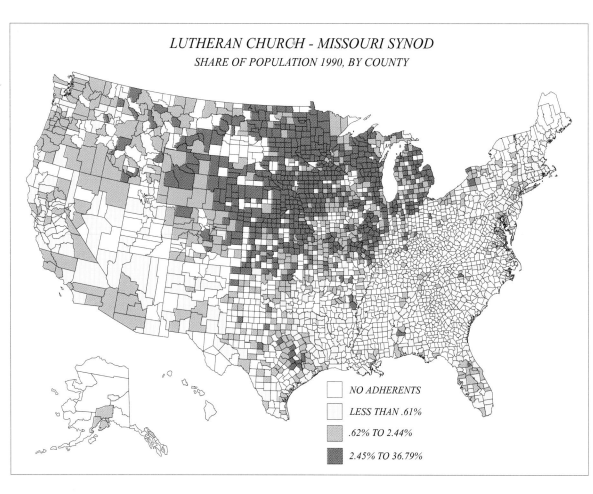

LUTHERAN CHURCH - MISSOURI SYNOD
SHARE OF POPULATION 1990, BY COUNTY

NO ADHERENTS
LESS THAN .61%
.62% TO 2.44%
2.45% TO 36.79%

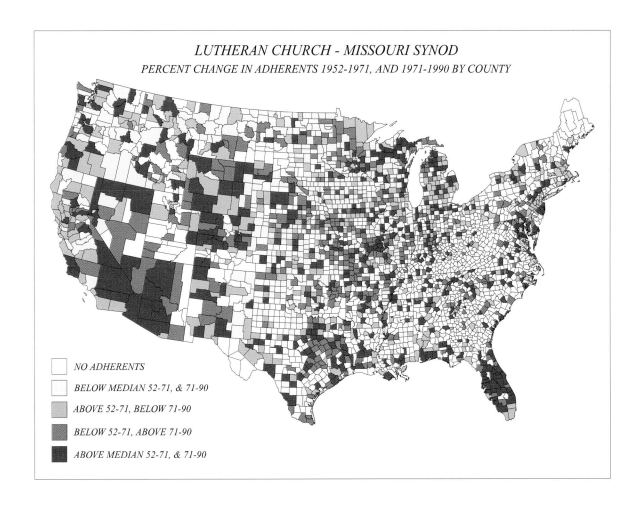

LUTHERAN CHURCH - MISSOURI SYNOD

PERCENT CHANGE IN ADHERENTS 1952-1971, AND 1971-1990 BY COUNTY

NO ADHERENTS
BELOW MEDIAN 52-71, & 71-90
ABOVE 52-71, BELOW 71-90
BELOW 52-71, ABOVE 71-90
ABOVE MEDIAN 52-71, & 71-90

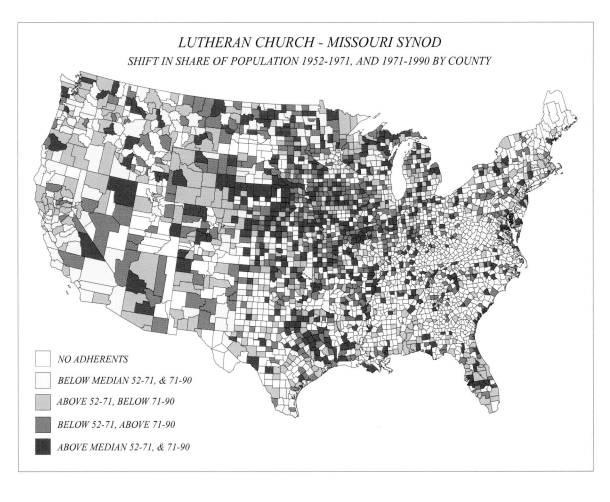

LUTHERAN CHURCH - MISSOURI SYNOD

SHIFT IN SHARE OF POPULATION 1952-1971, AND 1971-1990 BY COUNTY

NO ADHERENTS
BELOW MEDIAN 52-71, & 71-90
ABOVE 52-71, BELOW 71-90
BELOW 52-71, ABOVE 71-90
ABOVE MEDIAN 52-71, & 71-90

MENNONITE CHURCH

The various Mennonite bodies, most often thought of in the United States as "Pennsylvania Dutch," trace their origins to 16th Century Swiss and Dutch Brethren (Baptists) and to the leadership of Menno Simons. Mennonites, Hutterites, certain Brethren and Church of God bodies, and, of course, the Amish (named for the Swiss leader Jacob Amman) all are included in this theological family. The Mennonite Church, which is the largest Mennonite group, first was organized in the United States in 1683 at Germantown, Pennsylvania.

	1952	1971	1980	1990
Adherents:	66,652	108,048	118,239	154,257
Counties:	230	358	376	444

During the years 1952-1990, The Mennonite Church registered one of the most impressive rates of increase both in adherents (131.4%) and county coverage (93%) of any religious community in this *Atlas*. Moreover, the rate of growth in adherents was impressively high not just during the period of the so-called American religious revival (62.1% between 1952 and 1971), but also continued at a high level in the years between 1971 and 1990. In the more recent period, the growth rate reached over 42%, and the absolute number of new or added adherents actually exceeded that of the earlier period. This is one of the few groups of Continental European origins that registers such high sustained growth between 1952 and 1990.

The map of Total Adherents, 1990 shows a pattern that is common for religious communities that first settled in the Northeast. It reveals both a historic northeastern core area, and as a result of the general migration westward, two secondary cores in the Midwest and Far West. For this particular religious community, the Pennsylvania core is centered on the well known "Amish country" in Lancaster County, Pennsylvania. The clusters of high category counties in secondary cores, from Ohio to Iowa, and then reappearing in Oregon trace the historic path of 19th century migration. More recently developed clusters of counties in both California and Colorado, and in retirement locales in Florida, Arizona, and Texas, also are significant. In 1952, Lancaster County, Pennsylvania accounted for 19% of all adherents, and the state of Pennsylvania contained 38% of the denomination. In 1990, Lancaster County's portion has slipped to 13% of the church's total, while Pennsylvania's share of adherents has declined to 34%. Thus, growth in both adherents and counties has meant a gradual shift in this denomination's spatial center of gravity.

The map for Percent Change in Adherents, 1980-1990 confirms the impression that spatial shift has been occurring. Many counties in the top third of the distribution (beginning with a 155% change) are located outside the original northeastern core area. Moreover, the value ranges for the three categories on this map are uncommonly high, with fully two-thirds of

counties for this denomination growing at rates above the approximately 10% rate of the general population. Many counties in the middle third of the change distribution are located in the denomination's historic Pennsylvania core. This means that significant numerical increases have occurred there, as well as in other counties more recently entered. Among a religious community noted for large families this is not particularly surprising.

The map for Share of Population, 1990 indicates that even in its traditional core area, this community does not account for as much as 10% of any county's population. Thus, while these high category counties are located in virtually every locale where the Mennonite Church occurs, this church is not by itself a dominant cultural element anywhere. Rather, even in Pennsylvania's "Amish country," its cultural force is in connection with other denominations of similar life-style and theology, such as the Older Order Amish, and the Church of the Brethren.

The map for Percent Change in Adherents, 1952-1971 and 1971-1990 must be interpreted in the context of the extraordinarily high median county change values of 162.98% and 93.32% respectively. On the one hand, it is important to recognize that high percent change rates are not to be equated with high absolute values. Thus, when compared to the map of Total Adherents, 1990, it is clear that many counties that performed above the denomination's impressive median change rates in both periods actually have very small numbers of Mennonites (between 1 and 61 adherents) even in 1990. Additionally, given the high rates of change in both time periods, many counties that performed below the denomination's median county change rate in one or even both periods, were counties that significantly increased in adherents.

The map for Shift in Share of Population, 1952-1971 and 1971-1990 displays a very similar pattern. The median county share change rates are 2.07 and 1.68 respectively. These are among the highest share change rates for denominations in this *Atlas*. However, their high value in large part reflects the fact that small numbers of adherents, when augmented by relatively small numbers of adherents, will result in both high percent change rates and high change in share rates. This is especially so in the kinds of sparsely populated rural counties that are this denomination's typical home turf. Finally, both of these 1952-1971 and 1971-1990 maps exhibit change patterns that defy simple regional characterization.

In summary, the Mennonite Church grew impressively between 1952 and 1990. While that growth involved some spatial shift away from its traditional Pennsylvania core area, the core also retained its strength in absolute numbers. This general pattern of impressive numeric growth, accompanied by geographic expansion contrasts with the performance of other kindred communities like the Church of the Brethren, which contracted both spatially and numerically, and also experienced declines in its historic core area. The Mennonite Church, perhaps as a function of high rates of natural increase within its population, is an expanding though still small denomination.

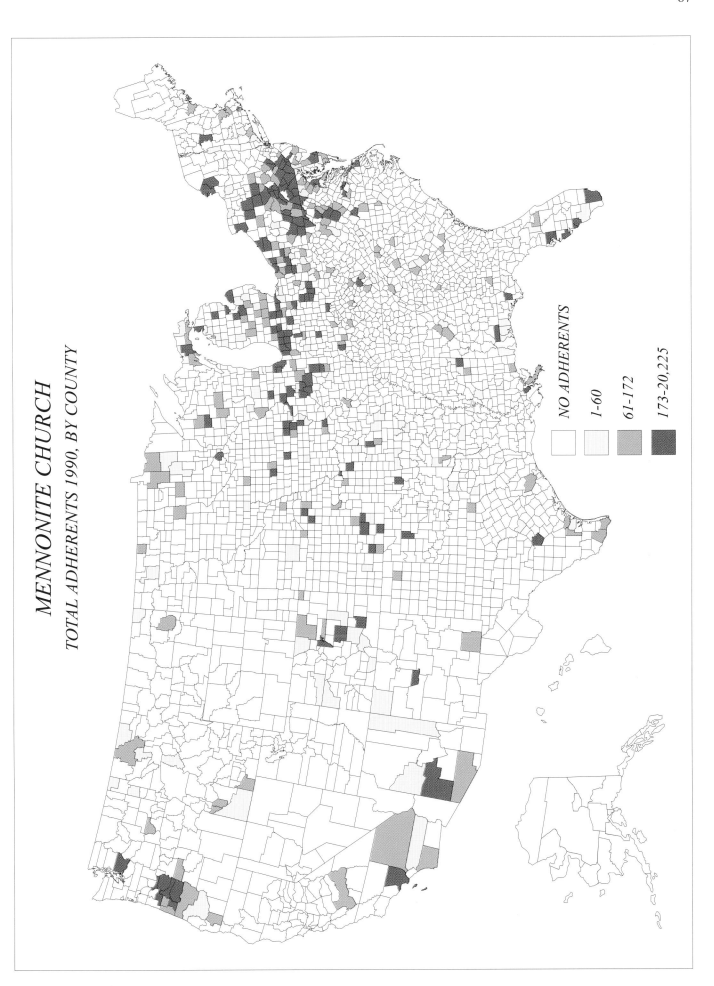

MENNONITE CHURCH
TOTAL ADHERENTS 1990, BY COUNTY

NO ADHERENTS

1-60

61-172

173-20,225

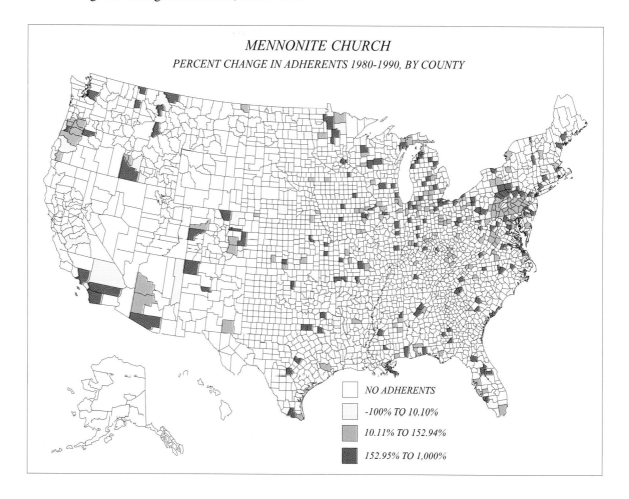

MENNONITE CHURCH
PERCENT CHANGE IN ADHERENTS 1980-1990, BY COUNTY

NO ADHERENTS
-100% TO 10.10%
10.11% TO 152.94%
152.95% TO 1,000%

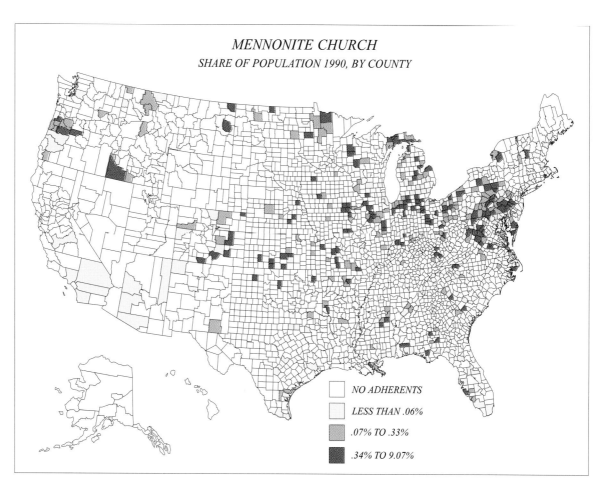

MENNONITE CHURCH
SHARE OF POPULATION 1990, BY COUNTY

NO ADHERENTS
LESS THAN .06%
.07% TO .33%
.34% TO 9.07%

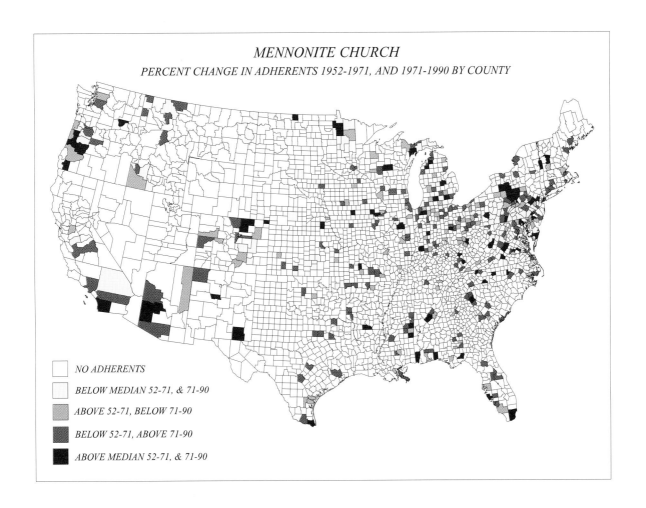

MENNONITE CHURCH

PERCENT CHANGE IN ADHERENTS 1952-1971, AND 1971-1990 BY COUNTY

NO ADHERENTS

BELOW MEDIAN 52-71, & 71-90

ABOVE 52-71, BELOW 71-90

BELOW 52-71, ABOVE 71-90

ABOVE MEDIAN 52-71, & 71-90

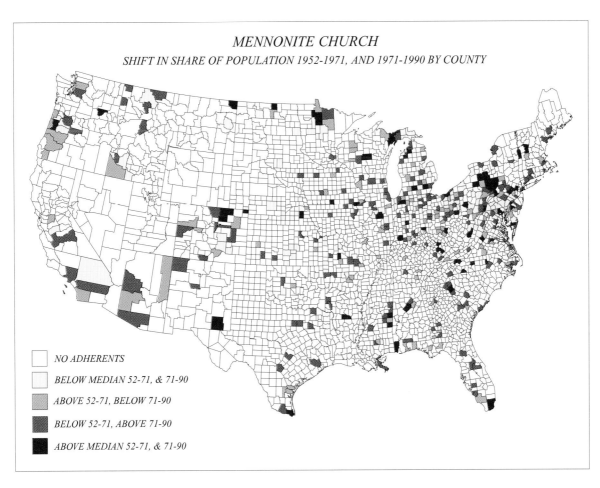

MENNONITE CHURCH

SHIFT IN SHARE OF POPULATION 1952-1971, AND 1971-1990 BY COUNTY

NO ADHERENTS

BELOW MEDIAN 52-71, & 71-90

ABOVE 52-71, BELOW 71-90

BELOW 52-71, ABOVE 71-90

ABOVE MEDIAN 52-71, & 71-90

MORAVIAN CHURCH IN AMERICA, UNITAS FRATRUM

While Moravian and Bohemian attempts to reform the Catholic Church can be traced as far back as the ninth century, this movement first took organizational expression in Bohemia in the mid-1450s. Here, followers of the martyrs John Hus and Jerome of Prague numbered several hundred thousand before the Reformation theologies of Luther and Calvin burst on the scene. These *Unitas Fratrum* (Church of Brethren) brought their evangelical brand of Pietism (German) to America in the early 1700s. Like so many other German evangelicals, they settled first in Pennsylvania. Eventually, two provinces of the denomination were created, North and South, the latter being centered in North Carolina. Statistics for the two provinces have been combined for all time periods in these data.

	1952	1971	1980	1990
Adherents:	48,618	57,121	53,647	52,519
Counties:	50	53	56	64

In most respects this small denomination has remained unchanged over the nearly forty year period encompassed by these studies. Between 1952 and 1971, the Moravian Church increased at a rate below that of the general population, and like many of the Protestant groups that initially settled along the northeastern seaboard, the Moravians decreased steadily between 1971 and 1990. As a result, for the entire 1952-1990 period they increased by only 8%, while experiencing a 25% increase in the number of counties occupied. These trends have produced a more thinly dispersed denomination in 1990 than existed in 1952.

The map for Total Adherents, 1990 reveals two historic core areas, one in Pennsylvania and one in North Carolina. Outside these two distinct core areas, the pattern of Moravian churches involves a scatter of counties across the Midwest from Ohio to the Dakotas. There are only four counties with Moravian adherents west of the Great Plains, and only three south of the Carolinas, and none of these are ranked in the high category on the map of Total Adherents in 1990.

The map for Percent Change in Adherents, 1980-1990 displays a general pattern of decline over the decade. Moravian communities experienced losses in most of their county locations, with an increase in adherents of less than 2% placing a county in the "high" change

category. Accordingly, counties that increased minimally as well as those of new entry all are contained in this upper third of counties. While some of these counties are located in the two traditional core areas adjacent to counties reporting losses, they are more often located in widely scattered places throughout the denomination's geographic distribution. Included are counties in Florida, Minnesota, Ohio, Arizona, and California.

The map for Share of Population, 1990 clearly reflects this denomination's small size, both nationally and more so in individual counties. A share of county population of .04% ranks among the high category of share counties. While some of these counties are located in Pennsylvania, a clustering of them in the Carolinas is much more noticeable. Elsewhere these counties are scattered in a pattern of isolated events.

The map of Percent Change in Adherents, 1952-1971 and 1971-1990 is based on median county percent change rates of 13.55% and -5%. Thus, in the context of a 65% increase in the general population between 1952 and 1990, at the county level Moravian congregations barely have held their initial numerical strength, and surely have not kept pace with population growth rates. As might be expected, counties performing at or above the respective median county percent change rates in both 1952-1971 and 1971-1990 are strongly in evidence in the two historic core areas. Outside these cores, such diverse locations as Detroit and Los Angeles also consistently report above median county change rate performances.

The map for Shift in Share of Population, 1952-1971 and 1971-1990 is based on median county share change rates of .89 and .76. These rates indicate that the relative position of the denomination at the county level consistently has been eroded. Because a rate of 1.00 indicates stability, counties that ranked above these median rates in both periods still may have been places of relative decline for the Moravian Church. This map clearly shows that especially outside the two historic core areas, the Moravians have not kept pace with the growth of the general population.

In summary, The Moravian Church in America appears to have attained its strongest numeric position by the end of the so-called religious revival or perhaps more accurately at the end of the Baby Boom. Since that time the Moravians have steadily declined both in absolute numbers and relative strength. At best, the Moravians have spread their distribution a bit in terms of counties occupied, but also have been diminishing in their traditional core areas.

MORAVIAN CHURCH IN AMERICA, UF
TOTAL ADHERENTS 1990, BY COUNTY

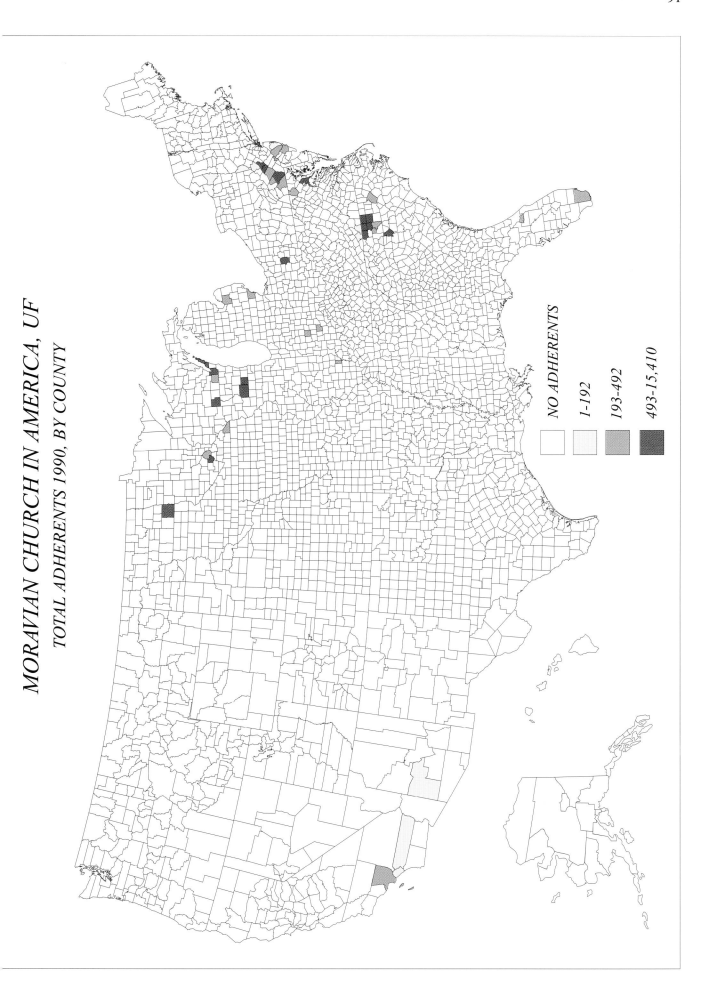

NO ADHERENTS

1-192

193-492

493-15,410

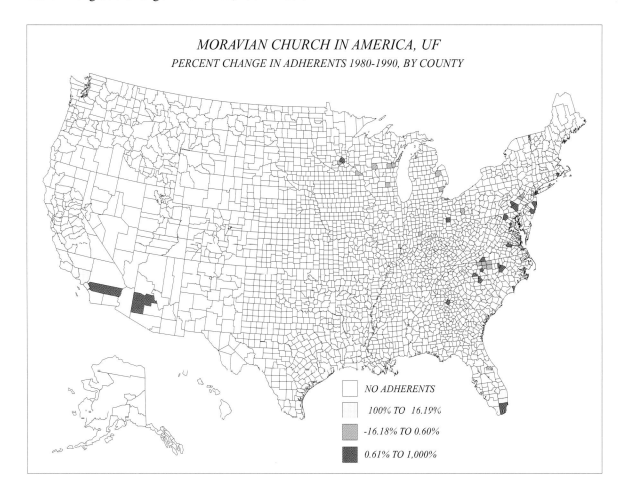

MORAVIAN CHURCH IN AMERICA, UF
PERCENT CHANGE IN ADHERENTS 1980-1990, BY COUNTY

NO ADHERENTS
100% TO 16.19%
-16.18% TO 0.60%
0.61% TO 1,000%

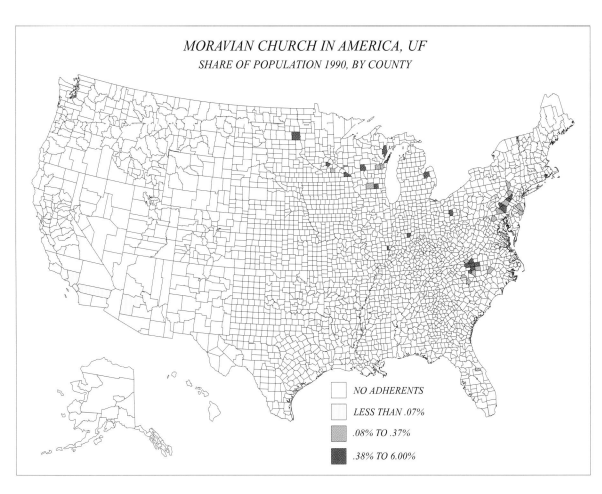

MORAVIAN CHURCH IN AMERICA, UF
SHARE OF POPULATION 1990, BY COUNTY

NO ADHERENTS
LESS THAN .07%
.08% TO .37%
.38% TO 6.00%

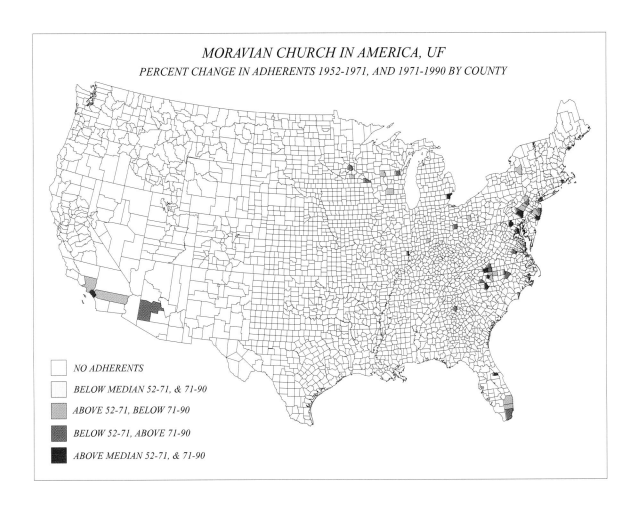

MORAVIAN CHURCH IN AMERICA, UF
PERCENT CHANGE IN ADHERENTS 1952-1971, AND 1971-1990 BY COUNTY

NO ADHERENTS
BELOW MEDIAN 52-71, & 71-90
ABOVE 52-71, BELOW 71-90
BELOW 52-71, ABOVE 71-90
ABOVE MEDIAN 52-71, & 71-90

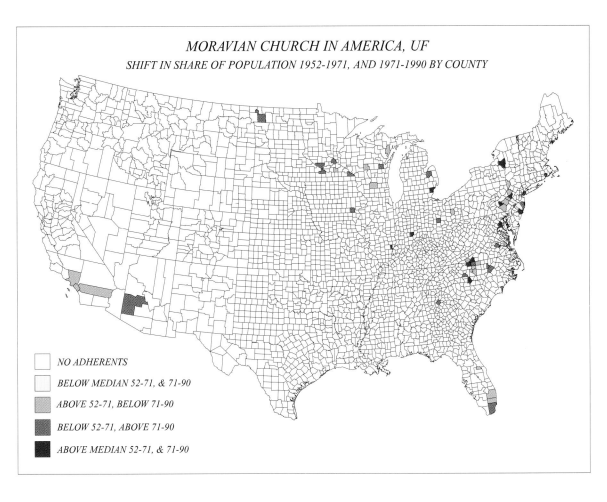

MORAVIAN CHURCH IN AMERICA, UF
SHIFT IN SHARE OF POPULATION 1952-1971, AND 1971-1990 BY COUNTY

NO ADHERENTS
BELOW MEDIAN 52-71, & 71-90
ABOVE 52-71, BELOW 71-90
BELOW 52-71, ABOVE 71-90
ABOVE MEDIAN 52-71, & 71-90

NORTH AMERICAN BAPTIST CONFERENCE

These German Baptists immigrated to America's shores in the middle 1800s, settling initially in Pennsylvania and New Jersey. Gradually, later waves of German immigration spread this small Baptist denomination into virtually all regions of the nation. Today, the North American Baptist Conference is organized into some twenty associations that convene annually. Theologically, the North American Baptist General Conference does not differ from other mainstream Baptist denominations. This is the smallest of the four Baptist denominations for which data are available for the entire nearly forty year period.

	1952	1971	1980	1990
Adherents:	35,431	50,555	51,726	54,010
Counties:	146	152	159	163

Over the entire 1952-1990 period, this Baptist denomination has grown in adherents by some 52.4%, but still numbers only a bit over 50,000 adherents. It also has increased its county coverage by 20%. As with so many other denominations, the growth of the 1952-1971 period (42.7%) was not matched in the later 1971-1990 period (6.8%). The total rate of change for this small German Baptist denomination (52.4%) approximates that for the national population during the same 1952-1990 period (65%). Generally, change patterns for these German Baptists very much follow those of many of the Continental European Protestant churches that have populated the American Midwest. Rapid growth during the period of the "revival" of the 1950s and 1960s, has been followed by very modest growth in the 1970s and 1980s.

The map of Total Adherents, 1990 clearly shows a denomination composed of small isolated clusters of counties. Much as they did in 1952, in 1990 these Baptists appear in metropolitan areas including Buffalo, Pittsburgh, Cleveland, Detroit, Chicago, Milwaukee, and Minneapolis- St. Paul. Larger clusters of counties are located in the Dakotas, and in the Seattle and Portland metropolitan areas.

Between 1980 and 1990, slightly more than half of the denomination's counties decreased in adherents. The middle third of counties on the map for Percent Change in Adherents, 1980-1990 ranges from an 18.6% decline to a just below a 14% increase. Those counties with the strongest performances (the upper third) are widely dispersed. They appear in the Buffalo and Chicago metropolitan areas, in the Dakotas, as well as in both California and

Washington. Counties experiencing the greatest declines (from 20% to 100% loss) are equally well dispersed. In the case of such a small and widely dispersed group there is a danger of over-interpreting "trends." However, the fact that strong and weak performing counties typically adjoin one another suggests that the same basic populations are shifting within their locales, most likely from urban into suburban counties.

The map for Share of Population, 1990 indicates that even in some of its strongest share of population counties, this denomination represents less than 1% of the population. Its strongest regional showing is in the Great Plains, especially in the Dakotas, where it attains nearly 18% of some county populations. While these counties are relatively small in total population, it is clear that this group constitutes a significant population element in the cultural mix of some counties in such areas.

The map for Percent Change in Adherents, 1952-1971 and 1971-1990 shows a pattern quite similar to the map for Percent Change in Adherents, 1980-1990. Strong and weak performing counties appear in all regions and typically are adjacent to one another. The median county percent change rate for 1952-1971 is a 39.21% increase, while the corresponding rate for 1971-1990 is -2%. Thus, while those counties performing above the median change rates in both periods almost certainly increased in adherents in both periods, there is no question that the greatest overall gains were during the so-called religious revival of the 1950s and 1960s.

The map for Shift in Share of Population 1952-1971 and 1971-1990 very much resembles the map for Share of Population, 1990. While there are isolated counties in all regions that performed above the denomination's median share rate in both periods, large clusters of such counties are found only in the core area of the Dakotas. The respective median share growth rates are 1.31 for 1952-1971 and 1.02 for 1971-1990. The places where these Baptists are gaining share, the Dakotas and northern Plains, are experiencing declining population. In this sense, the denomination represents a counter trend to the surrounding population dynamics.

In summary, by the early 1950s this was a relatively small ethnic denomination with a number of small clusters of counties and isolated county locations throughout the nation. While the rate of increase in adherents from 1952 to 1990 has been impressive (52.4%), for the more recent 1971-1990 period it has been, at best, modest (barely 7%). This change represents an absolute increase of only 20,000 people. Except for some counties in the core upper Plains states, this German Baptist denomination is a minor cultural element in most places where it is located.

NORTH AMERICAN BAPTIST CONFERENCE
TOTAL ADHERENTS 1990, BY COUNTY

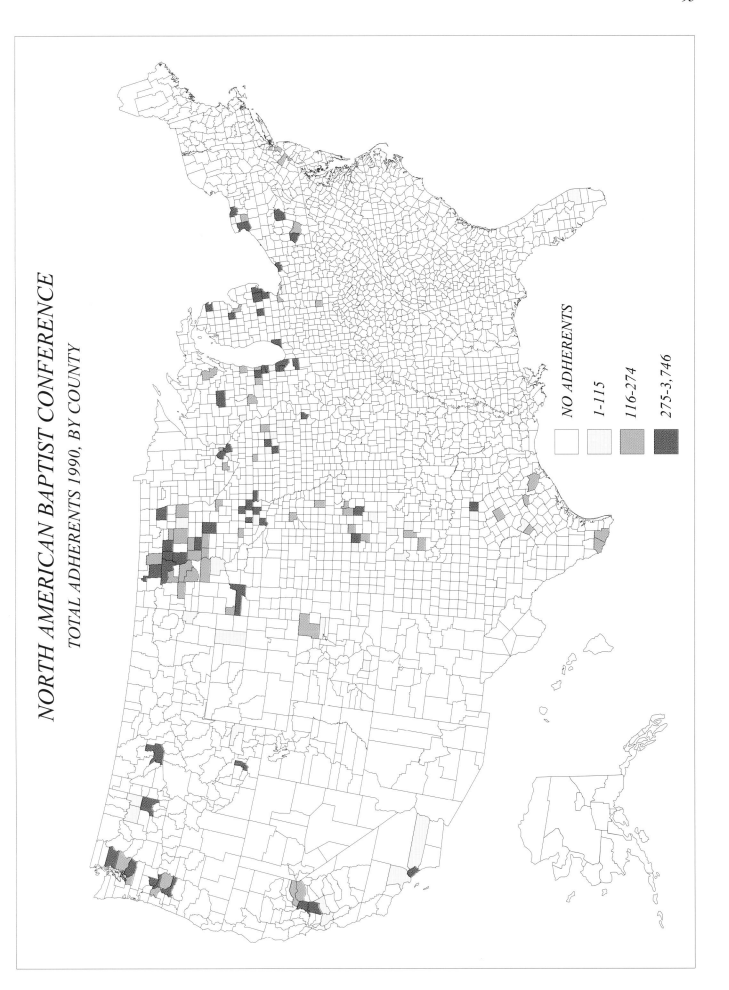

NO ADHERENTS

1-115

116-274

275-3,746

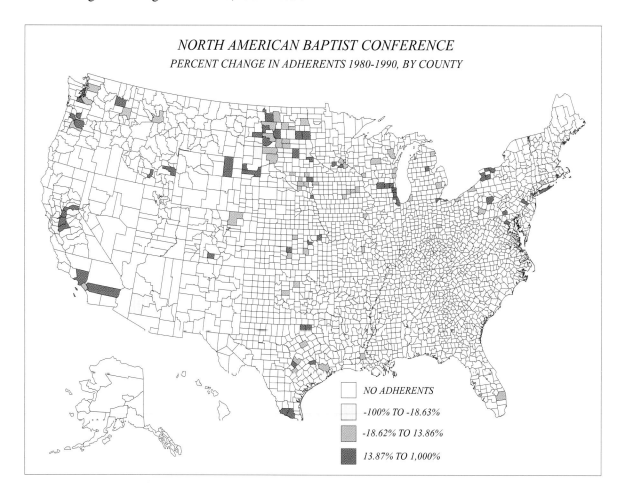

NORTH AMERICAN BAPTIST CONFERENCE
PERCENT CHANGE IN ADHERENTS 1980-1990, BY COUNTY

NO ADHERENTS
-100% TO -18.63%
-18.62% TO 13.86%
13.87% TO 1,000%

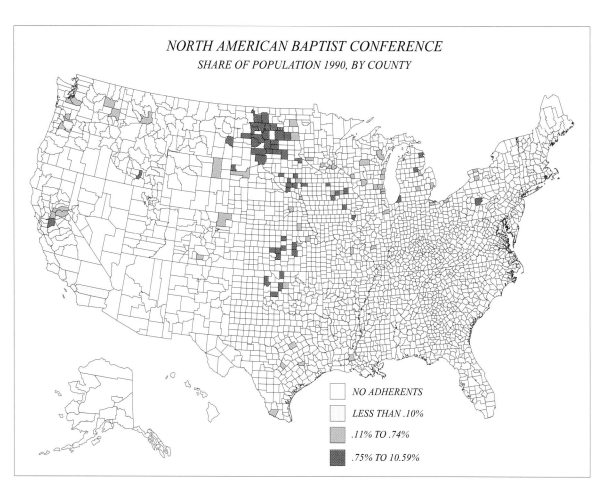

NORTH AMERICAN BAPTIST CONFERENCE
SHARE OF POPULATION 1990, BY COUNTY

NO ADHERENTS
LESS THAN .10%
.11% TO .74%
.75% TO 10.59%

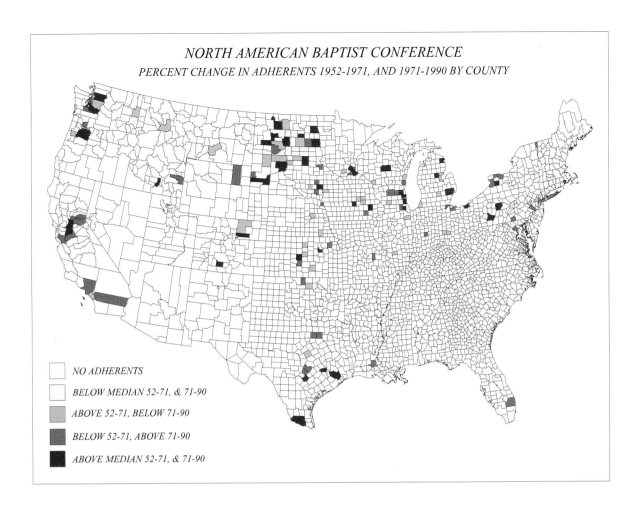

NORTH AMERICAN BAPTIST CONFERENCE

PERCENT CHANGE IN ADHERENTS 1952-1971, AND 1971-1990 BY COUNTY

NO ADHERENTS

BELOW MEDIAN 52-71, & 71-90

ABOVE 52-71, BELOW 71-90

BELOW 52-71, ABOVE 71-90

ABOVE MEDIAN 52-71, & 71-90

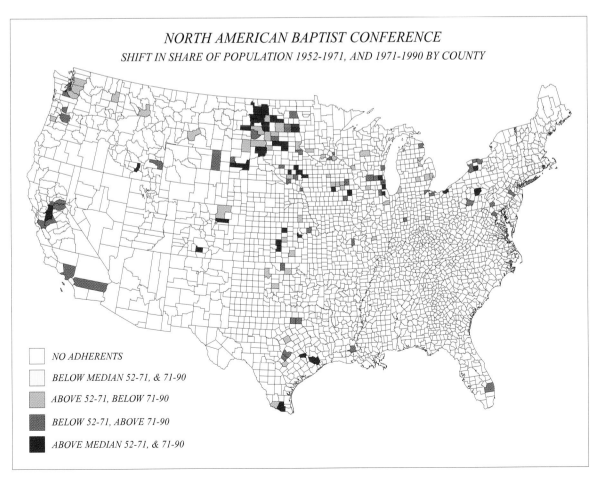

NORTH AMERICAN BAPTIST CONFERENCE

SHIFT IN SHARE OF POPULATION 1952-1971, AND 1971-1990 BY COUNTY

NO ADHERENTS

BELOW MEDIAN 52-71, & 71-90

ABOVE 52-71, BELOW 71-90

BELOW 52-71, ABOVE 71-90

ABOVE MEDIAN 52-71, & 71-90

PENTECOSTAL HOLINESS CHURCH, INC.

Pentecostalism encompasses a wide variety of native American denominations including the Churches of God, Assemblies of God, and other Pentecostal churches. All of these represent fundamentalist attempts to "purify" more traditional Baptist and Methodist forms of Protestantism. Denominations of this type are found in most states, and especially are prevalent in the South, Midwest, and West. In both polity and doctrine the Pentecostal Holiness Church is Methodist. In 1911, the Fire-Baptized Holiness Church, founded in 1898, merged with the Pentecostal Holiness Church, founded in 1899. Another group, the Tabernacle Pentecostal Church, joined the denomination in 1915. This series of mergers resulted in a denomination with two primary regional cores; one in the East centered in the Carolinas and Virginia, and the other in the southern Plains of Oklahoma and Texas.

	1952	1971	1980	1990
Adherents:	41,541	87,789	121,879	156,431
Counties:	371	489	459	509

Over the nearly 40 year period from 1952 to 1990 the Pentecostal Holiness Church grew in adherents by an impressive 276.6% and increased its county coverage by 37.2%. In the context of these long term trends, the decade of the 1970s was marked by a momentary spatial contraction, followed by a resumption of spatial expansion during the 1980s. Increases in the adherents have been sizable and continuous in all the periods in these data. Even though the absolute numbers remain modest, the rates of change in both adherents and counties place this denomination among the most impressive growth stories in this *Atlas*.

The map of Total Adherents, 1990 seems to depict a denomination of small churches (the middle third of counties begins with only 66 adherents per county). As noted previously, the history of organizational mergers is reflected in the presence of two distinct regional cores, one in the Southeast centered in Virginia and the Carolinas, and the other in the southern Plains of Oklahoma and Texas. Of these two cores, in 1990, the former accounts for more than half of this small denomination's adherents. Secondary clusters of high category counties appear in

California, Florida, and Alabama. On the whole, outside its two core areas, this denomination is thinly dispersed, primarily across the southern tier of states.

The map for Percent Change in Adherents, 1980-1990 indicates that growth during this decade was scattered throughout both the denomination's older core areas, as well as in more recently entered counties. Many individual counties that register in the bottom third on the map of Total Adherents, 1990 are in the top third of counties on this map of Percent Change in Adherents, 1980-1990. This is not a surprising pattern given the small absolute numbers involved.

The map for Share of Population, 1990 reveals that the Pentecostal Holiness Church, even in its strongest core areas, never represents as much as 5% of any county's population. In 1990, its strongest shares are in the two historic core areas, as well as in the Florida Panhandle. In two-thirds of its counties, this small group registers at or below one half of one percent of county populations.

The Maps for Percent Change in Adherents and Shift in Share of Population in 1952-1971 and 1971-1990 are virtually identical. The median county percent change in adherents rates are 136.57% for 1952-1971 and 58.82% for 1971-1990. Thus, counties performing at or above these median rates essentially doubled their original 1952 number of adherents in each period. Very few religious communities can make such a strong claim. The median county change in share rates are 2.10 and 1.28, indicating a similarly high positive movement. The maps clearly show that both percentage growth and increases in shares occurred across its geographic distribution. Said differently, this small denomination grew impressively both in its cores and on its margins.

In summary, although still relatively small in numbers in 1990, the Pentecostal Holiness Church registered a substantial continuous growth pattern over the entire 1952-1990 period. In 1990, it occupies over a third more counties than it did in 1952, and has become a frequently encountered church across the entire southern tier of the nation. However, its two historic core areas involving only five states still contain 67% of all adherents. While on a population share basis the group itself is a minor element, its cultural significance must be viewed in combination with other Pentecostals and Evangelicals in the Bible Belt.

PENTECOSTAL HOLINESS CHURCH, INC.
TOTAL ADHERENTS 1990, BY COUNTY

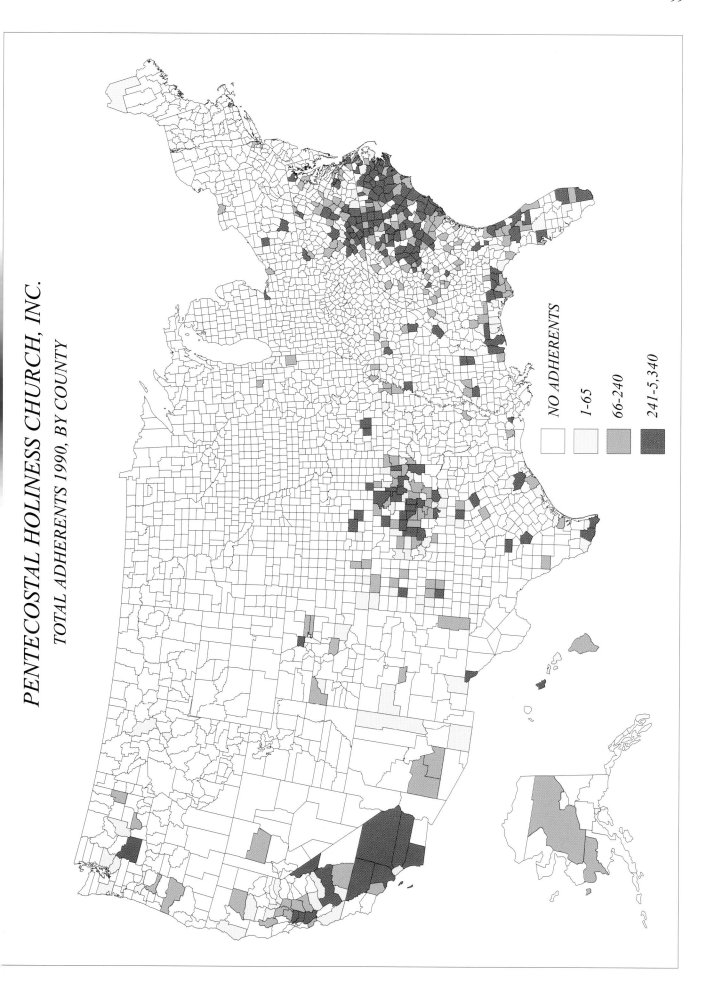

NO ADHERENTS

1-65

66-240

241-5,340

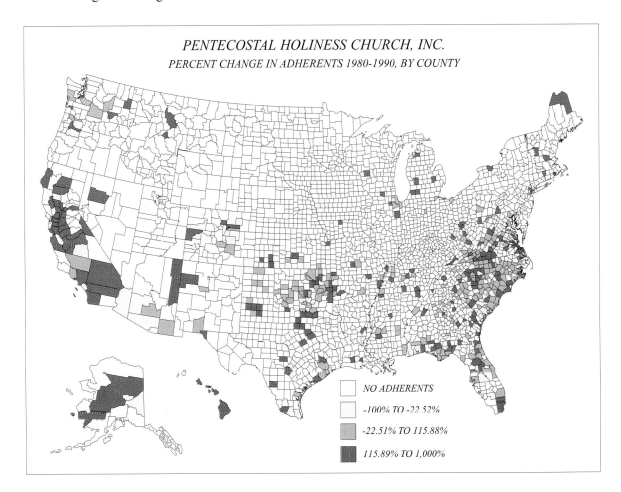

PENTECOSTAL HOLINESS CHURCH, INC.
PERCENT CHANGE IN ADHERENTS 1980-1990, BY COUNTY

NO ADHERENTS

-100% TO -22.52%

-22.51% TO 115.88%

115.89% TO 1,000%

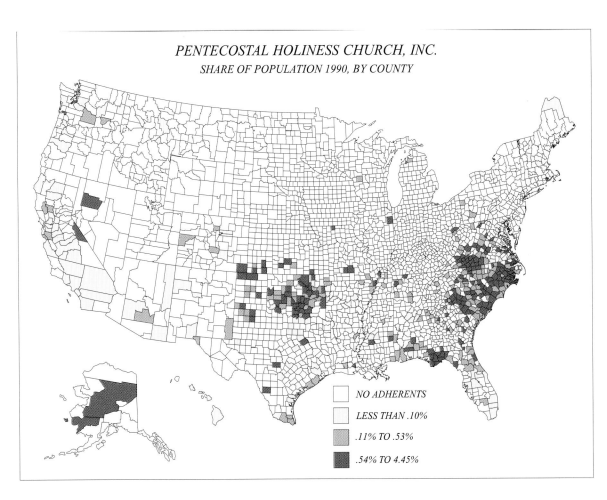

PENTECOSTAL HOLINESS CHURCH, INC.
SHARE OF POPULATION 1990, BY COUNTY

NO ADHERENTS

LESS THAN .10%

.11% TO .53%

.54% TO 4.45%

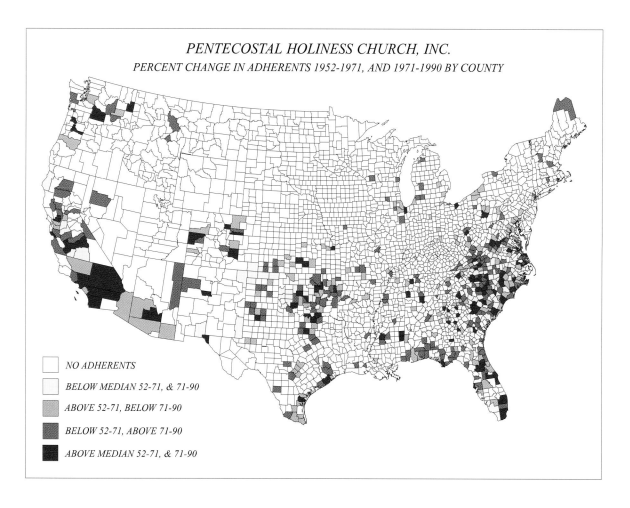

PENTECOSTAL HOLINESS CHURCH, INC.

PERCENT CHANGE IN ADHERENTS 1952-1971, AND 1971-1990 BY COUNTY

NO ADHERENTS

BELOW MEDIAN 52-71, & 71-90

ABOVE 52-71, BELOW 71-90

BELOW 52-71, ABOVE 71-90

ABOVE MEDIAN 52-71, & 71-90

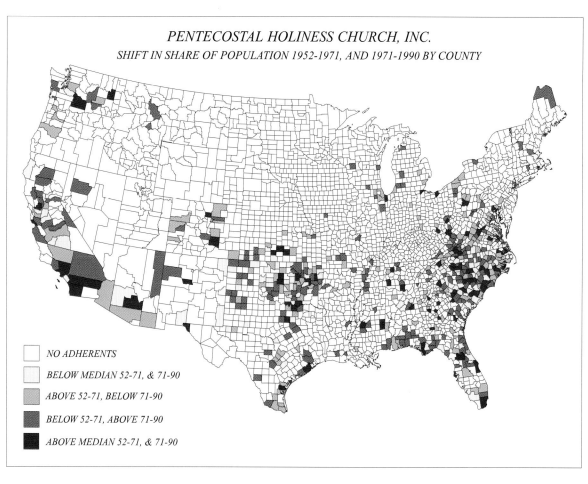

PENTECOSTAL HOLINESS CHURCH, INC.

SHIFT IN SHARE OF POPULATION 1952-1971, AND 1971-1990 BY COUNTY

NO ADHERENTS

BELOW MEDIAN 52-71, & 71-90

ABOVE 52-71, BELOW 71-90

BELOW 52-71, ABOVE 71-90

ABOVE MEDIAN 52-71, & 71-90

PRESBYTERIAN CHURCH (USA)

Presbyterianism refers to a form of church organization that is governed by presbyters, or representatives. Theologically, Presbyterians trace their origins to 16th century Calvinism. Their organizational beginnings are with John Knox and the Scottish Covenanters. The first American Presbyterian Synod was organized in Philadelphia in 1706. Successive migrations of Scotch-Irish, Welsh, English, Dutch, and Swiss peoples would make Presbyterianism one of the largest and most widely dispersed American Protestant denominational families.

The Presbyterian Church (USA) is the modern expression of the parent group from which the Cumberland Presbyterian Church divided in 1810, and with which some of that denomination reunited in 1906. It also is the same group from which the Presbyterian Church in the United States (the Southern Presbyterians) split in 1857. In 1858, the northern branch of American Presbyterianism, the United Presbyterian Church of North America (UPCNA) was formed through a merger of the Reformed Presbyterian Church and the Associate Presbyterian Church. In 1958, the UPCNA and the Presbyterian Church in the U.S.A. merged to become the United Presbyterian Church in the USA (UPCUSA). This merger extended the reach of the "Northern Presbyterians" into the Ohio Valley and West, making them a national church.

A 1983 merger united the two main branches of American Presbyterian that had been split by the Civil War. The Northern or national church (UPCUSA) contributed approximately two-thirds and the Southern Presbyterians (PCUS) approximately one-third of the adherents to the new merged denomination. Moreover, since many local churches had maintained affiliation with both denominations, the merged Presbyterian Church (USA) initially was somewhat smaller (by approximately half a million adherents) than the apparent sum of its two corponents. That fact has served to exaggerate the actual process of membership decline within American Presbyterianism.

Prior to the PCUSA merger, a division among the Southern Presbyterians (PCUS) resulted in the formation of a separate denomination, The Presbyterian Church in America. Founded in 1973, this denomination now numbering approximately 222,000 adherents is treated elsewhere in this *Atlas*. No adjustment for this division has been made in the 1952 and 1971 statistics for the merged PCUSA.

	1952	1971	1980	1990
Adherents:	3,415,837	4,687,228	4,005,950	3,545,264
Counties:	2,434	2,428	2,381	2,366

For the entire 1952-1990 period, these Presbyterians increased by only 3.8% of adherents, and lost 2.8% of their county locations. The Presbyterian Church is perhaps the leading example of those denominations that maintain stability of adherents over the long term only by virtue of their gains in the earlier 1951-1971 period. Even taking into consideration the problem of "double counting" local churches with dual affiliation before the merger, the 1971-1990 period has been one of decline for the Presbyterian Church. Between 1971 and 1990, the Presbyterian Church (USA) lost nearly a quarter of its adherents (-24.4%). This is the greatest extent of decline for any denomination in this *Atlas* during these years. The map of Total Adherents, 1990 clearly reflects the historic core areas of the two Presbyterian denominations

that merged in 1983. High category counties in the states of Virginia, North Carolina, and Florida delineate the southern core, while the Northern core stretches from New York and New Jersey, into the Great Lakes region through northern Illinois. Secondarily, there are bands of high category counties on the West Coast. It is little surprise that the Presbyterian Church (USA) ranks as the fifth most widely dispersed Protestant denomination in terms of number of counties. However, a third of its counties consist of relatively small communities, with less than 230 adherents.

The map of Percent Change in Adherents 1980-1990 reflects these losses. Over two-thirds of all counties lost adherents during the 1980s, with the weakest performing third of counties declining by over 20% of adherents. Because the strongest third of counties covers such a wide percentage range (-4.01% to +1,000%) it is difficult to characterize their distribution pattern. However, clearly there are more "high" performance counties in the population growth areas of the southern states from Virginia to Texas and on the West Coast than there are in the Northeast and Midwest.

The map for Share of Population, 1990 reveals a widely dispersed denomination claiming rather modest shares of county populations. The Presbyterian Church (USA) represents less then 2% of local populations in two-thirds of its counties, and in its "strongest" counties never accounts for as much as 17% of the county population. The high share counties appear to predominate in three different situations. First, they characterize both the southern and northern historic core areas. Second, in the central Plains where population out-migration is occurring the presence of high share counties suggests that the Presbyterians are persistent residents of this area. Third, growing population centers on the West Coast, and in Texas and Florida, seem to suggest that some Presbyterian growth accompanies population growth whether by reason of general migration or retirement.

The map for Percent Change 1952-1971 and 1971-1990 must be interpreted with care, as the respective median county change rates for the two periods are very different. For 1952-1971 the median county change rate is +22.19%, while between 1971 and 1990 it was -25.38%. Thus, many of the counties shaded red on this map actually may represent mere stability or even losses for the entire 1952-1990 period. One suspects that mortality, migration and even disaffiliation contribute to these highly dispersed, nation-wide change patterns.

The map for Shift in Share of Population is based on a median county change rate of 1.1 between 1952 and 1971, indicating that during the period of high growth in religious adherence, the Presbyterian Church (USA) simply held its ground. During the period of more stable adherence levels, the county median change rate of .64 reflects the substantial relative losses of this denomination. That quarter of counties that performed above these median county change rates in both time periods are strongly represented in the northern Plains. This is a region where population has been declining and in which the Presbyterian Church (USA) also lost adherents.

In summary, the 1983 merger reuniting the Presbyterian Church (USA) resulted in a truly national denomination that has been experiencing major losses in adherents. Some of this is only "apparent" loss reflecting the previous dual affiliation of many local churches prior to the merger. However, declines for this denomination are widely dispersed, suggesting that a major realigning of the position of American Presbyterianism in the scheme of American denominationalism may be underway.

PRESBYTERIAN CHURCH (U.S.A.)
TOTAL ADHERENTS 1990, BY COUNTY

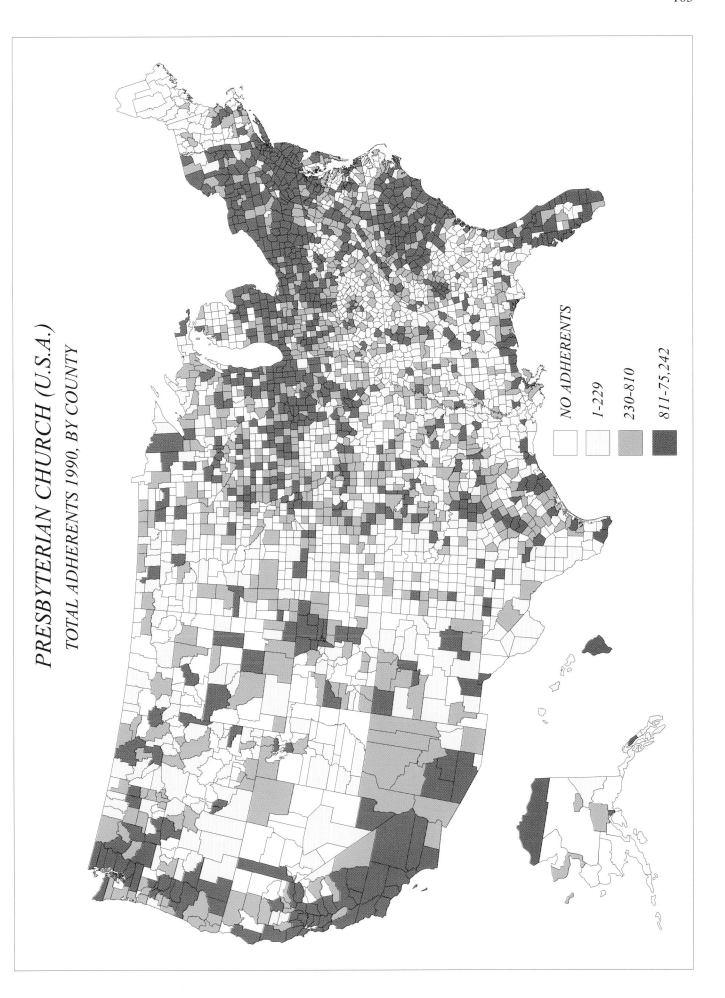

NO ADHERENTS

1-229

230-810

811-75,242

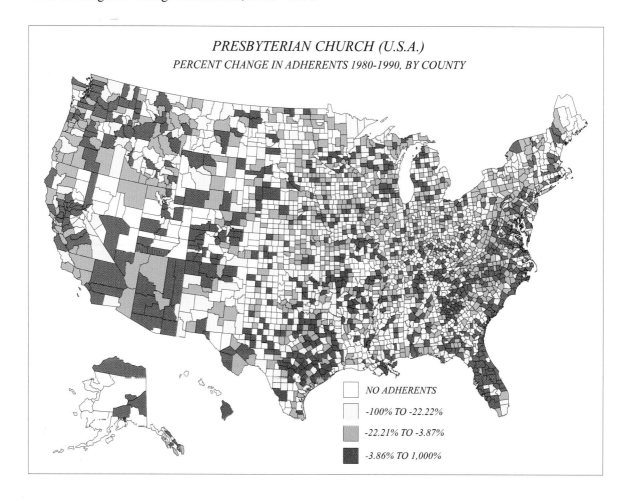

PRESBYTERIAN CHURCH (U.S.A.)

PERCENT CHANGE IN ADHERENTS 1980-1990, BY COUNTY

NO ADHERENTS

-100% TO -22.22%

-22.21% TO -3.87%

-3.86% TO 1,000%

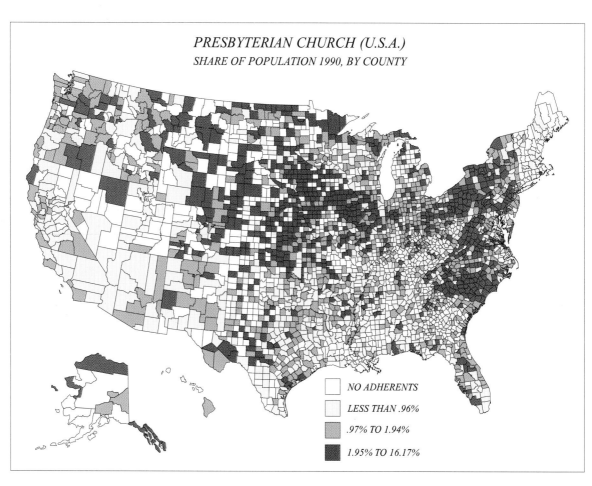

PRESBYTERIAN CHURCH (U.S.A.)

SHARE OF POPULATION 1990, BY COUNTY

NO ADHERENTS

LESS THAN .96%

.97% TO 1.94%

1.95% TO 16.17%

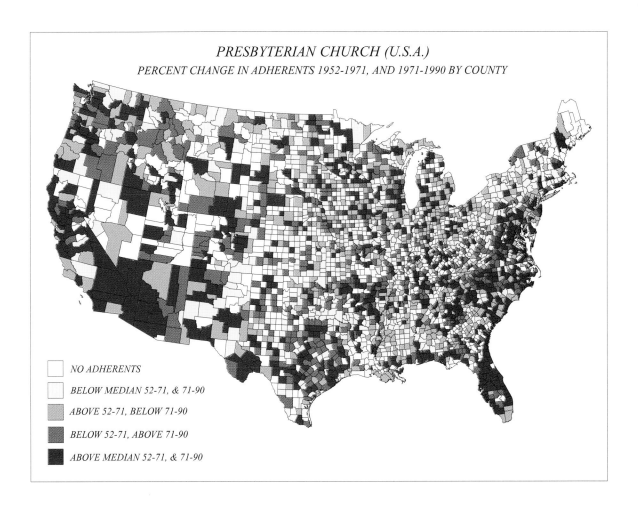

PRESBYTERIAN CHURCH (U.S.A.)

PERCENT CHANGE IN ADHERENTS 1952-1971, AND 1971-1990 BY COUNTY

NO ADHERENTS

BELOW MEDIAN 52-71, & 71-90

ABOVE 52-71, BELOW 71-90

BELOW 52-71, ABOVE 71-90

ABOVE MEDIAN 52-71, & 71-90

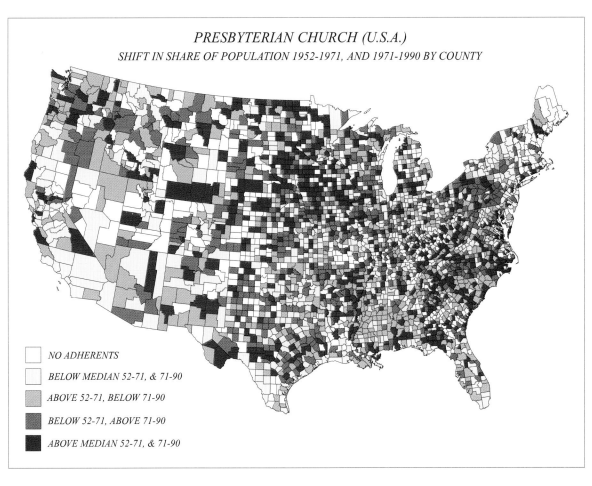

PRESBYTERIAN CHURCH (U.S.A.)

SHIFT IN SHARE OF POPULATION 1952-1971, AND 1971-1990 BY COUNTY

NO ADHERENTS

BELOW MEDIAN 52-71, & 71-90

ABOVE 52-71, BELOW 71-90

BELOW 52-71, ABOVE 71-90

ABOVE MEDIAN 52-71, & 71-90

THE REFORMED CHURCH IN AMERICA

The Reformed Churches (German, Swiss, and Dutch Calvinists) first were brought to America by the Dutch Palatines, who settled during the 1600s along New York's Hudson Valley, from New Amsterdam (later New York City) to Fort Orange (later Albany). By 1792 the group had separated from the parent denomination in Holland, and was known both as the Dutch Reformed Church in North America and as the Reformed Dutch Church in the United States of America. The name Reformed Protestant Dutch Church appeared in 1819, and the present name, Reformed Church in America, was adopted in 1867. This is the original denomination from which the Christian Reformed Church divided in the late 1850s.

	1952	1971	1980	1990
Adherents:	194,157	370,508	371,048	362,932
Counties:	150	203	208	232

The small denomination increased in adherents by 86.9% for the entire 1952-1990 period, yet experienced a modest decline in the most recent decade. This sequence of substantial growth between 1952 and 1971 followed by relative stability or decline between 1971 and 1990 is characteristic of many of the Continental European Protestant groups centered in the Northeast and Midwest. For the Reformed Church in America, these changes in adherents patterns occurred in the context of spatial expansion, even during the 1980s.

The denomination's two historic core areas of the Hudson-Mohawk Depression and western Michigan are readily apparent. In 1990, the four states of New York, New Jersey, Michigan, and Iowa account for 67% of the denomination's adherents. However, in 1990, the two midwestern core areas in Michigan and Iowa contain slightly more adherents (121,736) than the older core area in New York and New Jersey (totaling 121,257). Throughout the entire 1951-1990 period, that historic core has been decreasing in its share of the denomination's's adherents. Counties in the high adherents category in 1990 also are located in the metropolitan areas of Los Angeles, San Francisco, and Seattle. Counties in the lowest category of adherents are visible in the states of Texas, Florida, Oklahoma, Colorado, and New Mexico. The category limits for the map of Total Adherents, 1990 are higher than those for earlier years, and indicate that growth has been occurring throughout the denomination's locations.

The map for Percent Change in Adherents, 1980-1990 has two predominant features. First, the middle third of counties (-13.28% to +20.74%) indicates that during this decade, more counties increased than decreased, even though the denomination lost adherents on a national basis. Second, while the declining and modestly growing counties are distributed throughout the nation, they are more prevalent in the historic New York - New Jersey corridor.

Precisely because the patterns are so similar across geographic regions, it is suspected that natural decrease (aging) might be a significant factor within this denomination.

The map for Share of Population, 1990, as would be expected, shows that the highest third of share counties predominate in three areas, the upper Hudson Valley, western Michigan, and in Iowa. However, this "upper third" may represent as little as 1.3% of a county's total population.

The map for Percent Change in Adherents, 1952-1971 and 1971-1990 reveals the general spatial shift of this denomination away from the its oldest northeastern core area in the Hudson Valley. The median county change rates of 123.15% and 4.3% indicate that while the two time periods were quite different in their growth features, counties that performed at or above these median rates did, in fact, increase in adherents in both timeframes. However, most counties in the northeastern core area were below the median in both times periods, and thus, were loosing ground to other areas. The consistent "winners" are more apparent in the two midwestern clusters, as well as in the West and in Florida. The latter surely, to some extent, represent retirement populations.

The map for Shift in Share of Population 1952-1971 and 1971-1990 is based on median county change rates of 2.02 and .98 respectively. Thus, counties performing above the median grew aggressively in the earlier period and at least remained stable in the later period. When viewed along side other maps in this series, it is clear that the share patterns have several different meanings. Counties in the historic Hudson Valley core again register weak share performances either in both periods and or in the more recent period. This trend, of course, also reflects actual numeric loss for the Reformed Church. As would be expected, strong share performances are apparent in both the Midwest and the West. Finally, share performances that were above median level in 1952-1971 and below median rate in 1971-1990 are characteristic of most counties in the state of Florida, as well as counties in other retirement settings (California and Arizona). While the Reformed Church has grown in these places, this has not meant increased share because of the high rates of population growth in such locations.

In summary, this is a small ethnically distinct denomination that has several high density pockets of adherents. In the aggregate, it mirrors the national religious growth trend, with aggressive increases between 1952 and 1971, and relative stability in the more recent period. The Reformed Church's spatial features mirror the national population shifts to the Sunbelt, but depart from the national trends by increasing in the rural upper Midwest, where the general population is declining. The most dramatic feature of the trends for the Reformed Church in America is the diminishing of both the absolute strength and relative importance of its historic Hudson Valley core.

107

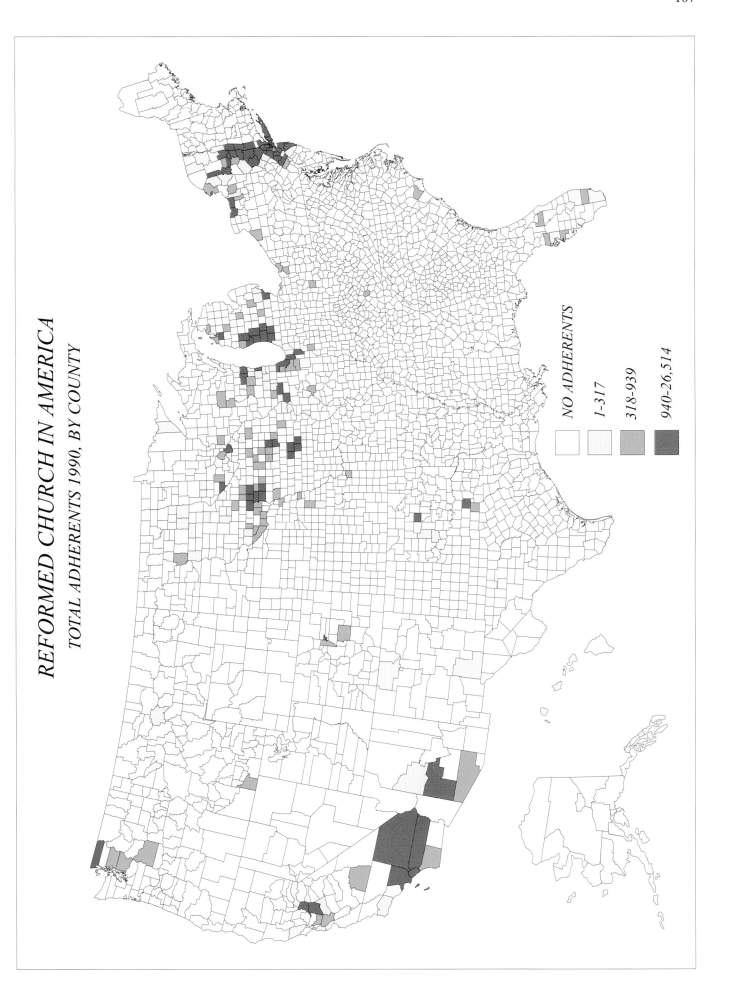

REFORMED CHURCH IN AMERICA
TOTAL ADHERENTS 1990, BY COUNTY

NO ADHERENTS
1-317
318-939
940-26,514

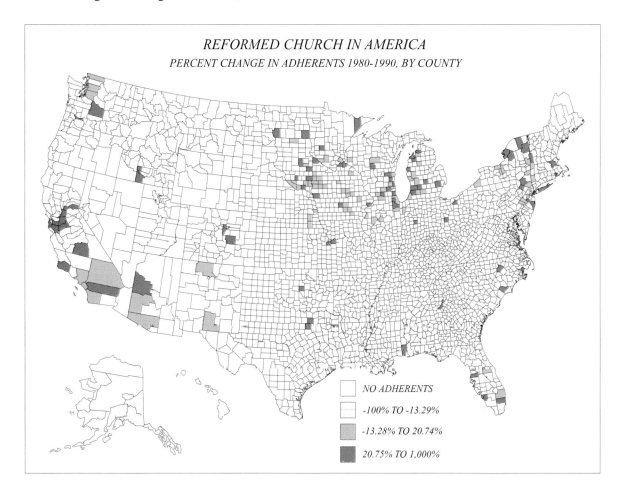

REFORMED CHURCH IN AMERICA
PERCENT CHANGE IN ADHERENTS 1980-1990, BY COUNTY

NO ADHERENTS
-100% TO -13.29%
-13.28% TO 20.74%
20.75% TO 1,000%

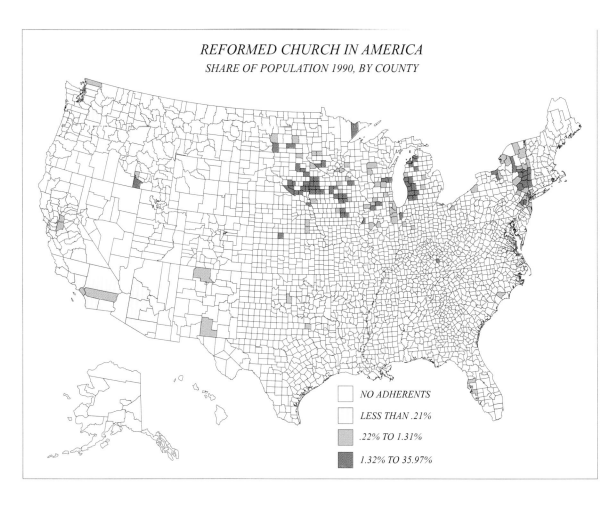

REFORMED CHURCH IN AMERICA
SHARE OF POPULATION 1990, BY COUNTY

NO ADHERENTS
LESS THAN .21%
.22% TO 1.31%
1.32% TO 35.97%

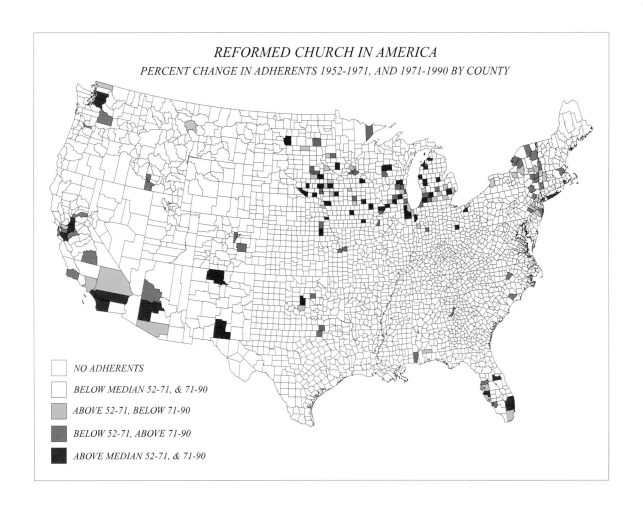

REFORMED CHURCH IN AMERICA

PERCENT CHANGE IN ADHERENTS 1952-1971, AND 1971-1990 BY COUNTY

NO ADHERENTS

BELOW MEDIAN 52-71, & 71-90

ABOVE 52-71, BELOW 71-90

BELOW 52-71, ABOVE 71-90

ABOVE MEDIAN 52-71, & 71-90

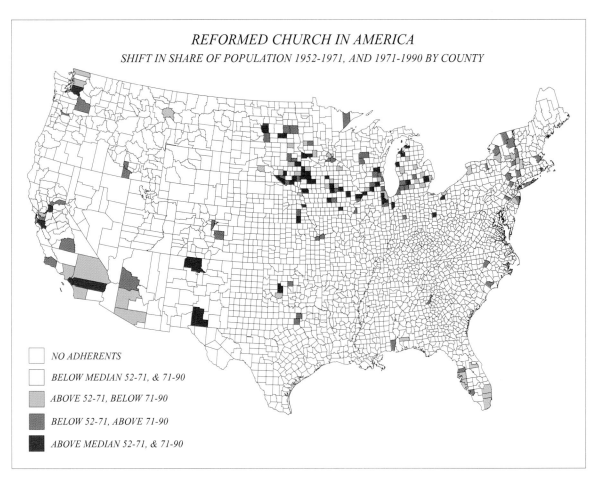

REFORMED CHURCH IN AMERICA

SHIFT IN SHARE OF POPULATION 1952-1971, AND 1971-1990 BY COUNTY

NO ADHERENTS

BELOW MEDIAN 52-71, & 71-90

ABOVE 52-71, BELOW 71-90

BELOW 52-71, ABOVE 71-90

ABOVE MEDIAN 52-71, & 71-90

SEVENTH-DAY ADVENTISTS

Adventism began as a movement within existing churches during the Great Awakenings of the early 1800s. This form of Protestantism, which focuses upon the second coming of Christ, first emerged as a distinct organization in upstate New York in the mid-1840s. Its most prominent early leader was the Baptist preacher William Miller (1782-1849), after whom the movement for a time was named. The Seventh-Day Adventists are the largest American denomination using the name "Adventist." They are theologically conservative, Bible-oriented Protestants who practice foot-washing and baptism by immersion, and they believe in the gift of prophecy. In the public mind they are frequently identified with their well-known *Watch Tower* publication.

	1952	1971	1980	1990
Adherents:	252,917	531,191	662,261	894,170
Counties:	1,466	1,624	1,734	1,781

Over the years encompassed by these data, this once sectarian group has taken on the appearance of a national denomination. With strong growth across both the 1952-1971 and 1971-1990 periods, the Seventh-Day Adventists have increased from 225,971 to 849,170 adherents (253.5%) and have expanded their geographic reach by over 300 counties.

The map for Total Adherents, 1990 reveals churches in virtually all regions of the nation, with the largest bands of contiguous counties along the West Coast, in Florida, Michigan, and in the metropolitan corridor stretching from southern New England into the Washington D. C. area. It is notable that nearly a quarter of the adherents are located in the state of California (206,894), with Los Angeles having the largest single concentration of Seventh-Day Adventists (54,000).

The map for Percent Change in Adherents, 1980-1990 confirms the impression of continuing rapid expansion for these Adventists. The median county change rate of 19.5% is well above that for the United States population. Moreover, this denomination's growth is not regionally confined. While counties in the upper third of the distribution (42.46% to 100%

increase) are evident in all regions, clearly areas across the Sunbelt from California to the Carolinas have experienced significant growth.

The map for Share of Population, 1990 shows a strong regional bias. Although the upper category ranges broadly from approximately .5% to 17.52% such counties are concentrated strongly in the western half of the nation. Included are states not only on the West Coast, but also locations throughout the interior West in Colorado, Wyoming, Montana, Kansas, Nebraska, and North Dakota. High category counties are evident elsewhere in a less continuous pattern.

The map for Percent Change in Adherents 1952-1971 and 1971-1990 is centered upon median county rates of 77.42% and 44.05%. Clearly, these rates reflect the substantial growth of the denomination. This map is very much a muted version of the map of Total Adherents, 1990, with the West, interior South, and Atlantic Coast corridor from Virginia to New England registering the highest sustained growth.

In contrast, the map for Shift in Share of Population 1952-1971 and 1971-1990 exhibits a much more widely dispersed pattern of clusters of counties in all regions. Clearly, in high population growth states like Florida and California high denominational growth rates do not translate into high share rates. This, in part, also reflects the small average size of Seventh-Day Adventist congregations.

In summary, over the nearly forty year period between 1952 and 1990, the Seventh-Day Adventists have undergone a fairly dramatic transformation. At mid-century, they were most readily classified as a relatively large but widely dispersed sect. However, by 1990, they number almost a million adherents and have spread into more counties (1,734) than such ranking denominations as the Evangelical Lutheran Church in America (ELCA) (1,620 counties) and the United Church of Christ (1,266 counties). Moreover, it is worth considering that this denomination's practice of adult baptism (children are not counted) yields a more conservative than liberal estimation of the number of adherents. In other words, these data very likely underestimate the actual size and growth of the Seventh-Day Adventists. Over the period 1952 to 1990, the Seventh-Day Adventists have become a major Protestant denomination of national scope and size.

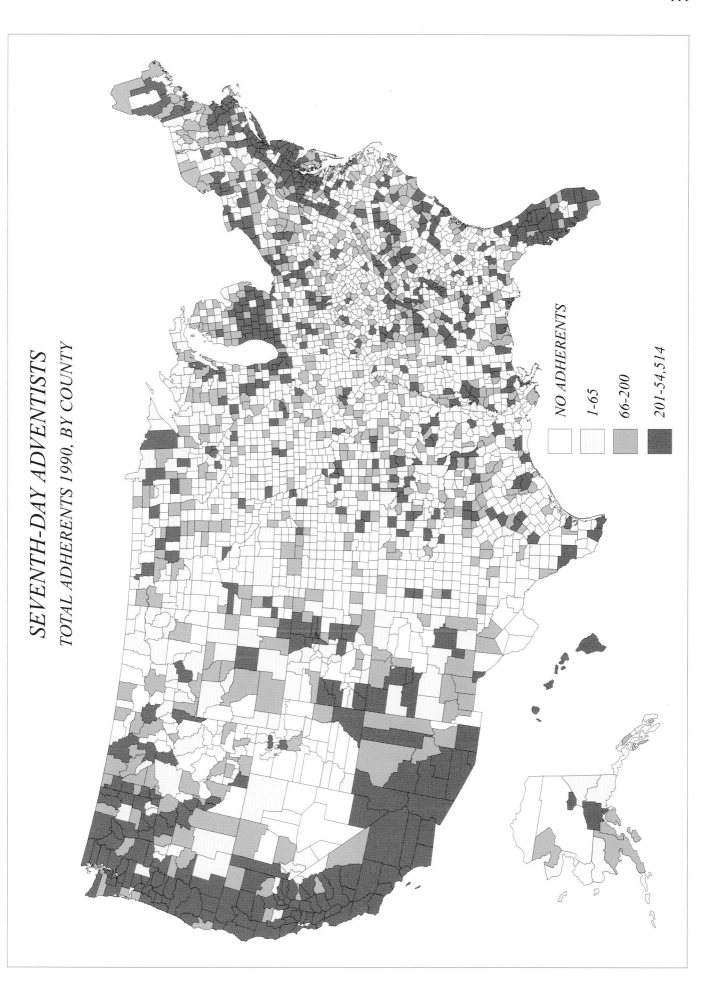

SEVENTH-DAY ADVENTISTS
TOTAL ADHERENTS 1990, BY COUNTY

NO ADHERENTS

1-65

66-200

201-54,514

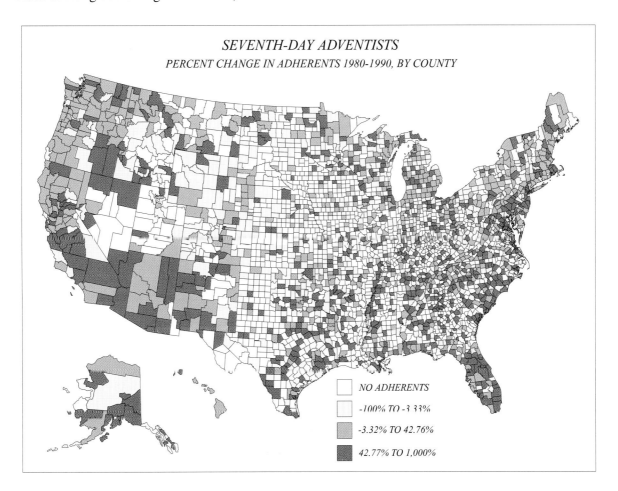

SEVENTH-DAY ADVENTISTS

PERCENT CHANGE IN ADHERENTS 1980-1990, BY COUNTY

NO ADHERENTS

-100% TO -3 33%

-3.32% TO 42.76%

42.77% TO 1,000%

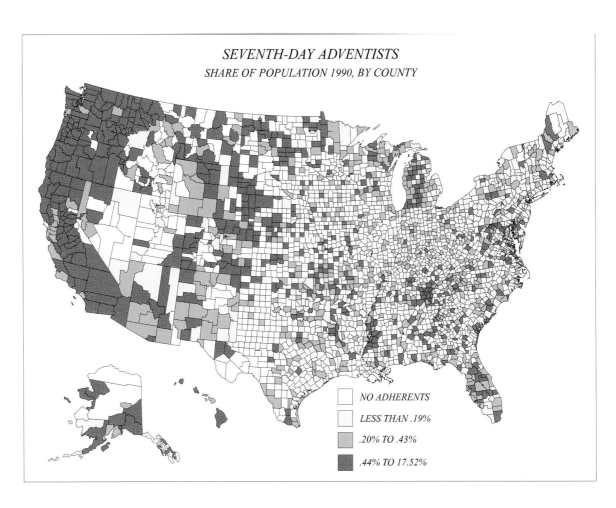

SEVENTH-DAY ADVENTISTS

SHARE OF POPULATION 1990, BY COUNTY

NO ADHERENTS

LESS THAN .19%

.20% TO .43%

.44% TO 17.52%

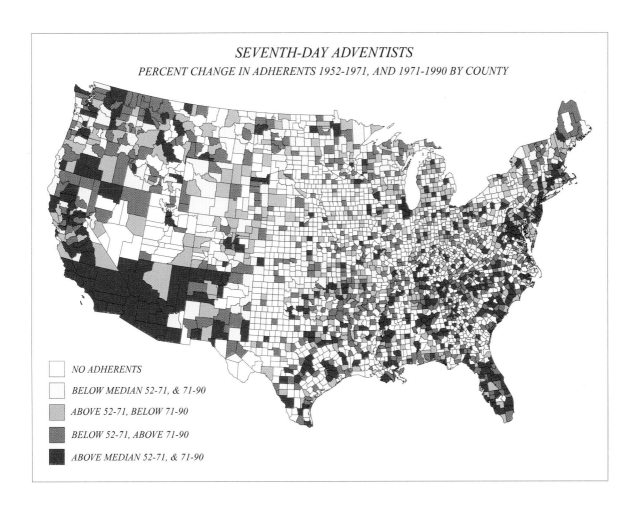

SEVENTH-DAY ADVENTISTS
PERCENT CHANGE IN ADHERENTS 1952-1971, AND 1971-1990 BY COUNTY

NO ADHERENTS

BELOW MEDIAN 52-71, & 71-90

ABOVE 52-71, BELOW 71-90

BELOW 52-71, ABOVE 71-90

ABOVE MEDIAN 52-71, & 71-90

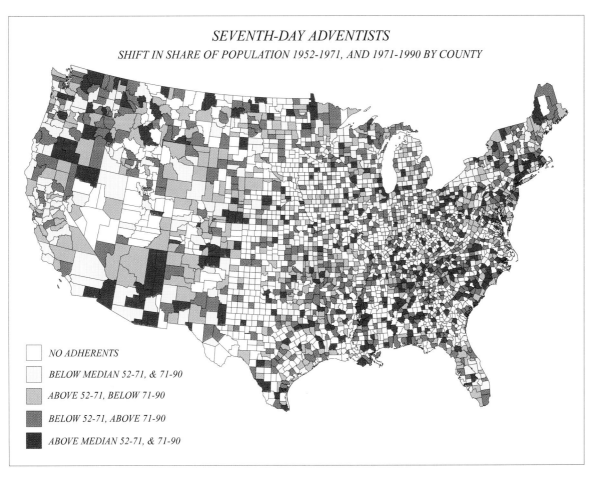

SEVENTH-DAY ADVENTISTS
SHIFT IN SHARE OF POPULATION 1952-1971, AND 1971-1990 BY COUNTY

NO ADHERENTS

BELOW MEDIAN 52-71, & 71-90

ABOVE 52-71, BELOW 71-90

BELOW 52-71, ABOVE 71-90

ABOVE MEDIAN 52-71, & 71-90

SEVENTH DAY BAPTIST GENERAL CONFERENCE

English in origin, these so-called Sabbatarian Baptists (because of their claim that the seventh day of the week is the Sabbath) first were organized in the United States at Newport, Rhode Island in 1672. Their organizer, Stephen Mumford, recruited other congregations from both New Jersey and Philadelphia. From these three original centers, the denomination spread west, creating a thinly dispersed scatter of churches which had entered 20 states by 1971 and increased to 28 states by 1990.

	1952	1971	1980	1990
Adherents:	6,425	6,178	6,145	6,439
Counties:	46	45	49	69

This is the smallest denomination in this *Atlas*. It is unique for having declined (-4%) during the years of general religious population increase (1952-1971), and only shows growth in the decade of the 1980s (5%). By 1990, it reported the same number of adherents it had in 1952. Yet, despite relatively small numbers and low rates of growth, there has been gradual spatial expansion since 1971, with 24 new counties representing a nearly 50% increase in counties.

The map of Total Adherents, 1990 reveals the unusually wide dispersion of counties for such a tiny sect. This group has extremely small local communions (two-thirds of them consist of less than 66 people). The typical event is an isolated county rather than clusters of counties, most of which represent single churches as there are only 83 churches across 69 counties.

The map for Percent Change in Adherents, 1980-1990 indicates that the 20 newly entered counties and growing counties are located predominantly in the Sunbelt. However, it must be remembered that when the numbers of adherents in counties are very small, slight increases in adherents register as large percentages. For one-third of this group's counties (see the map of Total Adherents, 1990) over the decade of the 1980s an increase of only three persons results in a 10% increase on this map of Percent Change in Adherents, 1980-1990!

It is little surprise that the map for Share of Population, 1990 indicates less than 5% as the upper limit of population share anywhere for this small group. The map for Percent Change in Adherents 1952-1971 and 1971-1990 is based on median county change rates of -6.81% and 56.71%. The map based on these median rates evidences a rather unique pattern. First, there are a small number of widely scattered counties performing above the median rates in both periods. Second, counties that bettered the median performance in the later more growth-oriented period also are largely isolated and scattered. This most likely reflects local congregational factors rather than denomination-wide trends. The absolute numbers behind these relative percent change patterns are very small. The trend, to the degree that such a limited number of counties can be viewed as demonstrating a trend, may be described as one moving away from the Northeast.

Finally, the map for Shift in Share of Population, 1952-1971 and 1971-1990 is based on median county rates of .81 and 1.50. The latter, no doubt, reflects the numerous counties of new entry during the 1980s. Without these "new" counties it is unlikely that the median county change rates would indicate a denomination with such small numbers as this one to be keeping pace with general population changes.

In summary, this is a small, theologically distinctive sect that for the entire 1952-1990 period remained stable in numbers while dispersing into many new counties, especially during the 1980s. This spurt in adherents and county coverage in the decade of the 1980s is not typical of the trend for most groups in this *Atlas*.

SEVENTH DAY BAPTIST GENERAL CONFERENCE
TOTAL ADHERENTS 1990, BY COUNTY

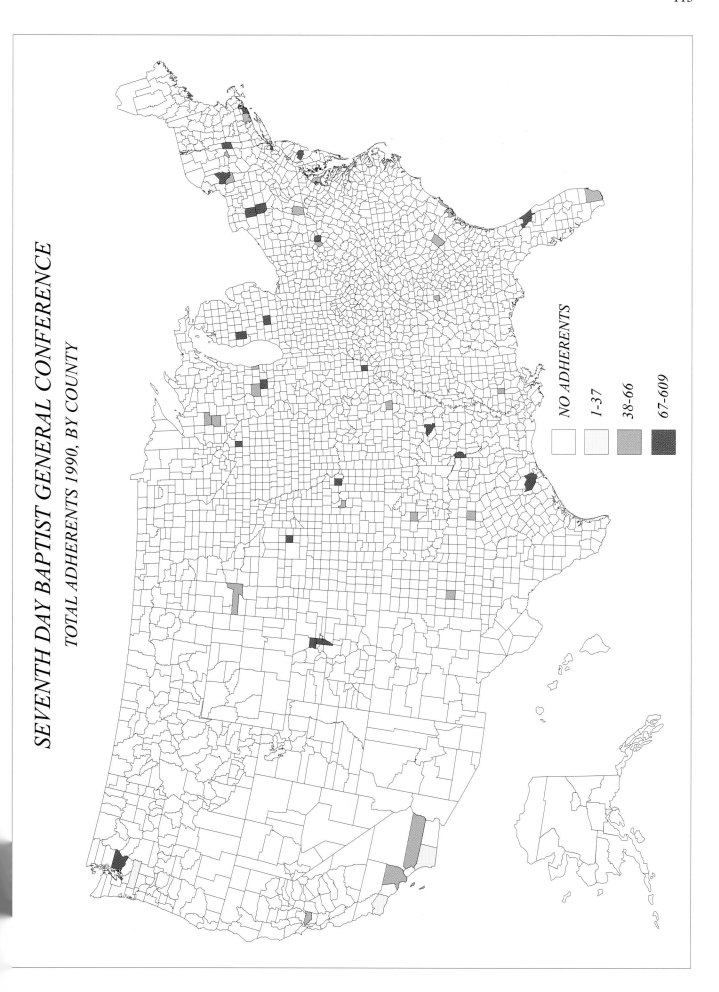

NO ADHERENTS

1-37

38-66

67-609

SEVENTH DAY BAPTIST GENERAL CONFERENCE

PERCENT CHANGE IN ADHERENTS 1980-1990, BY COUNTY

NO ADHERENTS

-100% TO -4.08%

-4.07% TO 1,000%

"NEW" COUNTIES

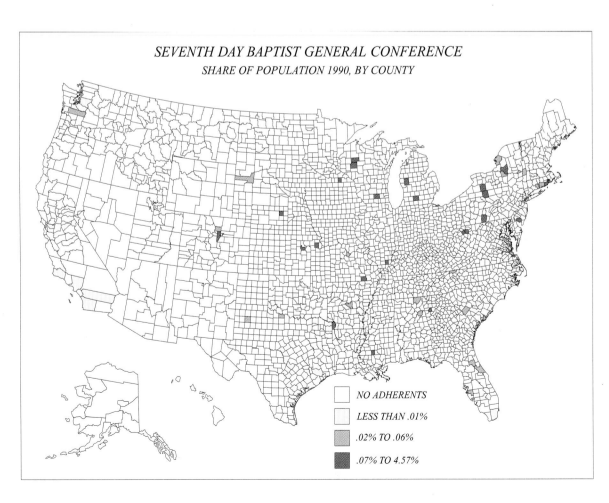

SEVENTH DAY BAPTIST GENERAL CONFERENCE

SHARE OF POPULATION 1990, BY COUNTY

NO ADHERENTS

LESS THAN .01%

.02% TO .06%

.07% TO 4.57%

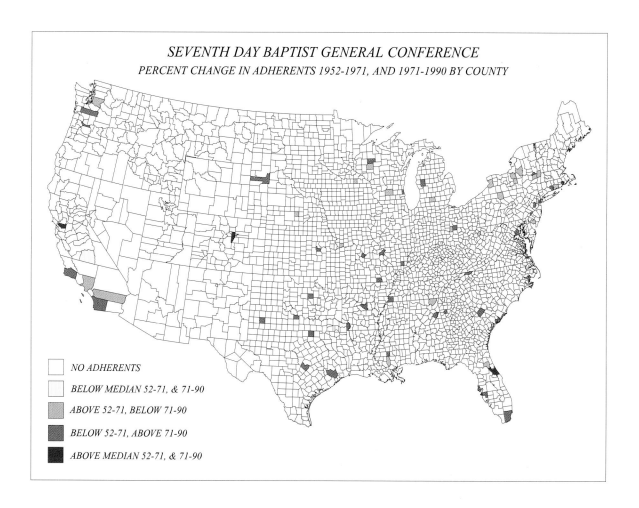

SEVENTH DAY BAPTIST GENERAL CONFERENCE
PERCENT CHANGE IN ADHERENTS 1952-1971, AND 1971-1990 BY COUNTY

NO ADHERENTS

BELOW MEDIAN 52-71, & 71-90

ABOVE 52-71, BELOW 71-90

BELOW 52-71, ABOVE 71-90

ABOVE MEDIAN 52-71, & 71-90

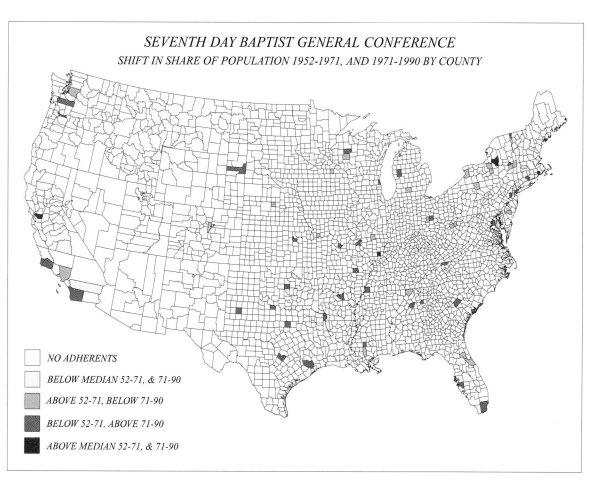

SEVENTH DAY BAPTIST GENERAL CONFERENCE
SHIFT IN SHARE OF POPULATION 1952-1971, AND 1971-1990 BY COUNTY

NO ADHERENTS

BELOW MEDIAN 52-71, & 71-90

ABOVE 52-71, BELOW 71-90

BELOW 52-71, ABOVE 71-90

ABOVE MEDIAN 52-71, & 71-90

SOUTHERN BAPTIST CONVENTION

There are twenty-some major Baptist denominations in the United States today. Most of these groups trace their lineage to the so-called left wing of the Continental Reformation in Europe, and the teachings John Smyth in England. In the colonies, of course, their founder was Roger Williams, who along with John Clarke, established Baptist churches in Newport and Providence, Rhode Island prior to 1650. During both the First and Second Great Awakenings, Baptism spread rapidly. However, the slavery issue and the impending conflict between North and South precipitated a break between northern and southern branches of the denomination, culminating in the formation of the Southern Baptist Convention in 1845.

	1952	1971	1980	1990
Adherents:	8,121,045	14,460,873	16,251,268	18,891,633
Counties:	1,788	2,212	2,365	2,495

Between 1952 and 1971 the Southern Baptist Convention became the largest American Protestant denomination, and between 1971 and 1990 it continued steadily to increase both in its number of adherents and in its geographical extent. For the entire period from 1952 to 1990, it registered a 132.6% rate of increase, gaining more than ten million adherents. The Southern Baptists also spread into more than 700 "new" counties, representing a 39.5% increase. This formerly southern denomination has become a national one, and has done so by growing at twice the rate of the general population. Clearly, this stands as the primary example of high and sustained growth by a large denomination over the entire period covered by this *Atlas*.

The map of Total Adherents, 1990 clearly reveals both the national extent of this denomination's coverage, and its traditional core area in the southern states. While over 80% of all counties on this map are occupied, counties reporting over 5,000 adherents are located almost exclusively south of a line formed by the metropolitan areas of Baltimore, Cincinnati, and St. Louis. They are located throughout the Old Confederacy from the Atlantic Coast to Texas. Such counties also appear in a somewhat less continuous pattern across the Southwest, from New Mexico and Arizona to southern California. Occasional high category counties are located in a diversity of other locales, including such diverse metropolitan areas as Spokane, Seattle, Detroit, and Cleveland. The smallest third of counties on this map represent as many as 1,014 adherents per county. This is twice the comparable category limit for the Evangelical Lutheran Church in America (ELCA) and ten times that of the Episcopal Church. The only other Protestant denomination with a comparable magnitude of adherents at the county level is the United Methodist Church, where the lower category reaches 1,023.

The map for Percent Change in Adherents, 1980-1990 is very much a reciprocal image of the map of Total Adherents, 1990. The top third of counties, representing those with increases in excess of 30%, mostly are located outside the traditional southern core area. They predominate throughout the western third of the nation, and in a northeastern corridor from the Ohio Valley to New England. Secondarily, there are clusters of high change rate counties in Texas, Florida, and even in the central Plains. Counties in the middle third of the distribution, representing increases from just under 8% to over 30%, are represented strongly in the traditional southern core region. Since many of these counties are in the high category on the map of Total Adherents, 1990, it can be concluded that a significant portion of this denomination's numerical growth in within its home turf. The weakest performing third of counties includes counties that increased as much as 7.4%, a rate approximately that of the increase in the general population.

The map showing Share of Population, 1990 reveals a much more compact version of the pattern on the map of Total Adherents, 1990. In spite of the Southern Baptist Convention's national distribution, they appear to be a dominant cultural force exclusively within their traditional Southern core area. There are no high category counties outside this region. Contiguous bands of high category counties, which at a minimum represent nearly a quarter of county population, begin in Virginia, and blanket much of Kentucky, Alabama, Mississippi, Louisiana, Texas, Oklahoma, and Missouri. Further reinforcing this impression of core region dominance is the ring of second level counties that surround the core, showing a general pattern of decline in population share as one moves further away from the Old South. For both this denomination and the Catholic Church, because people may commute from home to church across county lines, the upper limit on this map is above 100% of county population.

The map of Percent Change in Adherents 1952-1971 and 1971-1990 reveals a wide geographical dispersion of counties performing at or above the denomination's median county change rate in both time periods. As might be expected, given the denomination's overall growth trend, these median growth rates are quite high, 80.51% and 37.48% respectively. These counties appear throughout the western third of the nation, in the Ohio Valley, in New England, along the Gulf Coast from Florida to Texas, and even in the lower central Plains. However, it must be remembered that given the high levels of these median county change rates, many of the counties performing below the median in both times periods also experienced sizable rates of increase.

The map portraying Change in Share of Population 1952-1971 and 1971-1990 once again emphasizes several regions of new entry for the Southern Baptist Convention. Counties performing above the median county change rates of 1.73 and 1.12 for the two periods respectively predominate in the metropolitan corridors of New England, the Northeast, and Midwest. They also appear across Florida, and throughout the western third of the nation. Isolated high category counties in the older core southern region as well as bands of counties in both Oklahoma and Kansas may, in part, reflect Southern Baptist relative gains in a region of declining county populations. However, given the real gains in adherents for this denomination, 6.3 million adherents from 1952 to 1971 and 4.4 million adherents between 1971 and 1990, most of the counties shaded red on this map represent considerable increases in both absolute and relative terms.

In summary, the Southern Baptist Convention became the largest Protestant denomination in the years covered by these studies. It continued to grow at an impressive rate between 1971 and 1990 (31%) even as the national religious growth trend moderated (8.4% for all of the groups in this *Atlas*). While remaining a primary cultural force for its "home turf," the Southern Baptist Convention, by 1990, was present in over 80% of the nation's counties, and thus had become a truly national denomination.

119

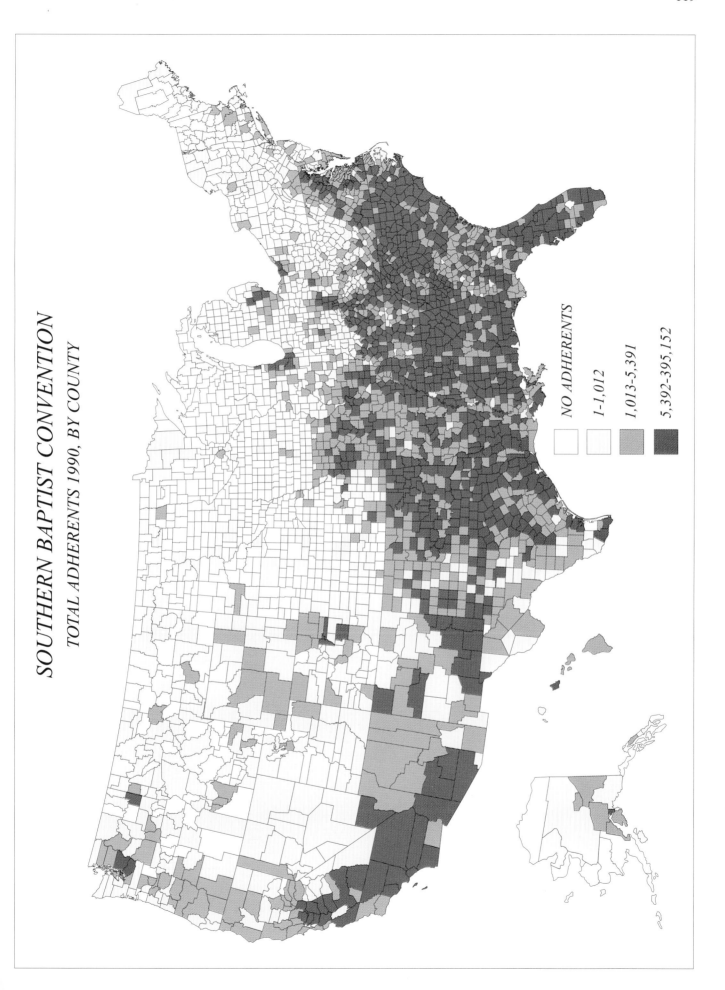

SOUTHERN BAPTIST CONVENTION
TOTAL ADHERENTS 1990, BY COUNTY

NO ADHERENTS

1-1,012

1,013-5,391

5,392-395,152

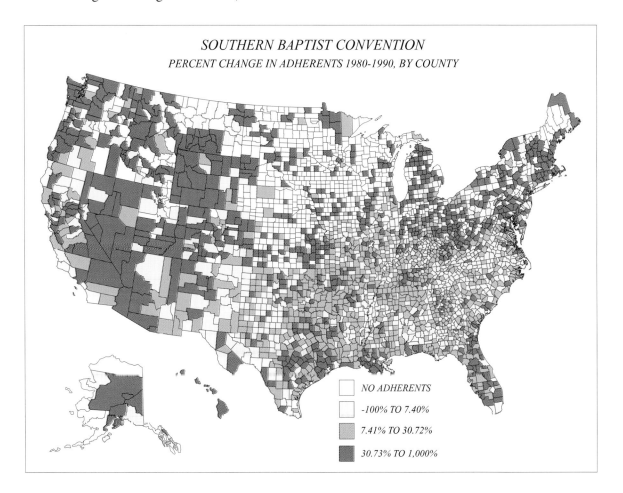

SOUTHERN BAPTIST CONVENTION
PERCENT CHANGE IN ADHERENTS 1980-1990, BY COUNTY

NO ADHERENTS

-100% TO 7.40%

7.41% TO 30.72%

30.73% TO 1,000%

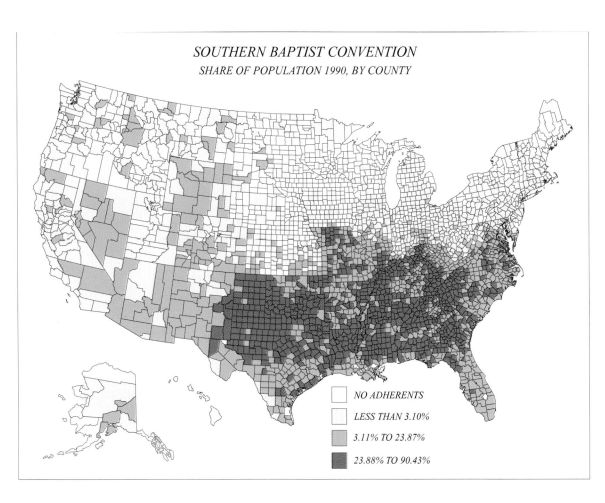

SOUTHERN BAPTIST CONVENTION
SHARE OF POPULATION 1990, BY COUNTY

NO ADHERENTS

LESS THAN 3.10%

3.11% TO 23.87%

23.88% TO 90.43%

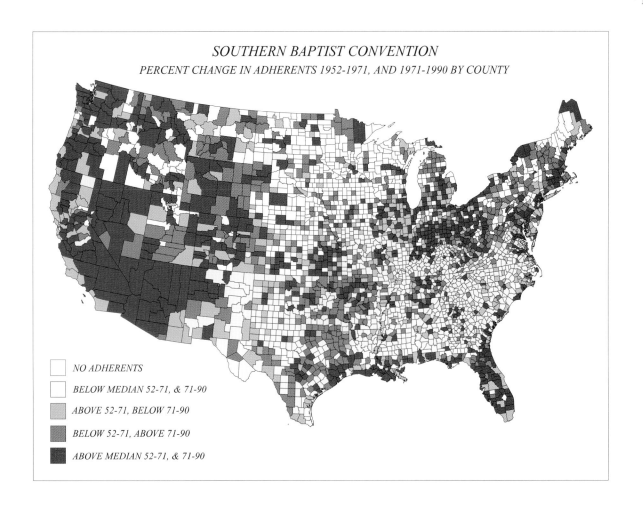

SOUTHERN BAPTIST CONVENTION
PERCENT CHANGE IN ADHERENTS 1952-1971, AND 1971-1990 BY COUNTY

NO ADHERENTS

BELOW MEDIAN 52-71, & 71-90

ABOVE 52-71, BELOW 71-90

BELOW 52-71, ABOVE 71-90

ABOVE MEDIAN 52-71, & 71-90

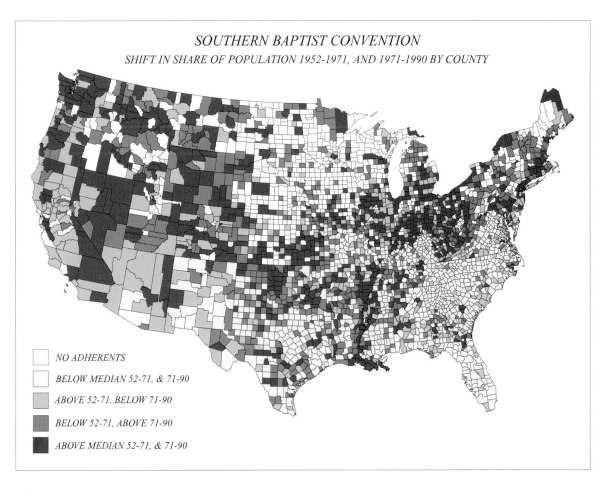

SOUTHERN BAPTIST CONVENTION
SHIFT IN SHARE OF POPULATION 1952-1971, AND 1971-1990 BY COUNTY

NO ADHERENTS

BELOW MEDIAN 52-71, & 71-90

ABOVE 52-71, BELOW 71-90

BELOW 52-71, ABOVE 71-90

ABOVE MEDIAN 52-71, & 71-90

UNITARIAN UNIVERSALIST ASSOCIATION

A 1961 merger between the American Unitarian Association and the Universalist Church of America brought together two bodies with similar theological outlooks, but different historical roots. Unitarianism emerged separately in both Europe and America during the 1700s. The American denomination began as a reform from within American Congregationalism. A codification of its views was provided by William Ellery Channing in 1819, and its first national conference was held in 1865. Universalist thought emerged from several different traditions in 18th century European Protestantism, especially in Germany and England. Its first congregation in America was founded by the British evangelist John Murray at Gloucester, Massachusetts in 1799.

	1952	1971	1980	1990
Adherents:	160,336	193,997	159,336	174,004
Counties:	365	520	511	541

The general trends for the Unitarian Universalists are somewhat complex. While increases in the level of adherents occurred in the years 1952 through 1971, this was followed by a sharp decline in the decade of the 1970s. To this extent the Unitarian Universalist's pattern conforms to that of other theologically liberal Protestant denominations that initially settled in the northeastern states. However, unlike those other denominations (most especially the Episcopalians, Presbyterians, and the United Church of Christ), during the 1980s, the Unitarian Universalists experienced a significant reversal of adherents trends, in which they grew at a rate equal to that of the general population. This growth is reported to be largely as a result of adherents switching from other denominations. Whatever the cause, this recent trend is an anomaly and casts doubt on the frequently heard claim that in recent decades only conservative forms of Protestantism have been growing.

The map of Total Adherents, 1990 reveals that the distribution pattern for the Unitarian Universalists is decidedly metropolitan. In fact, the Unitarian Universalist distribution greatly resembles that for the American Jewish population, with a general thinning of adherents outside the New York and New England core area. This denomination is found in only 541 counties, yet has representation in virtually all regions. One-third of all counties contain fewer than 64 adherents, suggesting a predominance of relatively small local congregations. Additionally, isolated counties rather than clusters of counties are characteristic.

Turning to the map for Percent Change in Adherents, 1980-1990, over one-third of all counties report declines. However, another third of counties report growth of more than 47%. These counties are widely distributed across the nation. The most striking areas of growth are across the middle South, from the Carolinas to metropolitan areas in Texas, and on the West Coast from San Francisco northward. During the 1980s these areas have been characterized by

general population growth. However, even the traditional northeastern cradle of this denomination contains a smattering of these high growth rate counties. Overall, the Unitarian Universalist growth pattern over the decade of the 1980s appears to be driven both by migration of adherents and by denominational switching. Unlike many other denominations, this growth pattern does not seem to reflect the relocation of adherents to retirement areas.

The map for Share of Population, 1990 is based on "high" category values ranging from .12% to only 4.21%, suggesting that places where the Unitarian Universalists represent a numerically significant element in the population mix are somewhat rare. Obviously, they continue to be most strongly represented as a proportion of county populations in the traditional northeastern region, and especially in the more rural counties of northern New England, the founding turf of Unitarianism.

A long term view of the patterns for the Unitarian Universalists is displayed on the map for Percent Change in Adherents, 1952-1971 and 1971-1990. The median county change rates are 208.47% and .62% respectively, the first of which reflects the substantial increase in numbers of counties during the earlier period. The traditional northeastern core region is characterized by performances consistently below the median county change rates, while counties performing consistently at or above these median rates are located further south and across the western half of the nation. However, the most common county level event is a mixed one, neither consistently above or below the median rates. It is clear that the small county level populations characteristic of this denomination create highly variable relative performances on this median county rate measure.

The map for Shift in Share of Population, 1952-1971 and 1971-1990 is based on median county rates of 2.05 and .81 respectively. The patterns on this map are quite similar to those just described for the map of Percent Change in Adherents over the same two time periods. Counties that performed at or above the median population share change rates in both time periods are relatively few in this denomination's traditional home region of New England. The greatest number of counties are of the mixed type, reporting at or above the median in one period and below it in the other. Moreover, it cannot be claimed that the latter exhibit a distinct regional trend. One is drawn to the conclusion that the dynamics of individual congregations and communities rather than denomination-wide policies or regional demographics are responsible for these patterns.

In summary, over the years 1952 through 1990 the Unitarian Universalists provide an interesting departure from the trends of many of its neighboring northeastern Anglo-Protestant denominations. Like most denominations in this Atlas, the Unitarian Universalists participated in the so-called religious revival of the 1950s and early 1960s. However, a resurgence of growth in adherents during the 1980s accompanied by increased county coverage represent a distinctive pattern.

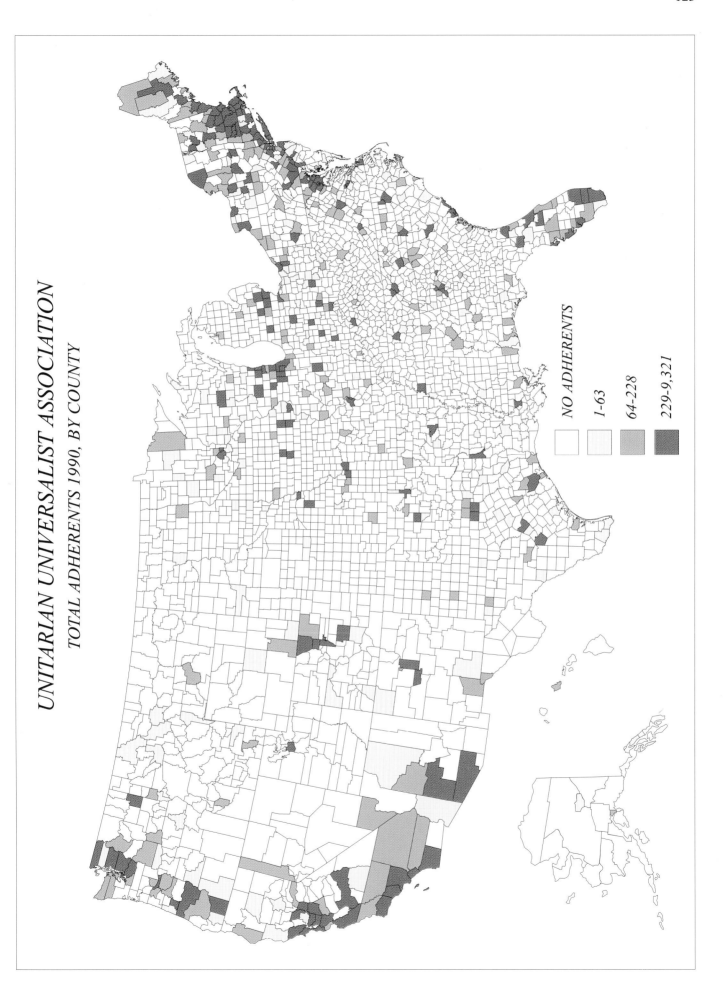

UNITARIAN UNIVERSALIST ASSOCIATION
TOTAL ADHERENTS 1990, BY COUNTY

NO ADHERENTS

1-63

64-228

229-9,321

123

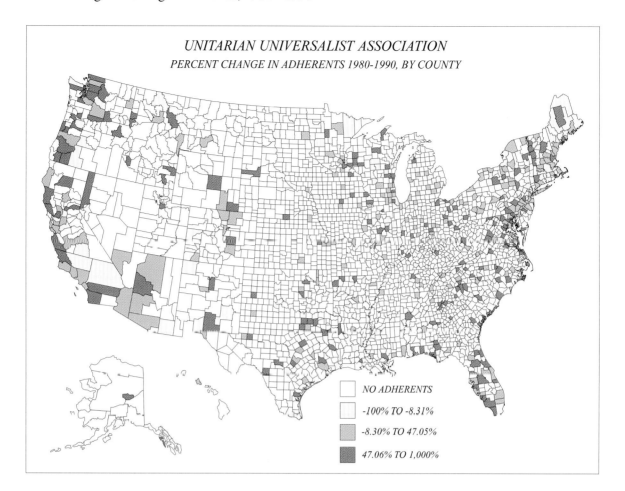

UNITARIAN UNIVERSALIST ASSOCIATION
PERCENT CHANGE IN ADHERENTS 1980-1990, BY COUNTY

NO ADHERENTS
-100% TO -8.31%
-8.30% TO 47.05%
47.06% TO 1,000%

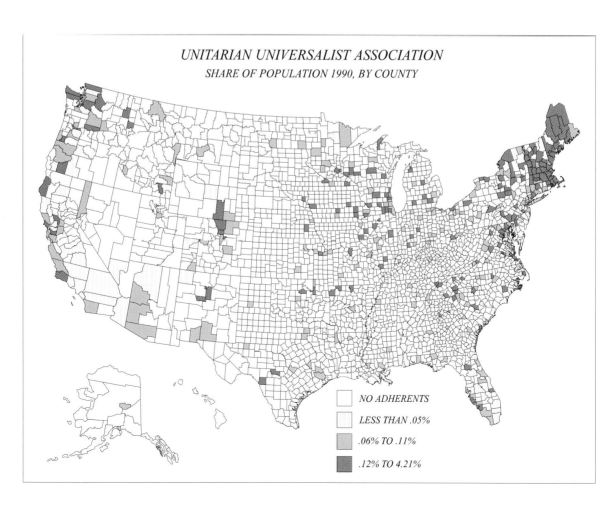

UNITARIAN UNIVERSALIST ASSOCIATION
SHARE OF POPULATION 1990, BY COUNTY

NO ADHERENTS
LESS THAN .05%
.06% TO .11%
.12% TO 4.21%

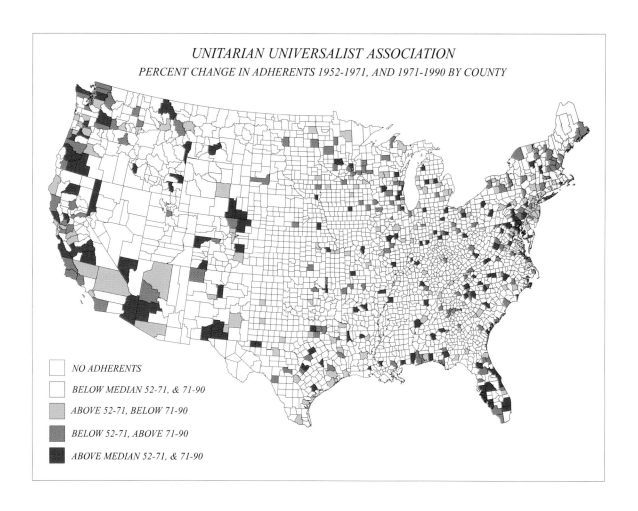

UNITARIAN UNIVERSALIST ASSOCIATION

PERCENT CHANGE IN ADHERENTS 1952-1971, AND 1971-1990 BY COUNTY

NO ADHERENTS

BELOW MEDIAN 52-71, & 71-90

ABOVE 52-71, BELOW 71-90

BELOW 52-71, ABOVE 71-90

ABOVE MEDIAN 52-71, & 71-90

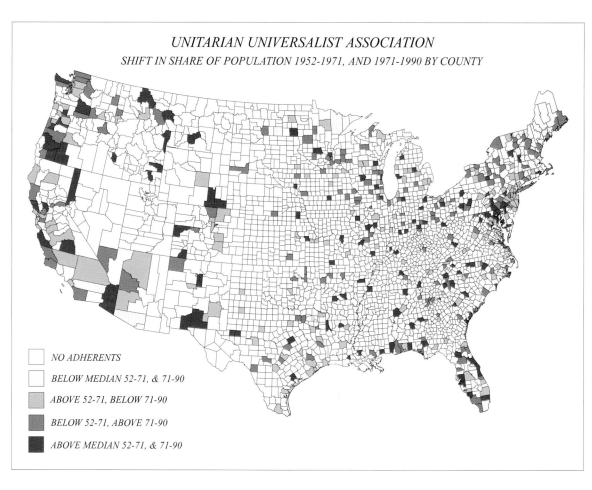

UNITARIAN UNIVERSALIST ASSOCIATION

SHIFT IN SHARE OF POPULATION 1952-1971, AND 1971-1990 BY COUNTY

NO ADHERENTS

BELOW MEDIAN 52-71, & 71-90

ABOVE 52-71, BELOW 71-90

BELOW 52-71, ABOVE 71-90

ABOVE MEDIAN 52-71, & 71-90

THE UNITED CHURCH OF CHRIST

The 1961 merger creating the United Church of Christ (UCC) involved two denominations that themselves had resulted from mergers, The Evangelical and Reformed Church, and the Congregational Christian Churches. Because these denominations had very different theological and ethnic traditions, as well as distinct settlement and geographic patterns in the United States, through this merger the UCC became a truly national denomination with a series of core geographic areas. A brief review of these organizational unions provides a context for the analysis of trends between 1952 and 1990.

The Evangelical and Reformed Church was created in 1934 through a merger of two Continental Protestant groups. The Reformed Church in the United States was composed of the eastern German, Swiss, and Dutch Calvinists, who arrived in the 1700s and settled along the eastern seaboard. Pennsylvania, and subsequently Maryland, Virginia, and Ohio became its primary core areas. The Evangelical Synod of North America was made up of German and Austrian Lutherans who settled during the mid-19th century in Missouri, and elsewhere in the upper Mississippi Valley throughout the upper Midwest.

The Congregational Christian Churches were formed in 1931.

Churches trace their origins to the voyage of the Mayflower in 1620 and developed throughout New England and elsewhere in the Northeast. The Christian Church was formed in 1808 by a merger of three relatively small groups, one Baptist, one Methodist, and one Presbyterian. Their congregations were located in New England, North Carolina, and Kentucky at the time of the 1931 merger with the New England-based Congregationalists.

Several groups of Congregational Churches did not participate in the 1961 UCC merger. The largest of these retained the name Congregational Christian Churches and is treated elsewhere in this *Atlas*. At the time of the split, the nonparticipating denomination consisted of some 300 congregations and approximately 100,000 adherents. No adjustment for this division has been made in the merged 1952 UCC data.

	1952	1971	1980	1990
Adherents:	2,009,642	2,296,566	2,075,227	1,970,607
Counties:	1,401	1,272	1,266	1,265

Typical of the pattern exhibited by most of the northeastern based Anglo-Protestant denominations, between 1952 and 1971 the United Church of Christ gained adherents at the same rate (14%) by which, in turn, it lost adherents between 1971 and 1990. For the entire nearly 40 year period covered by these studies, the UCC remained relatively stable in adherents (-1.9%) while gradually shrinking in its county coverage (-9.7%).

The map of Total Adherents, 1990 reveals a national pattern of distribution which is thinnest in the southern tier of states stretching from Virginia to New Mexico. Historic core areas of the merged denomination are easily discerned. They include the ancestral home of Congregationalism throughout New England, a pocket of former Christian Churches in the Carolinas, previous Reformed congregations in Pennsylvania, and the upper midwestern home of the Evangelical Synod. In 1990, the UCC also exhibits strength in the fast-growing states of the lower California, Texas, Arizona, Colorado, and Florida. It is noteworthy that the values of the upper limits of the upper two categories on the map of Total Adherents, 1990 indicate advances in size over what they were in 1952 (251 adherents per county as compared to 207, and 913 as compared to 762). The higher category limits for 1990 suggest that even as counties have been

lost during this period, a consolidation of strength has been occurring in a wide range of remaining counties.

The map for Percent Change in Adherents, 1980-1990 indicates a negative median county change rate (the middle third of counties ranges from -16.2% to only 3.28%). Thus, while the top third of counties experienced some relative growth, over half of all counties experienced decline in the decade of the 1980s. Aside from bands of high growth rate counties in suburban areas of New England and in retirement areas in Florida, it is difficult to discern strong regional patterns on this map. Rather, the impression is that different congregations or counties are charting independent courses. This pattern seems to reflect the distinctive character of the merged units of this denomination, which continue to stress local congregational autonomy and identity.

The map for Share of Population, 1990 greatly resembles the map of Total Adherents, 1990. In northern New England Pennsylvania, North Carolina, Missouri and to a degree in the Ohio Valley, traditional settlement cores once again register in the highest third of population shares in 1990. Understandably, where this denomination has followed general population growth and migration (Florida, California, Arizona, and elsewhere) its shares of population are less strong.

The map for Percent Change in Adherents 1952-1971 and 1971-1990 must be interpreted with care, as the median county change rates reflect very different trends; a 6.14% increase between 1952 and 1971, and a -12.69% decrease between 1971 and 1990. Thus, counties shown in red on this map, indicating performance above the median in both periods, may actually have declined in adherents. To some extent, this complex set of events may be illuminated by comparison with the several preceding maps. It is clear that some of the consistently high change rate areas, both in counties of new entry (Florida, Arizona, and Texas) as well as some of the older core areas (Pennsylvania, the Ohio Valley, and Minnesota) really have experienced percentage increase. However, the trends on this map are not easily characterized.

The map for Shift in Share of Population, 1952-1971 and 1971-1990 is a bit more easily interpreted. The median county shift in share values of .89 and .78 indicate that even when performing at or above the median rate of change for the denomination, the UCC may be declining in its share of population. This is an expected pattern for a denomination that remained stable as the general population grew. Several other trends are apparent. Some places of more recent entry for the UCC, such as Arizona, California, Colorado, and Florida are, in fact, places of better than median performance. Additionally, a scattering of counties in the upper Midwest suggest that in some places the UCC's population share also may be increasing in the context of thinning general populations.

In summary, while the UCC has remained relatively stable in size for the entire 1952-1990 period, the more recent decades reveal a decidedly negative trend. Moreover, a gradual decline in the denomination's total number of counties has occurred even as there has been expansion into counties outside the traditional core areas. This pattern, in part, seems to be a muted version of what has been transpiring in several other Anglo-Protestant denominations, including the Episcopal Church and the Presbyterian Church (USA). Clearly, those Protestant denominations representing America's oldest East Coast settlement have been undergoing both numeric decline and spatial shift. The UCC, as a denomination with more mixed historical backgrounds and geographic settlement patterns exhibits a less dramatic version of these changes.

UNITED CHURCH OF CHRIST
TOTAL ADHERENTS 1990, BY COUNTY

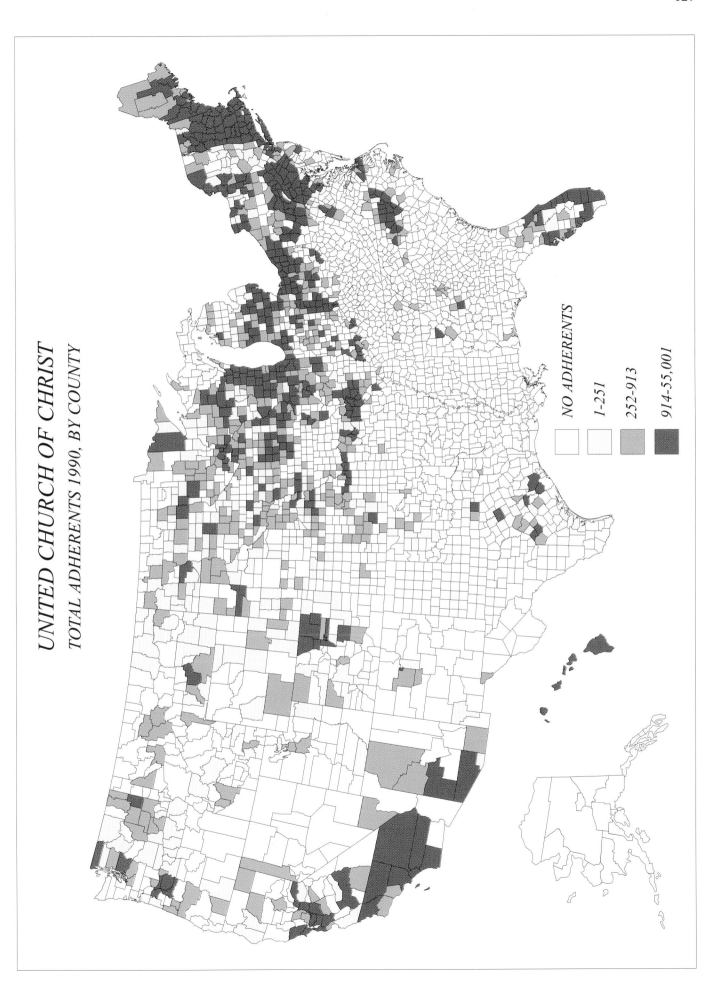

NO ADHERENTS

1-251

252-913

914-55,001

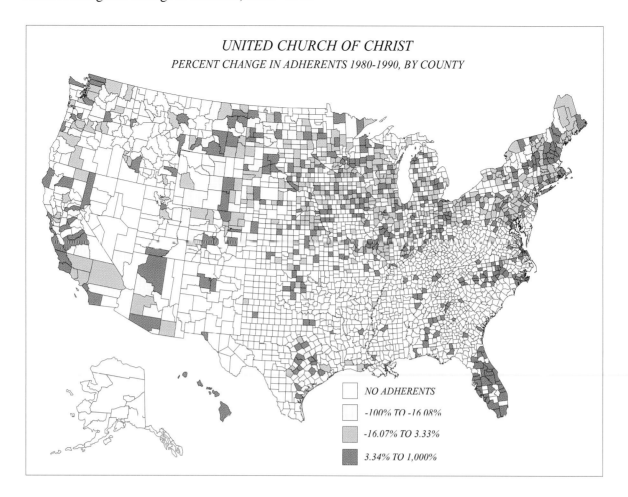

UNITED CHURCH OF CHRIST

PERCENT CHANGE IN ADHERENTS 1980-1990, BY COUNTY

NO ADHERENTS

-100% TO -16.08%

-16.07% TO 3.33%

3.34% TO 1,000%

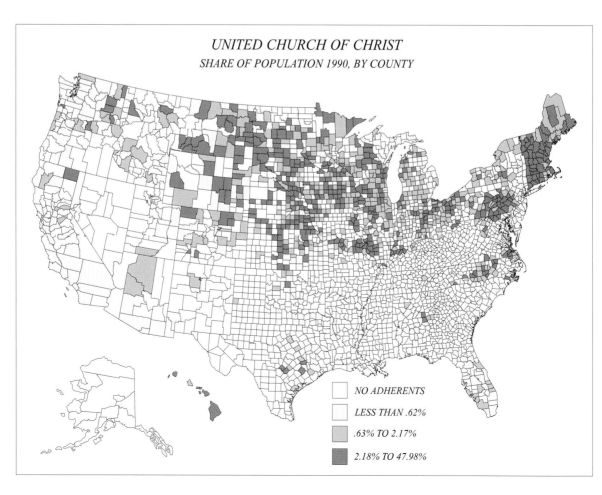

UNITED CHURCH OF CHRIST

SHARE OF POPULATION 1990, BY COUNTY

NO ADHERENTS

LESS THAN .62%

.63% TO 2.17%

2.18% TO 47.98%

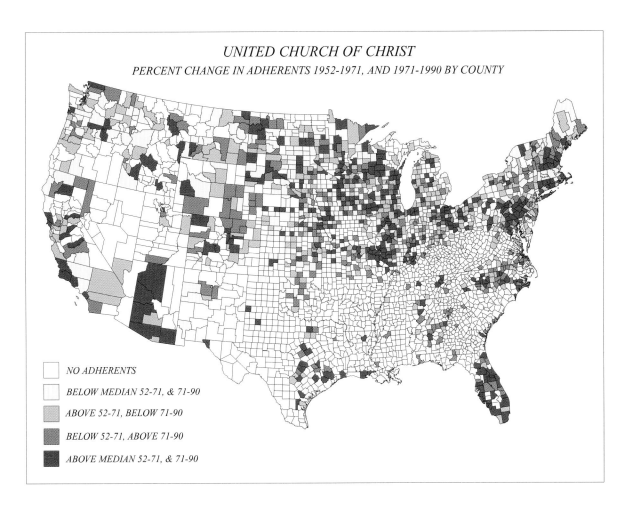

UNITED CHURCH OF CHRIST

PERCENT CHANGE IN ADHERENTS 1952-1971, AND 1971-1990 BY COUNTY

NO ADHERENTS

BELOW MEDIAN 52-71, & 71-90

ABOVE 52-71, BELOW 71-90

BELOW 52-71, ABOVE 71-90

ABOVE MEDIAN 52-71, & 71-90

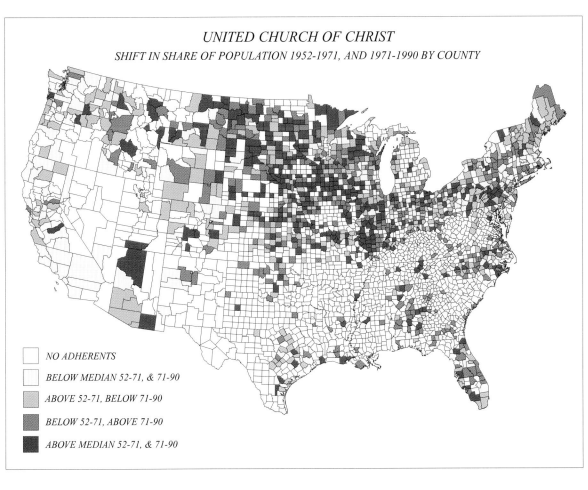

UNITED CHURCH OF CHRIST

SHIFT IN SHARE OF POPULATION 1952-1971, AND 1971-1990 BY COUNTY

NO ADHERENTS

BELOW MEDIAN 52-71, & 71-90

ABOVE 52-71, BELOW 71-90

BELOW 52-71, ABOVE 71-90

ABOVE MEDIAN 52-71, & 71-90

UNITED METHODIST CHURCH

Today, the United Methodist Church is numerically the second largest Protestant communion, and also, in terms of the number of counties in which adherents are reported, is the most widely dispersed denomination in this study. Originating during the early 1700s in England as an outgrowth of the Oxford Movement, and then transplanted to the colonies, Methodism expanded substantially during the Great Awakenings in the 18th and 19th centuries. Unified by a 1939 merger of three Methodist bodies, the United Methodist Church has remained a denomination of substantial proportions throughout the entire 1952-1990 period. Through a 1968 merger, the United Methodists absorbed a much smaller denomination, the Evangelical United Brethren. Because such large denominations have difficulty registering significant relative percentage change statistics in either direction, it is important to examine not just the rates of change (percentages), but the absolute numbers of persons they represent.

	1952	1971	1980	1990
Adherents:	9,509,244	11,542,198	11,540,616	11,077,728
Counties:	2,889	2,950	2,957	2,952

The United Methodist Church reported 9.5 million adherents in 1952, and having reached a peak size in 1971, reported just over 11 million adherents in 1990. This seemingly modest 16.5% increase in adherents represented a net gain of more than 1.5 million persons for the 1952-1990 period. Furthermore, by 1990 this denomination was situated in 2,952 counties, 96% of the national total. On the other hand, during the period 1952-1971, the United Methodists lost their position as the largest Protestant denomination, having been surpassed by the Southern Baptist Convention.

The 1990 distribution of the United Methodist Church mirrors the general distribution of population in the United States. The map of Total Adherents, 1990 shows heavy concentrations of Methodists in the old northeastern industrial core stretching from the Atlantic Coast to the Great Lakes, as well as a discontinuous series of clusters of counties across the South from the Carolinas and Florida through Georgia and Texas, and in California. The only distinct thinning of the Methodist distribution occurs in the Mountain West, most notably in the area known to be dominated by Mormonism.

Between 1980 and 1990, as might be expected from the general numerical trend, and as is shown on the map of Percent Change in Adherents, 1980-1990, more than two-thirds of all counties containing United Methodists experienced decline in adherents. The highest category includes counties that declined slightly, as well as those reporting growth. Not surprisingly, counties in this category typically are located across the Sunbelt. Conversely, the areas of greatest decline are most common throughout the denomination's 1990 numerical core area in the northeastern and midwestern states.

The map for Share of Population, 1990 depicts Methodism as a prominent element in areas characterized by declining total population. The classic case occurs in the central Plains, with other instances apparent in the Appalachians, and rural parts of the South. The highest category on this map represents a share of population (9.37% to 39.28%) not commonly encountered among Protestant denominations. Such shares of county populations unquestionably represent a prevailing level of cultural influence. The general pattern here contrasts with that portrayed on the map of Total Adherents, 1990 because areas where Methodism is most dominant in terms of population shares are not always those in which it is numerically strongest. Among such cases are the northeast industrial belt, California, and Florida. This suggests that Methodism is loosing ground relative to other religious groups and general population trends in such areas.

Longer term change patterns as portrayed on the map of Percent Change in Adherents, 1952-1971 and 1971-1990 reveal a somewhat different trend. In contrast to the 1952-1971 period, when the change rate for the median county for the United Methodists was 10.72%, between 1971 and 1990, the median county recorded a negative rate of -7.83 %. This means that during the more recent period, the gains of the earlier "religious revival" have been eroded in over half of this denomination's counties. Counties that consistently performed above the denomination's norm in both periods include retirement areas in Florida and Arizona, as well as areas of more general population growth including the Carolinas, and metropolitan areas in Texas. In contrast, consistent "losers" for the United Methodists are prevalent in the rural areas of the Appalachians, the central South, central Plains, as well as in the Ohio and Missouri Valleys. Generally, this category is most notable in nonmetropolitan areas of declining population.

The map for Shift in Share of Population, 1952-1971 and 1971-1990 reinforces the impression that Methodism is encountering difficulty keeping pace with the growth of other denominations and the general population. Areas of consistently high growth in the general population such as California and Florida display consistently declining shares of population for this denomination. Conversely, regions of general population decline, such as the Great Plains, register consistent increases in the United Methodist share of population. In this sense, they might be viewed as a "persisting" rather than an expanding communion (i.e. increases in population share reflect staying in places while others leave).

In summary, the United Methodists are a very large and very wide-spread denomination. Over the 1952-1990 period, the United Methodists have experienced numerically large but modest relative increases in adherents. However, despite the impressive national population growth between 1952 and 1990 and the very substantial regional redistribution of population, given its size and dispersion prior to mid-century, the 1990 distribution of adherents for the United Methodist Church is fundamentally the same as it was in 1952.

UNITED METHODIST CHURCH
TOTAL ADHERENTS 1990, BY COUNTY

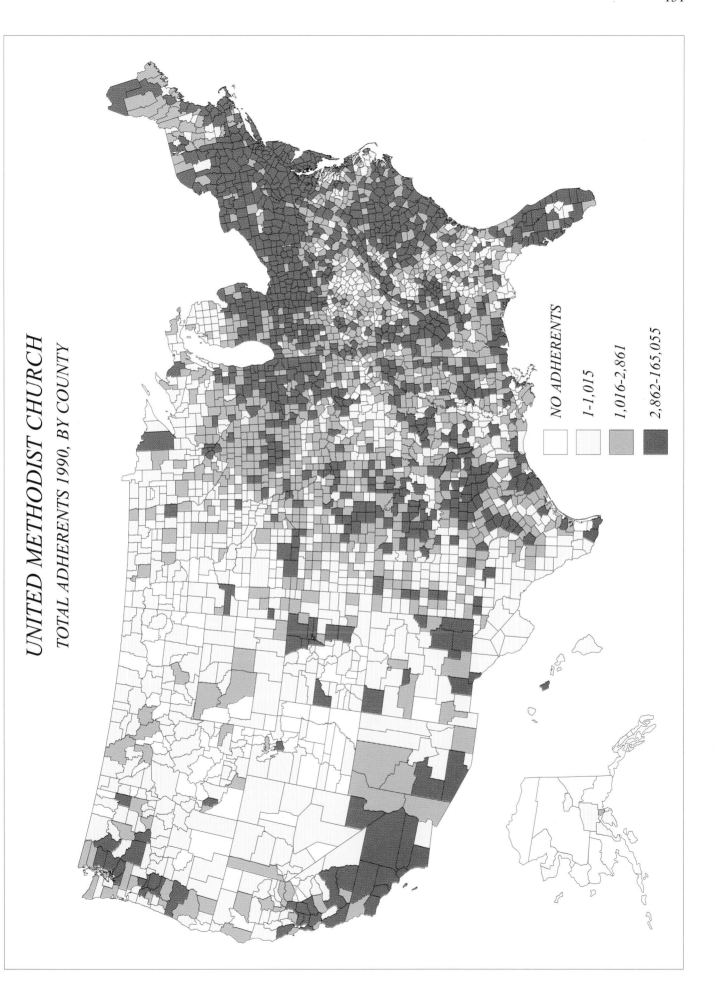

NO ADHERENTS

1-1,015

1,016-2,861

2,862-165,055

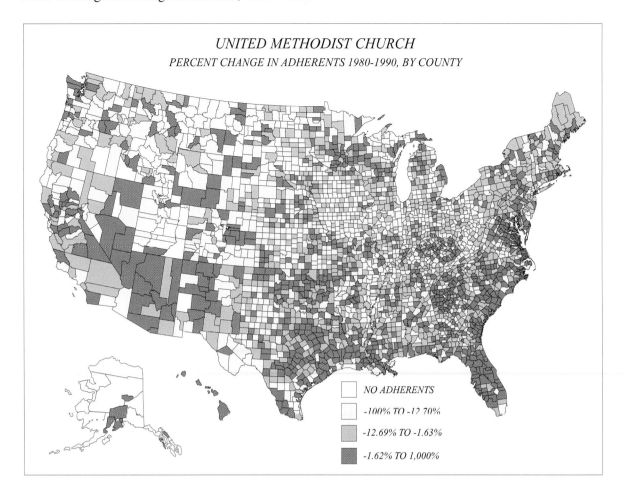

UNITED METHODIST CHURCH

PERCENT CHANGE IN ADHERENTS 1980-1990, BY COUNTY

NO ADHERENTS

-100% TO -12.70%

-12.69% TO -1.63%

-1.62% TO 1,000%

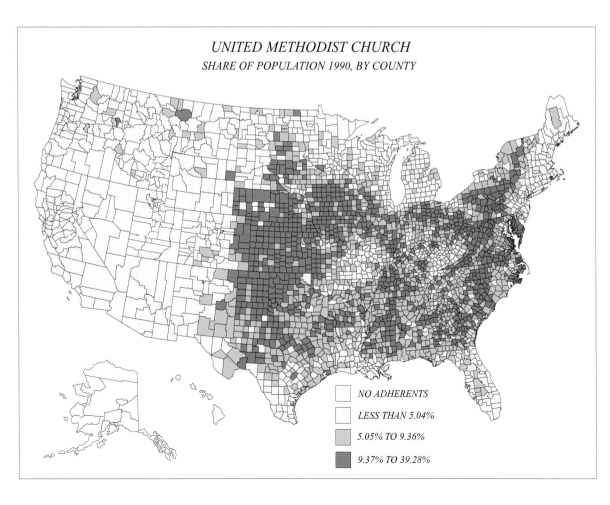

UNITED METHODIST CHURCH

SHARE OF POPULATION 1990, BY COUNTY

NO ADHERENTS

LESS THAN 5.04%

5.05% TO 9.36%

9.37% TO 39.28%

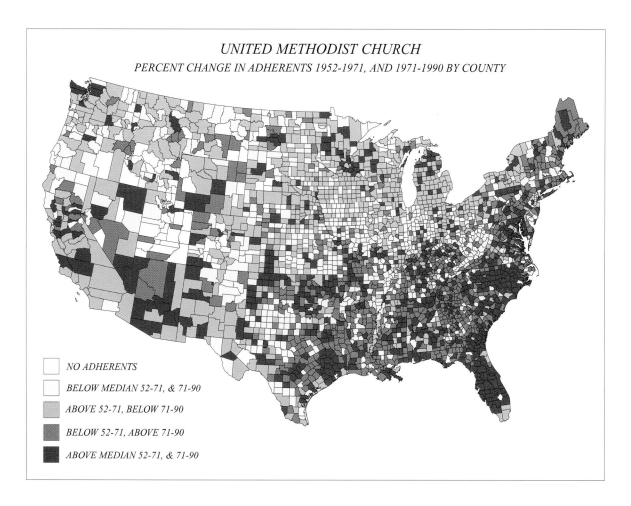

UNITED METHODIST CHURCH

PERCENT CHANGE IN ADHERENTS 1952-1971, AND 1971-1990 BY COUNTY

NO ADHERENTS

BELOW MEDIAN 52-71, & 71-90

ABOVE 52-71, BELOW 71-90

BELOW 52-71, ABOVE 71-90

ABOVE MEDIAN 52-71, & 71-90

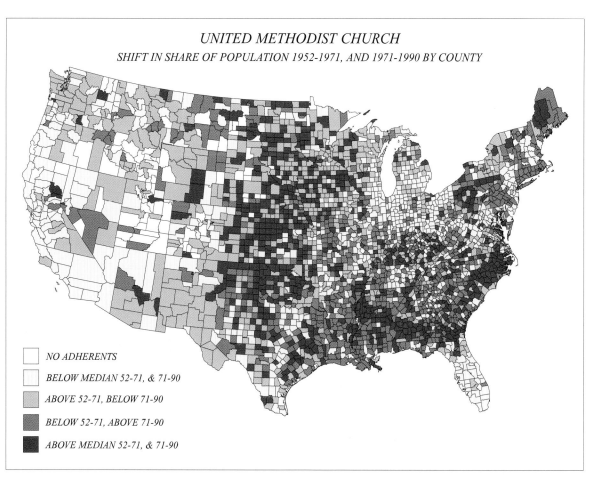

UNITED METHODIST CHURCH

SHIFT IN SHARE OF POPULATION 1952-1971, AND 1971-1990 BY COUNTY

NO ADHERENTS

BELOW MEDIAN 52-71, & 71-90

ABOVE 52-71, BELOW 71-90

BELOW 52-71, ABOVE 71-90

ABOVE MEDIAN 52-71, & 71-90

WISCONSIN EVANGELICAL LUTHERAN CHURCH

The Wisconsin Evangelical Lutheran Church was organized in 1850 as the First German Lutheran Synod of Wisconsin. Its federation and subsequent merger with German synods from Minnesota and Michigan in 1918 resulted in the name Joint Synod of Wisconsin and Other States. The present name was adopted in 1959. Although this denomination is doctrinally most similar to the Lutheran Church-Missouri Synod, it has remained aloof from that body, as well as from the several mergers that produced the American Lutheran Church (ALC), the Lutheran Church in America (LCA), and most recently, the Evangelical Lutheran Church in America (ELCA). The Wisconsin Evangelical Lutheran Church has objected to the theological heterogeneity inherent in these mergers, generally does not join ecumenical organizations, and thus, constitutes one of the more conservative expressions of Lutheranism in the United States. The Wisconsin Lutherans experienced a small schism during the 1960s, entailing a loss of perhaps 3% of their adherents at that time.

	1952	1971	1980	1990
Adherents:	316,692	381,735	403,854	418,820
Counties:	248	352	444	503

Over the 1952-1990 period the Wisconsin Evangelical Lutheran Church grew in adherents from 316,692 to 418,820 a 32.2% increase, while doubling in its spatial coverage from 248 to 503 counties. Significantly, this geographic expansion continued at a sustained pace, even as the rate of growth in adherents slowed during the years 1971-1980. These trends represent a conscious program of evangelism. The map of Total Adherents. 1990 shows that three traditional core areas have expanded. First, in the historic core states of Wisconsin, Minnesota, and Michigan, the Wisconsin Lutherans now occupy substantial clusters of counties that stretch from the Detroit metropolitan area across the Great Lakes region through to the border of the Dakotas. Second, a cluster of counties that initially was confined to the state of Arizona now extends into California. Third, there has been an increase in the number of counties reporting adherents in the vicinity of Seattle, Washington.

The map of Total Adherents, 1990 also indicates the incursion of this denomination into new locales, especially in the states of the Old South, Texas, and Florida, and in New England's metropolitan counties. The category size limits on the map of Total Adherents, 1990

are smaller than earlier versions of the adherents map for this denomination. This change implicitly reflects a reduction in the average size of congregations, and surely results from the many new and presumably smaller churches that now populate this denomination. The map for Percent Change in Adherents, 1980-1990 confirms these impressions. The traditional core areas register modest growth rate counties, while the areas of new entry, including Texas, Florida, California, and Colorado register the highest growth rates. It is significant that the upper third of the denomination's counties report 50% or greater increase in the decade of the 1980s.

As would be expected, in 1990, the Wisconsin Evangelical Lutheran Church's strongest shares of population are found in the historic core regions, especially in Wisconsin and Minnesota. However, high Wisconsin Lutheran shares also are reported in other places, especially where the general population is small, as in the Dakotas.

The map for Percent Change in Adherents, 1952-1971 and 1971-1990 indicates that counties performing below the denomination's median rates of 45.61% for 1952-1971 and 59.21% for 1971-1990 are widely distributed throughout the nation. However, counties that performed above the denomination's median change rate in both periods are predominantly outside the old core areas, and also are more often found in suburbs and small cities rather than in large metropolitan areas. Conversely, the original core region in Wisconsin, Illinois, and Minnesota contains a very significant number of counties that grew at rates well below the denominational median. Clearly, counties of new entry for this denomination predominate. The map for Shift in Share of Population, 1952-1971 and 1971-1990 conveys much the same image. The Wisconsin Evangelical Lutheran Church has been gaining in population share more rapidly in counties outside its traditional core area than within it.

In summary, during the entire 1952-1990 period the Wisconsin Evangelical Lutheran Church grew both in adherents and in its county coverage. However, its spatial expansion has continued unabated even as its growth in adherents slowed between 1971 and 1990. Migration to retirement areas, especially in Florida and Arizona, is only a part of this denomination's story. A continuous program of evangelism, as well as growth in the 1980s from congregations dissenting from the ELCA merger, both are involved in these growth trends. The Wisconsin Evangelical Lutheran Church was a regional denomination that significantly has changed its spatial characteristics over the years 1952-1990.

WISCONSIN EVANGELICAL LUTHERAN SYNOD
TOTAL ADHERENTS 1990, BY COUNTY

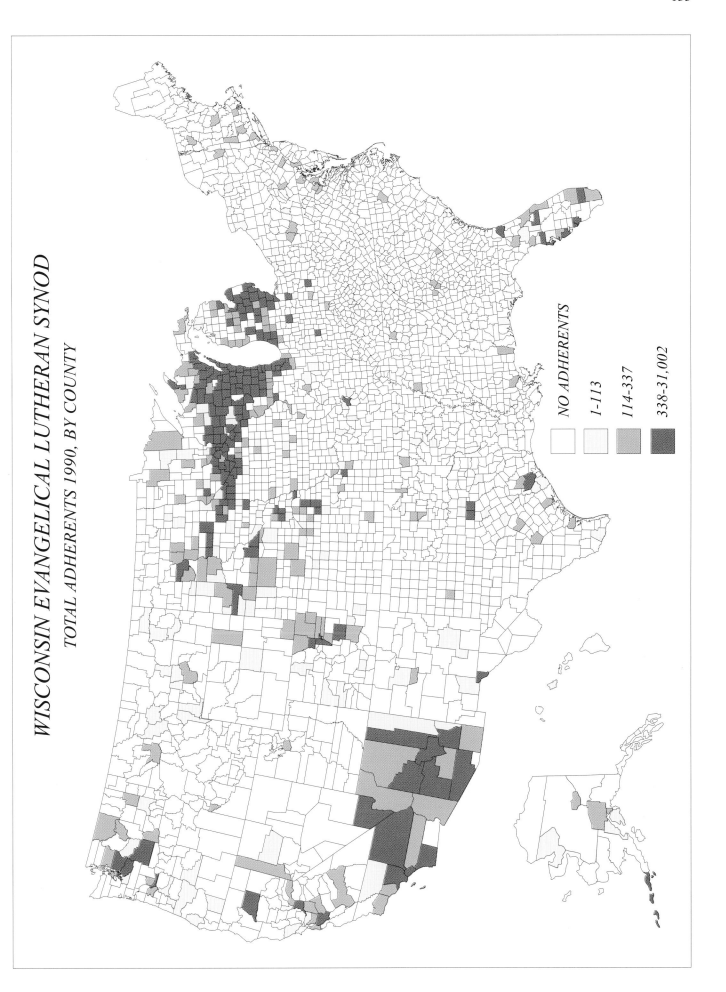

NO ADHERENTS

1–113

114–337

338–31,002

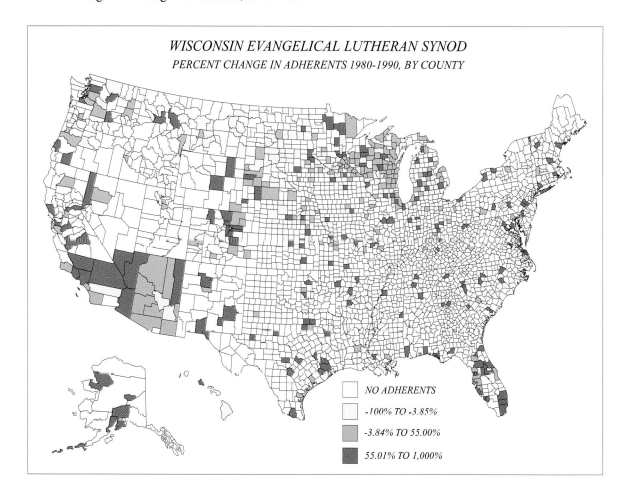

WISCONSIN EVANGELICAL LUTHERAN SYNOD
PERCENT CHANGE IN ADHERENTS 1980-1990, BY COUNTY

NO ADHERENTS

-100% TO -3.85%

-3.84% TO 55.00%

55.01% TO 1,000%

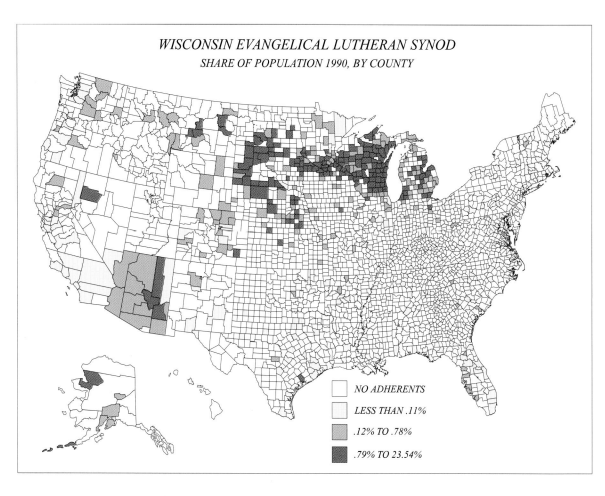

WISCONSIN EVANGELICAL LUTHERAN SYNOD
SHARE OF POPULATION 1990, BY COUNTY

NO ADHERENTS

LESS THAN .11%

.12% TO .78%

.79% TO 23.54%

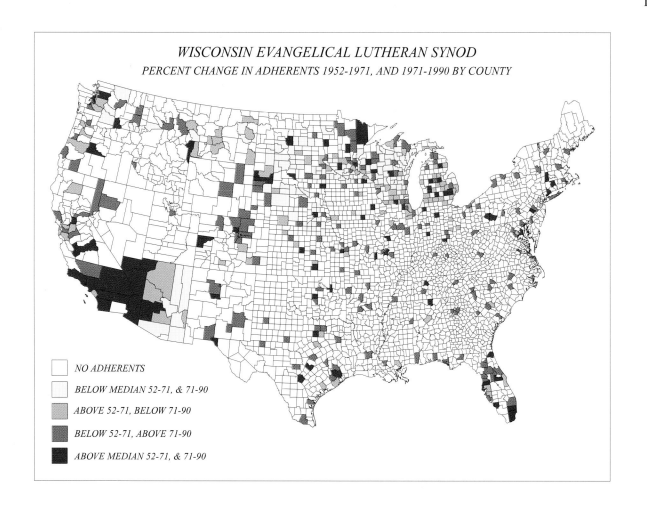

WISCONSIN EVANGELICAL LUTHERAN SYNOD
PERCENT CHANGE IN ADHERENTS 1952-1971, AND 1971-1990 BY COUNTY

NO ADHERENTS
BELOW MEDIAN 52-71, & 71-90
ABOVE 52-71, BELOW 71-90
BELOW 52-71, ABOVE 71-90
ABOVE MEDIAN 52-71, & 71-90

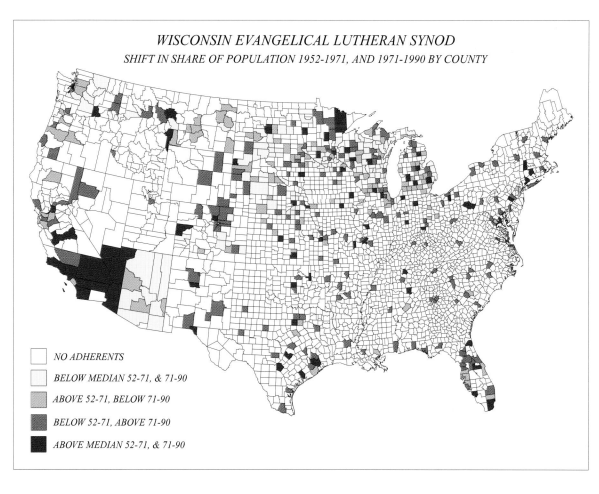

WISCONSIN EVANGELICAL LUTHERAN SYNOD
SHIFT IN SHARE OF POPULATION 1952-1971, AND 1971-1990 BY COUNTY

NO ADHERENTS
BELOW MEDIAN 52-71, & 71-90
ABOVE 52-71, BELOW 71-90
BELOW 52-71, ABOVE 71-90
ABOVE MEDIAN 52-71, & 71-90

DENOMINATIONAL MAPS: 1980 - 1990

ADVENT CHRISTIAN CHURCH

Adventism, with its theological focus on the second coming of Christ, began as a movement among established churches in the United States early in the 19th century. When, in the Spring of 1844, the second coming, as prophesied by William Miller did not occur, the movement coalesced into new organizations. Founded in 1860, the Advent Christian Church represents one such development. It is congregational in polity, and has a General Conference that meets every three years. Among its theologically distinct views is the claim that the dead are sleeping until the return of Christ. In 1964 the Advent Christian Church merged with a small Adventist sect, The Life and Advent Union. The merged body has been a member of the National Association of Evangelicals since 1987.

	1980	1990
Adherents:	35,448	23,794
Counties:	192	185

Between 1980 and 1990, the Advent Christian Church decreased from 35,488 adherents in 192 counties to 23,794 adherents in 185 counties. During this same period, it diminished from 358 to 329 churches. In 1990, this small sect's geographic features were distinctly bipolar, with a large cluster of adjacent counties stretching throughout the New England states,

and a second set of clusters of counties in the three southern states of North Carolina, Virginia, and Georgia. The church is headquartered in Charlotte, North Carolina, and maintains regional offices in both New Hampshire and Georgia, as well as in Texas and Idaho. In 1990, the New England states account for 5,566 adherents, while the three southern states total 6,664, together totaling 51% of the entire communion. The balance of counties are widely dispersed.

The map for Percent Change in Adherents, 1980-1990 is not readily interpreted in terms of the pattern of "winners" and "losers." This is because the upper third of counties ranges from counties that lost 18% of adherents to those that increased at high rates. Focusing on the first two-thirds of counties, it at least can be said that this small religious community lost adherents in virtually all geographic regions in which it had adherents.

The map for Share of Population, 1990 reveals that in two-thirds of its counties the Advent Christian Church does not reach as much as one fifth of one percent of the county population. This is not surprising for such a small and apparently declining communion.

In summary, this small branch of Adventism is declining in adherents (-32.9%) and churches (-8%) at substantial rates. The presence of a fair number counties in Florida and California (retirement communities?) suggests that aging may be a factor in these trends. The pattern of decline for the Advent Christian Church contrasts sharply with the growth of the Seventh-Day Adventists, a less extreme form of Adventism, that has continued to increase in adherents impressively (35%) during this same decade.

141

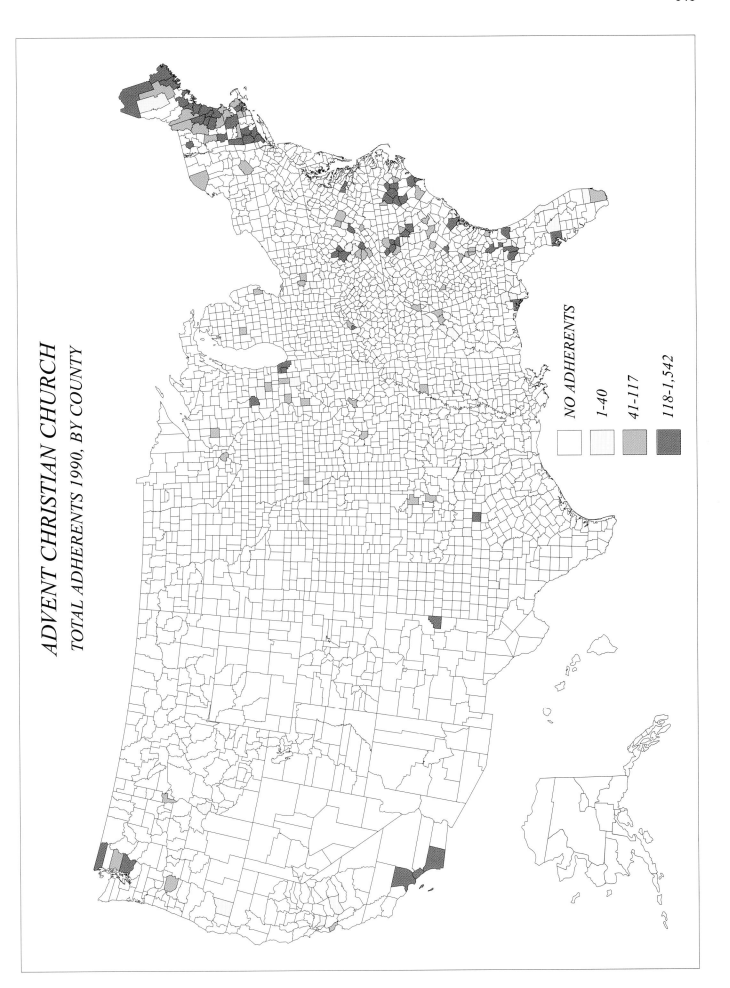

ADVENT CHRISTIAN CHURCH
TOTAL ADHERENTS 1990, BY COUNTY

NO ADHERENTS

1-40

41-117

118-1,542

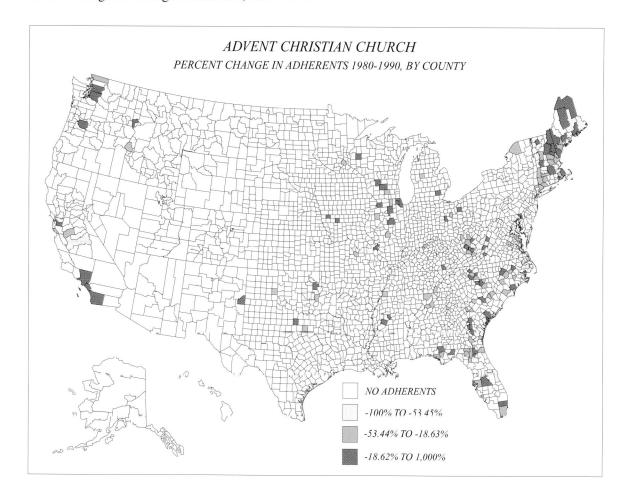

ADVENT CHRISTIAN CHURCH

PERCENT CHANGE IN ADHERENTS 1980-1990, BY COUNTY

NO ADHERENTS

-100% TO -53.45%

-53.44% TO -18.63%

-18.62% TO 1,000%

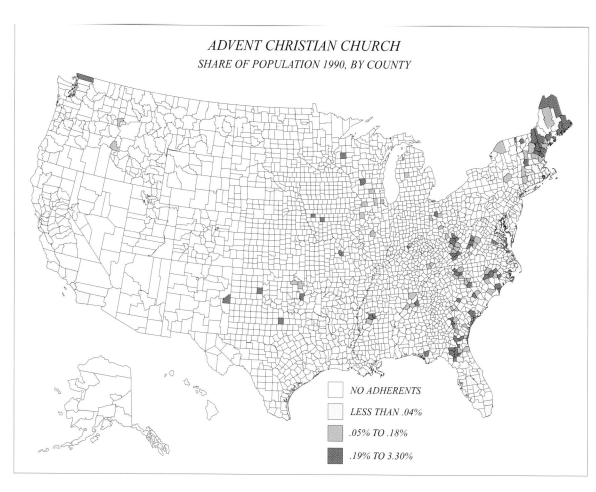

ADVENT CHRISTIAN CHURCH

SHARE OF POPULATION 1990, BY COUNTY

NO ADHERENTS

LESS THAN .04%

.05% TO .18%

.19% TO 3.30%

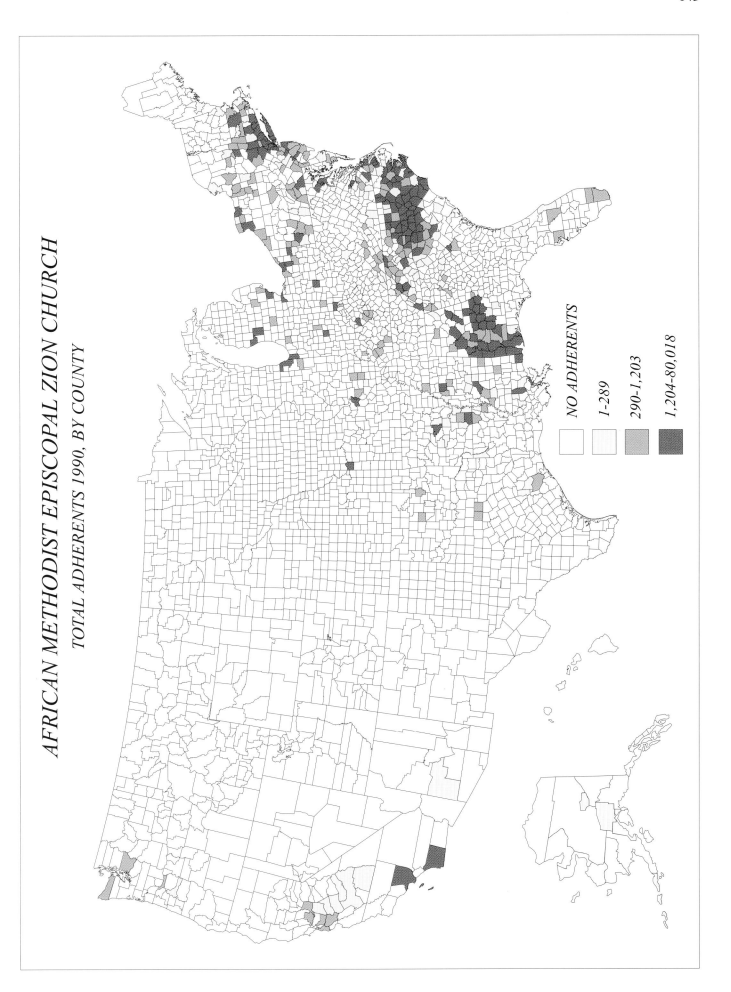

AFRICAN METHODIST EPISCOPAL ZION CHURCH

TOTAL ADHERENTS 1990, BY COUNTY

NO ADHERENTS

1-289

290-1,203

1,204-80,018

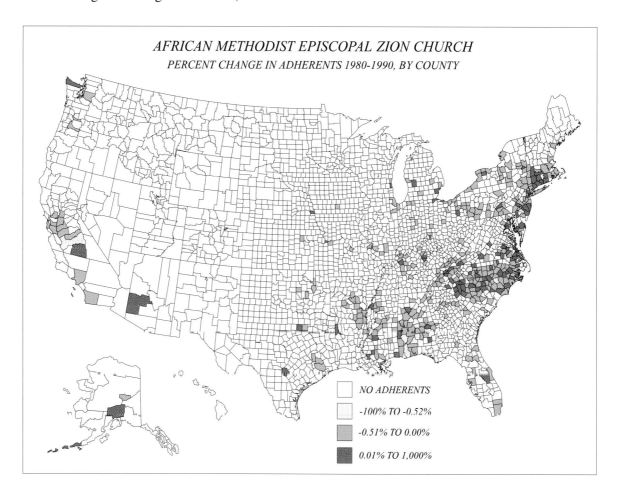

AFRICAN METHODIST EPISCOPAL ZION CHURCH
PERCENT CHANGE IN ADHERENTS 1980-1990, BY COUNTY

NO ADHERENTS
-100% TO -0.52%
-0.51% TO 0.00%
0.01% TO 1,000%

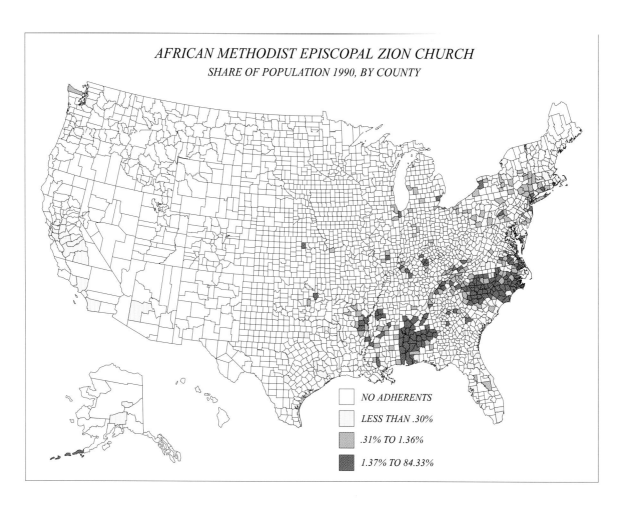

AFRICAN METHODIST EPISCOPAL ZION CHURCH
SHARE OF POPULATION 1990, BY COUNTY

NO ADHERENTS
LESS THAN .30%
.31% TO 1.36%
1.37% TO 84.33%

AFRICAN METHODIST EPISCOPAL ZION CHURCH

The African Methodist Episcopal Zion Church (the name Zion is taken from its first church, built in 1800) held its first annual conference in 1821. By 1880, given its rapid growth in the South, the church had founded Livingston College in Salisbury, North Carolina. Eventually, the church's work would be extended to the establishment of both home and foreign missions agencies, and the formation of Clinton Junior College in Rock Hill, South Carolina. Over time, the denomination has spread from its eastern seaboard origins to a widely dispersed pattern from coast to coast.

	1980	1990
Adherents:	1,092,389	1,141,650
Counties:	404	445

The AME Zion Church reported 1,092,723 adherents in 1,801 churches in 1980, and 1,142,016 adherents in 1,962 churches in 1990. However, a detailed inspection of the two data files reveals that for the great majority of counties, identical numbers of adherents are reported in both 1980 and 1990. This fact casts doubt upon the accuracy of the statistics and also cautions against an overly detailed analysis of these data. The aggregate increase in adherents of 4.5% lagged behind the United States population growth rate of 9.1% for the decade. The middle category on the map for Percent Change in Adherents, 1980-1990 is comprised of all those counties for which identical data were reported in the 1980 and 1990 studies. This reporting anomaly accounts for the disproportionate number of counties in the middle category on this map. At the national level, the growth reported is expressed by a 10% increase in counties, and a 9% increase in the number of AME Zion churches.

In 1990, the AME Zion Church has three distinct large clusters of contiguous counties. They are in the Boston to New York metropolitan corridor, in North Carolina, and in Alabama. Smaller clusters of counties characterize metropolitan centers in the Northeast and the midwestern Rustbelt cities. Included are virtually every major metropolitan area from Buffalo and Pittsburgh to St. Louis and Kansas City.

Compared with other Protestant denominations of similar size, the AME Zion church occupies an extremely small number of counties in 1990. Compare its 445 counties with more than double that number for such comparably sized groups as the American Baptist Churches and the Churches of Christ, with 1,000 and 2,400 counties respectively. It is difficult to escape the observation that this extent of spatial concentration for such a large religious community reflects historic patterns of racial discrimination and segregation in the United States. Indeed, this feature of the pattern for the AME Zion Church most resembles that for American Jews, a population of over five million situated in only 700 counties.

As we have already noted, generalizing about change trends from the adherents data supplied by this denomination is at best precarious. Yet, the impressive growth in the number of new churches and counties occupied during the decade of the 1980s suggests that some extent of upward social mobility for members of this denomination may be lessening historic patterns of spatial containment for this segment of the African American population.

ASSEMBLIES OF GOD

The term Pentecostal refers to a large family of American denominations that, while drawing their basic theology from Baptism and Methodism, also claim the literal truth of the Bible, and view divine healing and speaking in tongues as evidence of the work of the Holy Spirit. The General Council of the Assemblies of God, founded in Hot Springs, Arkansas in 1914 is the largest of these fundamentalist churches. While the Assemblies adhere to a congregational polity system, they also exhibit many presbyterial features, especially regarding such matters as ordination of clergy and missionary outreach activities. The denomination operates over a dozen colleges and Bible colleges in the United States, as well as hundreds of Bible schools abroad. While the Assemblies of God participated in earlier versions of the study *Churches and Church Membership in the United States*, fully comparable data for adherents became available for the first time in 1980. Accordingly, maps and analysis for only 1980 and 1990 are provided here.

	1980	1990
Adherents:	1,598,963	2,139,826
Counties:	2,424	2,546

Between 1980 and 1990, the Assemblies report growth from 1,598,963 adherents in 9,447 churches to 2,139,826 adherents in 11,149 churches. This is an increase of 33.8% in adherents during a period when both the general population and most religious bodies grew at much more modest rates. The Assemblies of God also expanded into 122 additional counties in the decade of the 1980s.

The map for Total Adherents, 1990 indicates that the upper third of counties (reporting a minimum of 457 adherents per county) are distributed across four regions. Some of these counties are found throughout the West and southwestern states, though not in the area dominated by Mormonism. Bands of high category counties are located throughout the South Central Interior, including east Texas, and of course, Arkansas, which is the denomination's point of origin. The Assemblies also report high category counties throughout Florida, and similar

strength across New England and the Northeast. Clearly, this is a denomination with a national distribution. While the smallest third of counties are modest in size (1 to 132 adherents), the upper two-thirds of counties reflect fairly sizable numbers of adherents. Moreover, the Assemblies of God are represented in 80% of all counties.

The map for Percent Change in Adherents, 1980-1990 provides a very different pattern that for Total Adherents, 1990. Counties in the highest category of change rate (minimally over 53% increase) are evident throughout the nation. However, for the most part they are outside of the several "core" areas apparent on the map for Total Adherents, 1990. The exceptions are in Florida, Arizona, New Mexico, and in southern New England. Nonmetropolitan counties seem to dominate this widely dispersed national growth pattern. Despite the overall trend of substantial growth (the median category reflects a median county rate of approximately 24% increase), a third of all counties for the Assemblies decreased in adherents between 1980 and 1990.

The map for Share of Population in 1990 again emphasizes the South Central Interior states and the founding state of Arkansas. Moreover, the predominance of high share counties in the central Plains, southern Pennsylvania, West Virginia, and the Northwest confirms the impression of a rural or small town rather than metropolitan character for this denomination. Moreover, in over two-thirds of all its county locations, the Assemblies of God account for less than 1.5% of total county population. Even in its strongest counties it never accounts for as much as 15% of county population. Thus, while this denomination is national in distribution, it is not a strong cultural element in most places where it is found. Rather, its cultural importance surely is in combination with other fundamentalist denominations, most clearly in the South Central Interior states, in the area thought of as the Bible Belt.

In summary, the Assemblies of God are a large and rapidly growing national denomination. While they rarely constitute a major proportion of county population, they do reflect the increasing significance of the fundamentalist branch of native Protestantism that organized at the beginning of the twentieth century. In terms of numbers of adherents, number of churches, and extent of counties occupied, this leading branch of Pentecostalism surely has developed into a ranking branch of American Protestantism.

ASSEMBLIES OF GOD
TOTAL ADHERENTS 1990, BY COUNTY

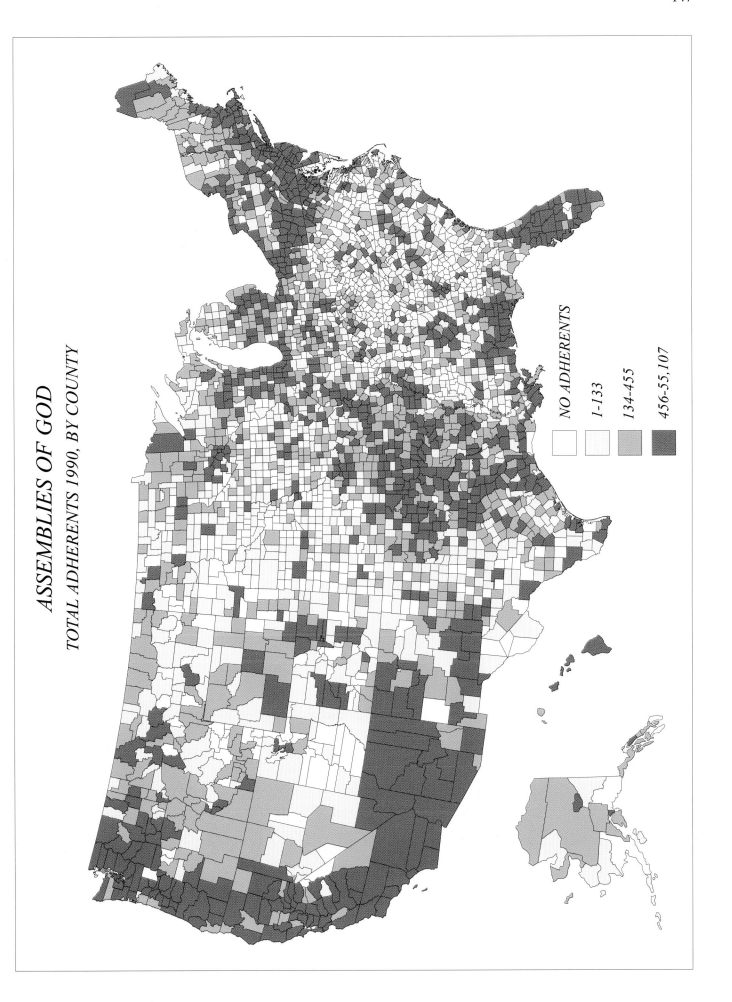

NO ADHERENTS

1-133

134-455

456-55,107

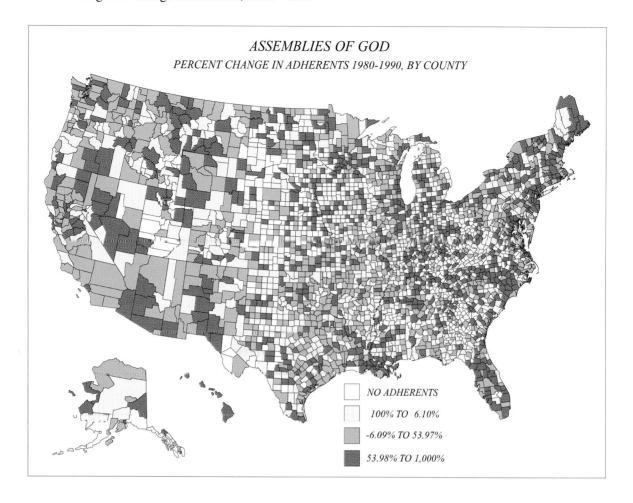

ASSEMBLIES OF GOD
PERCENT CHANGE IN ADHERENTS 1980-1990, BY COUNTY

NO ADHERENTS

100% TO 6.10%

-6.09% TO 53.97%

53.98% TO 1,000%

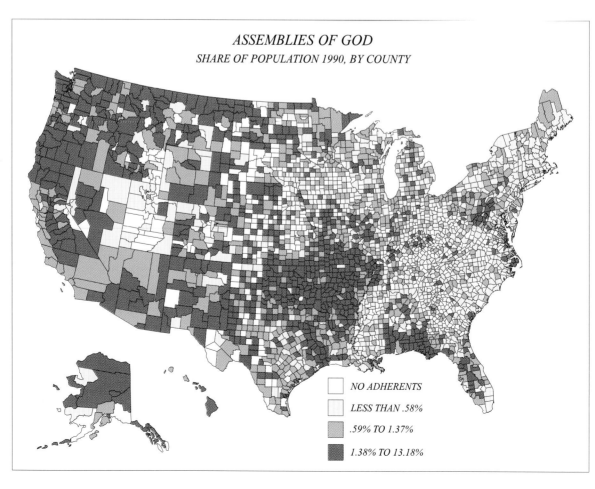

ASSEMBLIES OF GOD
SHARE OF POPULATION 1990, BY COUNTY

NO ADHERENTS

LESS THAN .58%

.59% TO 1.37%

1.38% TO 13.18%

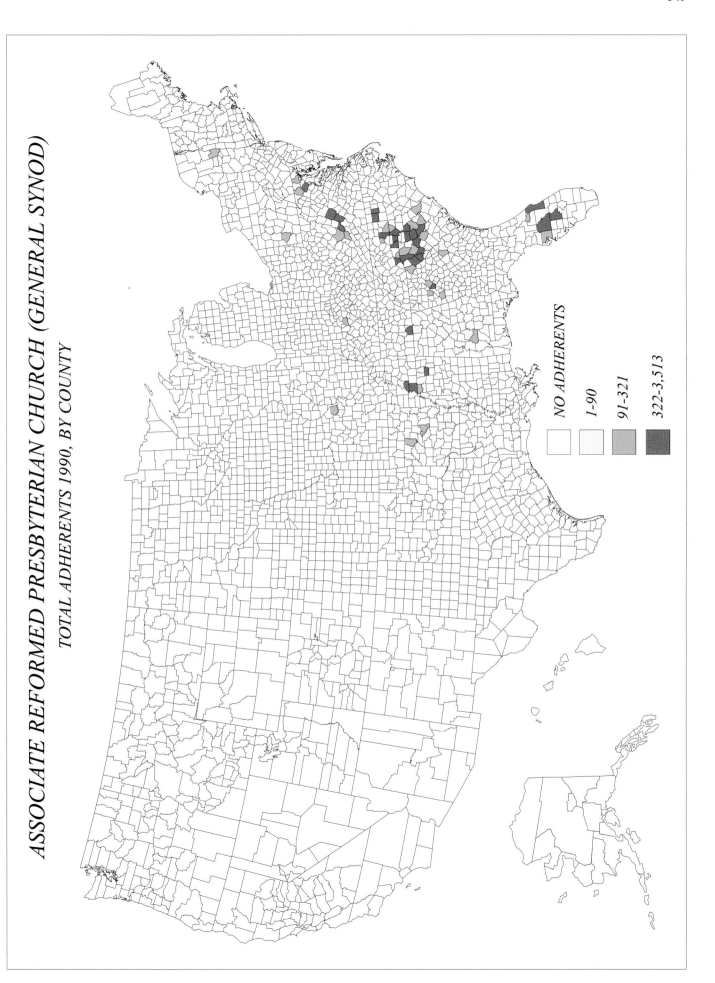

ASSOCIATE REFORMED PRESBYTERIAN CHURCH (GENERAL SYNOD)
TOTAL ADHERENTS 1990, BY COUNTY

NO ADHERENTS

1-90

91-321

322-3,513

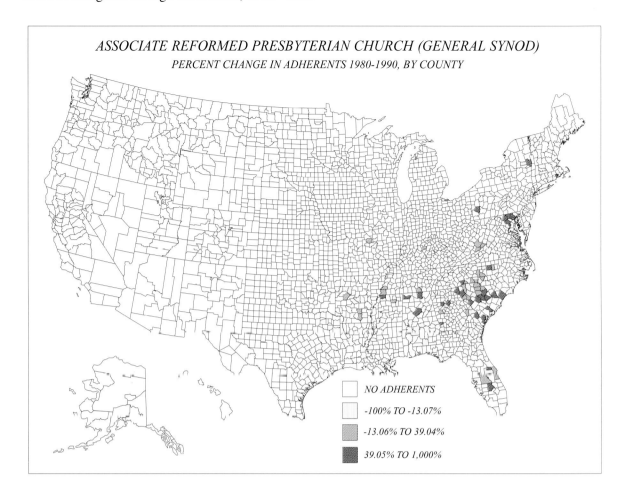

ASSOCIATE REFORMED PRESBYTERIAN CHURCH (GENERAL SYNOD)
PERCENT CHANGE IN ADHERENTS 1980-1990, BY COUNTY

NO ADHERENTS
-100% TO -13.07%
-13.06% TO 39.04%
39.05% TO 1,000%

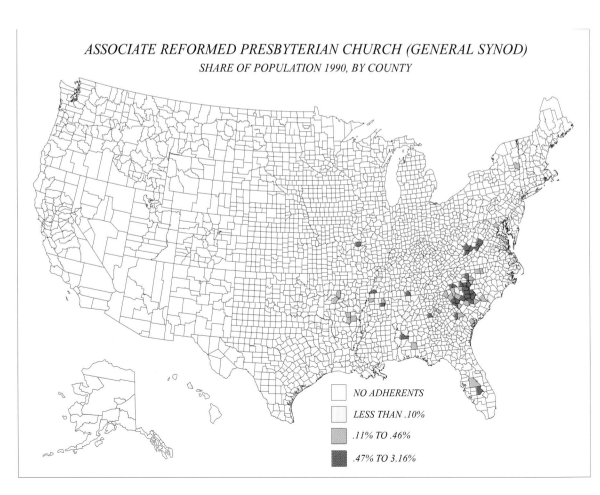

ASSOCIATE REFORMED PRESBYTERIAN CHURCH (GENERAL SYNOD)
SHARE OF POPULATION 1990, BY COUNTY

NO ADHERENTS
LESS THAN .10%
.11% TO .46%
.47% TO 3.16%

ASSOCIATE REFORMED PRESBYTERIAN CHURCH (GENERAL SYNOD)

Reformed Presbyterians trace their beginnings to Covenanters who immigrated from Scotland fleeing persecution during the 17th century. The Associate Presbyterians are followers of an 18th century secession movement in Scotland led by Ebner Erskine. An American branch was organized in 1801. By the mid-19th century theological disputes between "new light" and "old light" Presbyterians had created divisions within most branches of Presbyterianism. The Associate Reformed Presbyterian Church is a theologically conservative body that opted for independent status in the late 1850s, when most of these divisions were being healed.

	1980	1990
Adherents:	31,984	37,988
Counties:	68	86

Between 1980 and 1990, The Associate Reformed Presbyterian Church increased by 18.8% from 31,984 to 37,988 adherents. Similarly, it increased its spatial extent by 26.5%, from 68 to 86 counties, and also grew from 159 to 187 churches.

The map of Total Adherents, 1990 reflects the traditional southern origins of this small denomination, with 65% (24,558) of the 1990 adherents located in the two states of North and South Carolina. The entire denomination is contained in only eleven states. The numbers of adherents per county in the upper two-thirds of counties for this small denomination are comparable to those for much larger denominations. This suggests that this communion has expanded through the acquisition of "established" churches, most likely local churches in the northern and southern states dissenting from the 1983 merger that united the northern and southern branches of American Presbyterianism in the Presbyterian Church (U.S.A.).

The map for Percent Change in Adherents, 1980-1990 confirms the impression that this denomination is growing on its traditional turf. While counties in the upper third of the growth range (minimally a 39.05% increase) are located in virtually all states where the denomination is found, the greatest number of "high growth" counties are in the Carolinas. Moreover, strong growth rates (the median county rate being over 25%) are evident even in the middle third of counties. Finally, while the Carolinas also register the largest number of "high" population share counties, that share never is very great. These Associate Reformed Presbyterians never account for as much as 4% of any county population.

In summary, this small, theologically distinctive Presbyterian communion appears to have grown in adherents between 1980 and 1990 at a rate more than double that of the general population. This once ethnically (Scotch) and theologically distinctive branch of Presbyterianism has become a refuge for local churches, especially in the South, rejecting the consolidation of American Presbyterianism in the Presbyterian Church (U.S.A.). Nonetheless, because of its small population shares, the cultural impact of this church most likely is in combination with other Presbyterian churches.

BAPTIST MISSIONARY ASSOCIATION OF AMERICA

In the mid-19th century a movement within the Baptist churches coalesced around the writing of James R. Graves. Called Landmarkers, these fundamentalists argue that through the practice of Baptism, a succession of Baptist churches can be traced from the time of Christ, through the Middle Ages and the Protestant Reformation, to the present day. Thus, the true church is viewed as Baptist, not Protestant.

The Landmarkers, founded in 1905 as The Baptist General Association, changed their name to the American Baptist Association in 1924. In 1950, a division within the American Baptist Association resulted in the formation of the North American Baptist Association. In 1968, the present name which reflects its continuing missionary emphasis, Baptist Missionary Association, was adopted.

	1980	1990
Adherents:	274,515	289,919
Counties:	374	351

This denomination reported 274,515 adherents in 1,435 churches in 1980, and 289,919 adherents in 1,374 churches in 1990. The small decrease (4%) in the number of churches is reflected in a correspondingly small decline in its number of counties from 374 to 351.

However, this shrinkage is offset by a modest increase in the total number of adherents. If the term "Baptist" is commonly associated with the Bible Belt, then it is not surprising that these Landmarkers are centered in the heart of the Bible Belt region. Three states surrounding the lower Mississippi Valley, Texas (125,323 adherents), Arkansas (78,121), and Mississippi (39,295), account for more than 80% of this denomination's adherents. A smaller outlying cluster of counties containing almost 11,000 adherents is situated in Missouri.

As is suggested by the category values for the map of Percent Change in Adherents, 1980-1990, half of these counties gained adherents at more than a 10% rate (the median county value), and one-third of all counties grew by more than 20% during the decade. Increases in adherents are especially prevalent within the primary core area. This denomination is growing on its home turf.

The map for Share of Population, 1990 provides a slightly diminished version of the other two maps. Obviously, this group claims its highest shares of population in counties scattered throughout its primary or core locations. However, the fact that the highest third of share counties begins with a modest 1.8% of population suggests that these Landmarkers are not, by themselves, a salient cultural element. Rather, they contribute to a larger Baptist presence in their Bible Belt setting. For the decade of the 1980s, the Baptist Missionary Association of America exhibits a mixed pattern involving some shrinkage in geographic extent, coupled with substantial levels of growth in its formerly established locations.

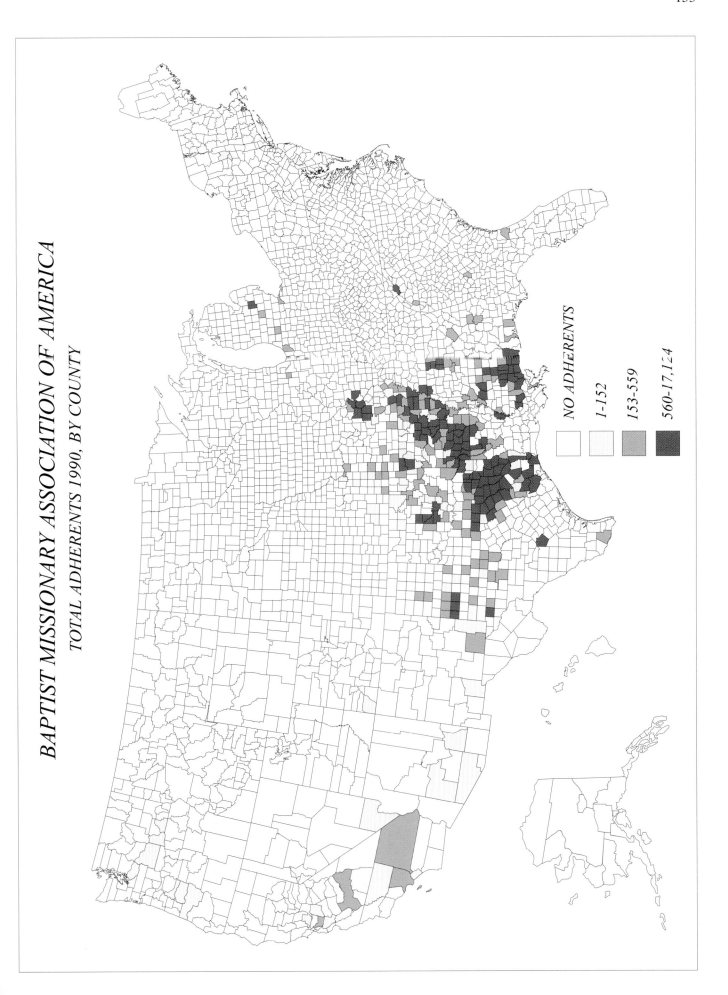

BAPTIST MISSIONARY ASSOCIATION OF AMERICA

TOTAL ADHERENTS 1990, BY COUNTY

NO ADHERENTS

1-152

153-559

560-17,124

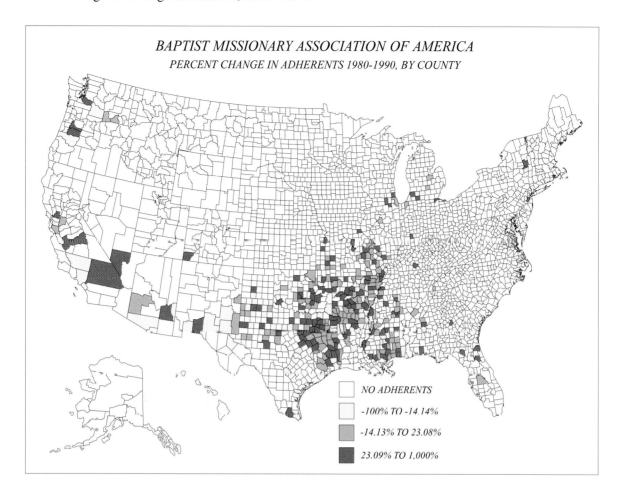

BAPTIST MISSIONARY ASSOCIATION OF AMERICA
PERCENT CHANGE IN ADHERENTS 1980-1990, BY COUNTY

NO ADHERENTS
-100% TO -14.14%
-14.13% TO 23.08%
23.09% TO 1,000%

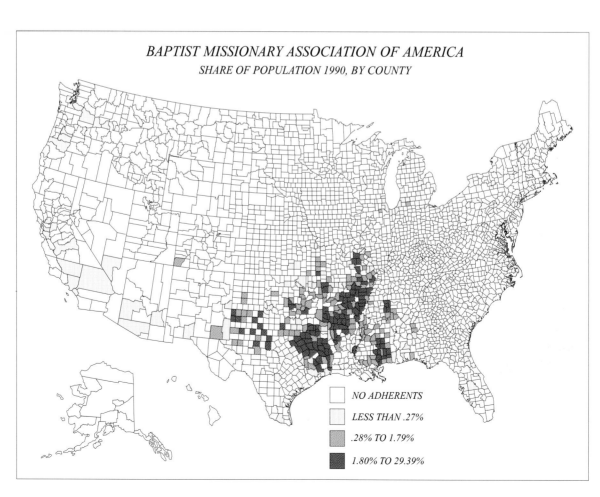

BAPTIST MISSIONARY ASSOCIATION OF AMERICA
SHARE OF POPULATION 1990, BY COUNTY

NO ADHERENTS
LESS THAN .27%
.28% TO 1.79%
1.80% TO 29.39%

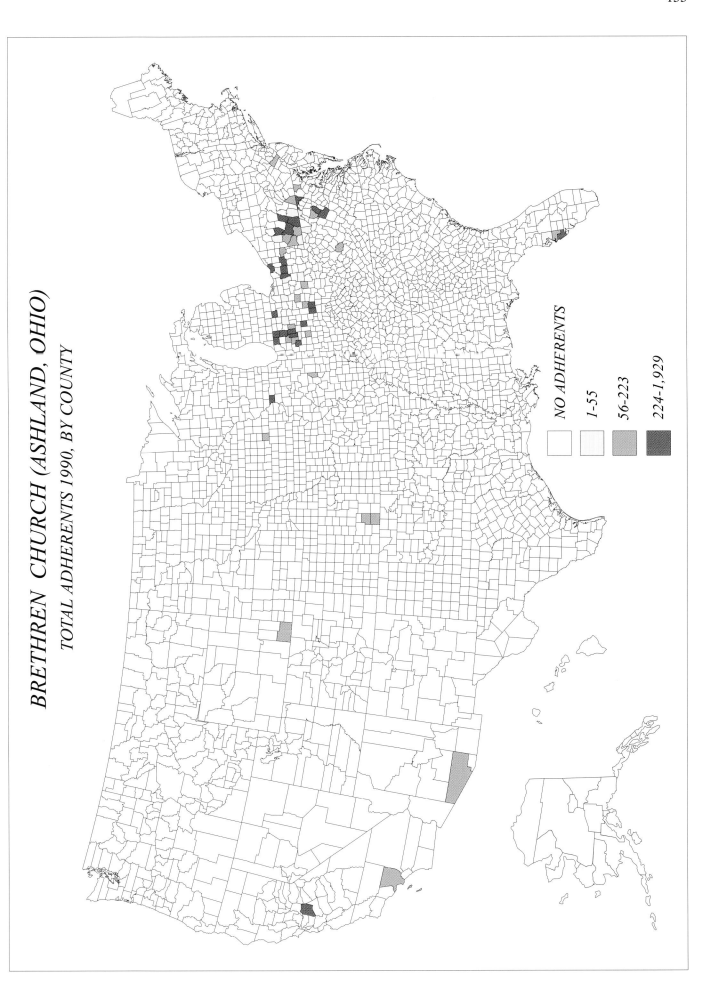

BRETHREN CHURCH (ASHLAND, OHIO)
TOTAL ADHERENTS 1990, BY COUNTY

NO ADHERENTS

1-55

56-223

224-1,929

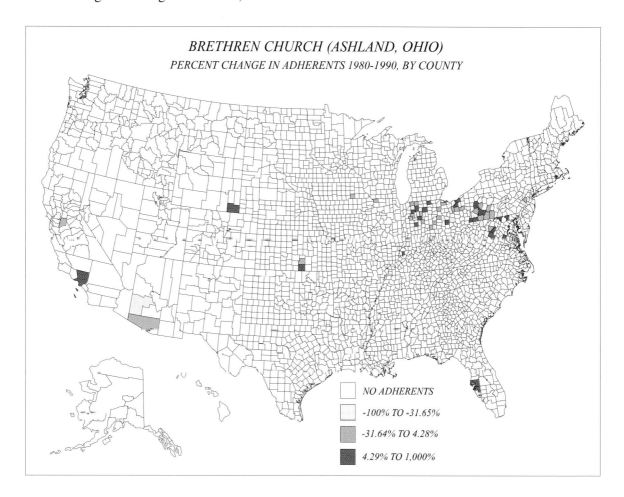

BRETHREN CHURCH (ASHLAND, OHIO)
PERCENT CHANGE IN ADHERENTS 1980-1990, BY COUNTY

NO ADHERENTS
-100% TO -31.65%
-31.64% TO 4.28%
4.29% TO 1,000%

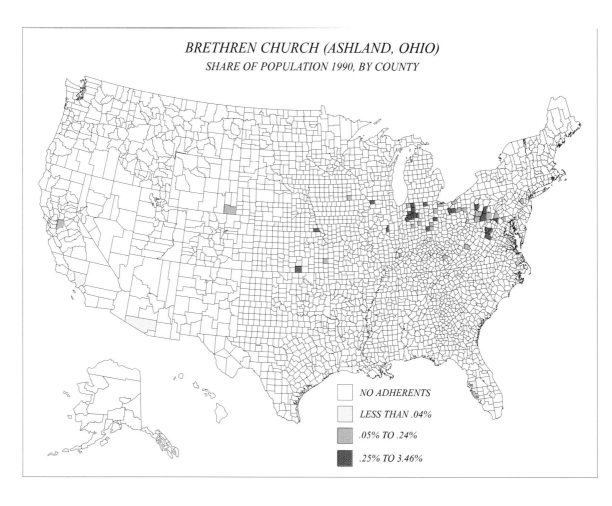

BRETHREN CHURCH (ASHLAND, OHIO)
SHARE OF POPULATION 1990, BY COUNTY

NO ADHERENTS
LESS THAN .04%
.05% TO .24%
.25% TO 3.46%

BRETHREN CHURCH (ASHLAND, OHIO)

Brethren churches are the descendants of German Pietists, with the largest American branch being the Church of the Brethren. The Brethren Church (Ashland, Ohio), also known as Progressive Brethren or Progressive Dunkers, was founded in 1882 as a modernizing departure from the conservative social practices of the parent body. The term "Dunkers" refers to the practice of baptism by immersion.

	1980	1990
Adherents:	18,372	16,331
Counties:	71	73

Between 1980 and 1990, the Brethren Church (Ashland, Ohio) decreased from 18,372 adherents to 16,331 adherents, while increasing from 120 to 124 churches. In 1990, adherents were reported in only two more counties (73) than in 1980. The map for Total Adherents, 1990 clearly delineates the three state core area for this small denomination. Indiana (5,307 adherents), Ohio (4,611), and Pennsylvania (2,089) contain 74% of all adherents in 1990, and there are but 7 counties reporting adherents outside these three states. This map also indicates that the average congregation is fairly small, with the middle third of counties representing between 56 and 223 adherents.

The map of Percent Change in Adherents, 1980-1990 shows that a third of all counties lost over 30% of adherents during the decade of the 1980s. In fact, the middle third of counties also represents those ranging from substantial decline (-31.64%) to virtual stability (+4.28%). Counties that either were declining or were stable predominate in the three core states of Indiana, Ohio, and Pennsylvania. Counties with positive growth rates are found on the edges of these core clusters, as well as in Florida, California, and Wyoming.

The map for Share of Population, 1990 reveals that the Brethren Church (Ashland, Ohio) does not represent as much as 3.5% of county population even in its core areas. In fact, even in counties within this core area, this religious community often represents less than one quarter of one percent of the county population.

In summary, this small sect had an overall pattern of moderate decline (-11%) between 1980 and 1990. In 1990, the three state area of Indiana, Ohio, and Pennsylvania contained nearly three quarters of all adherents. The Brethren Church (Ashland, Ohio) reports growth in adherents in counties on the fringes of its historic core locations, as well as in the widely separated states of California, Wyoming, and Florida. Clearly, because of small population shares, the cultural impact of this church must be understood in combination with other Brethren, Mennonite, and Amish churches with which it shares both theological tradition and geographic location in the United States.

CHRISTIAN AND MISSIONARY ALLIANCE

The Christian Alliance, a home missions society, and the Evangelical Missionary Alliance, a foreign missions society both were founded in New York City in the late 1880s under the leadership of A. B. Simpson. The present-day Christian and Missionary Alliance resulted from a merger of the two organizations in 1897. This group has a close doctrinal affinity with the Assemblies of God, some of whose original members were drawn from the Christian and Missionary Alliance.

	1980	1990
Adherents:	169,459	269,284
Counties:	601	722

Between 1980 and 1990, this evangelical communion grew from 169,450 adherents in 601 counties to 269,284 adherents in 722 counties. During this same period, the Christian and Missionary Alliance grew from 1,258 churches to 1,797 churches. This exceptional increase in the number of congregations has resulted from a policy decision to create new churches throughout this denomination's twenty-two districts across the nation. The map of Total Adherents, 1990 reveals a very distinctive distribution pattern. In addition to the historic core area centered around the states of New York and Pennsylvania, this evangelical denomination occupies substantial bands of counties along the West Coast, in the upper Midwest and Northwest, and in Florida. This unique spatial pattern, in large part, is explained by this church's missionary work with Native Americans and immigrant populations. Among the latter are significant efforts with Cambodians, Hmong, Haitians, Koreans, Laotians, Vietnamese, and Hispanics. Missionary work with America's most recent immigrant communities accounts for the substantial growth during the decade of the 1980s. As was noted previously, evangelism and new church "plantings" have been a policy of this denomination. The missionary character of the growth also explains why such small absolute sizes are present in the bottom third of counties.

Given this denomination's impressive growth, it is not surprising that even the weakest third of counties on the map for Percent Change in Adherents, 1980-1990 includes counties that grew in adherents. While "high" percentage counties are located in all geographic regions where the denomination is present, this is least so for its historic core area.

The map for Share of Population, 1990 indicates that the Christian and Missionary Alliance claims very modest shares of county populations nearly everywhere that it is located. Two-thirds of counties represent less than a third of a percent of county population. Moreover, the "high" share counties tend to be in rural settings. This is so even inside the historic core region, where the sparsely populated southern tier of New York and western Pennsylvania show greater shares than the more urbanized portions of these two states.

In summary, the Christian and Missionary Alliance has created an impressive counter trend to the general pattern of mainstream Protestant denominations. In an era of stability and decline, it has grown at substantial rates by extending its mission to ethnically diverse populations. While this pattern of aggressive evangelism directed at the most recent immigrant populations is characteristic of a number of groups in this Atlas, the Christian and Missionary Alliance is perhaps the most dramatic case of growth through these techniques.

CHRISTIAN AND MISSIONARY ALLIANCE
TOTAL ADHERENTS 1990, BY COUNTY

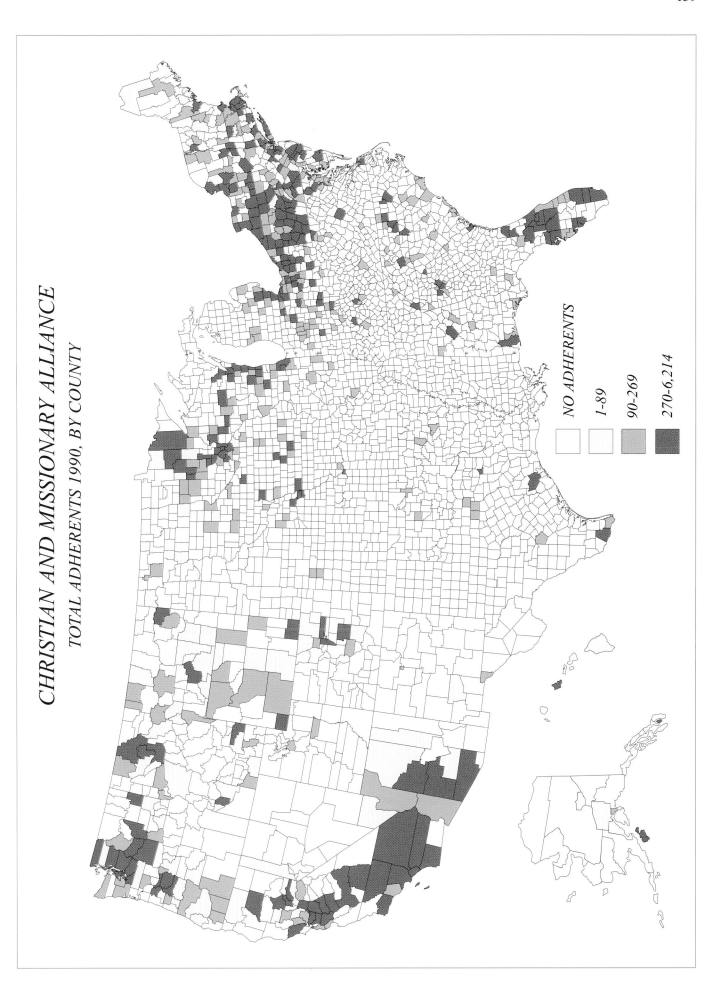

NO ADHERENTS

1-89

90-269

270-6,214

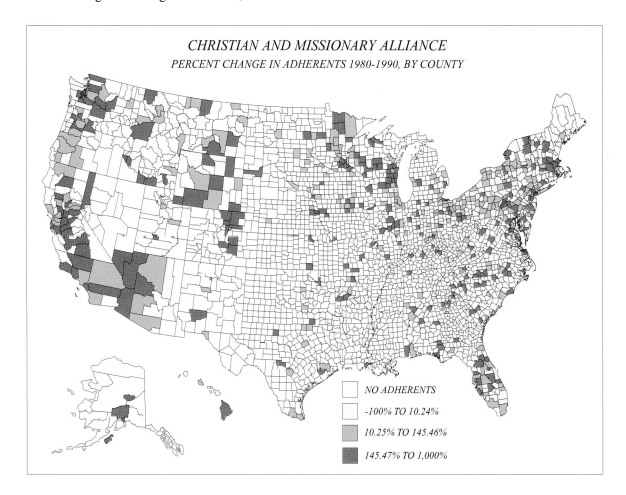

CHRISTIAN AND MISSIONARY ALLIANCE
PERCENT CHANGE IN ADHERENTS 1980-1990, BY COUNTY

NO ADHERENTS

-100% TO 10.24%

10.25% TO 145.46%

145.47% TO 1,000%

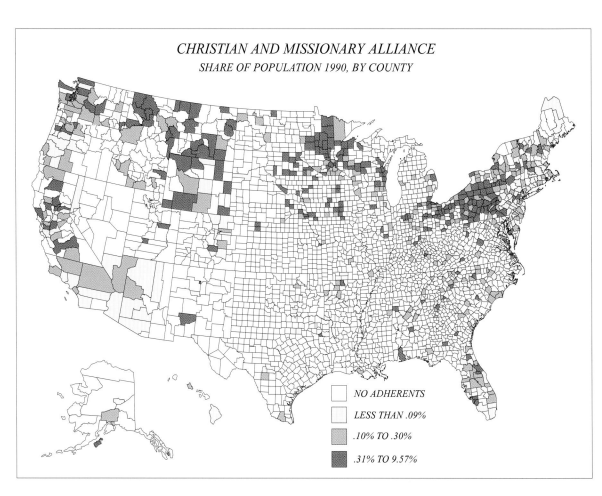

CHRISTIAN AND MISSIONARY ALLIANCE
SHARE OF POPULATION 1990, BY COUNTY

NO ADHERENTS

LESS THAN .09%

.10% TO .30%

.31% TO 9.57%

CHRISTIAN CHURCH (DISCIPLES OF CHRIST)
TOTAL ADHERENTS 1990, BY COUNTY

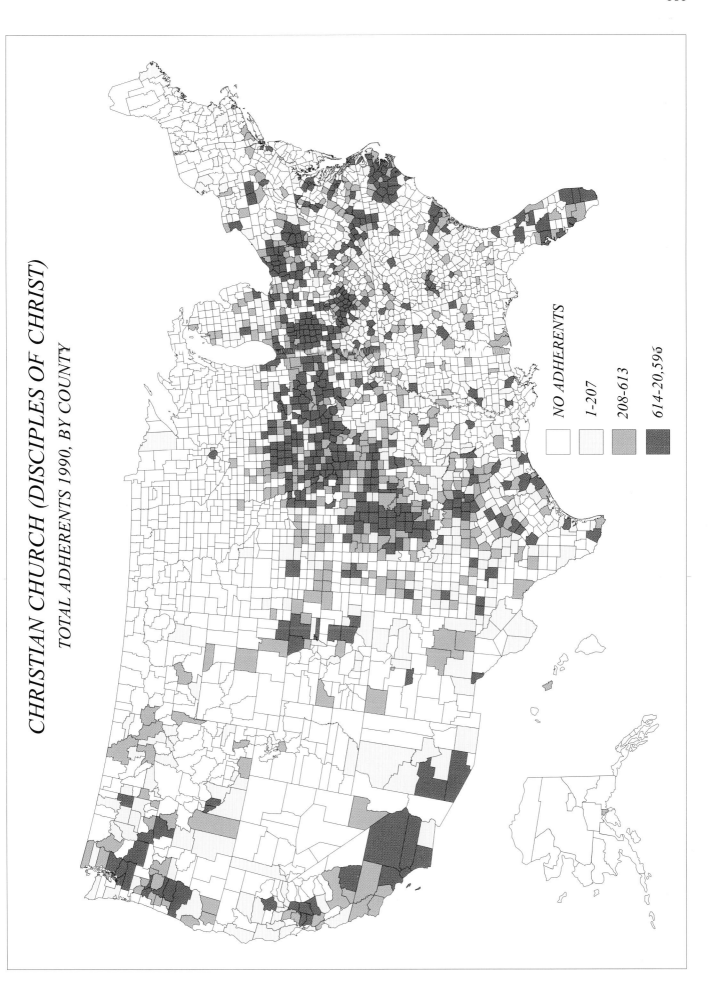

NO ADHERENTS

1-207

208-613

614-20,596

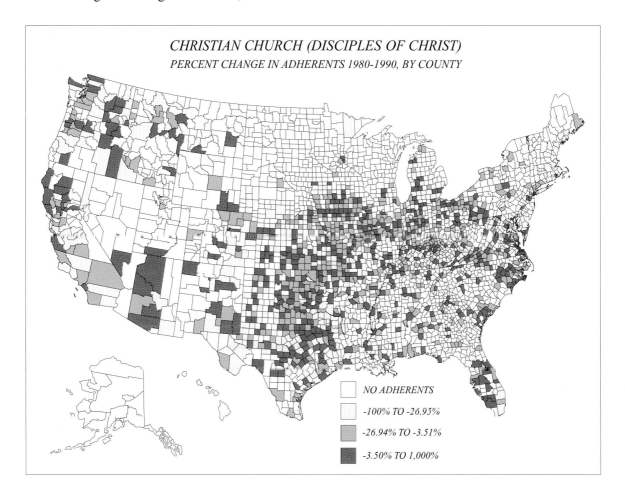

CHRISTIAN CHURCH (DISCIPLES OF CHRIST)
PERCENT CHANGE IN ADHERENTS 1980-1990, BY COUNTY

NO ADHERENTS
-100% TO -26.95%
-26.94% TO -3.51%
-3.50% TO 1,000%

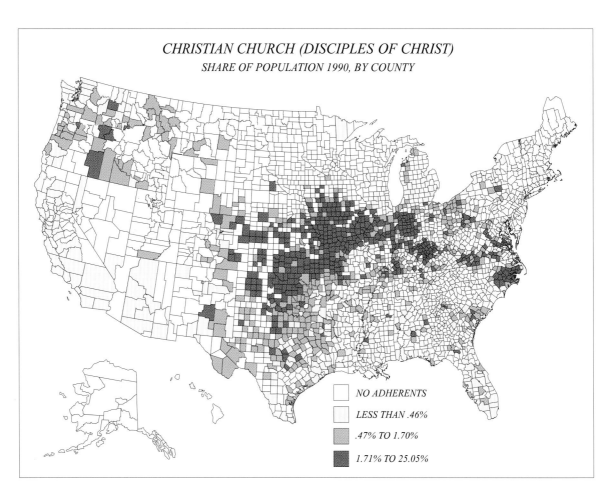

CHRISTIAN CHURCH (DISCIPLES OF CHRIST)
SHARE OF POPULATION 1990, BY COUNTY

NO ADHERENTS
LESS THAN .46%
.47% TO 1.70%
1.71% TO 25.05%

CHRISTIAN CHURCH (DISCIPLES OF CHRIST)

The Restoration Movement in American Protestantism emerged early in the 19th century as an attempt to "restore New Testament pattern and practice." While all four of its founders - Barton Stone, Thomas and Alexander Campbell, and Walter Scott - were Presbyterians, the Movement would spawn a new and large native American family of churches. The original parent body, The Christian Church (Disciples of Christ) first organized in 1839, with its first national convention in 1849. Unlike the Disciples, two other members of this family of churches, The Churches of Christ, and the Christian Churches and Churches of Christ continue to stress their status as fellowships rather than denominations. Rapid growth of Disciples churches after the Civil War transpired under a congregational form of polity. In 1968, a major reorganization resulted in a "representative government," with many local churches dissenting from this essentially presbyterial form of polity.

	1980	1990
Adherents:	1,211,889	1,037,205
Counties:	1,422	1,377

Between 1980 and 1990, the Disciples of Christ lost 14% of their adherents, while declining by only 3% of counties. During this same decade, their number of churches declined by 7%, from 4,324 to 4,035. The map for Total Adherents, 1990 reveals a denomination that spread from the Central Atlantic states into the Midwest and south central Great Plains. More urbanized portions of Florida, Arizona, and the West Coast also contain high category counties. Stated differently, historically, this 19th century American church appears to have settled widely in regions where other predominant Protestant denominational "turfs" were not established. Thus, they are least present in the upper Midwest (Lutheran), the Interior West (Mormon), New England (Congregational), and the Interior South (Baptist and Methodist). The Disciples' home turf in the American heartland also differs from that of their two kindred fellowships, the Churches of Christ which are situated more to the South, and the Christian Churches and Churches of Christ, which extend more to the West.

The map for Percent Change in Adherents, 1980-1990 indicates that in over two-thirds of its county locations this denomination lost adherents. Thus, there are declines even in those counties colored orange on this map. At best it can be said that all categories of change are widely dispersed. The trends here are across the denomination's entire distribution. They are not regional.

The map for Share of Population, 1990 clearly reaffirms the central Plains as "home turf" for the Disciples. Moreover, even in this region, they are not always a major component of county population, as the upper third of counties ranges from as little as 1.71% to over 25% of county populations. It is reasonable to suspect that the Disciples have their strongest share ratings in small town and rural portions of these Farm Belt states.

In summary, the Christian Churches (Disciples of Christ) rank among the 14 Protestant denominations in this Atlas that number in excess of a million adherents. They are present in over a third of all counties. In combination with the Churches of Christ, and Christian Churches and Churches of Christ, they comprise a major American Protestant faith community. However, in sharp contrast to the latter two groups, during the decade of the 1980s, the Disciples experienced substantial declines in adherents (-14%) while reporting less dramatic slippage in churches and counties. This general pattern of decline among the Disciples more closely resembles the pattern of loss for its longer established Anglo-Protestant progenitor, the Presbyterian Church (U.S.A.), than the prevailing growth trends among other native Protestant denominations.

CHRISTIAN CHURCHES AND CHURCHES OF CHRIST

The westward movement of the American frontier during the 19th Century spawned a native American branch of Protestantism known as The Restoration Movement. Initially recognizing only the authority of the New Testament and the autonomy of local congregations, this movement rejected denominational organization. However, in time, theological differences would shape three distinct organized branches of this Movement.

The most liberal of these bodies, the Christian Church (Disciples of Christ), gradually adopted a denominational style of organization that was formally shaped into a presbyterial type polity system during the 1960s. The other two branches of the movement continue to eschew the term "denomination," and also divided from each other during the 1920s over the issue of the use of instrumental music. The more conservative group known as the Churches of Christ uses only *a capella* music. The other communion, known as the Christian Church and Churches of Christ generally is viewed as more theologically moderate and does permit instrumental music in worship. These three native American branches of Protestantism also exhibit distinct spatial patterns.

	1980	1990
Adherents:	1,126,500	1,210,319
Counties:	1,584	1,524

In 1980, the Christian Churches and Churches of Christ reported 1,126,500 adherents in 1,584 counties, as compared to 1,210,319 adherents in 1,524 counties in 1990. Thus, a growth rate of 7.4%, approximating that for the United States population for the decade (9.1%), occurred in the context of some spatial contraction. As depicted on the map for Percent Change in Adherents, 1980-1990, during the decade of the 1980s, the overall pattern for these Christian Churches is one of increase. Fully a third of all counties register growth in excess of 27%, and the middle third of counties is centered on a 10% growth statistic. High growth counties are situated in nearly all regions of the nation.

The map of Total Adherents, 1990 reveals a pattern of high concentration across the Midwest and the West. The map for Share of Population, 1990 confirms the impression that the Corn Belt is home turf for this branch of the Restoration Movement. High population share counties mirror the map of Total Adherents, 1990, with the counties shaded orange stretching from western Pennsylvania into the southern and central Plains states.

These patterns may be compared with those for the non-instrumentalist branch of the Restoration Movement, the Churches of Christ. The midwestern orientation of the Christian Churches and Churches of Christ contrasts sharply with the more southern pattern for the Churches of Christ. The Christian Churches and Churches of Christ are smaller than the Churches of Christ (1,210,319 compared to 1,677,711 adherents), are considerably more spatially compact (1,524 as compared to 2,397 counties), and at their apex, achieve a less impressive share of county population (the upper limit of the top third of counties is 27.08% of population as compared to 64%). Nonetheless, the Christian Churches and Churches of Christ may be viewed as a sizable component of native Protestantism in the American Midwest that grew at a modest rate during the 1980s.

CHRISTIAN CHURCHES AND CHURCHES OF CHRIST

TOTAL ADHERENTS 1990, BY COUNTY

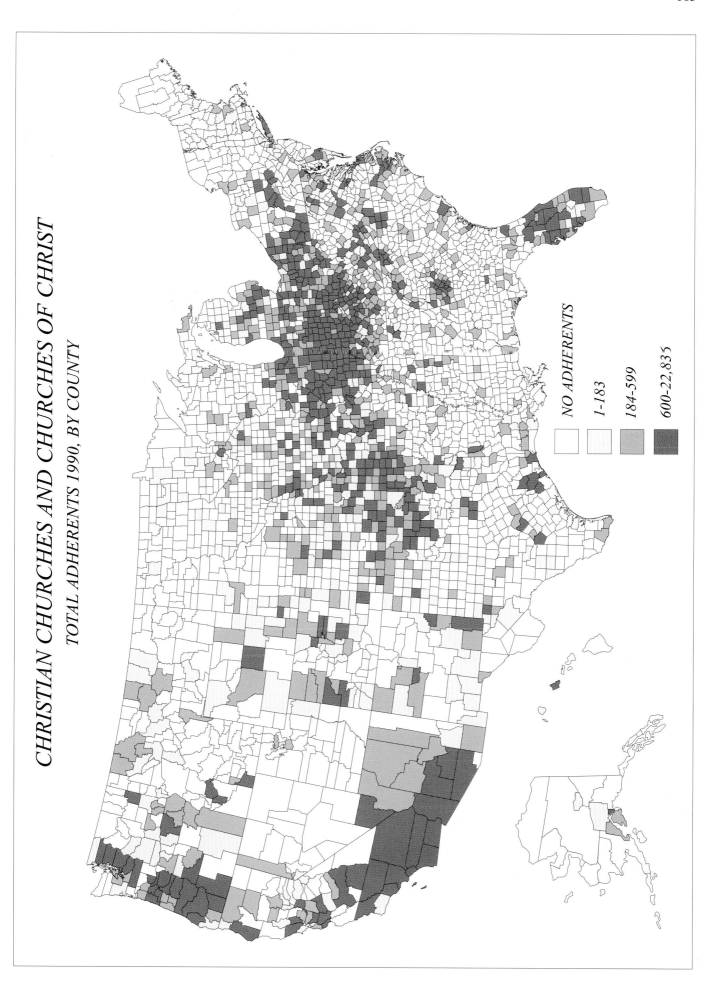

NO ADHERENTS

1-183

184-599

600-22,835

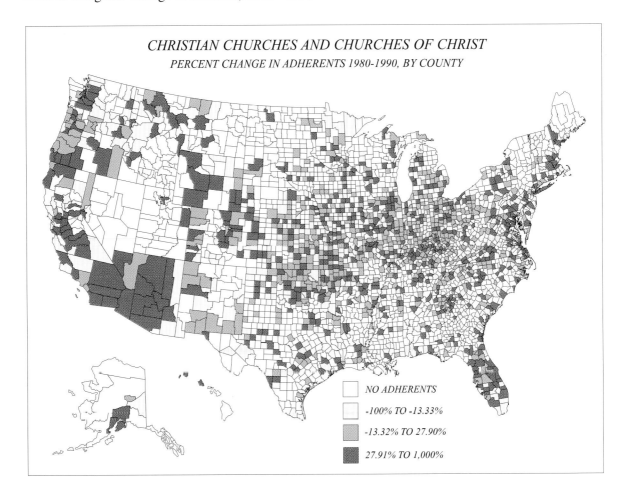

CHRISTIAN CHURCHES AND CHURCHES OF CHRIST
PERCENT CHANGE IN ADHERENTS 1980-1990, BY COUNTY

NO ADHERENTS
-100% TO -13.33%
-13.32% TO 27.90%
27.91% TO 1,000%

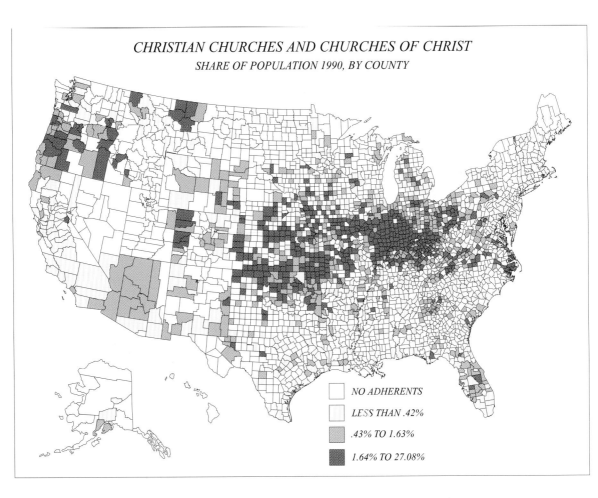

CHRISTIAN CHURCHES AND CHURCHES OF CHRIST
SHARE OF POPULATION 1990, BY COUNTY

NO ADHERENTS
LESS THAN .42%
.43% TO 1.63%
1.64% TO 27.08%

CHRISTIAN (PLYMOUTH) BRETHREN
TOTAL ADHERENTS 1990, BY COUNTY

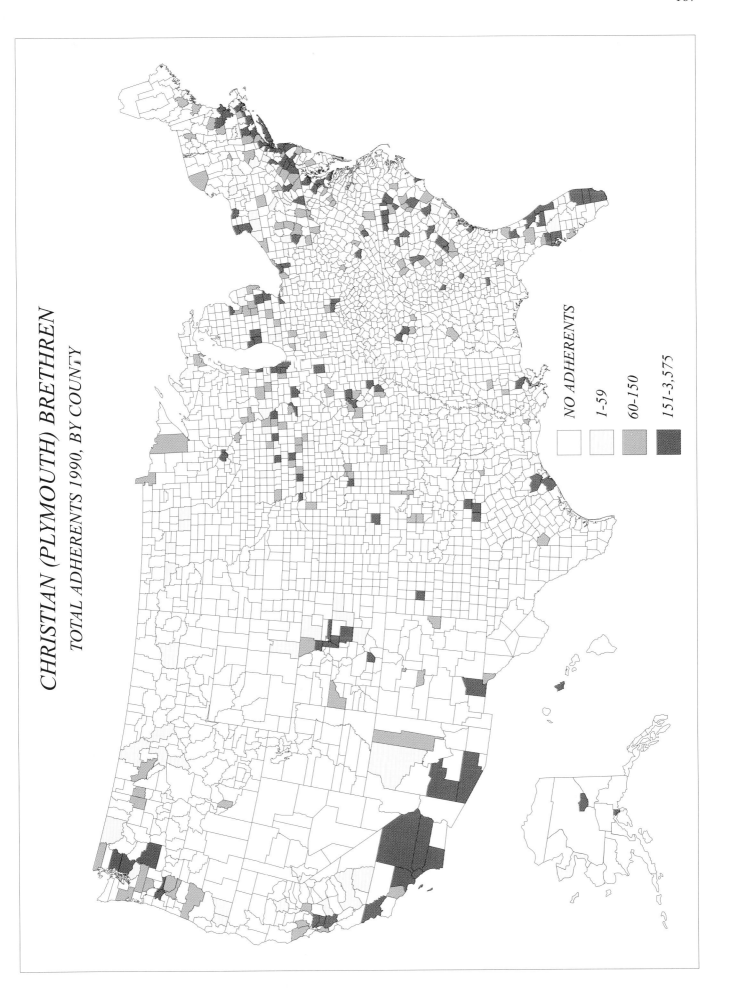

NO ADHERENTS

1-59

60-150

151-3,575

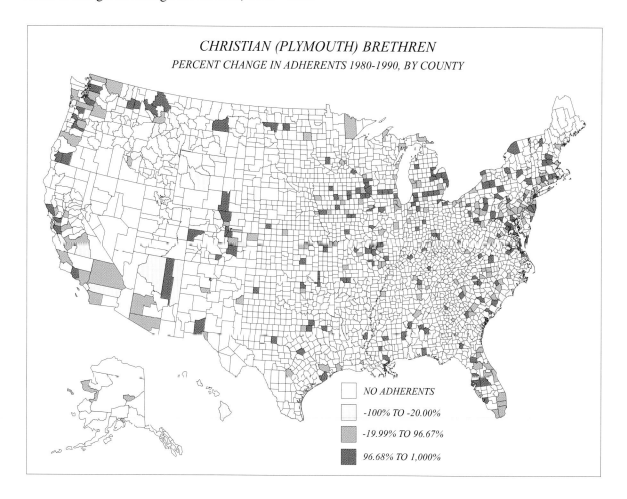

CHRISTIAN (PLYMOUTH) BRETHREN
PERCENT CHANGE IN ADHERENTS 1980-1990, BY COUNTY

NO ADHERENTS
-100% TO -20.00%
-19.99% TO 96.67%
96.68% TO 1,000%

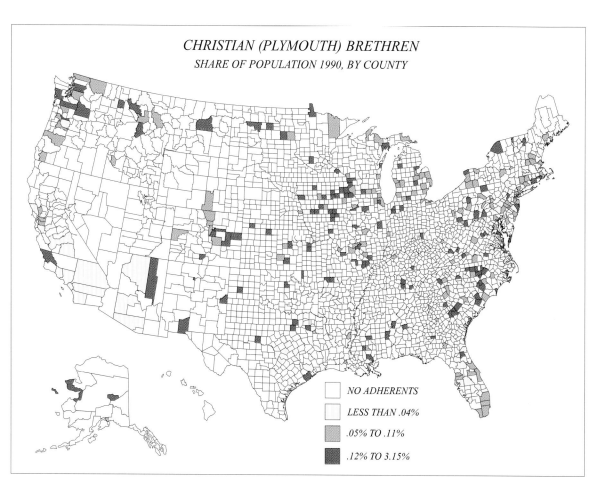

CHRISTIAN (PLYMOUTH) BRETHREN
SHARE OF POPULATION 1990, BY COUNTY

NO ADHERENTS
LESS THAN .04%
.05% TO .11%
.12% TO 3.15%

CHRISTIAN (PLYMOUTH) BRETHREN,

Founded in the British Isles in the 1820s, this evangelical religious movement gathers in assemblies (rather than churches) and holds meetings (not services). A division in England in 1848 between "exclusive" and "open" assemblies split the Brethren movements into two camps. In America, Brethren assemblies have been widely recognized for their founding of nondenominational Bible schools, colleges, and seminaries. In recent years, the open branch which has predominated in the United States by a factor of four to one, and it is that branch which has used the name "Christian Brethren." The Christian Brethren stress the autonomy of local congregations, and place great emphasis upon foreign missionary work. Their tradition of born-again Christianity very much resembles more evangelical Baptist forms of American Protestantism.

	1980	1990
Adherents:	65,490	84,966
Counties:	417	420

Between 1980 and 1990, the Christian (Plymouth) Brethren increased in adherents by an impressive 29.7% while remaining essentially spatially stable. These assemblies tend to be quite small in size, with the upper third of counties containing as few as only 152 adherents. Not surprisingly, the map for Share of Population, 1990 indicates that even in the places of their greatest absolute numbers, the Christian (Plymouth) Brethren never account for as much as 4% of a county's population.

The map for Percent Change in Adherents, 1980-1990 reveals a highly diffuse pattern of growth. High category counties are encountered in all regions where the Christian (Plymouth) Brethren are located. The small numbers involved in the adherents statistics allow modest absolute increases to represent impressively high relative change rates, with the upper third of counties reporting at least 130% increases.

There is a clear impression here that this small branch of evangelical Anglo-Protestantism has been growing in places where it has established its assemblies across the nation. The general pattern of spatial dispersal across a sizable number of counties is shared by a number of other smaller religious groups in this *Atlas*. Moreover, given the emphasis of this movement upon evangelism, the pattern of wide dispersal is quite understandable.

CHURCH OF GOD IN CHRIST, MENNONITE

There are a great diversity of Mennonite churches in the United States, ranging from the most conservative "Pennsylvania Dutch" Amish communities, to more conventional expressions of evangelical and fundamentalist Protestantism. The Church of God in Christ, Mennonite was founded in 1859 by the Ohio churchman John Holdeman, who believed that the Mennonite Church was in error in various matters of doctrine and practice. This is a conservative expression of the Mennonite tradition that follows nonconformity with the world in matters of dress, adornment, sports, and amusements.

	1980	1990
Adherents:	7,454	12,535
Counties:	51	61

This is the smallest of the communions in this *Atlas* providing data only for the 1980-1990 period. Between 1980 and 1990, the Church of God in Christ, Mennonite grew from 7,454 adherents in 66 churches to 12,535 adherents in 75 churches. While the map of Total Adherents, 1990 reveals a widely dispersed array of locations, it must be remembered that

most of these are fairly small assemblages, fully two-thirds of them less than 200 persons. Moreover, in 1990, 34% of all adherents (4,269) were located in the state of Kansas, with 10% are in a single place, McPherson County.

The substantial rate of increase in adherents between 1980 and 1990 (67%) must be viewed in the context of the relatively small absolute numbers involved. However, as seen on the map for Percent Change in Adherents,1980-1990, the growth pattern for the decade is widely dispersed. Counties reporting as much as a 50% increase in adherents are present even in that third of counties with the weakest change rates.

The map for Share of Population, 1990 again reflects the small size of this Mennonite community. Even in the top third of share counties this church may represent as little as nine-tenths of 1% of county population. These "high share" counties, as might be expected are especially prevalent in Kansas, where in at least one rural county they represent over 21% of county population.

In summary, the Church of God in Christ, Mennonite is a small group that grew in adherents at an impressive 67% rate between 1980 and 1990. In 1990 they consist of relatively small groupings of adherents in widely separated locations, except perhaps in the states of Oklahoma and Kansas, with Kansas accounting for 34% of all adherents.

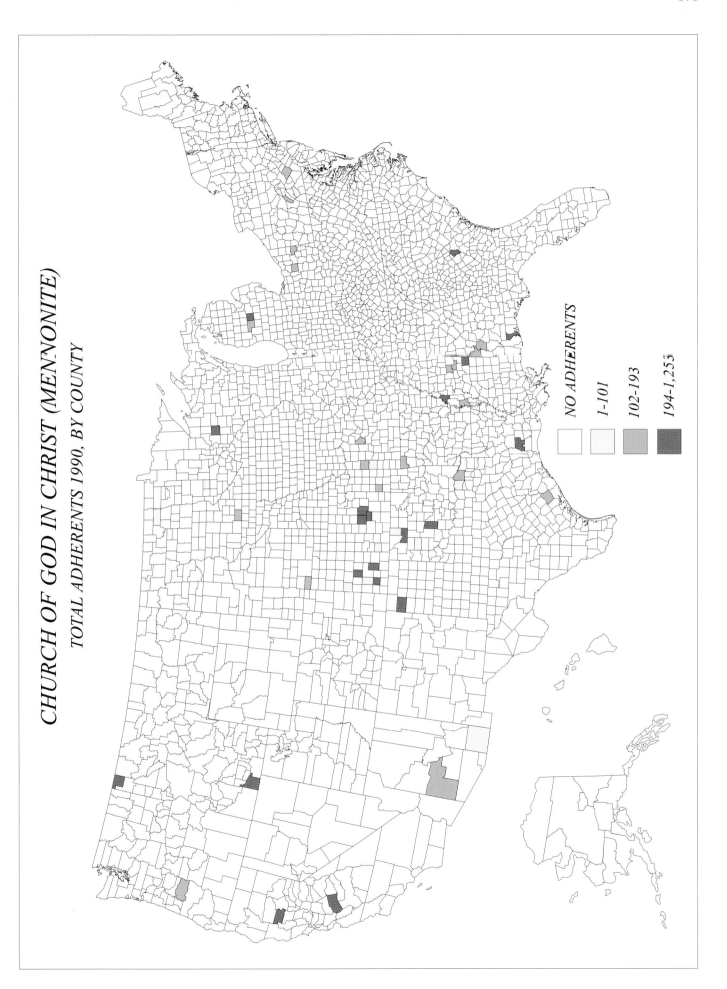

CHURCH OF GOD IN CHRIST (MENNONITE)

TOTAL ADHERENTS 1990, BY COUNTY

NO ADHERENTS

1-101

102-193

194-1,255

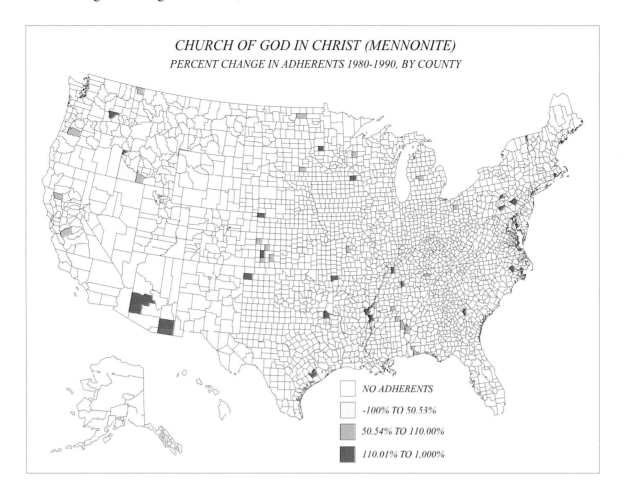

CHURCH OF GOD IN CHRIST (MENNONITE)
PERCENT CHANGE IN ADHERENTS 1980-1990, BY COUNTY

NO ADHERENTS
-100% TO 50.53%
50.54% TO 110.00%
110.01% TO 1,000%

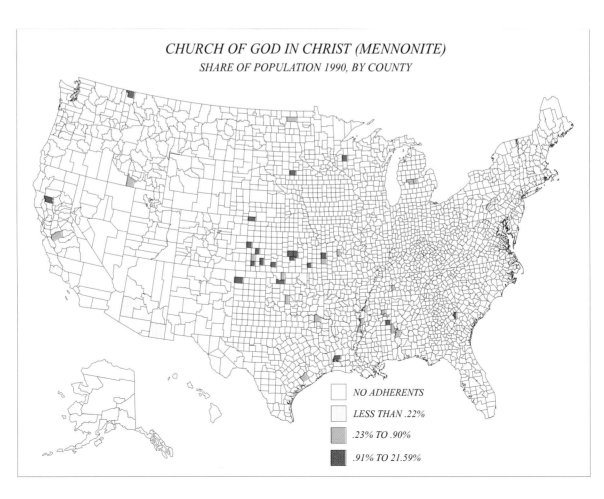

CHURCH OF GOD IN CHRIST (MENNONITE)
SHARE OF POPULATION 1990, BY COUNTY

NO ADHERENTS
LESS THAN .22%
.23% TO .90%
.91% TO 21.59%

173

CHURCH OF JESUS CHRIST OF LATTER-DAY SAINTS

TOTAL ADHERENTS 1990, BY COUNTY

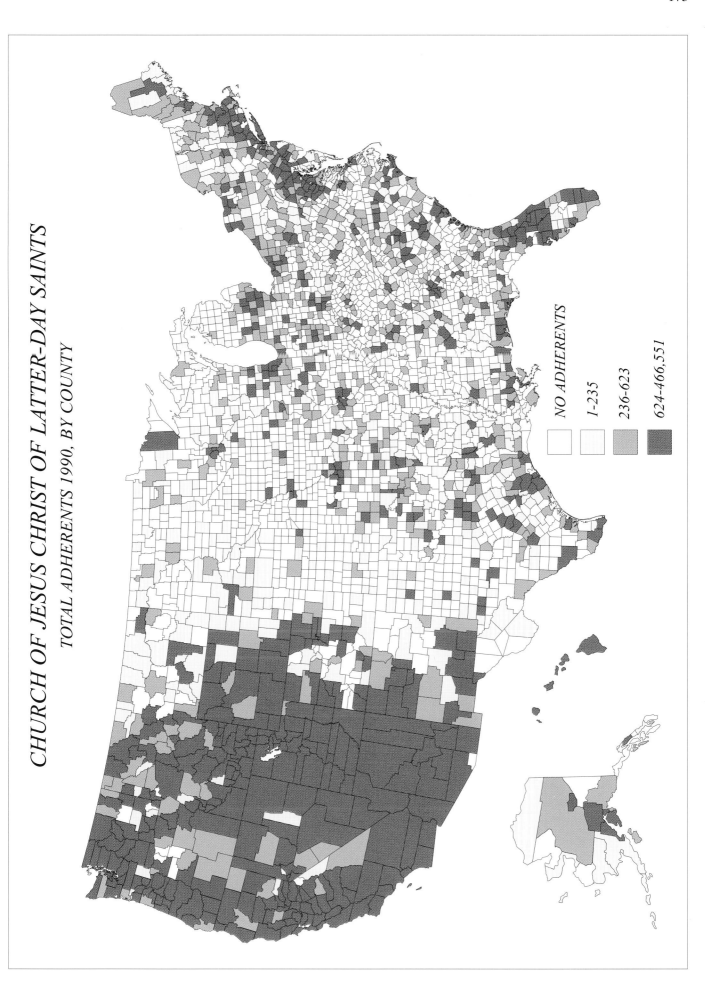

NO ADHERENTS

1-235

236-623

624-466,551

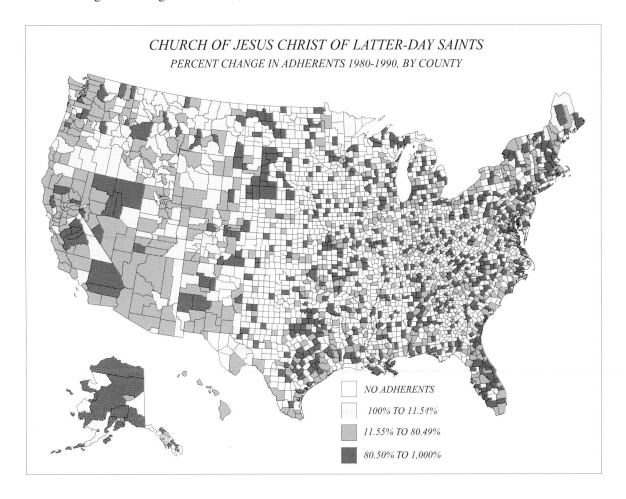

CHURCH OF JESUS CHRIST OF LATTER-DAY SAINTS
PERCENT CHANGE IN ADHERENTS 1980-1990, BY COUNTY

NO ADHERENTS
100% TO 11.54%
11.55% TO 80.49%
80.50% TO 1,000%

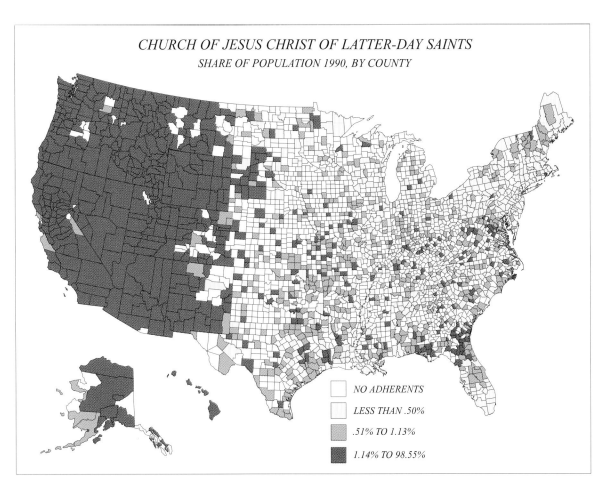

CHURCH OF JESUS CHRIST OF LATTER-DAY SAINTS
SHARE OF POPULATION 1990, BY COUNTY

NO ADHERENTS
LESS THAN .50%
.51% TO 1.13%
1.14% TO 98.55%

CHURCH OF JESUS CHRIST OF LATTER DAY SAINTS (MORMONS)

The Church of Jesus Christ of Latter-Day Saints is the largest of the five Mormon denominations tracing their heritage to the movement founded by Joseph Smith at Fayette, New York in 1830. Because it claimed a new scriptural source that departed from the New Testament, the Book of Mormon, and because Mormons engaged in social practices, especially polygamy, that were deemed sinful by most Christians, Mormons became the objects of brutal persecution and violence. Driven from New York, and subsequently through settlements in Ohio, Missouri, and Illinois, they eventually found peace and prosperity in Utah, where Mormonism remained the officially established religion until this territory gained statehood. The Mormons provided county level data only for western states in the 1952 and 1971 versions of the Church Membership Study. Thus, full national level change data are available for the first time for the 1980-1990 period.

	1980	1990
Adherents:	2,647,940	3,486,766
Counties:	1,502	1,646

Between 1980 and 1990, Mormon adherence grew by 30% from 2,647,940 to 3,486,766 adherents, and expanded in spatial extent by 10% from 1,502 to 1,646 counties. This means that by 1990, the Mormons were present in over half of all counties. During the decade of the 1980s, this major branch of Mormonism increased its number of local wards (churches) by 36%, from 6,771 to 9,208.

The map for Total Adherents, 1990 confirms the impression that Mormonism has become a nationally distributed faith community. While its weakest relative position seems to be through the Great Plains, where Lutherans (northern Great Plains), Methodists (central Great Plains), and Baptists (southern Great Plains) predominate, Mormonism has many high category counties throughout all other regions. Obviously, the western third of the nation is most consistently "Mormon" in character, as evidenced by the number of contiguous "high" category counties. Moreover, even the lowest third of counties reach as high as 235 persons per county. To the extent that counties are in many instances surrogate measures for local wards, the key for this map suggests that the average size is quite large.

Turning to the map for Percent Change in Adherents, 1980-1990, it is little surprise that the traditional western core area registers lower change rates than counties in other regions. The pervasive growth pattern is seen in the fact that the upper limit of the lowest third of counties is in excess of a 10% increase, and the median county growth rate is in excess of 50%. Moreover, in regions of the nation where Mormonism is less prevalent, counties with high change rates are clustered and contiguous, not isolated. This spreading of the faith by diffusion into adjacent counties clearly is a reflection of Mormonism's aggressive missionary stance.

The map for Share of Population, 1990 is best read in terms of two regional components. First, like the map of Total Adherents, 1990, the western third of the nation clearly is "home turf" for Mormonism. However, it is important to recognize that the top third of counties range from just over 1% to over 98% of county populations. Clearly, in many areas where Mormonism has experienced strong growth rates it still may be a small component of the general population. Indeed, as the key on the share map indicates, in two-thirds of its county locations, Mormonism barely exceeds 1% of county populations.

In summary, there is no question that in the decade of the 1980s Mormonism continued to represent one of American Christianity's success stories. In an era of generally modest religious population growth rates (8.4% for all denominations in this Atlas), The Church of Jesus Christ of Latter-Day Saints register impressive gains in terms of numbers of adherents (30%), counties newly entered (10%), and new wards (36%). These gains occurred in the context of a modest 9.1% growth rate for the general United States population, and surely are a product of a well-orchestrated program of evangelism.

CHURCH OF THE LUTHERAN BRETHREN OF AMERICA

Founded in 1900, the Church of the Lutheran Brethren of America practices a nonliturgical form of Lutheranism. These Bible-centered, missionary-oriented Lutherans stress the autonomy of local congregations and the importance of individual faith. Foreign missions and the "planting" of new churches at home are stressed by this small group.

	1980	1990
Adherents:	10,935	17,793
Counties:	82	87

Between 1980 and 1990, the Church of the Lutheran Brethren of America grew from 10,935 adherents in 82 counties, to 17,793 adherents in 87 counties. During these same years the denomination slightly increased its number of churches from 102 to 109.

The map of Total Adherents, 1990 shows a primary cluster of counties that stretch across Minnesota into North Dakota. A smaller group of counties stretch from southern New England to southern Pennsylvania. Similar patterns appear in Arizona and California, as well as Washington and Oregon. There are a few isolated counties elsewhere. This is a very small community of churches for which growth appears to be occurring across the full range of its locations.

The key for the map of Percent Change in Adherents, 1980-1990 indicates that growth has occurred even in the lower third of counties for this group. The exaggerated percentages in this distribution in part reflect the small absolute numbers involved. Consider that the middle category on the map of Total Adherents, 1990 represents from 102 to 164 persons per county.

In most cases the Share of Population rates for this Lutheran body are small (just over half of one percent for two-thirds of counties). The fact that this denomination reaches a 6.4% level of the population in at least one location reflects the rural character of its core region. Obviously, in its core region this very small denomination makes its cultural impact only in combination with the other Lutheran churches that so predominate in parts of the American Midwest.

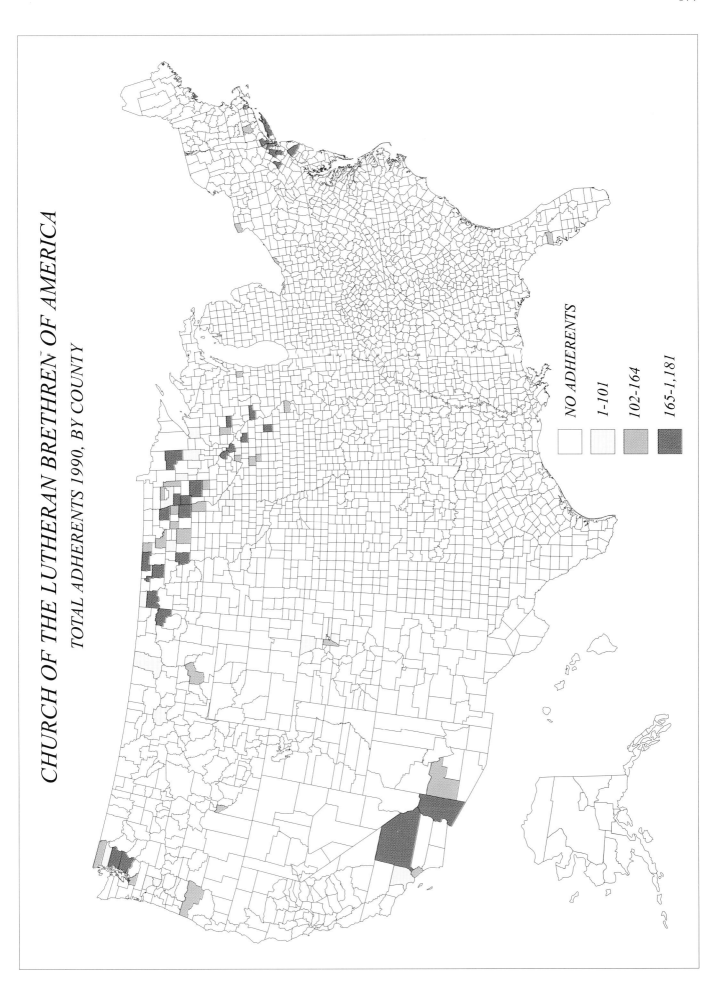

CHURCH OF THE LUTHERAN BRETHREN OF AMERICA
TOTAL ADHERENTS 1990, BY COUNTY

NO ADHERENTS

1-101

102-164

165-1,181

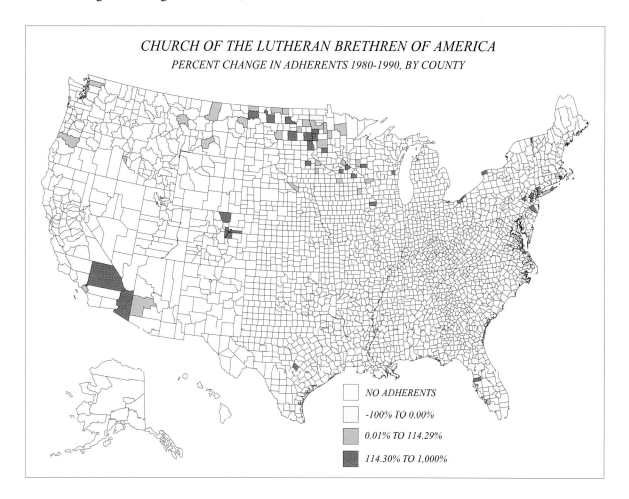

CHURCH OF THE LUTHERAN BRETHREN OF AMERICA
PERCENT CHANGE IN ADHERENTS 1980-1990, BY COUNTY

NO ADHERENTS

-100% TO 0.00%

0.01% TO 114.29%

114.30% TO 1,000%

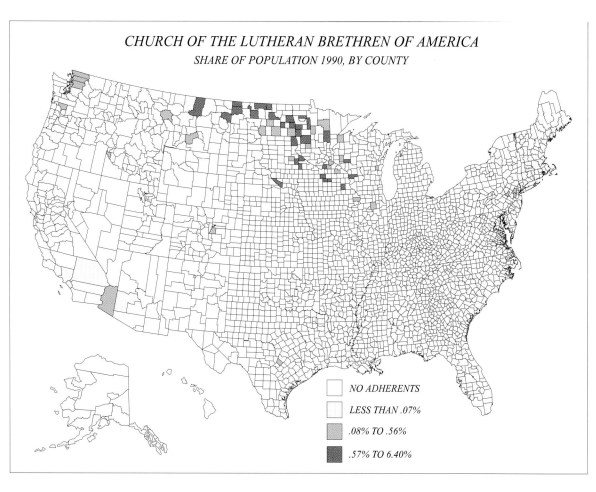

CHURCH OF THE LUTHERAN BRETHREN OF AMERICA
SHARE OF POPULATION 1990, BY COUNTY

NO ADHERENTS

LESS THAN .07%

.08% TO .56%

.57% TO 6.40%

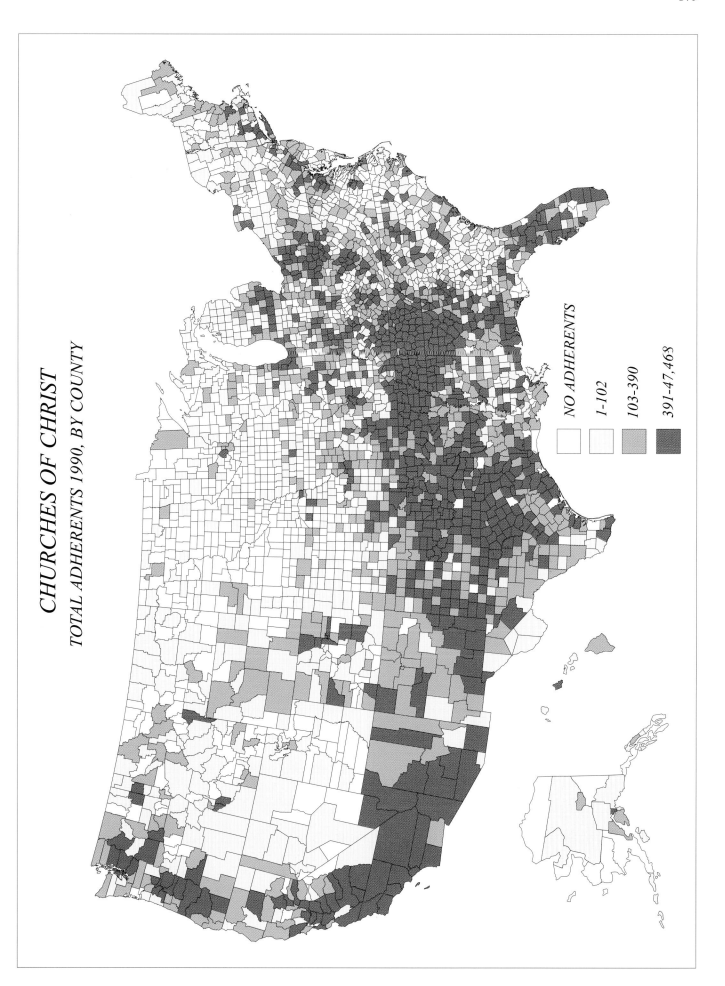

CHURCHES OF CHRIST
TOTAL ADHERENTS 1990, BY COUNTY

NO ADHERENTS

1-102

103-390

391-47,468

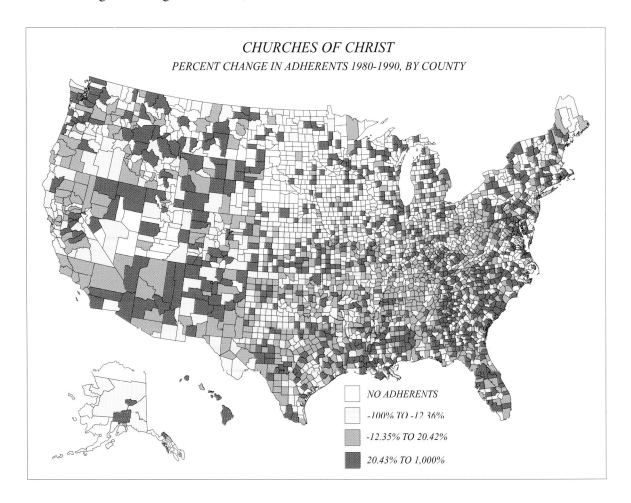

CHURCHES OF CHRIST
PERCENT CHANGE IN ADHERENTS 1980-1990, BY COUNTY

NO ADHERENTS

-100% TO -12.36%

-12.35% TO 20.42%

20.43% TO 1,000%

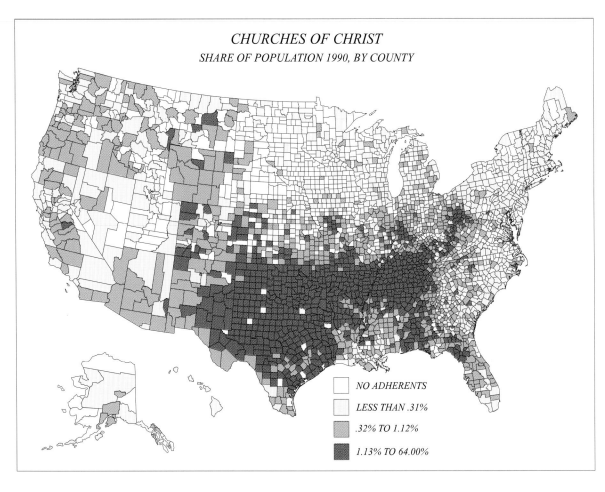

CHURCHES OF CHRIST
SHARE OF POPULATION 1990, BY COUNTY

NO ADHERENTS

LESS THAN .31%

.32% TO 1.12%

1.13% TO 64.00%

CHURCHES OF CHRIST

The 19th century Restoration Movement in American Protestantism has produced three distinct communities of churches. The Churches of Christ are at once the most widely dispersed geographically and the most conservative theologically. As compared to the Christian Churches (Disciples of Christ), and the Christian Churches, Churches of Christ, these Churches of Christ continue to reject the use of instrumental music in worship services, and also reject the notion of a connectional, denominational type organization. They stress the autonomy of the local congregations and the authority of the Bible.

	1980	1990
Adherents:	1,597,189	1,677,711
Counties:	2,345	2,397

Between 1980 and 1990, the Churches of Christ increased slightly from 1,597,189 adherents in 2,345 counties, to 1,677,711 adherents in 2,397 counties. These numbers represent almost half a million more adherents and five hundred more counties than are reported by the Christian Churches and Churches of Christ, the group from which these Churches of Christ divided. However, these aggregate statistics also mask some important parts of the story. As seen in the value ranges for the map of Percent Change in Adherents, 1980-1990, in their top third of counties, these Churches of Christ grew minimally at better than twice the population change rate for the nation (20% increase compared to the national rate of just over 9%). Moreover, these high growth counties are not confined to any single geographic region.

In contrast, both the map of Total Adherents, 1990 and the map for Share of Population, 1990 reveal distinctive regional features. These maps more clearly reflect the Churches of Christ's historic origins in the Tennessee Valley, as well as subsequent migrations to the Midwest, and westward to Texas and Oklahoma. Across that region, high level counties, some with sizable numbers of adherents and significant shares of county populations, form a large contiguous block. State level statistics confirm that the adherents pattern is distinctively concentrated. The three states of Tennessee (218,996), Texas (380,948), and Alabama (118,561) account for 42% of all adherents. This is a substantial proportion given that the Churches of Christ report adherents in 2,397 or 78% of the nation's 3,073 counties.

In summary, this is the largest and most theologically conservative of the three major American Restoration churches. It exhibits a distinctively regional distribution pattern much like that of the Southern Baptist Convention. Yet, with only one-tenth the number of adherents of the Southern Baptists, these Churches of Christ most often are a secondary cultural element in their home turf of the American South.

CONGREGATIONAL CHRISTIAN CHURCHES, NATIONAL ASSOC. OF

Organized in 1955, the National Association of Congregational Christian Churches is the largest branch of Congregationalism that did not participate in the 1957 merger between the Congregational Christian Churches and the Evangelical and Reformed Church that formed the United Church of Christ. Congregationalism, which began in America with the New England Separatists and Puritans, claims a pure democratic form of church polity emphasizing local church autonomy. This denomination views itself as the carrier of that tradition.

	1980	1990
Adherents:	119,002	98,457
Counties:	215	217

Between 1980 and 1990, this denomination decreased from 119,002 adherents in 215 counties to 99,110 adherents in 217 counties. However, during this same period the denomination's number of churches increased from 381 to 399. The pattern of declining numbers of adherents in the context of increasing numbers of churches is not typical. In this instance it suggests that even as more Congregational (or UCC) churches decide to affiliate with this denomination, the adherents gained thereby do not keep pace with a declining base of adherents. Alternatively, this pattern of declining adherents but increasing spatial dispersion may be symptomatic of an aging population moving into retirement locations.

The map for Total Adherents, 1990 provides a faint shadow image of the distribution map for the United Church of Christ. The clustering of counties from New England through the Great Lakes region and into the Midwest is the historic turf of Congregationalism. Florida, and especially California, complete this denomination's distribution pattern. In fact, 46% of all adherents are situated in just five states: California, Massachusetts, Connecticut, Maine, and Michigan.

The map for Percent Change in Adherents, 1980-1990 must be read in light of the fact that all three categories on the map include counties that experienced declines. This pattern closely resembles that of other Anglo-Protestant denominations such as the Presbyterian Church (U.S.A.), the Episcopal Church, and the United Church of Christ. The declines for such groups are throughout their spatial distribution rather than regional in character.

Finally, the map for Share of Population, 1990 indicates that these Congregationalists account for less than half of a percent of population in two-thirds of counties where they are encountered. It is likely that the National Association of Congregational Christian Churches makes a cultural impact only in those areas occupied by the other branches of Congregationalism, especially the United Church of Christ. Clearly, the 1980s have been a period of significant decline in adherents for this community of Congregationalists.

CONGREGATIONAL CHRISTIAN CHURCHES, NATIONAL ASSOCIATION OF

TOTAL ADHERENTS 1990, BY COUNTY

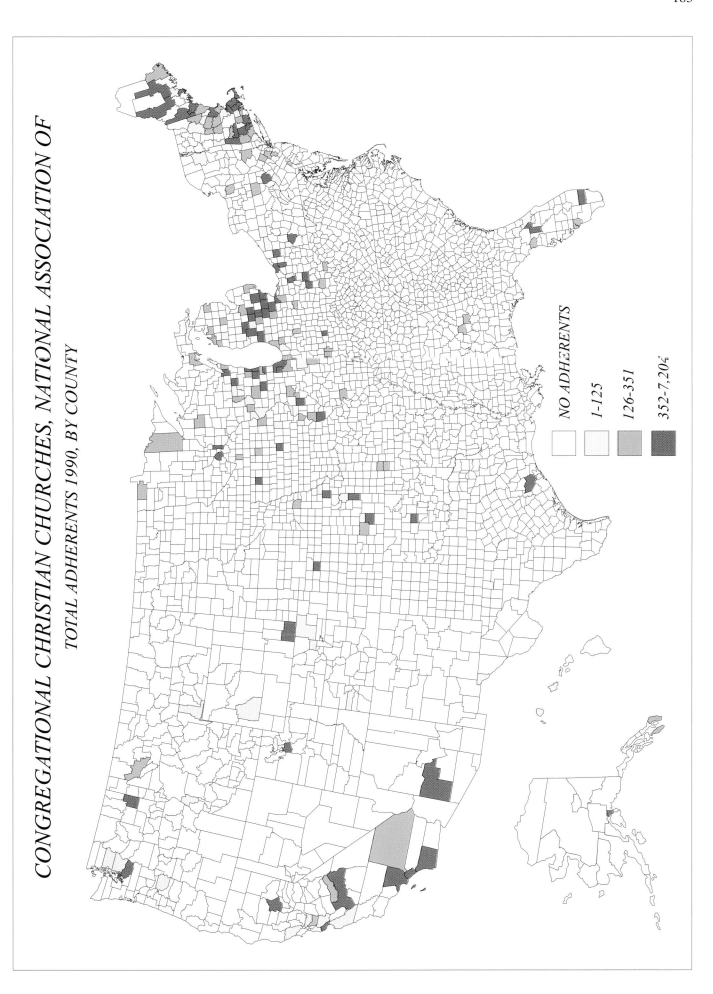

NO ADHERENTS

1-125

126-351

352-7,204

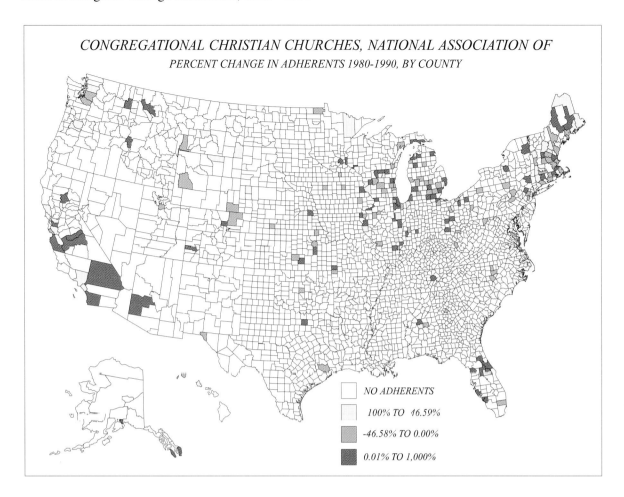

CONGREGATIONAL CHRISTIAN CHURCHES, NATIONAL ASSOCIATION OF
PERCENT CHANGE IN ADHERENTS 1980-1990, BY COUNTY

NO ADHERENTS

100% TO 16.59%

-46.58% TO 0.00%

0.01% TO 1,000%

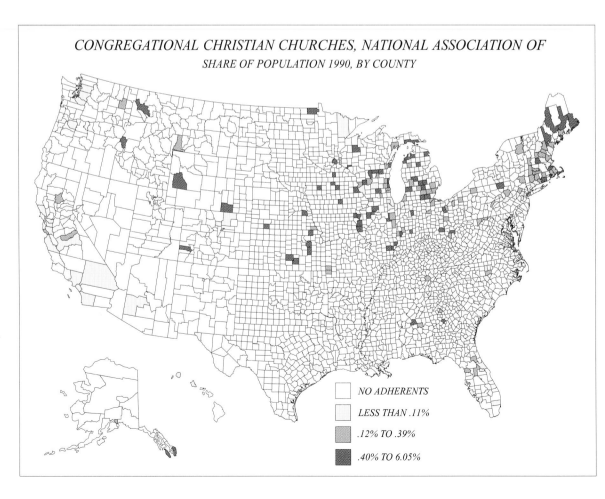

CONGREGATIONAL CHRISTIAN CHURCHES, NATIONAL ASSOCIATION OF
SHARE OF POPULATION 1990, BY COUNTY

NO ADHERENTS

LESS THAN .11%

.12% TO .39%

.40% TO 6.05%

CONSERVATIVE CONGREGATIONAL CHRISTIAN CONFERENCE

TOTAL ADHERENTS 1990, BY COUNTY

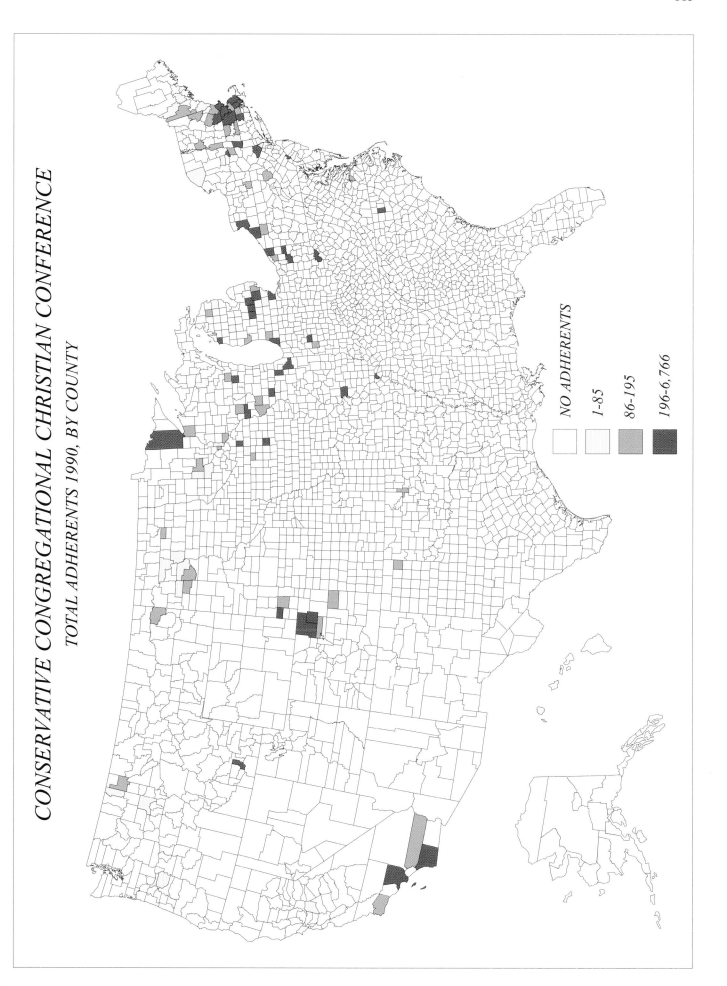

NO ADHERENTS

1-85

86-195

196-6,766

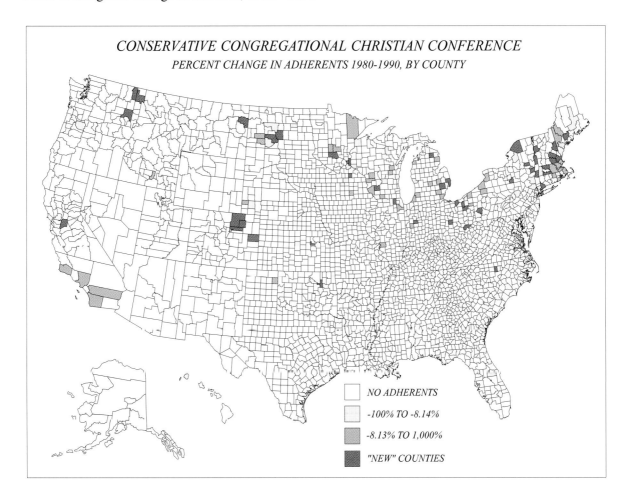

CONSERVATIVE CONGREGATIONAL CHRISTIAN CONFERENCE
PERCENT CHANGE IN ADHERENTS 1980-1990, BY COUNTY

NO ADHERENTS
-100% TO -8.14%
-8.13% TO 1,000%
"NEW" COUNTIES

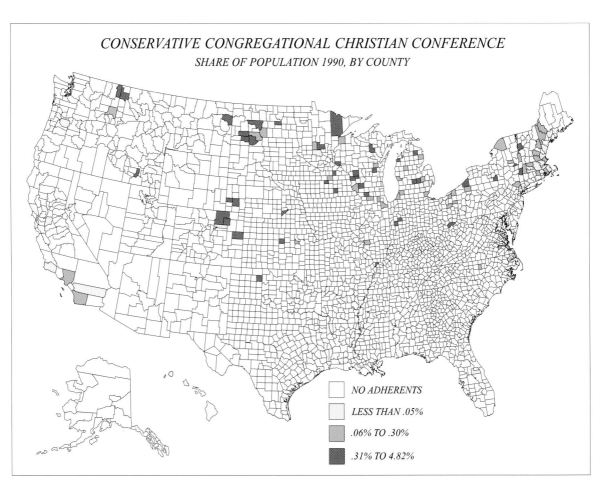

CONSERVATIVE CONGREGATIONAL CHRISTIAN CONFERENCE
SHARE OF POPULATION 1990, BY COUNTY

NO ADHERENTS
LESS THAN .05%
.06% TO .30%
.31% TO 4.82%

CONSERVATIVE CONGREGATIONAL CHRISTIAN CONFERENCE

This denomination emerged as a direct response to the involvement of New England Congregationalism in organizational mergers and merger discussions during the 1930s and 1940s. In the aftermath of Congregationalism's merger with the Christian Churches (1931), H. B. Sandine began a series of efforts resulting in the formation in 1945 of the Conservative Congregational Christian Fellowship. Viewing the pending merger with the Evangelical and Reformed Church as a clear departure from congregational principles, the Fellowship reorganized as a Conference in 1948.

	1980	1990
Adherents:	27,781	35,574
Counties:	92	127

In 1980, this denomination reported 27,781 adherents in 92 counties, while in 1990, it reported 35,574 adherents in 127 counties. Additionally, during the decade, these Conservative Congregationalists grew from 128 to 177 churches.

The map of Total Adherents, 1990, much like that for the National Association of Congregational Christian Churches, generally resembles the distribution of the larger Congregational (now UCC) body from which it emerged. Small pockets of counties reach from the New England states across the Great Lakes region and into the upper Midwest. The denom-ination also appears in California, Oregon, and Washington. The only departure from the antic-ipated pattern is a pronounced cluster of counties in northern Colorado and western Nebraska. Generally, major metropolitan areas predominate in this denomination's county pattern.

The map for Percent Change in Adherents, 1980-1990 reveals that "losers" (the third of counties in the middle third of counties) and "gainers" (assumedly most of the counties that are new to the distribution during the decade (those colored orange) all are pre-sent in all regional settings. This mixed pattern suggests that growth is a function of established congregations (defections from the UCC?) joining the denomination.

The map for Share of Population, 1990 shows that these Conservative Congregationalists fail to account for as much as 5% of county populations, and in fully two-thirds of their county locations represent slightly less than a third of a percent of population. However, it is not sur-prising that "higher" share counties seem to be in more rural isolated counties, and not so much in Congregationalism's historic New England core area.

Overall, the trend for this branch of Congregationalism very much resembles that for the National Association of Congregational Christian Churches. Both groups have their origins in opposition to mergers in which the larger Congregational body participated. Historically, the opposition to mergers has been grounded in a strong sense of the integrity of a "gathered" church and local congregational autonomy. Such views are not particularly conducive to growth through evangelism. Thus, the lack of a strong growth trend is not unanticipated.

EVANGELICAL LUTHERAN SYNOD

The Evangelical Lutheran Synod was founded in 1918 by a merger of several Norwegian churches under the name the Norwegian Lutheran Church. The present name, Evangelical Lutheran Synod, was adopted in 1958. This communion, which stresses the autonomy of local churches, maintained fellowship with both the Wisconsin and Missouri Synods until 1963, when it severed relations with the Missouri Synod because of doctrinal issues. The Evangelical Lutheran Synod operates Bethany Lutheran College and Bethany Lutheran Theological Seminary.

	1980	1990
Adherents:	20,044	21,523
Counties:	73	92

In 1980, the Evangelical Lutheran Synod reported 20,044 adherents in 73 counties, and in 1990, reported 21,523 adherents in 92 counties. During the decade, this denomination also grew from 110 to 126 churches.

The map of Total Adherents, 1990 clearly delineates the historic center of gravity of this ethnic Lutheran church in the upper midwestern states. Only four states outside this region contain multiple numbers of counties for this denomination. They are Washington, Oregon, California, and Florida.

The map for Percent Change in Adherents, 1980-1990 indicates that strong growth is occurring in many of the counties outside the midwestern core region. Migration to retirement communities, especially in Florida, California, New Mexico, and Arizona seems to be a factor in this trend.

The map for Share of Population, 1990 indicates that in two-thirds of the counties it occupies, this small Lutheran denomination accounts for no more than half a percent of the population. The Evangelical Lutheran Synod, then, like several other smaller Lutheran bodies in this *Atlas*, derives its cultural significance from its combination with other Lutheran bodies that are the dominant faith community in the upper Midwest.

EVANGELICAL LUTHERAN SYNOD
TOTAL ADHERENTS 1990, BY COUNTY

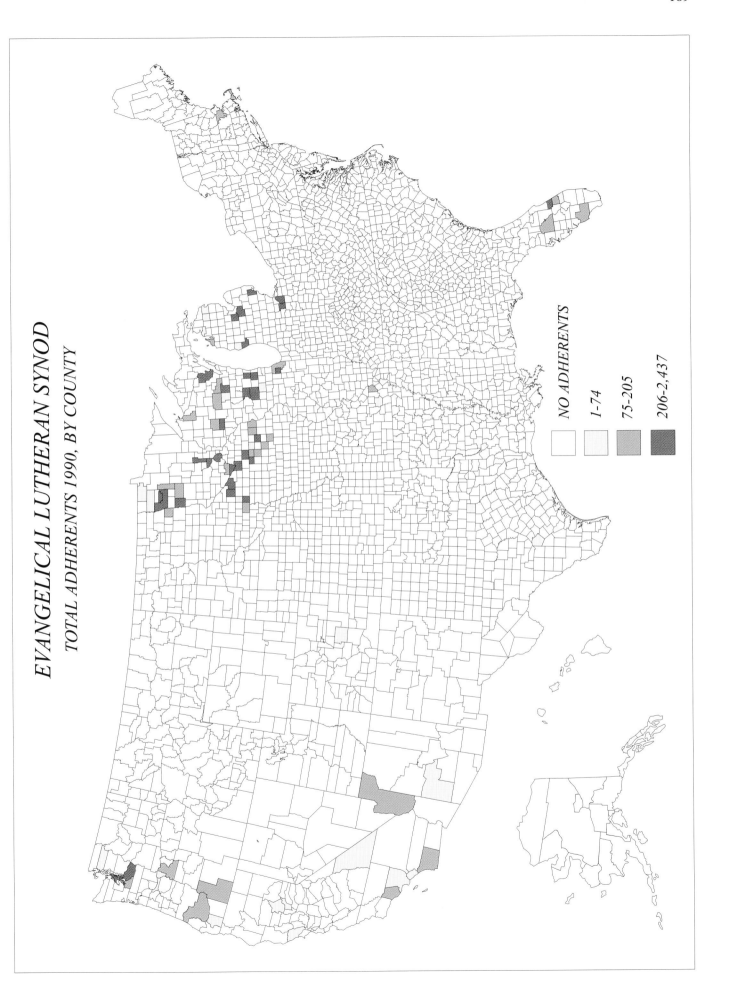

NO ADHERENTS

1–74

75–205

206–2,437

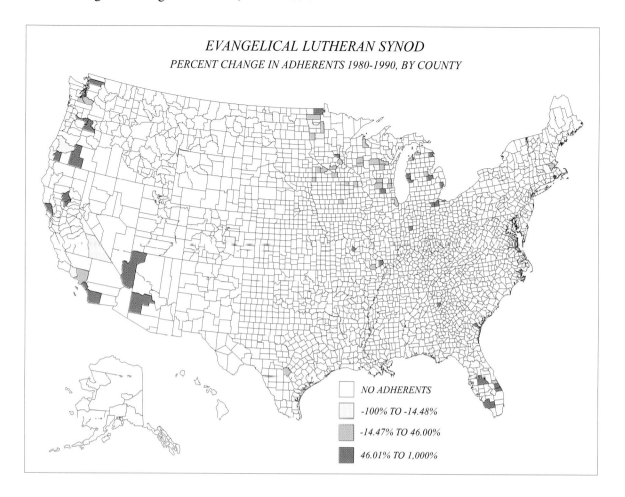

EVANGELICAL LUTHERAN SYNOD
PERCENT CHANGE IN ADHERENTS 1980-1990, BY COUNTY

NO ADHERENTS

-100% TO -14.48%

-14.47% TO 46.00%

46.01% TO 1,000%

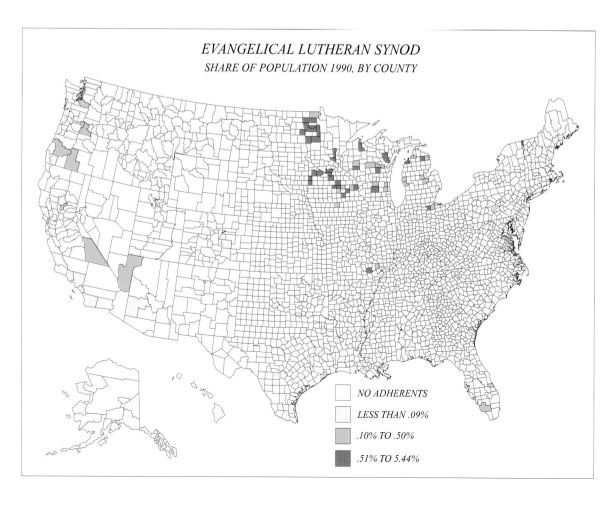

EVANGELICAL LUTHERAN SYNOD
SHARE OF POPULATION 1990, BY COUNTY

NO ADHERENTS

LESS THAN .09%

.10% TO .50%

.51% TO 5.44%

EVANGELICAL METHODIST CHURCH
TOTAL ADHERENTS 1990, BY COUNTY

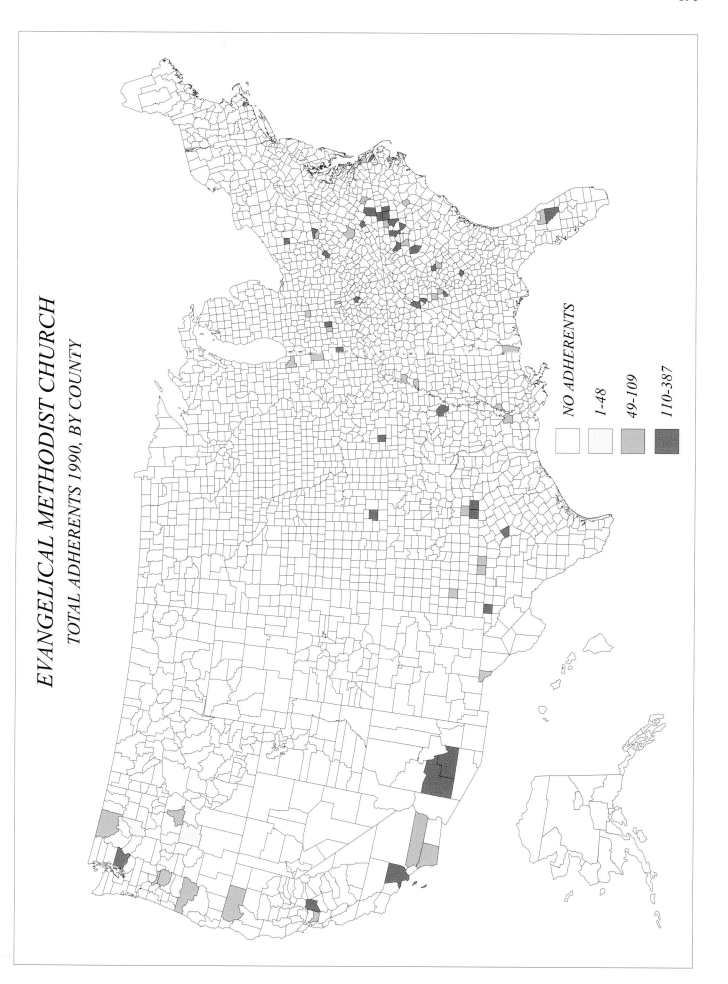

NO ADHERENTS

1-48

49-109

110-387

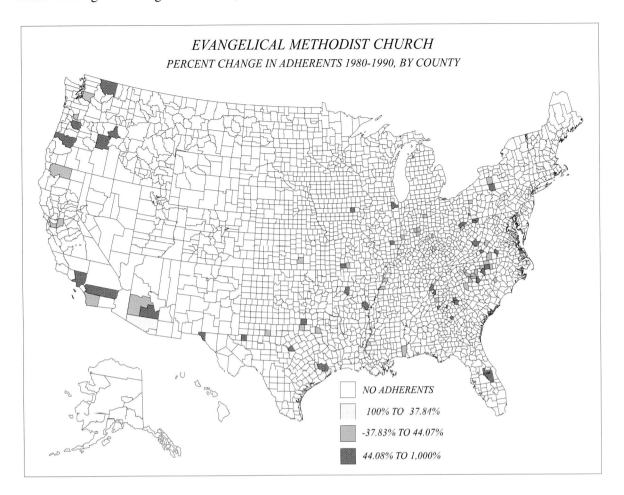

EVANGELICAL METHODIST CHURCH
PERCENT CHANGE IN ADHERENTS 1980-1990, BY COUNTY

NO ADHERENTS
100% TO 37.84%
-37.83% TO 44.07%
44.08% TO 1,000%

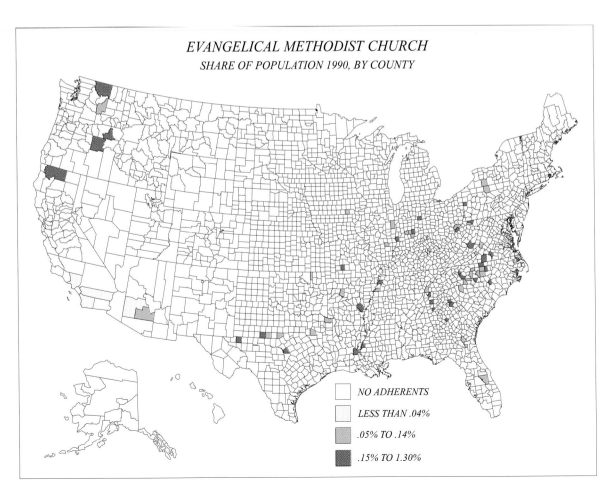

EVANGELICAL METHODIST CHURCH
SHARE OF POPULATION 1990, BY COUNTY

NO ADHERENTS
LESS THAN .04%
.05% TO .14%
.15% TO 1.30%

EVANGELICAL METHODIST CHURCH

This small Methodist denomination was founded in 1946. While it subscribes to a fundamentalist interpretation of Wesleyan theology, it adheres to a strictly congregational form of polity in which local autonomy is stressed. This evangelistic communion has remained relatively stable, reporting 11,788 adherents in 100 counties in 1980 and 11,105 adherents in 104 counties in 1990. During this decade it reports a net gain of one church.

	1980	1990
Adherents:	11,788	11,105
Counties:	100	104

The map of Total Adherents, 1990, reveals a core cluster of counties that stretches from northern Georgia to southern Virginia, and is centered in the Carolina Piedmont. Elsewhere, there is a scatter of paired and isolated counties across the southern tier of states and along the West Coast. Unlike the map of Total Adherents 1990, which indicates a distinct core area, the map for Percent Change in Adherents, 1980-1990 indicates no clear regional characteristic to patterns of loss and gain. Moreover, roughly equal numbers of counties report losses and gains in adherents.

Like the Percent Change map, the Share of Population map for this small Methodist denomination does not exhibit a regional pattern. Both inside and outside its core region, this group never accounts for as much as 2% of county populations. The general pattern is one of stability. This may be viewed either as an accomplishment for a small denomination that now is a half century from its founding, or as a cause for questioning the long-term viability of such a small group that is both geographically and organizationally diffuse.

FREE LUTHERAN CONGREGATIONS, THE ASSOCIATION OF

Established in 1962 as an expression of Scandinavian revival movements, this independent association of Lutheran churches also entailed dissent from the American Lutheran Church (ALC) merger. Over the next four decades other local congregations, especially from the former Evangelical Lutheran Church and the Suomi Synod, wishing to remain outside of the larger "merged" bodies joined these Free Lutherans. These churches stress the primacy of the Bible and recognize no earthly synodical authority.

	1980	1990
Adherents:	14,462	27,316
Counties:	75	118

Originally located primarily in the states of Minnesota and North Dakota, these Free Lutherans reported 14,462 adherents in 75 counties in 1980, and 27,316 adherents in 118 counties in 1990. During this same period, the Association increased from 131 to 203 churches.

The map for Total Adherents, 1990 confirms the notion that this Association is a remnant of other midwestern branches of Lutheranism. Minnesota alone accounts for 46% (12,420) of its adherents, and the four states of Minnesota, North Dakota, South Dakota, and Wisconsin represent 74% of adherents (20,225). Across its distribution, this Association appears to be situated primarily in rural and small town locations.

The map for Percent Change in Adherents, 1980-1990 highlights the movement of entire churches into the denomination with counties colored orange on the map indicating "new" counties since 1980. Many of these reflect defections of "established" congregations dissenting from the most recent Lutheran (ELCA) merger. Similarly, the exaggerated growth rates in the other two-thirds of counties also reflect this special growth pattern. It is clear from the map that new churches have joined the Association from both "near and far."

As would be expected for a denomination of relatively small size, the map depicting share of population shows the Association of Free Lutheran Congregations typically to represent less than 1% of county populations. Despite its small town and rural character, this denomination never accounts for as much as 10% of county populations.

In summary, it seems reasonable to suggest that this 20th century branch of Lutheranism symbolizes a remnant of the Scandinavian Lutheran tradition in the United States. Additionally, the impressive growth rate for this denomination also reflects its role as a refuge for local congregations dissenting from organizational mergers within American Lutheranism. In this sense, this Lutheran group occupies a similar position in its denominational family to that of the Presbyterian Church in America, which has absorbed churches dissenting from the recent Presbyterian merger (the Presbyterian Church, U.S.A.). Understandably, the core area for these Free Lutheran Congregations is but a faint reflection of the traditional upper midwestern home of American Lutheranism and especially of the largest merged Lutheran denomination, The Evangelical Lutheran Church in America (ELCA).

FREE LUTHERAN CONGREGATIONS, THE ASSOCIATION OF

TOTAL ADHERENTS 1990, BY COUNTY

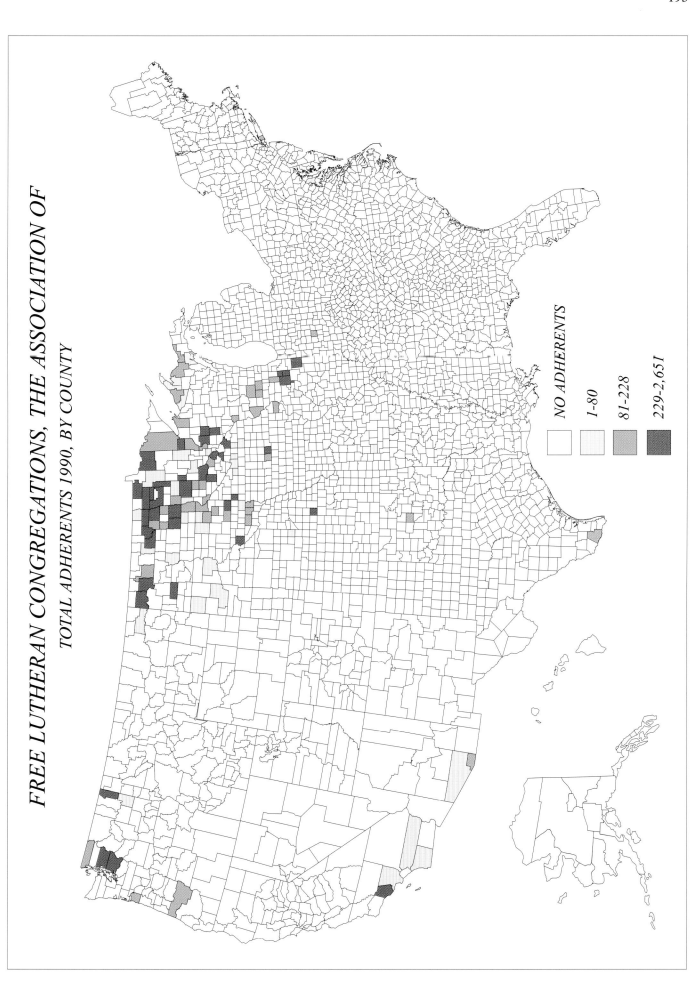

NO ADHERENTS

1-80

81-228

229-2,651

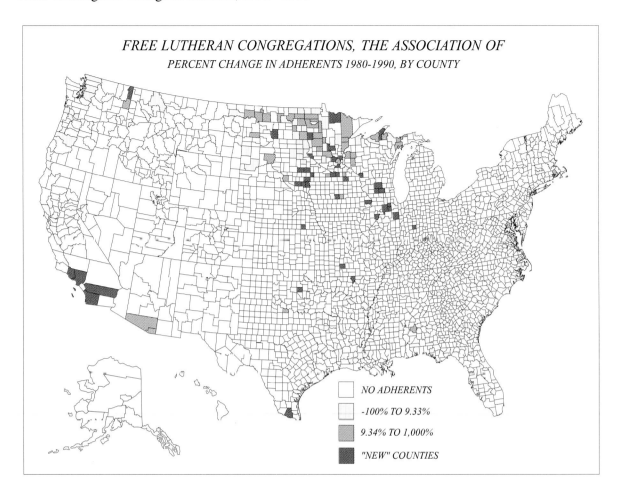

FREE LUTHERAN CONGREGATIONS, THE ASSOCIATION OF
PERCENT CHANGE IN ADHERENTS 1980-1990, BY COUNTY

NO ADHERENTS

-100% TO 9.33%

9.34% TO 1,000%

"NEW" COUNTIES

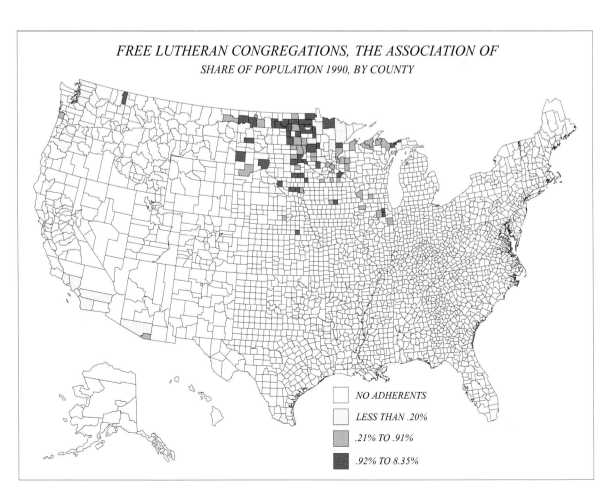

FREE LUTHERAN CONGREGATIONS, THE ASSOCIATION OF
SHARE OF POPULATION 1990, BY COUNTY

NO ADHERENTS

LESS THAN .20%

.21% TO .91%

.92% TO 8.35%

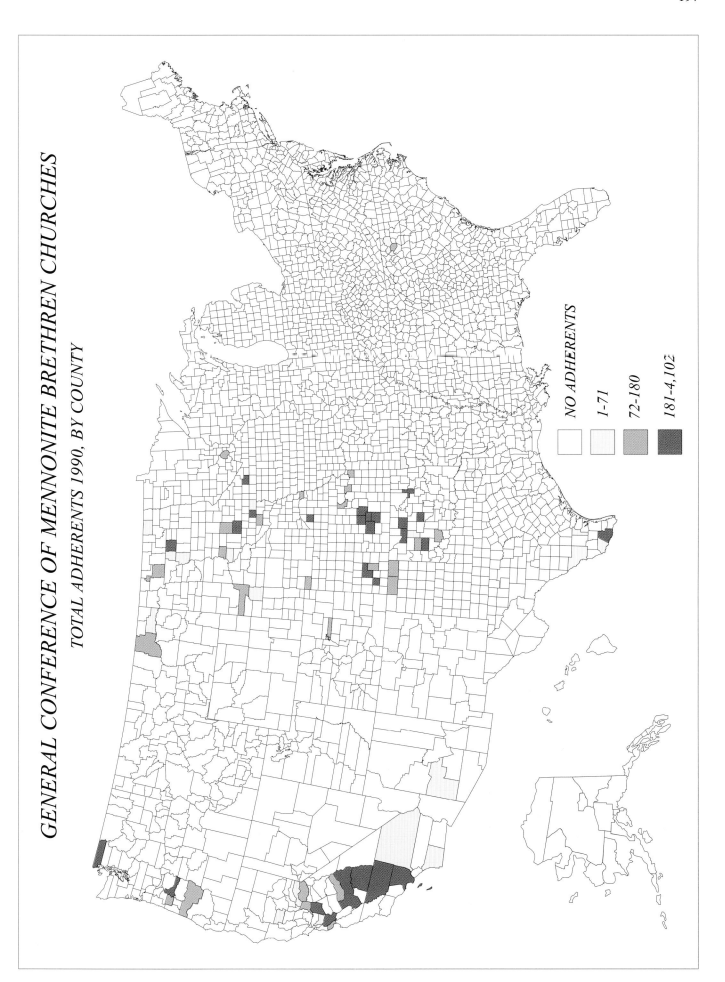

GENERAL CONFERENCE OF MENNONITE BRETHREN CHURCHES

TOTAL ADHERENTS 1990, BY COUNTY

NO ADHERENTS

1-71

72-180

181-4,102

197

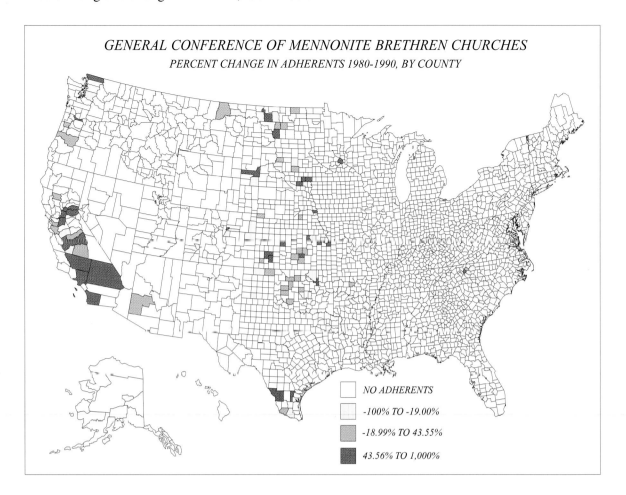

GENERAL CONFERENCE OF MENNONITE BRETHREN CHURCHES
PERCENT CHANGE IN ADHERENTS 1980-1990, BY COUNTY

NO ADHERENTS
-100% TO -19.00%
-18.99% TO 43.55%
43.56% TO 1,000%

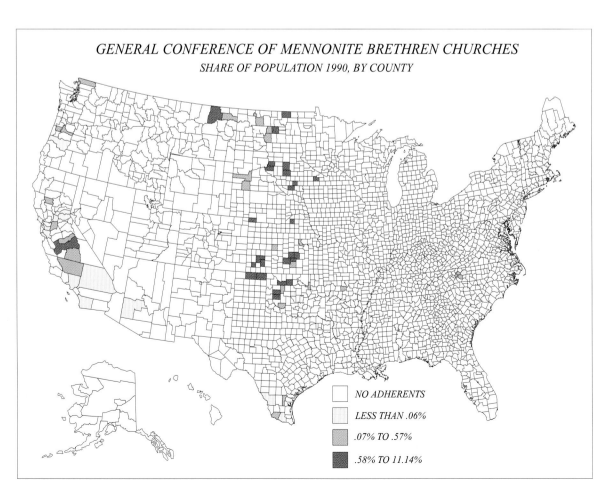

GENERAL CONFERENCE OF MENNONITE BRETHREN CHURCHES
SHARE OF POPULATION 1990, BY COUNTY

NO ADHERENTS
LESS THAN .06%
.07% TO .57%
.58% TO 11.14%

GENERAL CONFERENCE OF MENNONITE BRETHREN CHURCHES

This branch of the Mennonite churches traces its origins to German-speaking Ukrainian Pietists who immigrated to the United States in the 1860s and 1870s. Prayer and Bible study are the focus of their tradition and their polity is congregational. Original settlements in Kansas spread throughout the Pacific Coast and into Canada. In 1960, the Krimmer Mennonite Brethren Church merged with this denomination. These Brethren still conduct services in European languages, as well as in Vietnamese, Mandarin, and Hindi.

	1980	1990
Adherents:	19,268	22,097
Counties:	79	78

Between 1980 and 1990, the General Conference of the Mennonite Brethren Churches increased in adherents by 14%, while reporting in one less county. During this same period they grew from 202 to 257 churches. The map of Total Adherents, 1990 clearly indicates that this is a widely dispersed midwestern and western branch of Pietist/Amish Protestantism. The three states of California (9,186 adherents), Kansas (4,534), and Oklahoma (3,603) account for 78% of all adherents. Secondary clusters of counties are located on the West Coast in Oregon and Washington, and in the southern (Texas) and northern (the Dakotas, Wyoming, and Minnesota) reaches of the Great Plains.

The map for Percent Change in Adherents, 1980-1990 shows that counties losing adherents (-100% to -19%) and those gaining at impressive rates (43.6 to 1,000%) both are widely dispersed. However, it also must be remembered that this group is characterized by small local communities. The map of Total Adherents, 1990 reveals that two-thirds of all counties number less than 181 people. Thus, small absolute changes in numbers translate into very high percentages.

The map for Share of Population, 1990 indicates that for this group even the highest third of share counties may represent as little as just over half of one percent of a county's total population. These are minuscule county shares. The latter include some urban locations, such as the Twin Cities, Denver, and San Jose. However, both in California and throughout the nation's mid-section, many rural counties are in evidence.

In summary, this small Pietist sect experienced modest growth in adherents during the 1980s (14%), while maintaining a stable geographic pattern. Their growth, seen most clearly in the addition of 55 new congregations, reflects missionary and outreach work with diverse immigrant populations. In 1990, two clusters of counties, the first in California, and the second in Kansas and Oklahoma, account for nearly four in five of all adherents.

LATVIAN EVANGELICAL LUTHERAN CHURCH IN AMERICA

The Baltic states of Latvia, Estonia, and Lithuania were absorbed into the Soviet Union after the Second World War. However, ethnic immigrant churches survived in the United States even as their homelands had ceased to be independent political entities. It is too soon to know the consequences for these ethnic churches of the recent demise of the Soviet Union and the liberation of their homelands.

	1980	1990
Adherents:	13,617	14,299
Counties:	50	49

In 1980, this communion reported 13,617 adherents in 50 counties, while in 1990, 14,299 adherents are reported in 49 counties. Additionally, the number of churches decreased from 61 to 56. Because there was little immigration to expand these churches for the period under study here, it may be argued that relative stability represents a positive trend.

The map for Total Adherents, 1990 reveals a pattern of wide dispersal, which in most cases, no doubt, represents one church per county. Metropolitan areas in the Northeast and Midwest seem to predominate. This pattern departs from the midwestern and rural shape of much of American Lutheranism, and reflects 20th rather than 19th century immigration. Accordingly, the denomination's largest population is located in Westchester County, New York, and the most tightly clustered counties are in the New York to Boston corridor.

While the aggregate statistics reflect a stable denomination, the county level data provide a very different picture. Counties that lost adherents during the 1980s extend into the upper third of counties (the lower limit is -11.43%). It is hard to escape the impression that these declines represent the passing of a generation.

The map for Share of Population, 1990 must be read in the context of its value limits. These Latvian Lutherans do not account for as much as a third of a percent of county populations. The image of a highly distinctive small ethnic church persists. The presently unfolding events in Eastern Europe may well have enormous influence on the future growth or decline for this small community of American churches during the next decade.

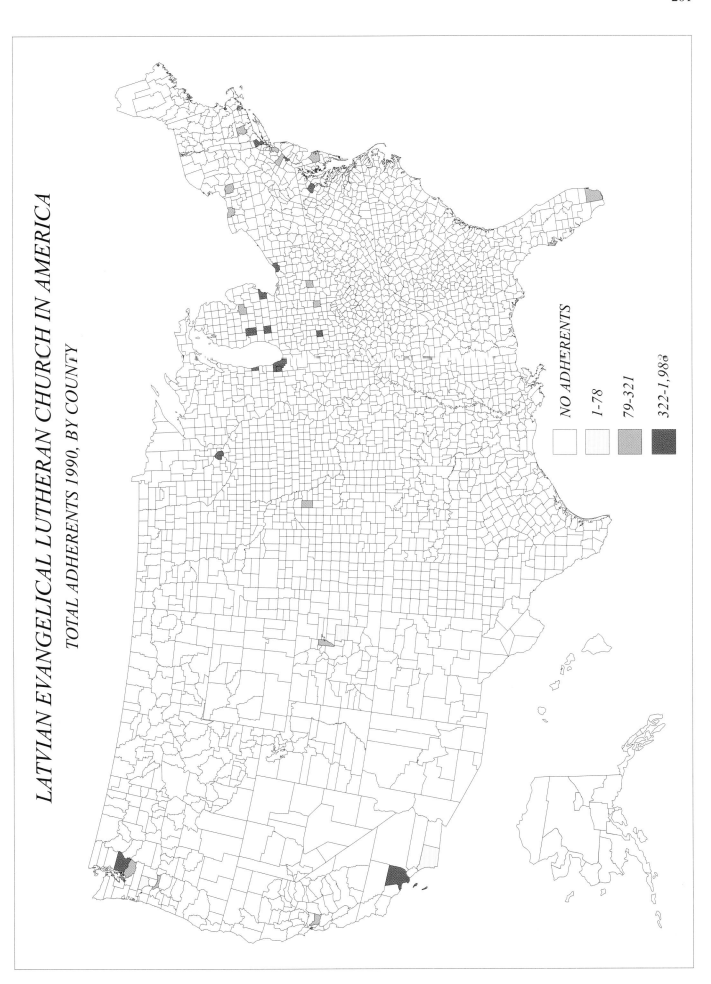

LATVIAN EVANGELICAL LUTHERAN CHURCH IN AMERICA

TOTAL ADHERENTS 1990, BY COUNTY

NO ADHERENTS

1-78

79-321

322-1,983

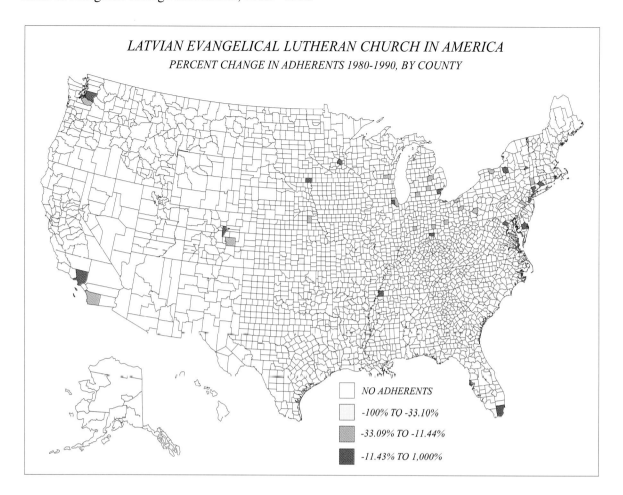

LATVIAN EVANGELICAL LUTHERAN CHURCH IN AMERICA
PERCENT CHANGE IN ADHERENTS 1980-1990, BY COUNTY

NO ADHERENTS
-100% TO -33.10%
-33.09% TO -11.44%
-11.43% TO 1,000%

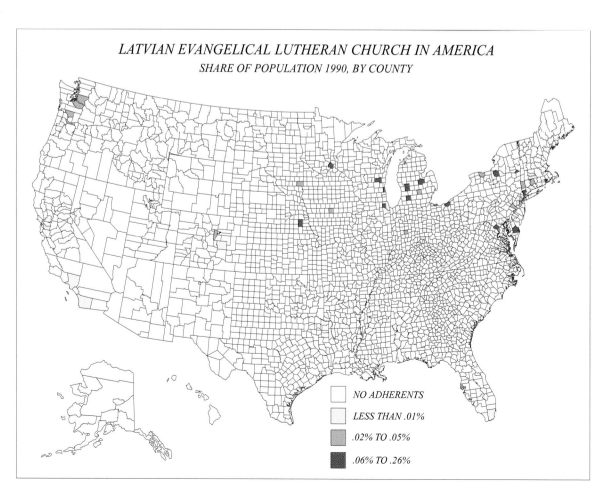

LATVIAN EVANGELICAL LUTHERAN CHURCH IN AMERICA
SHARE OF POPULATION 1990, BY COUNTY

NO ADHERENTS
LESS THAN .01%
.02% TO .05%
.06% TO .26%

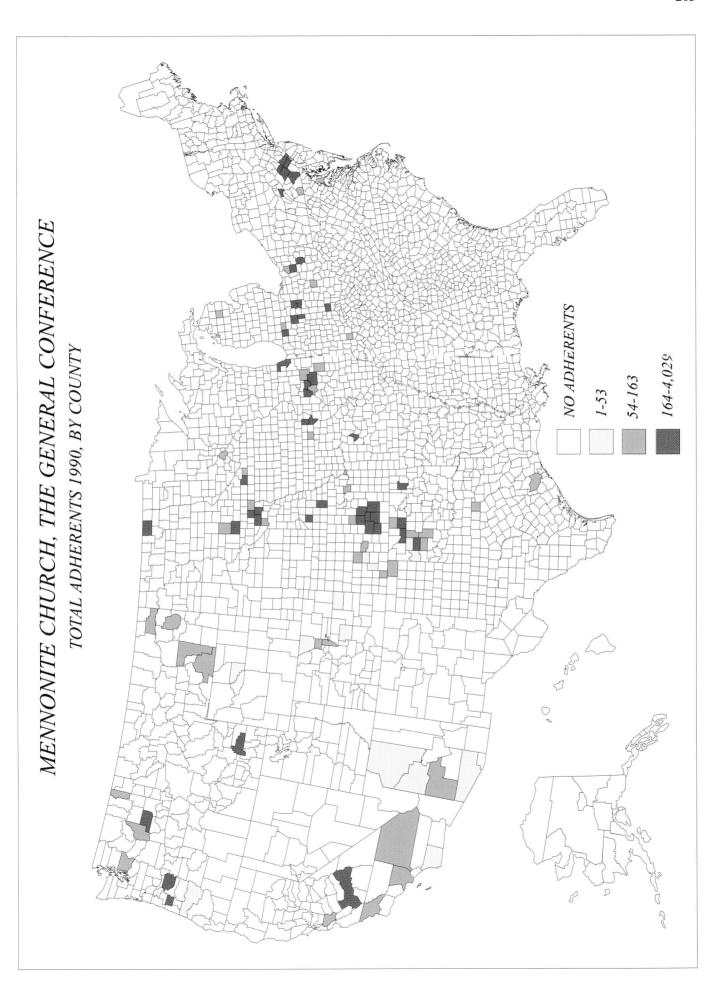

MENNONITE CHURCH, THE GENERAL CONFERENCE
TOTAL ADHERENTS 1990, BY COUNTY

NO ADHERENTS

1-53

54-163

164-4,029

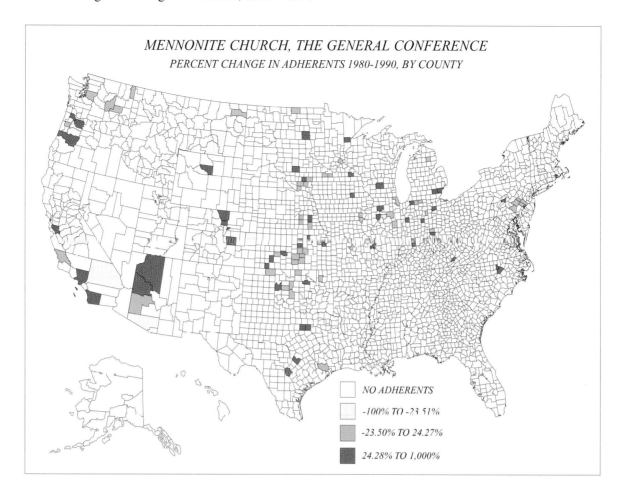

MENNONITE CHURCH, THE GENERAL CONFERENCE
PERCENT CHANGE IN ADHERENTS 1980-1990, BY COUNTY

NO ADHERENTS
-100% TO -23.51%
-23.50% TO 24.27%
24.28% TO 1,000%

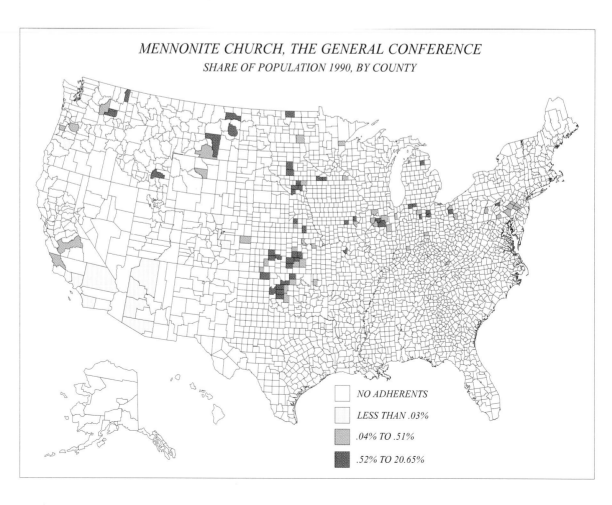

MENNONITE CHURCH, THE GENERAL CONFERENCE
SHARE OF POPULATION 1990, BY COUNTY

NO ADHERENTS
LESS THAN .03%
.04% TO .51%
.52% TO 20.65%

MENNONITE CHURCH, THE GENERAL CONFERENCE

Mennonite churches, following the teachings of Menno Simons (1496-1561), first settled in Germantown, Pennsylvania in 1683. Successive waves of European migration brought many varieties of this tradition to these shores, especially from Germany and Switzerland. The Mennonite Church, General Conference was established in 1860 by independent congregations wishing to cooperate in missionary work.

	1980	1990
Adherents:	46,891	40,951
Counties:	113	134

Between 1980 and 1990, the Mennonite Church, General Conference decreased in adherents (-12.%) while expanding in its spatial extent (18.6% more counties). At the same time, its number of churches also increased from 202 to 257. The map of Total Adherents, 1990 provides a clear record of this community's gradual westward migration in the United States. Isolated clusters of counties appear first in eastern Pennsylvania, followed by some in Ohio, Indiana, and Illinois. Finally, scattered clusters of counties appear in both the central Great Plains and on the West Coast. It is notable that the single Plains state of Kansas contains one-third of the entire church, 13,326 adherents.

This denomination is characterized by very small individual communities, with a median number of adherents per county of just over one hundred. The small absolute numbers have an obvious impact on relative numbers, a fact that must be considered when viewing the map for Percent Change in Adherents, 1980-1990. While it is true that fully half of all counties experienced growth (the middle category on the change map is centered on 1% increase), these growth statistics tend to mask the reality of an aggregate pattern involving an increase in counties but a decline in adherents of over 10%. In this context, high growth counties are widely dispersed throughout the Midwest and Plains states, as well as in the far West. While these counties appear predominately in rural locations, some metropolitan areas are present, among them Dallas and Denver. These varied patterns may reflect the fertility trends of individual families, since local groups are of such small size.

Finally, as might be expected, The Mennonite Church, General Conference does not typically account for a significant share of county population. In two-thirds of counties where it is found, it represents a maximum of about half of one percent of the population. Only in one small area of the state of Kansas does it account for a significant share of population.

On balance, this theologically and culturally distinctive church appears to be widely dispersed. Over the decade of the 1980s it did not replenish its flock even at a growth rate equal to that of the general population. At the same time, the spatial features of this Mennonite community seem to reflect dispersion. The increase in the number of churches and counties during the 1980s appear to be a geographic transplanting of a diminishing faith community. It remains to be seen if this will result in numeric growth during the 1990s.

MISSIONARY CHURCH

The Missionary Church was formed by a 1969 merger of two Mennonite communities both of which originated in the context of the Holiness revivals of the late 19th century. The Missionary Church Association, founded in 1889, and the United Missionary Church, founded as the Mennonite Brethren in Christ in 1883, were headquartered in Indiana and Ohio respectively. Today, The Missionary Church is theologically evangelical and is congregational in its polity. A substantial world missions program is maintained in conjunction with the Missionary Church of Canada.

	1980	1990
Adherents:	30,697	38,580
Counties:	128	123

Between 1980 and 1990, The Missionary Church grew from 30,697 adherents in 128 counties to 38,580 adherents in 123 counties. During this same period, it increased from 277 to 303 churches.

The map for Total Adherents, 1990 reveals a small denomination with very few truly "core" areas. As would be expected from its organizational history, the Missionary Church is centered in Indiana (14,009 adherents), with spillover into Michigan (7,192), and Ohio (3,030).

These three states contain 61% of the denomination's adherents. Elsewhere, counties with adherents appear in isolation or in clusters of two or three counties. Included are the states of Iowa and Kansas, as well as portions of the Pacific Northwest known to be the home of other Mennonite bodies. Counties in Southern California account for an additional 10% of the denomination's adherents.

The map for Percent Change in Adherents, 1980-1990 has several noteworthy features. First, it is clear that the small absolute values on the map of Total Adherents, 1990 (the median county value is just over 100 persons per county) has created rather exaggerated percent change rates on the map of Percent Change in Adherents, 1980-1990. Nonetheless, this denomination grew by 25% over the decade of the 1980s, while losing a few counties. The fact that high growth counties are present in all regions where the denomination is found, even in the Great Plains states, suggests that local evangelism is a key to this growth.

The map for Share of Population, 1990 indicates that these small religious communities never account for as much as 3% of county population. Like several other small branches of the Mennonite faith included in this Atlas, this small distinctive community appears to be increasing either by natural increase or by the absorption of new families into the faith. Migration into retirement areas (Florida, Arizona, and perhaps California) also seems to be contributing to the spatial expansion of the Missionary Church.

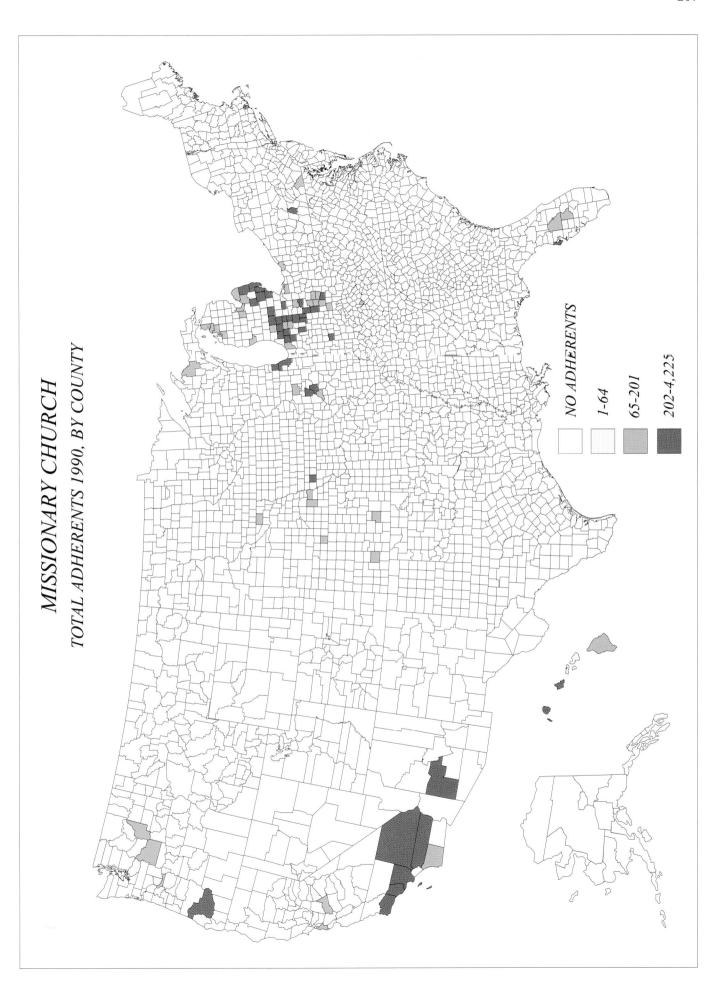

MISSIONARY CHURCH

TOTAL ADHERENTS 1990, BY COUNTY

NO ADHERENTS

1-64

65-201

202-4,225

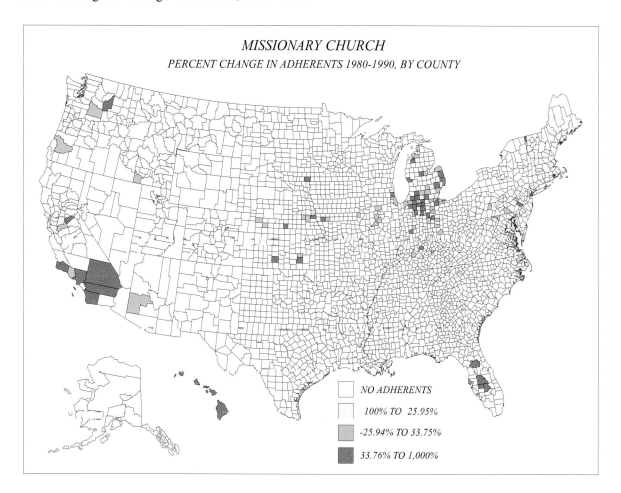

MISSIONARY CHURCH
PERCENT CHANGE IN ADHERENTS 1980-1990, BY COUNTY

NO ADHERENTS
100% TO 25.95%
-25.94% TO 33.75%
33.76% TO 1,000%

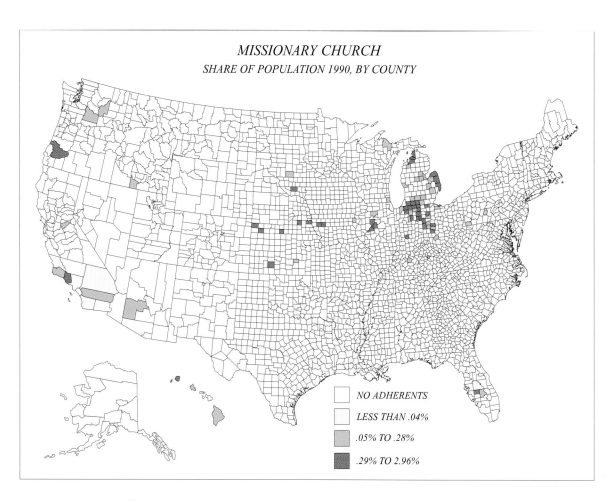

MISSIONARY CHURCH
SHARE OF POPULATION 1990, BY COUNTY

NO ADHERENTS
LESS THAN .04%
.05% TO .28%
.29% TO 2.96%

209

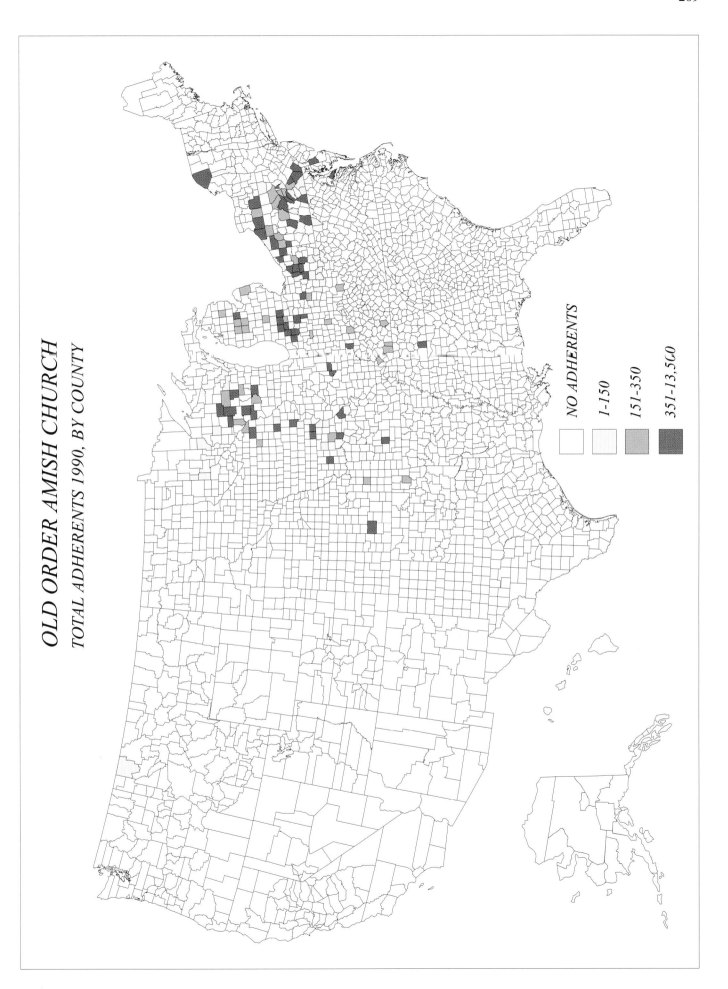

OLD ORDER AMISH CHURCH

TOTAL ADHERENTS 1990, BY COUNTY

NO ADHERENTS

1-150

151-350

351-13,560

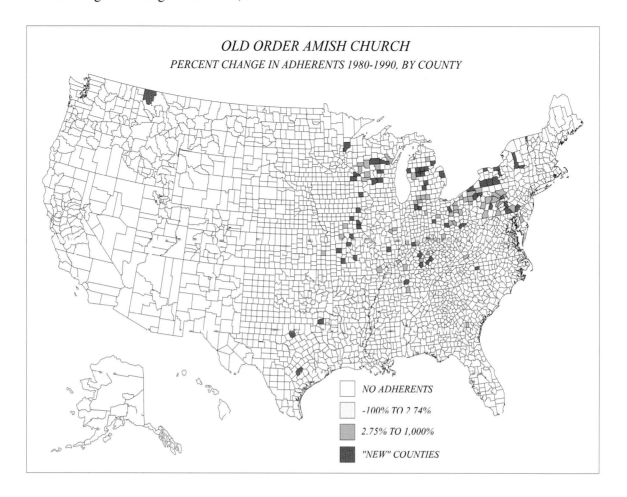

OLD ORDER AMISH CHURCH
PERCENT CHANGE IN ADHERENTS 1980-1990, BY COUNTY

NO ADHERENTS

-100% TO 2.74%

2.75% TO 1,000%

"NEW" COUNTIES

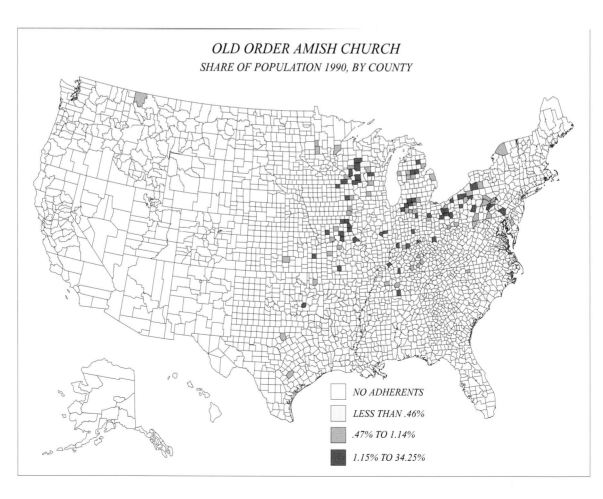

OLD ORDER AMISH CHURCH
SHARE OF POPULATION 1990, BY COUNTY

NO ADHERENTS

LESS THAN .46%

.47% TO 1.14%

1.15% TO 34.25%

OLD ORDER AMISH

Amish communities take their name from the 17th century Swiss Mennonite bishop Jacob Aman. Today, this branch of the Mennonite churches continues to represent theological conservatism and the preservation of a traditional life-style. In America, the two major expressions of this unique rejection of "modernity" in both religious and secular affairs are the Conservative Amish Mennonite Church and the Old Order Amish Mennonite Church.

	1980	1990
Adherents:	85,676	121,750
Counties:	107	166

The study *Churches and Church Membership in the United States, 1990* cautions that very rough estimates were employed in the enumeration for this community. Settlements established before 1987 were estimated at 150 persons per congregation. Those established in 1987 and 1988 were estimated at 100 adherents each. The newest settlements created in 1989 and 1990 were estimated to have 50 adherents. Based on these approximations, between 1980 and 1990, the Old Order Amish report increases from 85,676 adherents in 535 churches to 121,750 adherents in 830 churches. This apparent gain in adherents of 42.1% was accompanied by a 55% rate of increase in counties reporting adherents.

The map of Total Adherents, 1990 reveals clusters of counties that stretch from western New York, throughout Pennsylvania, into northeastern Ohio and Indiana, as well as Michigan and Minnesota. Isolated counties and pairs of counties are scattered among the eastern Plains states and as far south as Tennessee. The three states of Ohio (35,200 adherents), Pennsylvania (30,550), and Indiana (22,300) account for 72% of all Old Order Amish adherents.

The map for Percent Change in Adherents, 1980-1990 provides three very distinct classes of events. The highest category (colored orange) consists of all counties that entered the distribution between 1980 and 1990. The greatest preponderance of these "new" counties are outside the core states of Ohio, Pennsylvania, and Indiana. The lowest growth category represents counties that were present in the distribution in 1980, and over the decade either lost adherents or remained virtually stable (+2.74%). Many of these are in the traditional three state core area. Finally, the middle group of counties were present in 1980 and report positive change statistics between 1980 and 1990. These counties, with widely varying growth rates, from 2.75% to 1000%, are scattered throughout the distribution.

The map for Share of County Population, 1990 suggests that in all but a very few locations, the Old Order Amish are a very minor portion of county populations. The upper third of counties may represent as little as 1.15% of county population. Thus, even in "Pennsylvania Dutch" country, the Old Order Amish report very modest population shares, and therefore, their assumed contribution to the local culture is in combination with other theologically similar groups.

In summary, it is probably accurate to assume that some portion of the 42% growth in adherents reported by the Old Order Amish is a reflection of the enumeration technique rather than "real" growth. It must be remembered that the method of enumeration for this community entailed very general approximations. Given this proviso, growth seems to be largely outside the denomination's traditional core areas. Although three states - Indiana, Pennsylvania, and Ohio - still contain nearly two-thirds of all adherents, this community does appear to be shifting its center of gravity westward. Clearly, for this denomination, interpretation is best limited to general patterns rather than more specific features of these distributions.

PRESBYTERIAN CHURCH IN AMERICA

Initially named the National Presbyterian Church, The Presbyterian Church in America was formed in the mid-1970s through a schism within the Presbyterian Church in the United States (the so-called Southern Presbyterians). These Presbyterians objected to the growing liberalism of the parent body, and also were opposed to the movement that ultimately resulted in the reunion of the northern and southern branches of American Presbyterianism (The Presbyterian Church, U.S.A.). Additionally, during the 1980-1990 period, the Presbyterian Church in America absorbed a kindred body known as the Reformed Presbyterian Church, Evangelical Synod. As a result, the Presbyterian Church in America which claimed 86,631 adherents in 505 churches in 1980, reports having increased to 221,295 adherents in 1,161 churches in 1990.

	1980	1990
Adherents:	86,631	221,295
Counties:	252	530

In 1990, clusters of high category counties are found in four places: in Pennsylvania, Maryland, and Virginia; in Carolina and Tennessee; in Arkansas and Alabama; and finally, in Florida. Owing to the unique circumstances of the several merger events, the upper third of counties on the map of Percent Change in Adherents, 1980-1990 are identified as "new counties." While "new" counties, assumedly from the merger, are present in all of the new denomination's four core areas, they also are widely dispersed outside those cores. Obviously, this map must be interpreted differently than those for other denominations both because the growth in the number of counties reporting adherents is so large (more than doubling the earlier number), and because so much of the "growth" can be attributed to established churches dissenting from the merger of the two mainline Presbyterian denominations in 1985. It is noteworthy that in 1990 the share of county populations reaches a substantial level of 13.38%.

On balance, the general distribution of the Presbyterian Church in America very much resembles a shadow of that for the former Presbyterian Church in the United States (the Southern Presbyterians). However, by virtue of its merger with the Reformed Presbyterian Church, Evangelical Synod, this denomination is found in more areas than might be expected. The Presbyterian Church in America, while much larger, bears some resemblance to the Free Lutherans, in that both provide a refuge for local churches objecting to organizational mergers among larger bodies in their respective denominational families.

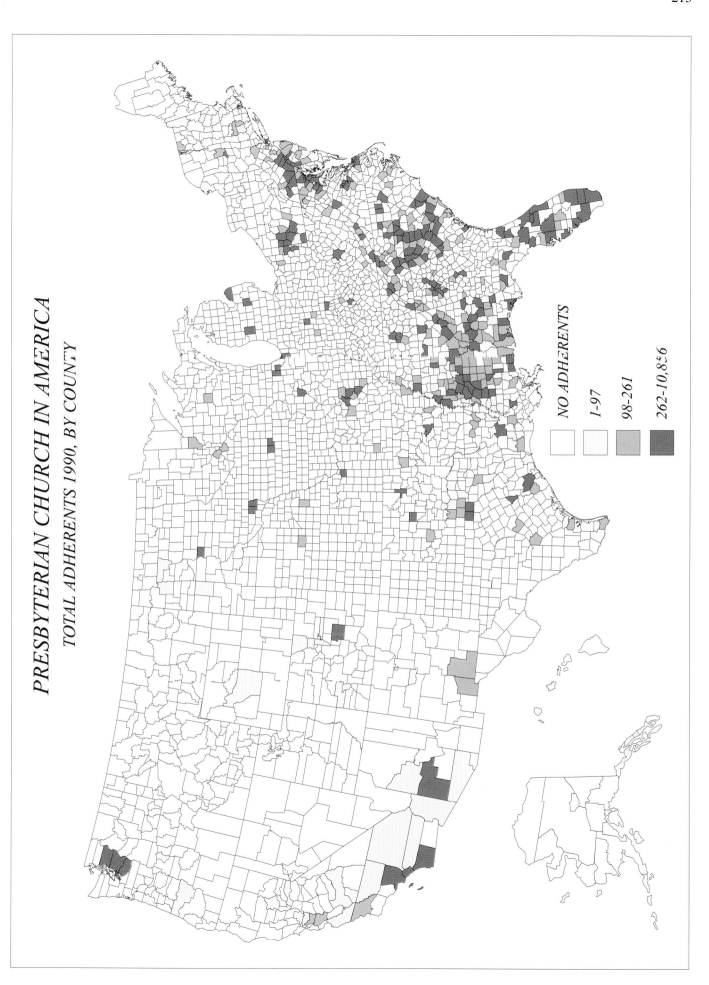

PRESBYTERIAN CHURCH IN AMERICA

TOTAL ADHERENTS 1990, BY COUNTY

NO ADHERENTS

1-97

98-261

262-10,856

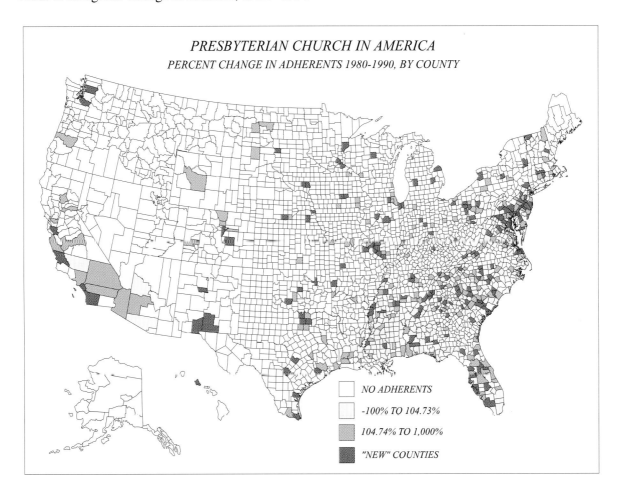

PRESBYTERIAN CHURCH IN AMERICA
PERCENT CHANGE IN ADHERENTS 1980-1990, BY COUNTY

NO ADHERENTS

-100% TO 104.73%

104.74% TO 1,000%

"NEW" COUNTIES

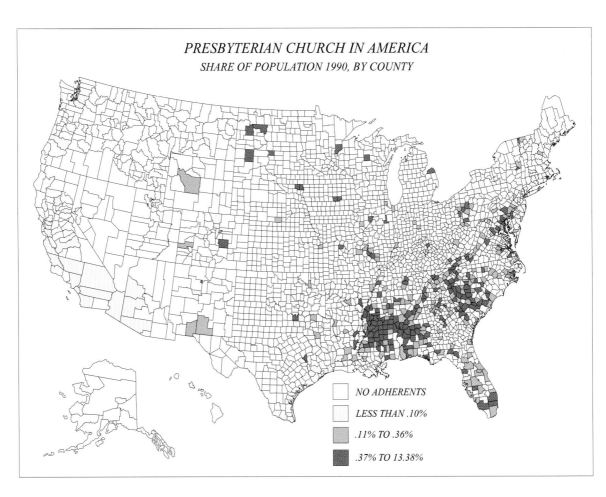

PRESBYTERIAN CHURCH IN AMERICA
SHARE OF POPULATION 1990, BY COUNTY

NO ADHERENTS

LESS THAN .10%

.11% TO .36%

.37% TO 13.38%

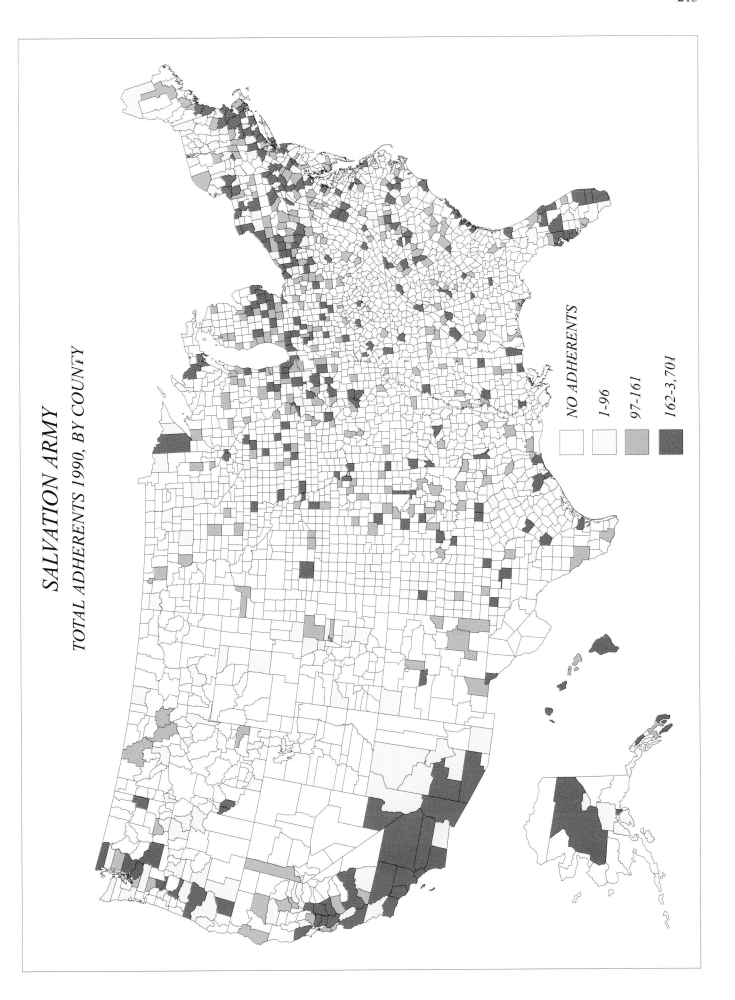

SALVATION ARMY

TOTAL ADHERENTS 1990, BY COUNTY

NO ADHERENTS

1-96

97-161

162-3,701

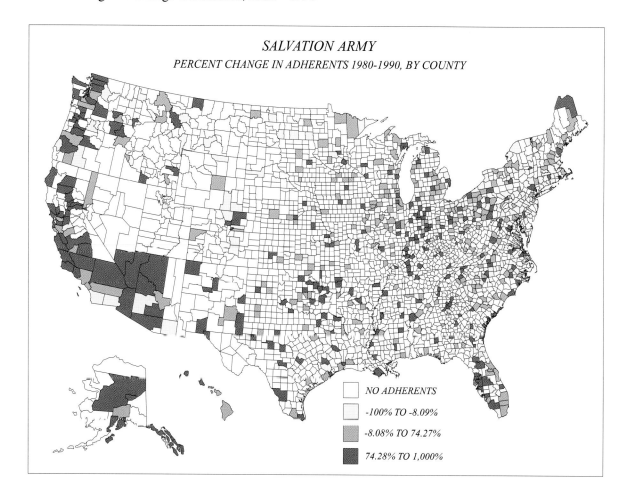

SALVATION ARMY

PERCENT CHANGE IN ADHERENTS 1980-1990, BY COUNTY

NO ADHERENTS

-100% TO -8.09%

-8.08% TO 74.27%

74.28% TO 1,000%

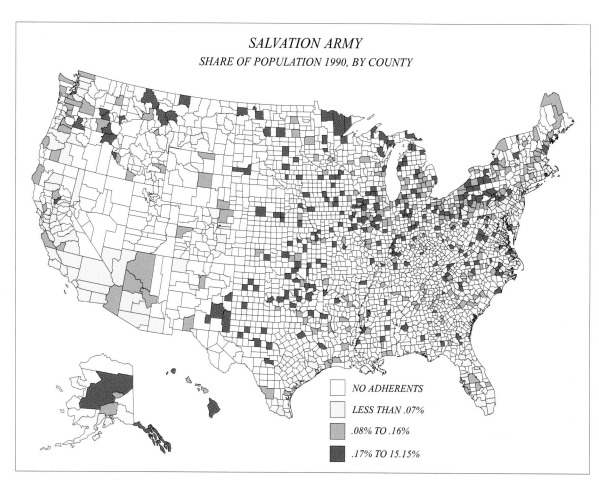

SALVATION ARMY

SHARE OF POPULATION 1990, BY COUNTY

NO ADHERENTS

LESS THAN .07%

.08% TO .16%

.17% TO 15.15%

SALVATION ARMY

The Salvation Army plays a dual function both as a church and a social agency. Originating as a missionary movement among established churches in England in the 1860s, by 1878 this Christian Mission changed its name to the Salvation Army and adopted a military style of organization. The movement came to America in the 1880s, and today is headquartered in Verona, New Jersey. Commissioned officers in the Salvation Army are much like clergy in other denominations. Similarly, soldiers, like members and adherents in other churches, render voluntary service. With corps and divisions in all fifty states, the Salvation Army operates a large network of hospitals, children's camps, community centers, and family service bureaus.

	1980	1990
Adherents:	144,032	136,752
Counties:	730	761

Between 1980 and 1990, the Salvation Army decreased from 144,032 to 136,752 adherents, while expanding from 730 to 761 counties. It also increased from 1,076 to 1,167 communities during the decade of the 1980s. Two-thirds of the counties in which the Salvation Army is present report having less than 161 adherents. This is a somewhat unique distribution having a great many more counties than might be expected given such a small number of adherents.

Clearly, this is a geographically wide-spread missionary and social out-reach organization composed of small local units that serve larger populations. The largest concentrations of Salvation Army adherents are in the major metropolitan areas, including Boston, Chicago, Detroit, Miami, Los Angeles, Seattle, and elsewhere.

The map of Percent Change in Adherents, 1980-1990 indicates that like the Army itself, both increases and declines are widely dispersed. The strongest performances are outside the metropolitan areas, while the weakest relative performances are concentrated in the northeastern quadrant of the nation. Generally, small absolute numbers have translated into very large change rates.

It is not surprising that the map for Share of Population, 1990 exhibits rather modest percentages. This thinly-spread group nowhere constitutes a significant share of county population. In two-thirds of counties, the Salvation Army represents less than one-fifth of one percent of the population. "High" shares seem to be situated disproportionately in rural and/or small town settings. Conversely, the smallest shares of county populations are in the kinds of places most associated in the public mind with the Salvation Army and its work - big cities.

In summary, this unique religious and social welfare organization maintained a pattern of relative stability between 1980 and 1990. Because of the extent of its social outreach programs, it is not surprising that its number of adherents (soldiers) may decline even as it reports operations in more counties.

219

APPENDIX

TABLE 7A

UPPER LIMITS OF CATEGORIES FOR MAPS OF TOTAL ADHERENTS
1990

DENOMINATION	Adherents per county		
	lower	middle	upper
American Baptist Churches in the U.S.A.	320	1,084	76,010
Baptist General Conference	113	307	16,502
Brethren in Christ Church	48	140	3,412
Catholic Church	617	3,990	3,077,114
Christian Reformed Church	142	399	43,473
Church of God (Anderson, Indiana)	60	171	8,672
Church of God (Cleveland, Tennessee)	101	339	15,323
Church of the Brethren	81	242	9,644
Church of the Nazarene	84	257	19,002
Cumberland Presbyterian Church	82	263	4,469
Episcopal Church	123	498	50,674
Evangelical Congregational Church	139	624	6,820
Evangelical Lutheran Church in America	487	2,097	160,979
Free Methodist Church of North America	36	116	2,704
Friends	30	129	4,445
International Church of the Foursquare Gospel	61	204	65,280
Jewish Population	285	1,320	501,700
Lutheran Church - Missouri Synod	240	893	83,205
Mennonite Church	60	172	20,225
Moravian Church in America, UF	192	492	15,410
North American Baptist Conference	115	274	3,746
Pentecostal Holiness Church, Inc.	65	240	5,340
Presbyterian Church (U.S.A.)	229	810	75,242
Reformed Church in America	317	939	26,514
Seventh-Day Adventists	65	200	54,514
Seventh Day Baptist General Conference	37	66	609
Southern Baptist Convention	1,012	5,391	395,152
Unitarian Universalist Association	63	228	9,321
United Church of Christ	251	913	55,001
United Methodist Church	1,015	2,861	165,055
Wisconsin Evangelical Lutheran Synod	113	337	31,002

TABLE 7B

UPPER LIMITS OF CATEGORIES FOR MAPS OF TOTAL ADHERENTS
1990

DENOMINATION	Adherents per county		
	lower	middle	upper
Advent Christian Church	40	117	1,542
African Methodist Episcopal Zion Church	289	1,203	80,018
Assemblies of God	133	455	55,107
Associate Reformed Presbyterian Church (General Synod)	90	321	3,513
Baptist Missionary Association of America	152	559	17,124
Brethren Church (Ashland, Ohio)	55	223	1,929
Christian and Missionary Alliance	89	269	6,214
Christian Church (Disciples of Christ)	207	613	20,596
Christian Churches and Churches of Christ	183	599	22,836
Christian (Plymouth) Brethren	59	150	3,575
Church of God in Christ (Mennonite)	101	193	1,253
Church of Jesus Christ of Latter-Day Saints	235	623	466,551
Church of the Lutheran Brethren of America	101	164	1,181
Churches of Christ	102	390	47,468
Congregational Christian Churches, National Association of	125	351	7,204
Conservative Congregational Christian Conference	85	195	6,766
Evangelical Lutheran Synod	74	205	2,437
Evangelical Methodist Church	48	109	387
Free Lutheran Congregations, The Association of	80	228	2,651
General Conference of Mennonite Brethren Churches	71	180	4,102
Latvian Evangelical Lutheran Church in America	78	321	1,988
Mennonite Church, The General Conference	53	163	4,029
Missionary Church	64	201	4,225
Old Order Amish Church	150	350	13,500
Presbyterian Church in America	97	261	10,856
Salvation Army	96	161	3,701

TABLE 8A

UPPER LIMITS OF CATEGORIES FOR MAPS OF PERCENT CHANGE IN ADHERENTS
1980-1990

DENOMINATION	percent change	
	lower	middle
American Baptist Churches in the U.S.A.	-19.01	2.90
Baptist General Conference	-12.99	42.86
Brethren in Christ Church	-49.41	10.96
Catholic Church	-5.58	25.93
Christian Reformed Church	-5.77	32.44
Church of God (Anderson, Indiana)	-30.32	23.10
Church of God (Cleveland, Tennessee)	9.09	74.74
Church of the Brethren	-29.20	2.21
Church of the Nazarene	-5.52	36.79
Cumberland Presbyterian Church	-26.84	10.20
Episcopal Church	-26.59	4.62
Evangelical Congregational Church	-18.69	20.87
Evangelical Lutheran Church in America	-9.54	12.48
Free Methodist Church of North America	-24.69	33.09
Friends	-8.33	200.00
International Church of the Foursquare Gospel	10.10	698.17
Jewish Population	-21.80	49.26
Lutheran Church - Missouri Synod	-6.38	14.43
Mennonite Church	10.10	152.94
Moravian Church in America, UF	-16.19	.60
North American Baptist Conference	-18.63	13.86
Pentecostal Holiness Church, Inc.	-22.52	115.88
Presbyterian Church (U.S.A.)	-22.22	-3.87
Reformed Church in America	-13.29	20.74
Seventh-Day Adventists	-3.33	42.76
Seventh Day Baptist General Conference	-4.08	1,000.00
Southern Baptist Convention	7.40	30.72
Unitarian Universalist Association	-8.31	47.05
United Church of Christ	-16.08	3.33
United Methodist Church	-12.70	-1.63
Wisconsin Evangelical Lutheran Synod	-3.85	55.00

TABLE 8B

UPPER LIMITS OF CATEGORIES FOR MAPS OF PERCENT CHANGE IN ADHERENTS
1980-1990

DENOMINATION	--------percent change--------	
	lower	middle
Advent Christian Church	-53.45	-18.63
African Methodist Episcopal Zion Church	-.52	0.00
Assemblies of God	-6.10	53.97
Associate Reformed Presbyterian Church (General Synod)	-13.07	39.04
Baptist Missionary Association of America	-14.14	23.08
Brethren Church (Ashland, Ohio)	-31.65	4.28
Christian and Missionary Alliance	10.24	145.46
Christian Church (Disciples of Christ)	-26.95	-3.51
Christian Churches and Churches of Christ	-13.33	27.90
Christian (Plymouth) Brethren	-20.00	96.67
Church of God in Christ (Mennonite)	50.53	110.00
Church of Jesus Christ of Latter-Day Saints	11.54	80.49
Church of the Lutheran Brethren of America	0.00	114.29
Churches of Christ	-12.36	20.42
Congregational Christian Churches, National Association of	-46.59	0.00
Conservative Congregational Christian Conference	-8.14	1,000.00
Evangelical Lutheran Synod	-14.48	46.00
Evangelical Methodist Church	-37.84	44.07
Free Lutheran Congregations, The Association of	9.33	1,000.00
General Conference of Mennonite Brethren Churches	-19.00	43.55
Latvian Evangelical Lutheran Church in America	-33.10	-11.44
Mennonite Church, The General Conference	-23.51	24.27
Missionary Church	-25.95	33.75
Old Order Amish Church	2.74	1,000.00
Presbyterian Church in America	104.73	1,000.00
Salvation Army	-8.09	74.27

224   Atlas of Religious Change in America, 1952 - 1990

TABLE 9A

UPPER LIMITS OF CATEGORIES FOR MAPS OF SHARE OF POPULATION
1990

DENOMINATION	percent share		
	lower	middle	upper
American Baptist Churches in the U.S.A.	.71	2.01	53.97
Baptist General Conference	.13	.58	8.16
Brethren in Christ Church	.02	.16	1.97
Catholic Church	3.84	15.08	116.27
Christian Reformed Church	.06	.41	26.41
Church of God (Anderson, Indiana)	.08	.29	6.14
Church of God (Cleveland, Tennessee)	.22	.74	9.80
Church of the Brethren	.13	.56	19.42
Church of the Nazarene	.23	.58	6.43
Cumberland Presbyterian Church	.24	.81	5.53
Episcopal Church	.46	.99	33.71
Evangelical Congregational Church	.09	.55	2.45
Evangelical Lutheran Church in America	.99	4.95	77.36
Free Methodist Church of North America	.04	.15	4.47
Friends	.02	.11	17.02
International Church of the Foursquare Gospel	.08	.33	11.54
Jewish Population	.34	1.11	24.21
Lutheran Church - Missouri Synod	.61	2.44	36.79
Mennonite Church	.06	.33	9.07
Moravian Church in America, UF	.07	.37	6.00
North American Baptist Conference	.10	.74	10.59
Pentecostal Holiness Church, Inc.	.10	.53	4.45
Presbyterian Church (U.S.A.)	.96	1.94	16.17
Reformed Church in America	.21	1.31	35.97
Seventh-Day Adventists	.19	.43	17.52
Seventh Day Baptist General Conference	.01	.06	4.57
Southern Baptist Convention	3.10	23.87	119.90
Unitarian Universalist Association	.05	.11	4.21
United Church of Christ	.62	2.17	47.98
United Methodist Church	5.04	9.36	39.28
Wisconsin Evangelical Lutheran Synod	.11	.78	23.54

TABLE 9B

UPPER LIMITS OF CATEGORIES FOR MAPS OF SHARE OF POPULATION
1990

DENOMINATION	lower	middle	upper
Advent Christian Church	.04	.18	3.30
African Methodist Episcopal Zion Church	.30	1.36	84.33
Assemblies of God	.58	1.37	13.18
Associate Reformed Presbyterian Church (General Synod)	.10	.46	3.16
Baptist Missionary Association of America	.27	1.79	29.39
Brethren Church (Ashland, Ohio)	.04	.24	3.46
Christian and Missionary Alliance	.09	.30	9.57
Christian Church (Disciples of Christ)	.46	1.70	25.05
Christian Churches and Churches of Christ	.42	1.63	27.08
Christian (Plymouth) Brethren	.04	.11	3.15
Church of God in Christ (Mennonite)	.22	.90	21.59
Church of Jesus Christ of Latter-Day Saints	.50	1.13	98.55
Church of the Lutheran Brethren of America	.07	.56	6.40
Churches of Christ	.31	1.12	64.00
Congregational Christian Churches, National Association of	.11	.39	6.05
Conservative Congregational Christian Conference	.05	.30	4.82
Evangelical Lutheran Synod	.09	.50	5.44
Evangelical Methodist Church	.04	.14	1.30
Free Lutheran Congregations, The Association of	.20	.91	8.35
General Conference of Mennonite Brethren Churches	.06	.57	11.14
Latvian Evangelical Lutheran Church in America	.01	.05	.26
Mennonite Church, The General Conference	.03	.51	20.65
Missionary Church	.04	.28	2.96
Old Order Amish Church	.46	1.14	34.25
Presbyterian Church in America	.10	.36	13.38
Salvation Army	.07	.16	15.15

TABLE 10

MEDIAN COUNTY PERCENT CHANGE RATES AND SHIFT IN SHARE OF POPULATION RATES
1952-1971 AND 1971-1990

DENOMINATION	--median percent change--		--median shift in share--	
	1952-1971	1971-1990	1952-1971	1971-1990
American Baptist Churches in the U.S.A.	14.36	-11.00	1.01	.80
Baptist General Conference	218.96	43.45	2.47	1.29
Brethren in Christ Church	97.67	132.43	1.62	1.71
Catholic Church	52.63	21.80	1.40	1.10
Christian Reformed Church	68.08	25.30	1.34	1.07
Church of God (Anderson, Indiana)	72.10	3.24	1.44	.86
Church of God (Cleveland, Tennessee)	221.21	78.99	2.70	1.43
Church of the Brethren	5.36	-23.72	.87	.68
Church of the Nazarene	96.54	34.33	1.63	1.12
Cumberland Presbyterian Church	5.53	-21.28	1.05	.64
Episcopal Church	29.01	-17.35	1.08	.67
Evangelical Congregational Church	19.00	1.92	1.07	1.01
Evangelical Lutheran Church in America	33.84	-1.25	1.23	.91
Free Methodist Church of North America	8.00	-3.42	.87	.83
Friends	305.26	41.73	3.49	1.19
International Church of the Foursquare Gospel	122.76	409.45	1.71	3.78
Jewish Population	9.09	130.77	.81	1.60
Lutheran Church - Missouri Synod	60.92	5.73	1.40	.95
Mennonite Church	162.98	93.32	2.07	1.68
Moravian Church in America, UF	13.55	-5.05	.89	.76
North American Baptist Conference	39.21	-.20	1.31	1.02
Pentecostal Holiness Church, Inc.	136.57	58.82	2.10	1.28
Presbyterian Church (U.S.A.)	22.19	-25.38	1.11	.64
Reformed Church in America	123.15	4.30	2.02	.98
Seventh-Day Adventists	77.42	44.05	1.45	1.17
Seventh Day Baptist General Conference	-6.81	56.71	.81	1.50
Southern Baptist Convention	80.51	37.48	1.73	1.12
Unitarian Universalist Association	208.47	.62	2.05	.81
United Church of Christ	6.14	-12.69	.89	.76
United Methodist Church	10.72	-7.83	1.03	.81
Wisconsin Evangelical Lutheran Synod	45.61	59.21	1.19	1.27